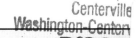

WAY BANK.　　　　　PARK PLACE.　　　　　　　　　　　　　　　　　　MURRAY STREET.

TY, COMMENCING AT THE ASTOR HOUSE.

CHEMICAL BANK.　　　　CHAMBER STREET　　　　IRVING HOUSE.

TY, COMMENCING AT THE ASTOR HOUSE

HOSPITAL.

TY, COMMENCING AT THE ASTOR HOUSE.

[For description, see page 173.]

BROADWAY

BROADWAY

A HISTORY OF
NEW YORK CITY
IN THIRTEEN MILES

FRAN LEADON

W. W. NORTON & COMPANY
Independent Publishers Since 1923
NEW YORK   LONDON

FRONTISPIECE:

Lower Broadway, looking south from Fulton Street, 1899.

Copyright © 2018 by Fran Leadon

FIRST EDITION

For information about permission to reproduce selections
from this book, write to Permissions,
W. W. Norton & Company, Inc., 500 Fifth Avenue,
New York, NY 10110

For information about special discounts for bulk purchases,
please contact W. W. Norton Special Sales
at specialsales@wwnorton.com or 800-233-4830

Manufacturing by Quad Graphics Fairfield
Book design by Barbara M. Bachman
Production manager: Anna Oler
Maps by Teresa Fox

LIBRARY OF CONGRESS CATALOGING-IN-PUBLICATION DATA
NAMES: Leadon, Fran, 1966– author.
TITLE: Broadway : a history of New York City in thirteen miles / Fran Leadon.
DESCRIPTION: New York, NY: W. W. Norton & Company, 2018. | Includes
bibliographical references and index.
IDENTIFIERS: LCCN 2017052699 | ISBN 9780393240108 (hardcover)
SUBJECTS: LCSH: Broadway (New York, N.Y.)—History. | Broadway (New York,
N.Y.)—Buildings, structures, etc.—Guidebooks. | New York (N.Y.)—History. | New
York (N.Y.)—Buildings, structures, etc.—Guidebooks.
CLASSIFICATION: LCC F128.67.B7 L43 2018 | DDC 974.7/1—dc2
LC record available at https://lccn.loc.gov/2017052699

W. W. Norton & Company, Inc.,
500 Fifth Avenue, New York, N.Y. 10110
www.wwnorton.com

W. W. Norton & Company Ltd.,
15 Carlisle Street, London W1T 3QT

1 2 3 4 5 6 7 8 9 0

For Leigh
Blue Sky Coming

A walk through Broadway revives recollection; makes life flow backward for the hour; lifts the curtain from scenes of the past; recreates feelings often pleasant, oftener painful,—all ghosts of the dead years that shimmer through our darkened memory.

—JUNIUS HENRI BROWNE, 1869

CONTENTS

MILE 3

HOUSTON STREET TO UNION SQUARE

———

MILE 4

UNION SQUARE TO HERALD SQUARE

———

MILE 5

HERALD SQUARE TO COLUMBUS CIRCLE

———

MILE 6

COLUMBUS CIRCLE TO 79TH STREET

———

MILE 7

79TH STREET TO 106TH STREET

———

MILE 8

106TH STREET TO 122ND STREET

———

MILE 9

122ND STREET TO 143RD STREET

———

MILE 10

143RD STREET TO 165TH STREET

———

MILE 11

165TH STREET TO 179TH STREET

———

"A SORT OF
GEOGRAPHICAL
VIVISECTION"

A NOTE ON STRUCTURE

"THE BEST WAY OF FINDING OUT THE INSIDE OF AN ORANGE
is by cutting it through the middle," William Henry Rideing wrote in
Harper's New Monthly Magazine in December of 1877, "and if, in a sort
of geographical vivisection, a scalpel should be drawn down the middle of New York, it would fall into the channel formed by Broadway."

This book takes up Rideing's suggestion and not only flays Manhattan south to north along its most vital street but also examines
Broadway mile-by-mile from Bowling Green to Marble Hill. Exactly
where one of those miles ends and another begins is, it turns out, an
inexact science. Milestones set up to measure Manhattan's length in
1769 were famously inaccurate, compressing the distance between
the miles so that the island became over fourteen miles long. Adjustments were made and new series of milestones erected, each time
with similar miscalculations. Measurements became standardized
when John Randel Jr., the remarkably scrupulous surveyor of the 1811
Commissioners' Plan, spaced the city's grid of streets so that twenty
blocks equaled one mile.

But it doesn't always pay to be so precise, and Broadway's miles
are often best measured according to matters of personal routine: the
distance from home to the subway; from your favorite coffee shop to

your favorite park; from the Flatiron Building to the Times Building; from the Ansonia to the Apthorp. In the 1840s, lawyer and diarist George Templeton Strong was in the habit of walking up Broadway from his Wall Street office to his sweetheart's home on Union Square, a distance that he measured not in miles but in how many cigars (four) he could smoke along the way.

Today, measurements taken by a GPS device, the odometer in a car, or Google Maps will each give slightly different mile demarcations. For our purposes, it seemed best to embrace imprecision—to push and pull the miles a bit—for the sake of the story.

PREFACE

Broadway began in the early seventeenth century as a muddy path running through the Dutch colony of New Amsterdam and out the settlement's back door, where it dissolved in the farms that lay north of town. Over the next two hundred years the farms gradually disappeared and Broadway grew in length, absorbing older roads in the process, until it had become New York City's "Path of Progress," its legendary traffic and unrelenting commotion, lively public squares, and impressive mansions, hotels, stores, theaters, and churches providing ample evidence of American virtue and industry. Walt Whitman was just one of many poets to compare Broadway to a river—a "mighty ever-flowing land-river" in Whitman-speak— flowing through the heart of America's great metropolis.

"Broadway represents the national life," journalist Junius Henri Browne wrote soon after the Civil War. In order to see America, he suggested, all that was required was a station point along Broadway. "Take your stand there," Browne advised, "and Maine, and Louisiana, the Carolinas, and California, Boston, and Chicago, pass before you." In 1896, illustrator Valerian Gribayedoff, a Russian immigrant, described Broadway as "a kind of animated mirror, looking back at you with its myriad faces in the same mood in which you regard it." By the end of the nineteenth century, Broadway's mirror had reflected, along with millions of merchants, bankers, politicians, pickpockets, preachers, and prostitutes, the faces of George and Martha Washington, Abraham and Mary Todd Lincoln, Alexander and Elizabeth Hamilton, Lafayette, John Jacob Astor, Edgar Allan Poe, P. T. Barnum, John James Audubon, Ralph Waldo Emerson, Margaret

Fuller, Lydia Maria Child, Henry James, Emma Goldman, Stephen Crane, and even (supposedly but not quite) the exiled Louis Philippe I, king of the French.

During the twentieth century, Broadway became a state of mind as much as a street, a ribbon of light that song-and-dance man George M. Cohan celebrated as the most American of American places. And yet Broadway has always had a pronounced dark side, and the dark side grew proportionally with the street until the Great White Way became emblematic of a certain social carelessness, even dissolution, a "street of broken dreams" beset by crime, loneliness, and urban decay. In 1930, playwright William Anthony McGuire's famous declaration—"Broadway's a great street when you're going up. When you're going down take Sixth Avenue"—needed no further explanation.

More recently Broadway has been spruced up and lined with pricey cafes, family-friendly theaters, and festive pedestrian plazas. Most people experience Broadway in fragments—a shopping trip to Herald Square, a cup of coffee near Union Square six months later, a stroll down the West Side the following year, a hike up the stairs from Broadway to Fort Tryon Park five years after that—but those who walk its entire length in one day-long jaunt, from Bowling Green all the way up to Marble Hill, are often surprised to find that Broadway is the one thread that keeps the city stitched together in time and space. This story, a south-to-north journey up one famous street, follows that thread back into America's deep memory.

MILE 1

BOWLING GREEN TO
CITY HALL PARK

CHAPTER 1

SOARING THINGS

———

I T HAPPENED FOR THE FIRST TIME NOT ON BROADWAY BUT on Wall Street. It was a rainy, overcast afternoon, October 28, 1886, and a group of revelers—army veterans, firemen, and a contingent of Columbia and City College students—peeled off onto Wall Street from Broadway, where they had been marching in a parade celebrating the dedication of the Statue of Liberty. They were in high spirits and making noise. Office workers heard the commotion and as a practical joke began dumping used ticker tape from their windows onto the street below. "Every window," the *New York Times* reported the next day, "appeared to be a paper mill spouting out squirming lines of tape."

Ticker-tape parades didn't really become a Broadway tradition until 1899, when Admiral George Dewey, the hero of Manila Bay, was welcomed back to the city at the end of the Spanish-American War. But Broadway processions were hardly a new idea: There had been celebrations, military parades, and funerals up and down Broadway since at least as far back as the Colonial era. Many of those parades, long forgotten, were nothing if not ambitious: An 1825 parade marking completion of the Erie Canal began and ended at the Battery and took in not only Broadway but also the Bowery and Greenwich, Canal, Grand, Broome, and Pearl streets, a tour of cheer and hoopla that took five hours to complete.

In 1842 a parade inaugurating the Croton Aqueduct wound its way from the Battery up Broadway two and a half miles to Union Square, then turned around and headed south down the Bowery, detoured to the east along Grand Street, and returned along East Broadway and Chatham Street (present-day Park Row) to City Hall Park. Fully 15,000 people marched in the parade while 200,000 spectators, "crowded to suffocation," the *New York Tribune* reported, watched from the sidewalks—at a time when the city's population was less than 400,000. The mass of people and festive floats took over two hours to pass a single spot along the route. The parade was so long—six miles in total—that by the time John Aspinwall Hadden, a young soldier marching at the head of the parade, completed the circuit and returned to City Hall Park, the tail end of the procession was still visible slowly making its way up Broadway.

The 1858 "Cable Carnival" celebrating the first successful connection of the Atlantic Cable included as its centerpiece a Broadway parade hailing Cyrus W. Field, a wealthy local paper merchant and the driving force behind the cable project, as a conquering hero. As Field was trundled up Broadway, he was accompanied by the crew of the steam frigate *Niagara*, one of two ships that had unspooled the cable across the ocean. They carried a scale model of the ship and marched just behind a wagon loaded with a huge coil of the cable itself. Then came the inevitable aldermen, policemen, firemen, and representatives of trade societies that were part of every Broadway parade, plus 2,000 laborers then occupied in the construction of Central Park, their hats festooned with sprigs of evergreen.

Thousands of people watched from rooftops and balconies along the parade route, hoping for a glimpse of the renowned Field; one balcony collapsed under the weight of spectators. It took six hours for the procession to make its way from Bowling Green to a reception at the Crystal Palace at Fifth Avenue and 42nd Street, where Field said he was overwhelmed by the "vast crowd testifying their sympathy and approval; praises without stint and friends without number!" He was hailed as "Cyrus the Great," "Gallant Cyrus," and the "Columbus of America."

Cyrus W. Field in 1858, following his Atlantic Cable triumph.

Broadway gave itself over to cable mania. The famous Broadway jewelers Tiffany & Company struck a commemorative gold coin in Field's honor and bought miles of leftover cable from Field and cut it into short strands to sell as souvenirs. A musical production, *Love and Lightning, or the Telegraph Cable,* was performed at Laura Keene's Theatre, on Broadway near Bleecker Street. A special service was held at Trinity Church. Archbishop John J. Hughes buried a written tribute to Field in the cornerstone of St. Patrick's Cathedral, then under construction on Fifth Avenue. The "Atlantic Telegraph Polka" briefly became a dance craze.

That evening the city's Common Council gave a banquet in Field's honor at the swank Metropolitan Hotel at the corner of Broadway and Prince Street, with a dinner menu featuring turtle soup, lobster, salmon, oysters on the half shell, stewed terrapin, wild duck with olives, lamb tenderloin, broiled English snipe, and chartreuse of partridge with Madeira sauce. The table was ornamented with ice sculptures approximating the shapes of Queen Vic-

The "Cable Carnival" procession passes up Broadway.

toria, President James Buchanan, and Field himself. The celebration continued into the night, with a second procession down Broadway by torchlight. There were illuminations, fireworks, and strings of colored lanterns, lending Broadway "a carnivalesque appearance which it is almost impossible to describe," one reporter for the *New York Herald* raved.

In the late nineteenth century Fifth Avenue began to vie with Broadway as the city's uptown parade route, and Broadway parades became truncated, typically encompassing only the street's first mile between Bowling Green and City Hall Park. But as Broadway parades got shorter in length, the advent of ticker tape gave them a thrilling new vertical dimension. Between 1900 and 1970 the city was absolutely besotted with ticker tape: Over those seventy years, through two world wars and the Great Depression, ticker tape rained down on Broadway, cascading from windows high above the street and gathering in drifts along the curbs. (Budget cutbacks and the general urban malaise of the 1970s and '80s turned ticker-tape parades—the ticker tape replaced with shredded sheets of 8½-by-11-inch paper—into exceedingly rare events.)

But during its golden era, if someone was famous, even temporarily, they had a good chance of entering the city through a storm of paper. Theodore Roosevelt, Charles Lindbergh, Jesse Owens, Amelia Earhart, Albert Einstein, Winston Churchill, Harry S. Truman, Dwight D. Eisenhower, and John F. Kennedy were obvious choices for adulation, but throngs also assembled in Broadway to cheer Douglas "Wrong Way" Corrigan, Prince Gustav Adolf of Sweden, President-elect Júlio Prestes de Albuquerque of Brazil, and German airship designer Hugo Eckener. (Einstein insisted on an impromptu detour from Broadway to the Lower East Side, where Jewish immigrants greeted him with something approaching euphoria. "New York has been kind, most kind," he told reporters the next day. "Your city's landscape is not the landscape of a town. It is more like the landscape of a mountain in its impressiveness.") Gertrude Ederle, the first woman to swim the English Channel, was honored with a parade in 1926; two weeks later so was Amelia Corson, the *second* woman to swim the Channel.

The ticker-tape parade was the unlikely byproduct of a contraption invented in 1863 by Edward A. Calahan and improved upon by Thomas Edison. By the 1880s the stock ticker, an intricate brass machine about the size of a modern-day coffeemaker, was a fixture in virtually every office along Broadway. Each machine, resolutely ticking the day away, churned out continuous paper ribbons of stock quotes upon which fortunes were won and lost, but the tape itself was worthless the moment it was read. Office wastepaper bins constantly overflowed with the stuff, and it was only a matter of time before someone decided to hurl it from a window. Whoever was the first to throw it on that fateful day in 1886—the *Times* blamed "imps of office boys"—probably justified it later by saying something like "but it was just *sitting* there."

Of course, ticker-tape parades required launching pads for the projectiles—the higher the better, really—so that the ticker tape unfurled in long streams as it soared downward. And so ticker-tape parades never would have happened without the advent of tall buildings, and tall buildings never would have been possible without elevators and steel.

THERE HAD BEEN a few buildings of seven or even eight stories on Broadway as early as the 1850s, but heights were limited because load-bearing masonry walls had to thicken with each additional floor. By law, a ten-story building required walls 6 to 7 feet thick at ground level, a restriction that severely reduced the size and value of ground-floor rental spaces, which became as dark as dungeons. And building heights were limited to the number of stairs a tenant or customer was willing to climb. Elevators existed, but weren't generally trusted. That changed at the 1853 New York World's Fair, when inventor Elisha Otis dramatically unveiled a new safety device that acted as a brake in the event a supporting cable of an elevator car failed. Otis demonstrated his invention by riding a platform high up into the rafters of the Crystal Palace and then ordering the supporting ropes cut. The brakes caught the platform, Otis removed his top hat and took a bow, and contractors began installing the Otis safety elevator in buildings.

The following year English engineer Henry Bessemer developed a technique for forcing oxygen through molten pig iron to remove carbon and other impurities, creating, for the first time, consistently strong steel. The "Bessemer process" allowed for the eventual mass production of steel beams and columns, substantially lowering the cost of steel construction. In New York, where Manhattan's narrowness made land scarce, the idea that offices might be stacked one upon the other promised a real-estate revolution. On Broadway, first iron (wrought and cast) and then steel construction transformed the street into a vertiginous canyon.

Among the first to dream of Broadway as a vertical landscape was none other than Cyrus W. Field, who, in the summer of 1881, acquired the decaying Washington Hotel (originally the historic eighteenth-century Archibald Kennedy house) at the foot of Broadway, tore it down, and began building one of the street's earliest tall office buildings that employed an interior frame—iron in this case—for its structural support.

Twenty-three years after he had sutured America to Europe through the Atlantic Cable, Field, at sixty-one, was no longer "Cyrus the Great." As the maligned president of the New York Elevated Railroad Company, he was regularly flayed in the press, his once sterling reputation sullied by questionable dealings with financiers Jay Gould and Russell Sage. The *Real Estate Record & Builders' Guide* labeled Field not merely a "crank" but a crank "with no moral sense"—quite an about-face for someone who had once been among the most popular men in America. Field's late-career foray into construction was, in essence, a comeback attempt—a chance, even, at redemption.

It was called the Washington Building or the Field Building, and its address, No. 1 Broadway, seemed to promise great things. Field invited six architects to submit renderings and, with input from his wife Mary, selected Edward Hale Kendall's design as the competition winner.

Kendall's submission was a nine-story mass of brownstone and brick in the then-fashionable Queen Anne style, with entries at two corners accessed by cascading stairs guarded by iron dragons. The Washington Building was completed in 1882, but Field couldn't stop fussing with it. Perhaps he had been goaded into a kind of architectural arms race when the Produce Exchange, a massive palazzo in maroon brick designed by the great architect George B. Post, began rising at No. 2 Broadway, just across the street, or maybe he just wanted the extra square footage, but Field ordered Kendall to add two more floors and then, in 1886, two more, pushing the overall height to 258 feet—only 2 feet shy of the Tribune Building on Park Row, then the world's tallest building. Kendall crowned the finished building with a steeply pitched roof reminiscent of a Swiss chalet, with projecting turrets, balconies, bay windows, and, at the very top, a cylindrical tower enclosed in glass that jutted like a lighthouse high above the roof. Accessed by a winding stair, the tower functioned as an observation deck and, with its unobstructed views of the harbor, quickly became a tourist attraction. Visitors arriving in the city were often so eager to climb to the top of Field's building they went there as soon as their ships docked—even before checking into their hotels. Field himself ascended to his roof as often as he could.

"If I had the time I could spend all day gazing out on that beautiful scene," he remarked wistfully in January of 1887, five months before he lost his entire fortune because of the machinations of Gould and Sage, who dumped their stock in the Manhattan Railway Company just after Field had bought 70,000 shares at a margin of 80 percent, driving down the price and forcing Field to sell the stocks back to Gould for a fraction of their original price.

Field kept to himself what he thought about when he gazed from the Washington Building roof out over the harbor, but no doubt he considered the passage of time and the twists and turns that had brought him in his autumn years to a rooftop at the point where Broadway begins. As he watched ships steaming through the Narrows, ferries plying the rivers, and families of weeping immigrants arriving at the Battery and embracing loved ones, perhaps Field's mind wandered back to that morning in 1858 when he had processed up Broadway past thousands of smiling people shouting his name.

ON A HOT AUGUST MORNING in 1893, French novelist Paul Bourget arrived in New York from Southampton after seven days at sea. "Leaning over the ship's rail on the side toward New York," he wrote, "I succeed in distinguishing a mass of diminutive houses, an ocean of low buildings, from the midst of which rise, like cliff-bound islets, brick buildings, so daringly colossal that, even at this distance, their height overpowers my vision. I count the stories above the level of the roofs; one had ten, another twelve." He called New York's emerging skyline "gigantic, colossal, enormous," and an "apparition."

During his first week in the city he went to the top of the Equitable Building at the corner of Broadway and Pine Street and was overwhelmed by its "hum of life" and the thousands of people coming and going. He called the Equitable a "gigantic palace" and a "human beehive" and began to wonder if New Yorkers were even human.

Cyrus W. Field's Washington Building (far left) in 1900.

"At what time of day do they die here?" he wondered. "At what time do they love? At what time do they think? At what time, indeed, are they men, nothing but men . . . and not machines for locomotion?"

PEOPLE HAD BEGUN calling the tallest of the new buildings "Sky-Scrapers." The Chicago architect Louis Sullivan insisted that they should inspire architects to do their very best work: A skyscraper, Sullivan wrote in 1896, "must be every inch a proud and soaring thing."

By then it was becoming possible to trace the path of Broadway from far out in the harbor, just by following the profiles of its skyscrapers. Field's Washington Building was still clearly visible from the decks of incoming ships, but it had been superseded in height and stature by the Bowling Green Offices, Empire Building, Home Life Insurance Building, Union Trust Building, Manhattan Life Building, American Surety Company Building, and St. Paul Building—a march of progress in glass and steel that was to culminate, in 1913, with construction of the wondrously Gothic Woolworth Building on Broadway opposite City Hall Park.

Today the Woolworth Building still presides over Broadway, its creamy terra-cotta quoins, brackets, and finials catching the first rays of the morning sun as it rises over the park, but many of those early skyscrapers that Bourget found so heroic proved to be, like most buildings in New York, surprisingly ephemeral: The pioneering Tower Building, the first skyscraper with a steel "skeleton" that supported its exterior walls as well as its interior floors, was demolished in 1914; Post's majestic Produce Exchange was torn down in 1957, followed the next year by his Tower-of-Pisa-like (minus the lean) St. Paul Building. Even the mighty Singer Building succumbed to the wrecking ball, in 1968. The Washington Building, which in 1921 had been stripped of its terra-cotta ornaments, covered with limestone, and renamed the International Merchant Marine Company Building, is still there at the foot of Broadway, although today the view from its roof is very different than it was in Field's day. But the street that begins at its front door is very much the same as it was four hundred years ago. As the buildings along its edges have come and gone, Broadway itself has remained, virtually identical in its width, shape, and trajectory to the muddy path that was first surveyed there in the early seventeenth century.

CHAPTER 2

MUD AND FIRE

Broadway was among the very first streets—maybe the first path of any kind—laid out after the Dutch colony of New Amsterdam was established at the southernmost tip of Manhattan in 1624. Broadway may have been the work of surveyor Cryn Fredericksz, who was sent over shortly after the first boatload of settlers—mostly desperate Wallonian refugees—arrived. The Dutch West India Company, a hugely powerful business consortium—think Walmart with its own navy—planned New Amsterdam as the centerpiece of the larger New Netherland colony, and provided Fredericksz with plans that described a network of straight streets within a fortified perimeter.

For reasons that remain lost to time, Fredericksz's orthogonal plan was never carried out. Instead, New Amsterdam grew up around concentric streets that resembled an incomplete version of the Grachtengordel, the remarkable system of canals the Dutch had recently completed in the center of Amsterdam. New Amsterdam's version of the Grachtengordel was somewhat less than remarkable, but included a coherent system of streets that originated from the East River front, where ships anchored, and radiated in ever-larger quarter-circles across the island's toe. The westernmost street was called the Heere Straat (Gentlemen's, or Lord's, Street) or Brede

Wegh (Broad Way) and ran along the Hudson River edge, following a primordial ridge of sand and gravel. In 1653, New Amsterdam's director-general, Peter Stuyvesant, built a wall across the northern boundary of the settlement as a defense against possible British invasion from the north, with a path called the Cingel running along the inside. The Brede Wegh began in an open space in front of Fort Amsterdam, passed through the settlement and out the main gate in the wall, and continued to the Commons, New Amsterdam's communally owned pasture located half a mile north of town.

The Brede Wegh was, as advertised, broad—80 feet wide—but also short, coming to an abrupt dead end at the Commons. The street's generous width allowed for the daily passage of the colony's livestock from town to the Commons and back, and as houses and taverns were built along it, the Brede Wegh gradually became New Amsterdam's main street.

When the long-feared British invasion finally came in 1664, Stuyvesant's wall was of no help. Freezing colonists had already pilfered many of its wide oak boards for firewood, and the British could have simply walked *through* it, as the local Lenape Indians were in the habit of doing. Instead, they took the colony simply by anchoring a frigate off Fort Amsterdam and threatening Stuyvesant with wholesale slaughter. Stuyvesant reluctantly surrendered and retired to his estate north of town. New Amsterdam became New York, the Cingel became Wall Street, and the Brede Wegh became the Broad Way.

THE BROAD WAY—the name was gradually combined into one word and eventually lost its definite article—was unpaved, poorly maintained, and muddy. Hogs foraged in the middle of the street, heedless of oncoming wagons. Gangs of Caribbean pirates infested the taverns clustered around the rechristened Fort James at the foot of the street. The remains of Stuyvesant's wall were torn down in 1699, and in the early eighteenth century the city began extending along Broadway north of Wall Street.

Beginning in 1673, a group of tanners and shoemakers bought up the old Cornelius van Tienhoven farm between Wall Street and the

Commons, and in 1696 partitioned the land into streets and building lots. It was known as the "Shoemakers' Land," and when coupled with the development of the neighboring Jan Jansen Damen farm, added some 53 acres of urban fabric to a city that, in its entirety, consisted of only about 200 acres of developed land. In 1719 a ropewalk—a long, narrow rope factory—was added to the north end of Broadway, where the street terminated at the Commons, and soon the entire east side of the street was thriving as a commercial and industrial center.

Broadway's west side, meanwhile, remained almost completely undeveloped, as everything north of Wall Street had been given over to the 200-acre "Queen's Farm"—the property of Queen Anne. Trinity Church, the Anglican parish built in 1698 at the T where Wall Street ended at Broadway, became the wealthiest landowner in New York, when, in 1705, Anne gave her farm to the church. For many years afterward, Trinity chose not to develop its land, and it wasn't until the 1790s that Broadway's west side, the former farm subdivided into streets and building lots by then, caught up to the bustling activity on the other side of the street.

But that initial difference between Broadway's two sides—wealthy Trinity on one side and tradesmen and manufacturers on the other— evolved into a cultural divide that resonated, as we shall see, into the nineteenth century and colored generations of New Yorkers' perception of the street.

IN 1733 A FEW wealthy families who had built mansions at the foot of Broadway convinced the city's Common Council to let them close a cattle market that had occupied the open space in front of Fort James and replace it with an enclosed green for private games of ninepins. Soon wealthy merchants and ship captains built fine houses surrounding what became known as Bowling Green or the "Parade." They included Archibald Kennedy, who in 1760 built a wide, two-story mansion at the corner of Broadway and State Street facing Bowling Green, its rear lawn sloping down to the Hudson River. The house was in the prevailing Georgian mode; symmetrical, with Classical details on the inside and a front façade dominated by a Palladian window on the second floor. Its address, No. 1 Broadway, was the most coveted in the city. When Kennedy died in 1763, the house passed to his son Archibald Jr., a captain in the Royal Navy.

Other wealthy residents built houses on Broadway until the street, which linked Fort George (formerly Fort James), Trinity Church, and the Commons, where British soldiers were housed in barracks, became a kind of linear allegory of royal power. But Broadway also included the shops and houses of less wealthy artisans and tradesmen and featured two well-known taverns—George Burns's, 115 Broadway, and Abraham de la Montagne's, opposite the Commons—that became centers of revolutionary activities, and as the city edged closer to the events of 1776, Broadway became a corridor of protest.

IN 1765, PARLIAMENT passed the Stamp Act, the first tax levied directly on American colonists, who generally viewed the act, which required the use of specially stamped paper imported from England for everything from newspapers to playing cards, as an egregious imposition, "unconstitutional and oppressive." The first shipment of stamped paper arrived in the city on October 24. When a crowd of protestors refused to let the ship dock and unload its cargo, Lieutenant-Governor Cadwallader Colden slipped the shipment into Fort George at night.

On October 31, a group of prominent merchants gathered at Burns's tavern to draft a nonimportation agreement that bound them to a boycott of British goods. The act took effect the next day, and by seven o'clock in the evening a large group of protestors had gathered on the Commons. A "moveable Gallows" was erected, the *New York Post-Boy* reported, and Colden, "whose public Conduct . . . has unhappily drawn upon himself the general Resentment of his Country," was hung in effigy. The dummy held a piece of stamped paper and was outfitted with a drum on its back, while at its side hung a likeness of Satan, the "Deceiver of Mankind." A second group of torch-wielding protestors paraded its own Colden effigy through the streets to Fort George, where they broke into Colden's carriage house, stole his coach, and with Colden's effigy seated inside, rolled it up Broadway to the Commons. Along the way they met the first group of protestors with its gallows and effigies heading south from the Commons to the fort.

"The whole Multitude then returned to the Fort," the *Post-Boy* reported, "and though they knew the Guns were charged, and saw the Ramparts lined with Soldiers, they intrepidly marched with the Gallows, Coach, & c. up to the very Gate, where they knocked, and demanded Admittance."

The protestors had designs on the despised shipment of paper inside the fort, but when they couldn't get in made do with "many Insults to the Effigy" and then tore down the wooden fence surrounding Bowling Green. They piled up the fence pickets, effigies, and Colden's coach and two sleighs and soon a roaring bonfire illuminated the walls of the fort and the front façade of the Kennedy mansion. "[It] soon kindled to a great Flame," the *Post-Boy* reported, "and reduced the Coach, Gallows, Man, Devil, and all to Ashes."

Colden received several death threats over the next few days, and on November 4 he asked Captain Kennedy to move the paper onto a British warship anchored in the harbor for safekeeping. Kennedy refused—Colden said it was because Kennedy was afraid a mob would burn down his house if he complied—and Colden, eager to be rid of the paper, agreed to turn the shipment over to the Common Council, and the paper, seven crates in all, was carted up to City Hall on Wall Street.

The Stamp Act was repealed in May of 1766, and in gratitude the Common Council commissioned a gilded statue of King George III. Fabricated in Britain, the monument, which depicted the king astride a rearing stallion, arrived in the city in July of 1770 and was placed in the middle of Bowling Green.

FIVE YEARS LATER came the first shots at Lexington and Concord, the Battle of Bunker Hill, and the yearlong siege of British-occupied Boston. When the British finally evacuated in March of 1776, filing onto ships and disappearing into the Atlantic, no one knew where they would turn up next. General George Washington guessed they would sail for New York, the strategically vital key to controlling the Hudson River Valley. As Washington and his ragtag Continental Army marched from Boston to New York, anxious New Yorkers, fled in such numbers that by the time Washington arrived, on April 13, 1776, the city had been practically abandoned.

The city's deserted buildings included the Kennedy mansion and, two doors up, lawyer William Smith's house at No. 5 Broadway. (Kennedy, a loyalist, had departed the city ahead of Washington's arrival. Later that summer he was captured and confined in Morristown, New Jersey, and later immigrated to England to become the 11th Earl of Cassilis.) Washington's exhausted army took possession of both houses, plus others in the vicinity of Bowling Green. Washington stayed at first in Smith's house but, when his wife Martha joined him four days later, moved to the vacated Abraham Mortier estate north of town.

The British, it turned out, had reconnoitered at Halifax, Nova Scotia, where they dropped off evacuating Boston loyalists, took on supplies, and awaited reinforcements. In June, British warships under the command of General William Howe set sail for New York and by the end of the month began arriving in clusters off Sandy Hook, New Jersey, in New York's lower harbor.

On July 2, Howe, aboard the flagship *Greyhound*, led the fleet toward the Narrows, the passageway between Brooklyn and Staten Island that leads into New York's upper harbor. Howe was trying to land his troops on Staten Island, but to those watching from lower Manhattan it seemed Howe was intent on the immediate obliteration of the city, and a general panic ensued. From a hall window in the Kennedy house Colonel Henry Knox and his wife Lucy watched the ships advance "with a fair wind and rapid tide" as "distress and anxiety" prevailed in the streets.

"The city in an uproar, the alarm guns firing, the troops repairing to their posts, and every thing in the [height] of bustle," Knox wrote to his brother William. Then both the wind and tide turned and most of Howe's fleet remained on the far side of the Narrows.

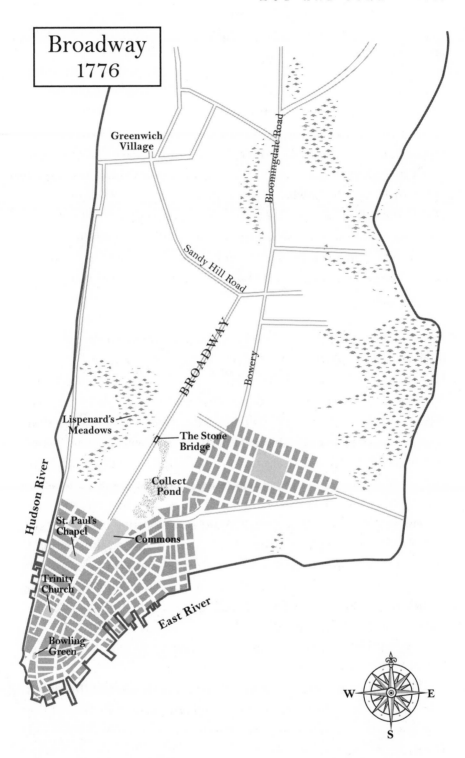

Broadway
1776

Greenwich
Village

Bloomingdale Road

Sandy Hill Road

BROADWAY

Bowery

Lispenard's
Meadows

The Stone
Bridge

Collect
Pond

Hudson River

St. Paul's
Chapel

Commons

Trinity
Church

East River

Bowling
Green

W E

S

Later that evening the ships managed to get through the Narrows and Howe was able to land his troops.

ON JULY 6, THE FIRST COPIES of the Declaration of Independence arrived from Philadelphia. On the evening of July 9, Washington ordered the document read aloud to his troops assembled on the Commons, and afterward a raucous crowd of soldiers and civilians rushed down Broadway to Bowling Green. Ropes were thrown around the gilded statue of George III and, following a series of hopeful cracking noises, king and horse hit the ground with a resounding thud. The leaden statue was hacked up and sent to a forge in Connecticut, where it was melted down into bullets to use against the redcoats.

THE BRITISH FINALLY took New York on September 15, two weeks after its victory at the Battle of Brooklyn. The Continental Army, having narrowly escaped Brooklyn by recrossing the East River to Manhattan under cover of darkness and a lucky morning fog, retreated to Harlem Heights in upper Manhattan, where Washington commandeered the evacuated loyalist Robert Morris's grand Georgian mansion, built ten years earlier on a hill just to the east of the Kingsbridge Road. The house faced south, its front portico affording expansive views of Manhattan's farms and villages and, ten miles to the south, New York City, its skyline then an outline of ship masts and church spires. On September 22, Washington wrote to John Hancock, president of the Second Continental Congress.

"I have nothing in particular to communicate to Congress respecting the Situation of our Affairs," Washington began, before revealing a startling development: "On Friday night, about Eleven or Twelve Oclock, a Fire broke out in the City of New York, near the New or St Pauls [sic] Church, as It is said, which continued to burn pretty rapidly till after Sun rise the next morning. I have not been Informed how the Accident happened, nor received any certain account of the damage. Report says many of the Houses between the Broadway and the River were consumed."

The fire started just east of the Battery, in or near a sketchy tavern known as the Fighting Cocks at the foot of Whitehall Street—not as far north as St. Paul's, as Washington initially believed. Fanned by a stiff southerly wind, the fire rapidly ate its way north, consuming everything between Whitehall and Broad streets, the east side of Broadway from Bowling Green almost to Wall Street, and the west side of the street from Morris Street to Trinity Church.

Joseph Henry, an American soldier who had been captured by the British during the American attack on Quebec, watched the fire from the deck of a British prison ship anchored in the harbor some four miles south of the city. No sooner had Henry seen the fire begin on Whitehall Street than he saw Trinity Church burst into flames. The fire burned so brightly, Henry wrote, that the deck of his ship was lit up "as at noon day."

"If we could have divested ourselves of the knowledge that it was the property of our fellow citizens which was consuming, the view might have been esteemed sublime, if not pleasing," he added.

British sailors stationed in the harbor were hastily ordered onto boats and hustled into town to join soldiers fighting the fire, which roared north along the Hudson River edge, destroying everything between Broadway and Greenwich Street, but sparing most of the buildings along the west side of Broadway north of Trinity. St. Paul's Chapel was saved only because a few stalwart citizens climbed onto its roof and extinguished embers as they fell. The Kennedy mansion was also saved.

The wind died down soon after sunrise the next morning. An improvised firefighting brigade made up of citizens and British soldiers and sailors gradually got the upper hand, and by eleven o'clock had checked the fire's progress. The flames were extinguished just before reaching King's College (renamed Columbia College after the war) on Barclay Street. In all, some 493 houses were destroyed—about one-quarter of the entire city. Trinity Church was especially hard hit, losing not only its seventy-eight-year-old church, but also two schools, its library, the rector's house, and 536 pounds in annual rents from 246 destroyed houses that sat on church property between Broadway and Greenwich Street.

Washington's army had plundered much of the town before their retreat, even removing church bells to melt into cannon or, as the accusations later went, to prevent sounding the alarm when the fire broke out. It was never proven conclusively who set the fire, or whether it was an act of nature or design. There were multiple reports of incendiaries found with matchsticks soaked in liquid rosin, and allegations that British soldiers and sailors had thrown suspected American agents into the flames and hung others from lampposts. The British blamed the catastrophe on a nefarious design perpetrated by Washington himself, who attributed the fire to the work of "some good honest fellow" and apparently considered the destruction of New York a fair price to pay for denying the British the use of a functioning city. ("Had I been left to the dictates of my own judgment," Washington wrote to his cousin Lund Washington, "New York should have been laid in Ashes.")

But the British occupied the compromised city throughout the long war and didn't give it up until November 23, 1783, when Washington rode victorious down Broadway to Fort George to reclaim the city.

BROADWAY WAS QUICKLY REBUILT after the war, and by 1790 had blossomed into a lively thoroughfare lined with poplars and dominated by the spire of a rebuilt Trinity Church. New York had been designated the national capital the year before, with City Hall appropriated as the capitol building. Chief Justice John Jay, Treasury Secretary Alexander Hamilton, Senator Ralph Izard of South Carolina, Senator James Gunn of Georgia, and others in the innermost circle of the federal government moved into townhouses on Broadway in the vicinity of Bowling Green. In 1790, President George Washington himself moved from 3 Cherry Street to the Alexander Macomb mansion at 39-41 Broadway, one block north of Bowling Green. Isaac Sears, a leader of the Sons of Liberty, took over the Kennedy mansion until, disgraced by debt and corruption, he fled to China. (Secretary of State Thomas Jefferson rented a house on Maiden Lane.)

Fort George had been demolished and Government House, a fine palazzo in the Americanized Federal style (a patriotic rebranding of the Neoclassical Georgian mode), was built in its place. It was intended to serve as the permanent national capitol building, but by the time Government House was finished in 1791, New York had already lost the capital to Philadelphia, and Washington and his cohort had settled their accounts, packed up, and left the city. ("All persons having demands against the Household of the PRESIDENT of the United States, are requested to exhibit their accounts for settlement, at his late Dwelling in Broad-Way, before the 15th of September," proclaimed one notice in a local newspaper.)

The capitulation to Philadelphia rankled New Yorkers for years afterward, and in the absence of national-capital status, they were determined that New York should at least triumph over Philadelphia as America's preeminent commercial metropolis. New York, after all, had a deeper harbor than Philadelphia and more direct access to the open ocean—and it had Broadway, and no street in Philadelphia could compare.

Though still barely a mile in length, Broadway was already the envy of every other American city. William Winterbotham, visiting from England in 1795, thought Broadway was delightful, the "most convenient and agreeable part of the city," and noted that the ruins of the Great Fire had been cleared away and replaced with "elegant brick houses" with brick sidewalks in front.

At the Bowling Green end of Broadway were the well-appointed homes of merchants, lawyers, and physicians, while its upper reaches, north of the Commons, were sparsely settled, consisting of humble frame dwellings and shops where tanners, cartmen, and unskilled laborers lived and worked. In between, north of Wall Street but south of the Commons, was a vibrant mix of stores selling dry goods (textiles), jewelry, and shoes, the shops and dwellings of tradesmen and artisans—carpenters, coopers, tinsmiths, cabinetmakers, distillers, saddlers, and makers of soap and candles—and the mansions of wealthy merchants. John Jacob Astor, then amassing a fortune in the fur trade, lived at No. 149, but his next-door neighbor was one John B.

Nash Jr., an ironmonger; Nash's father, a fabricator of tinplate, lived just a few blocks to the south. There were no theaters on Broadway yet, but there were hints of the street's later cultural exuberance in the famous City Hotel just north of Trinity Church, a circulating library across from the hotel, and the many booksellers who opened shops along that stretch of the street.

Broadway was full of life, but wasn't especially beautiful. Foraging hogs, garbage, and good old American dirt remained intractable problems. Broadway wasn't yet paved, and since drainage was a poorly understood art, the roadbed quickly became a foul stew of mud and horse manure. And aside from Government House, Trinity Church and St. Paul's Chapel, Broadway wasn't architecturally impressive. In 1797, New York surpassed Philadelphia for the first time in the total tonnage of imports and exports moving through its port, but for the next twenty years that advantage remained tenuous. As the nineteenth century dawned, it occurred to politically astute merchants and members of the city's Common Council that if New York was ever going to vanquish Philadelphia once and for all, it had better look the part.

"We certainly ought . . . to possess at least one public edifice which shall vie with the many now erected in Philadelphia," alderman Wynant van Zandt Jr. argued at a meeting of the Common Council in 1803. New York was prosperous and growing—between 1790 and 1800 the population almost doubled, from 33,131 to 60,489—but still lacked grand public buildings and even basic sanitation. Dead cats, the *Boston Gazette* reported that year, lay in the streets "in every part of the city."

In 1803 the Common Council, with Van Zandt in charge of the building committee, began construction of a new City Hall at the center of the Commons, hoping it would improve the city's image. The Commons, for almost two hundred years the site of political insurgencies and public executions, was benignly reconstituted as "the Park," a triangular public space lined with gravel walks and shaded by elms and willows. Critics condemned the new City Hall as a "bottomless pit of finance"—it ended up costing half a million dollars—but even before its completion City Hall had helped dispel the long-held notion that New York was nothing more than Philadelphia's backward cousin. John Lambert, visiting from England in 1807, walked up Broadway and dutifully admired City Hall and its lovely new park, but what really struck him was the vitality of Broadway itself.

CHAPTER 3

PROMENADE

—

I N A CITY WITHOUT MANY PUBLIC AMUSEMENTS—SINCE ITS
opening in 1798 the Park Theatre, on Chatham Street opposite City
Hall Park, had been practically the only show in town—social promenading was a favorite pastime, and with its shade trees and brick
sidewalks no street was better for walking than Broadway. On week-
days between eleven in the morning and three in the afternoon the
city's "genteel" residents took to the street, John Lambert noted, until
Broadway became "as much crowded as the Bond-street in London."
On Sundays chains were fastened across the street on either side of
Broadway's three churches, Grace, Trinity, and St. Paul's, to prevent
traffic from disturbing services. Afterward men and women strolled
down Broadway to the Battery to catch the ocean breezes. It was
how they kept up with each other, how they did business, and how
they fell in love.

"[Dressed] in their best [young women] would generally walk
together keeping [to] the inside of the street going down and the outside going up," resident John J. Sturtevant remembered. "Somewhere
on the line they would see their John Henry or Mary Jane as the case
might be; if John Henry had pluck and Mary Jane's companion was
complaisant he would join her and the companions would separate
so giving them a good time."

"Yes, everyone walked in those days," journalist John Flavel Mines remembered, "and, as I grew out of boyhood towards manhood, I used to think that the rosebud garden of Broadway on a crisp autumn afternoon was lovely beyond compare."

One of the first things tourists did when they arrived in New York was to go for a walk on Broadway. "We walked everywhere, and saw everything," George Kirwan Carr, a young British second lieutenant, visiting with fellow soldiers in 1832, wrote in his diary. "[We] were much delighted with the 'flash' dresses of the Ladies—Pink Satin, bonnets & feathers, and boots to match of the same material, at 10 o'clock in the Morning walking in Broadway!"

Carr and his mates should not have been surprised that Broadway's "Ladies" were so well dressed. Broadway's stores got the first pick of imported dry goods arriving by ship only a few blocks away, and its daily promenade became a parade of the latest Parisian fashions. Broadway "might be taken for a French street, where it was the fashion for very smart ladies to promenade," English travel writer Frances Trollope observed in 1829. "The dress is entirely French; not an article (except perhaps the cotton stockings) must be English, on pain of being stigmatized as out of the fashion."

The "Broadway Belle" draped in Parisian shawls and trimmed in Irish lace became a stock New York character. In 1825, McDonald Clarke, the "Mad Poet of Broadway," published *Afara; or, the Belles of Broadway*, a rhapsody of evening on Broadway, when stores closed and the daily promenade came to an end.

> *Broadway became a desert—one, two, three,*
> *Pealed, unnoticed, from the steeple's throat;*
> *The sun was wasting his rich rays—ah, me,*
> *That he should deign to shine on shawl and coat,*
> *Unvandervoort or Scofield born—and night,*
> *Stole out upon the scene as well arrayed,*
> *As if the day had seen that precious sight,*
> *Fashion's unbending exquisite parade,*
> *And wore a clear, blue mantle—star inwrought,*
> *And looked as if her dress—could not be bought.*

Broadway may have been the city's most fashionable street, but only its west side, the Trinity side, was considered safe for Society. The cultural divide between Broadway's two sides had festered until by the early nineteenth century the west side was known as the "dollar side" of the street, while the east side, at least in the blocks north of Wall Street, was denigrated as the low-end "shilling side."

Shillings, a holdover from the British currency used in the colonies before the Revolution, remained in circulation in the United States even after the new American currency was introduced in 1792. Shillings were valued differently depending on the state: In Georgia and South Carolina they were worth 21 cents; in Pennsylvania, Delaware, New Jersey, and Maryland, only 13½ cents. The so-called York shilling used in New York, North Carolina, Ohio, and Michigan was the least valuable of all, worth only 12½ cents, or eight to the dollar. (Shillings remained common in New York until after the Civil War, and were still occasionally seen even into the early twentieth century.)

The distinction between Broadway's two sides has most often been attributed to the quality of morning sunlight falling on the dollar side, where crisp morning rays highlighted to greater advantage the merchandise on display in its shop windows, while the shilling side remained in shadow until late morning. But the comparative intensity of morning light doesn't fully explain why the east side of the street would have been relegated to second-class status. The noon sun, after all, fell equally on both sides of the street, and storefronts along the shilling side received better light in the afternoons than those on the dollar side. The perception that the east side of Broadway was déclassé was undoubtedly a vestige of the class distinction that in the 1600s had set the Trinity side of the street apart from the shoemakers and rope manufacturers on the opposite side.

The dollar side was a thin façade anyway, as just behind its impressive churches and mansions lay blocks of decrepit buildings, many of them owned and rented by Trinity. Church Street, one block west of Broadway, had been the epicenter of an eighteenth-century red-light district called the Holy Ground, a disreputable area of wood-frame dwellings, gambling houses, and brothels that by the early nineteenth century had attracted the largest concentration of blacks in the city and was known locally as Coontown.

Blacks liked to promenade on Broadway every bit as much as whites did, but had to endure stares and comments as they walked up and down the street. "On one occasion we met in Broadway a young negress in the extreme of fashion," Trollope wrote, "and accompanied by a black *beau*, whose toilet was equally studied; eye-glass, guard-chain, nothing was omitted; he walked beside his sable goddess uncovered, and with an air of the most tender devotion."

Black parishioners from Zion African M. E. Church, at the southwest corner of Church and Leonard streets, were not warmly received when they adjourned to Broadway following Sunday evening services. One anonymous letter to the editor of the *New York Evening Post* in 1825 accused Zion's congregation of rude manners and insobriety, and hinted that they might be forcibly stopped from congregating on Broadway if they didn't walk a straighter line.

And God forbid if whites and blacks were ever seen promenading together. "If a white person were to walk arm in arm with a black, in Broadway or any other of the leading streets in New York, he would probably be hooted and pelted by the populace," English visitor Isaac Candler noted in 1824. "I was once conversing in one of the streets of Paris with a New York citizen, when two genteelly dressed persons, the one a white the other a black walked by us in the way I have mentioned. My acquaintance instantly calling my attention to them, [and] expressed his astonishment and abhorrence at a white man's so degrading himself."

IN THE 1830s AND '40s, Broadway underwent a radical transformation, as commercial concerns made inroads into its first mile. Mansions were pulled down or converted to boardinghouses and offices, and John Jacob Astor built the palatial Astor House hotel on Broadway one block north of St. Paul's Chapel. But the Broadway Belles didn't go away; if anything, their numbers increased and their dress became more ostentatious.

"Heaven save the ladies, how they dress!" Charles Dickens exclaimed in 1842. "We have seen more colours in these ten minutes, than we should have elsewhere, in as many days. What various parasols! what rainbow silks and satins! what pinking of thin stockings, and pinching of thin shoes, and fluttering of ribbons and silk tassels, and display of rich cloaks with gaudy hoods and linings!"

Dickens, visiting New York for the first time, was gazing down at Broadway from his window at the Carlton House hotel on the corner of Broadway and Leonard Street. The city tried to put its best foot forward for Dickens's much-anticipated visit, staging an elaborate "Boz Ball" in his honor and inviting him to dinner parties, but the city couldn't hide its warts, and there was much to see on Broadway besides the latest fashions. Despite its reputation as America's most fashionable thoroughfare, Broadway featured scenes of desperation that rivaled anything in Dickens's own writing.

The vicissitudes of the city's economy—the disastrous Panic of 1837, the recession of 1840, and the "mini-panic" of 1841—hadn't slowed the steady influx of new residents, and by 1840 New York City's population had reached 312,710, almost four times larger than Baltimore, then the second-largest American city. (Philadelphia, fading as a serious rival to New York, had slipped to third place.) As the city expanded, and as the divide between rich and poor grew ever wider, alarming numbers of indigent men and women gathered each day on Broadway. The same month as Dickens's visit, the *New York Aurora* described a crowd of two hundred indigent women, both black and white, plus a few men, "ragged cripples mostly," waiting at the entrance of the city's almshouse in City Hall Park for handouts of food and firewood.

"Twice a week they come—on Tuesday from one side of the town, on Saturday from the other," the *Aurora* reported. "They are scenes for a Dickens, and all men and women looked pale, woe-be-gone and desolate . . . What a contrast was this to . . . the brilliant groups that were passing up and down the sunny side of dear Broadway!"

That the destitute gathered in such numbers on Broadway, the undisputed epicenter of the city's wealth and power, was not lost on essayist Lydia Maria Child, who had moved to the city from rural Massachusetts the year before Dickens's visit. Slavery had been illegal in New York since 1827, but New York's prosperity was still in large part based on the exportation of Southern cotton and therefore on slave labor.

"There, amid the splendour of Broadway, sits the blind negro beggar, with horny hand and tattered garments, while opposite to him stands the stately mansion of the slave trader, still plying his bloody trade," Child observed in 1841. Broadway, too, was an increasingly dangerous place, especially after dark, when the street was crowded with con artists, pickpockets, prostitutes, and gangs. "It's a pity we've no street but Broadway that's fit to walk in of an ev'ng," George Templeton Strong wrote in his diary in the fall of 1840. "The street is always crowded, & whores & blackguards make up about two thirds of the throng."

And Broadway was still extraordinarily filthy. Street cleaning was sporadic at best, and piles of garbage and horse manure were routinely left to fester at the curb. When the wind kicked up, the street virtually disappeared in blinding dust storms; when it rained it became a sea of mud. Hogs still rooted along Broadway, just as they had in Dutch times. Soon after his arrival, Dickens went for a tour of the city and was startled when two "portly sows," followed by a "select party of half-a-dozen gentlemen-hogs," followed along behind his carriage.

"These are the city scavengers, these pigs," Dickens wrote in *American Notes for General Circulation,* an unsparing account of his trip published later that year. "Ugly brutes they are; having, for the most part, scanty, brown backs, like the lids of old horse-hair trunks; spotted with unwholesome black blotches. They have long, gaunt legs, too, and such peaked snouts, that if one of them could be persuaded to sit for his profile, nobody would recognize it for a pig's likeness. They are never attended upon, or fed, or driven, or caught, but are thrown upon their own resources in early life, and become preternaturally knowing in consequence."

Broadway's hogs were an embarrassment, but more alarming, the city had no storm-water or sewer system, and no workable system for providing fresh water for drinking, washing, and bathing. (Wooden water pipes laid under some streets in 1790, and iron pipes laid under Broadway and the Bowery in 1829 and fed from a cistern on 13th Street, were woefully out of date and had never worked well in the first place.) For centuries the city had relied on cisterns, springs, and communal wells for fresh water, but whatever local water sources remained in Manhattan had long since been irrevocably soiled or covered up. No surprise, then, that cholera swept through the city every few years.

The Croton Aqueduct, which brought fresh water from Westchester County directly into the city, was as ambitious in scope as the Erie Canal, which had opened seventeen years earlier and brought the lucrative markets of the West into New York's sphere of influence. The Croton River was dammed to form an artificial lake of some 400 acres, and every day 17 million gallons of fresh water flowed, by gravity alone, thirty-three miles through an arched brick, stone, and cast-iron aqueduct into upper Manhattan, emptying into a 32-acre "Detaining or Clarifying Reservoir" at 86th Street, in the middle of what would later become Central Park.

From there the water flowed downhill to a 4-acre "Distributing Reservoir" at the corner of 40th Street and Fifth Avenue (a site that would later become the New York Public Library), and finally into a complex grid of iron supply pipes laid beneath every street in the city. Most streets had one pipe, and some had two, but Broadway, because of its width and centrality, had three. At Bowling Green, City Hall Park, and Union Square, Croton water erupted in jets from a glorious new novelty: decorative fountains.

On Friday, October 14, 1842, the waters of the Croton flowed unimpeded beneath the city for the first time, and New Yorkers devoted themselves to a day of celebration, just as they had when the Erie Canal opened in 1825. Business was suspended, even on hectic Wall Street, and everyone, it seemed, pressed into Broadway. Normally reserved citizens lost themselves in sheer joy at the sudden abundance of what had for generations been a scarce and precious commodity.

"Then the water leaped joyfully and went on its mission of love,"

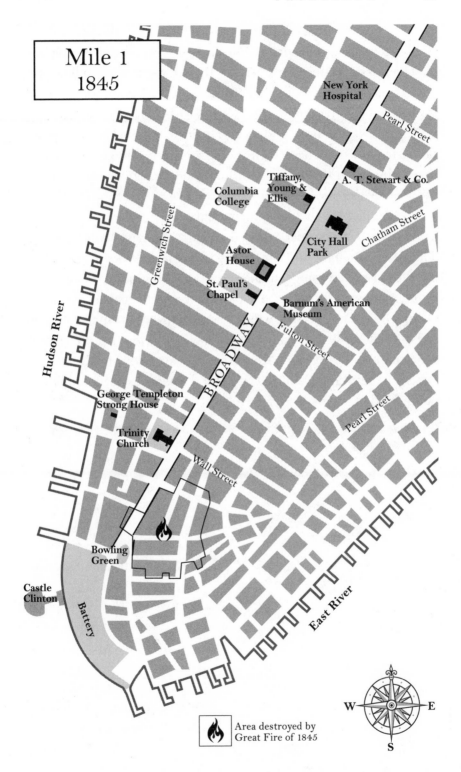

Mile 1
1845

New York Hospital

Pearl Street

Tiffany, Young & Ellis

A. T. Stewart & Co.

Columbia College

Chatham Street

Astor House

City Hall Park

St. Paul's Chapel

Greenwich Street

Barnum's American Museum

Fulton Street

Hudson River

BROADWAY

Pearl Street

George Templeton Strong House

Trinity Church

Wall Street

Bowling Green

Castle Clinton

Battery

East River

Area destroyed by
Great Fire of 1845

W E
S

Child wrote. "Concealed, like good deeds, it went all over the city, and baptized it in the name of Purity, Temperance, and Health."

The fire department, made up in those days of brave and boisterous volunteer "fire laddies" who dressed in red sweaters and black leather hats and carried themselves with considerable swagger, turned out in full force, and in high spirits, for the Croton celebration. Many of them had taken the temperance pledge, but even the hard drinkers in the department had good reason for rejoicing over the aqueduct's completion.

For decades the fire department had been fighting a losing battle against what newspapers tended to call "the devouring element." The city was simply too big for the beleaguered volunteers to keep up with the increasing number, and alarming scale, of fires that regularly destroyed entire city blocks. It was the calamitous losses of the Great Fire of 1835, which had destroyed much of the financial district between Broadway and the East River, that precipitated construction of the Croton Aqueduct. At least with a ready supply of water, the thinking went, the city stood a chance. But it didn't turn out quite that way.

CHAPTER 4

FIRE AND PROGRESS

———

By THE 1840s, BROADWAY'S FIRST MILE HAD CHANGED irrevocably. The headquarters of shipping, insurance, coal, finance, and railroad companies had moved in, along with dry goods "jobbers" (middlemen in the wholesale textile trade), lawyers, brokers, architects, and engineers. As more and more of Broadway's dwellings were torn down, converted to commercial uses, or turned into boardinghouses for visitors and European immigrants, residents moved uptown to Bond Street, Washington Square, Union Square, and Gramercy Park. But holdouts remained: Lawyer George Templeton Strong, resisting the northward migration of his peers, lived a solitary existence in a small extension built behind his parents' house at 108 Greenwich Street, one block west of Broadway.

Strong was twenty-five in the summer of 1845. He was a partner in his father's Wall Street law firm of Strong, Bidwell & Strong, but was never very active in the practice and rarely appeared in court. He spent much of his spare time at favorite haunts along Broadway's first mile, going to concerts at the Broadway Tabernacle, lectures at Peale's Museum, and meetings at the Union Club and Trinity Church, where he was a member of the vestry. In summer, Strong and his pals gorged themselves on strawberry ice cream and concoctions of frozen lemonade and rum within the leafy confines of Contoit's

New-York Garden, a verdant "pleasure garden" on Broadway near Leonard Street.

Few people outside Strong's immediate family knew that he was steadily compiling the most extraordinary diary in the city's history. Eventually encompassing four thick, bound volumes brimming with caricatures and imaginative sketches of medieval castles and futuristic flying contraptions, Strong's journal, written in a neat, nearly microscopic hand, documented everyday life in New York City beginning in 1835, when he was a fifteen-year-old Columbia College student, and ending just before his death in 1875.

Strong complained strenuously in his journal as, one-by-one, his neighbors left downtown and German and Irish immigrants moved in. But the cardinal points of Strong's everyday life still aligned along a very short but reassuringly stable east-west path connecting his home on Greenwich Street, Trinity Church, and his Wall Street office. Other than summer vacations to Long Island or Saratoga, Strong's world was neatly inscribed along that line. But that was all about to change.

STRONG WAS ASLEEP at home in the wee hours of July 19, 1845, when a fire began in a whale-oil warehouse on New Street, a narrow alley running parallel to Broadway, one block east of Bowling Green. The fire quickly spread to a chair factory and then to a warehouse. Volunteer fire brigades arrived, uncoiled their hoses, and began pumping water from curbside hydrants, an important feature of the new Croton water system. As was the custom, several firemen, including Francis Hart Jr. of Engine Company No. 22, climbed onto the roofs of neighboring buildings and began wetting them down. It was a bad fire, but nothing out of the ordinary. No one realized that potassium nitrate—"saltpeter," an extremely volatile compound then used in the manufacture of fireworks and gunpowder and employed as a food preservative—was stored in the warehouse.

At half past three in the morning the warehouse exploded, shaking Strong's house, he wrote in his diary, "like an earthquake" and practically throwing him from his bed. When he looked out his window toward Broadway, he saw a "broad column of intense red flame, that made the moon look pale."

Hart, positioned on the roof of a building at the corner of Broad Street and Exchange Place when the warehouse exploded, felt the building falling under him. "[The] roof moved around so that a corner of it caught on the opposite side of Exchange Street and was thrown off into that street," Hart said later. "As far as I could judge the whole roof that I was on moved in one piece, and the walls under it crumbled down beneath it." Somehow Hart survived, his only injury a twisted ankle.

The warehouse exploded at least three more times, sending flaming debris scattering over the rooftops and igniting many of the buildings on Broadway and Broad Street. Strong threw on his clothes and ran to Broadway, where a large crowd had already gathered.

The fire burned south to Bowling Green, destroying houses, offices, and hotels along the way. Soon the entire east side of Broadway between Whitehall Street and Exchange Place—the same stretch of the street that had been destroyed in the Great Fire of 1776—was in flames. To the east of Broadway the fire spread all the way to William Street, while occupants of buildings as far away as Water, Front, and Pearl streets hauled goods out onto the street, just as they had during the Great Fire of 1835. Then the wind picked up, and the fire leapt across Broadway and ignited six houses on the street's west side.

The fire raged through the night and into the next morning, and everyone panicked, hurling their belongings into the streets and gathering in confused crowds in Bowling Green and on the Battery. "Drays, carts and wheelbarrows, hastily loaded with the most incongruous cargoes, are pushing through the dense crowd in every direction," the *Tribune* reported in a special edition published at dawn. "Irish women, with a bed in one hand and two or three naked children in the other, run to deposit them on the [side] walk." Soon the sidewalk in front of Trinity Church was piled with beds, tables, bureaus, chairs, clocks, and kettles. Burning papers floated high into the air over the harbor and landed as far away as Staten Island.

By ten o'clock in the morning Broadway was a tunnel of fire.

The heat was so intense in the middle of the street, the *Tribune* reported, "not even the daring firemen could venture upon the burning pavement." The volunteers of Engine Company No. 8 stationed themselves at the corner of Broadway and Morris Street, but could maintain their position only if another company doused them with water. Police prevented crowds from entering Broadway, but Strong persuaded them to let him through. Walking north, he found Broadway a "chaos of ruin and smoke" and eerily deserted except for a few firemen.

By half past ten the fire had reached the roof of a building at the southeast corner of Greenwich and Morris streets, only 300 yards south of the Strong family home and even closer to Trinity Church. But the fire spread no further, and by noon was under control, but not before much of Broadway between Bowling Green and Trinity had been reduced to a field of hissing ruins. About a dozen people were killed.

That night hundreds of refugees camped on the Battery. Three days later small patches of fire were still burning in at least twenty different spots. The *Evening Post* likened the scene to a prairie fire.

The fire had destroyed 217 buildings—34 of them on Broadway. The losses on Broadway included Cornelius Vanderbilt's office and the Waverley, Bowling Green, and Adelphi hotels. The fire displaced at least 400 residents and businesses, while the total loss was estimated at $5 million to $8 million—$151 million to $242 million in today's dollars.

"Bank notes of the denomination of five dollars would not burn as rapidly in a common fireplace as property was consumed by this conflagration," John Doggett Jr., publisher of *Doggett's Directory*, wrote in a special supplement rushed to press shortly after the fire.

Many New Yorkers felt thoroughly chastened for having believed that the era of the "Great Fires" was over. "[Our] bountiful supply of Croton Water does not afford us an absolute protection against the devouring element," the *Tribune* lamented the day after the fire, as if considering the possibility for the first time.

But the Great Fire of 1845 didn't prostrate Broadway the way the

Great Fire of 1776 had. Progress was already changing Broadway, the fire only hastening an ongoing process of demolition and construction. Even those who had suffered steep losses in the fire practically rejoiced at the chance to rebuild, seeing the fire not so much as a reversal but as an opportunity. Diarist and one-time mayor Philip Hone, then serving as president of American Mutual, one of six fire insurance companies bankrupted by the fire, vowed that the city's economy wouldn't miss a beat.

"Throw down our merchants ever so flat, they roll over once, and spring to their feet again," Hone wrote in his diary. "Knock the stairs from under them, and they will make a ladder of the fragments, and remount."

The *Tribune* predicted that the city wouldn't be "crushed nor stunned by" the fire, that businesses would quickly relocate and reopen. Sure enough, within days of the fire, the *Evening Post* reported seeing piles of bricks stacked in the streets, ready for rebuilding, while an "abundance of capital [was] lying in wait."

The age when Broadway's first mile was a tree-lined promenade was rapidly fading into the past. It wasn't a sentimental era, and favorite landmarks were torn down with barely a second thought. Even the old Kennedy mansion at No. 1 Broadway was irreversibly altered in 1849, its roof shorn off and a third story added, and the once-grand house became the Washington Hotel, someone's scheme for cashing in on its Revolutionary War backstory.

For even the most long-established families, to continue living on or near Broadway's first mile seemed increasingly out of step with the times. Three years after the fire, even George Templeton Strong, having married the daughter of a real-estate speculator, built a new house on 21st Street, facing Gramercy Park, and left Greenwich Street behind forever.

Broadway was a juggernaut by 1845, a bustling commercial thoroughfare. But there was still something homogenous about its architecture. Aside from City Hall, the Astor House hotel, and St. Paul's Chapel, it lacked civic monuments. That all changed in 1846, with the completion of a majestic new church and a remarkable store.

————————

IN 1839, FOLLOWING a winter of heavy snowfall, parishioners began noticing worrisome cracks in the walls and ceiling of Trinity Church, a relatively new structure built in 1790 as the replacement for the original church lost in the Great Fire of 1776. Trinity's vestry hired architect Richard Upjohn, a former cabinetmaker from England, as a consultant, and Upjohn reported that the church was beyond saving. Instead of repairing the old church, Upjohn was allowed to tear it down and design a new church in its place. It was the most important commission of his career.

Upjohn was under the spell of English architect Augustus Welby Northmore Pugin, who in writings and pattern books championed the Gothic Revival mode as the one true style of Christian architecture. In 1841, Pugin published *The True Principles of Pointed or Christian Architecture*, an obsessive how-to book full of Gothic brackets, quoins, ogees, and arches, plus drawings of an "Ideal Church."

Pugin's Ideal Church was a soaring, dramatically vertical version of the Gothic Revival, with a long central nave beneath a pitched roof and a graceful spire towering over the main entrance. Upjohn, thirty-nine in 1841 but virtually untested as an architect, was just beginning to design the new Trinity when *The True Principles* was published. Upjohn had already designed a very similar Gothic structure with soaring, arched ceilings, a long central nave, and a tower and spire on the Broadway end of the building. But then Pugin's Ideal Church came along, and Upjohn copied many of its features, including, almost note-for-note, its tower and slender spire.

The site, on Broadway at Wall Street, could not have been more public, and Upjohn's every move was closely scrutinized. He built a temporary office in Trinity's churchyard, close by the graves of Alexander Hamilton and Robert Fulton, and went about methodically demolishing the old church, uncovering seventeenth-century burial vaults in the process. Construction of the new church began in 1841, and George Templeton Strong paid regular visits to the site, admiring the "cunningly carved" brownstones littering the churchyard. By 1844 the tower was far enough along that Strong could scramble up a rickety ladder to the top and enjoy panoramic views from what was then a dizzying height—281 feet above the ground and the city's tallest structure.

It took five full years to complete the new Trinity. Even before its consecration it was hailed as the finest Gothic Revival structure America had ever seen. "It rivals the accurate taste of the best works of the fourteenth century, and is carried out upon a scale which we had deemed it impossible to adopt, in a country where architecture is in so chaotic a state," Boston architect Arthur D. Gilman wrote in the *North American Review.*

Trinity Church in 1900.

Trinity was consecrated on the Feast of the Ascension, May 21, 1846. Nearly two hundred clergy led a procession up Broadway from Bowling Green to the new church, which was packed to the gills. Strong couldn't find a seat.

Six months later, on September 20, 1846, the most magnificent retail store America had ever seen opened at the corner of Broadway and Reade Street, ten blocks north of Trinity. One thousand people per hour, for twelve straight hours, passed through the doors of A. T. Stewart & Company on that first day, and for the next thirty years the store was so successful Stewart never bothered to put a sign on the building.

Alexander Turney Stewart, a physically unassuming, book-ish Irish protestant immigrant from a village near Belfast, was the wealthiest dry goods merchant in the city, worth a reported $800,000—$25,000,000 in today's dollars—in an era when dry goods accounted for about one-third of all American imports. Stew-art's mercantile innovations included fixed pricing—before Stewart, everyone haggled—and it was Stewart, more than anyone else, who, by seeing to his customers' comfort, turned shopping into a social ritual. And it was Stewart who made Broadway's east side safe for business when he breached social protocol and built his new store not only on the shilling side of Broadway but on a block *above* City Hall Park, at a time when that stretch of the street was an unfashionable wilderness of daguerreotype studios, oyster saloons, music publish-ers, corset-makers, and thread-and-needle stores.

Customers flocked to Stewart's for its vast inventory of imported dry goods, its fair prices, and its considerate staff. The store con-sisted of long, open showrooms with counters staffed by friendly, efficient clerks who, when asked, brought out bolt after bolt of won-drous imported wool, silk, linen, and lace. Stewart's sold dry goods directly from the case—ready-to-wear clothing hadn't caught on yet—and so at the top floor, out of sight, were long wooden tables where hundreds of women worked as seamstresses, watched over by stern male supervisors.

But it was the store itself, immediately christened the "Marble Palace," that stopped traffic. It was designed by the firm of Trench

& Snook and was five stories high—still tall for its time. Its exterior was off-white Tuckahoe marble quarried in Westchester County, the façades composed in a fresh new style cribbed from the Italian Renaissance that came to be known as the Italianate mode and gradually took over the city's mid-century architecture. Interior walls and ceilings were frescoed, and the showrooms were organized around a grand, circular stair that swept around a skylit central rotunda. And there were bells and whistles, including an elevator and a spacious lounge for the exclusive use of women shoppers.

The store's ground-floor windows along the Broadway and Reade Street sides were imported French plate glass, each pane measuring a then-unimaginable 6 by 11 feet. Philip Hone scoffed at the extravagance, predicting that children would break the windows with marbles or snowballs. But the windows, protected at night with roll-down iron shutters, survived. Henry James, in his memoir *A Small Boy and Others,* recalled childhood excursions down Broadway to Stewart's, which, he wrote, exerted a kind of gravitational pull on his aunt. The windows especially, James wrote, were "notoriously fatal to the female nerve."

CHAPTER 5

BARNUM

———

"BROADWAY WAS THE FEATURE AND THE ARTERY, THE JOY and adventure of one's childhood," James wrote, while fondly recalling Saturday visits to the American Museum's "dusty halls of humbug," its lecture hall smelling of peppermint and oranges.

The American Museum was an institution that since its founding as a scientific "cabinet" in 1790 had moved repeatedly, its collection of stuffed birds, wax figures, minerals, fossils, and paintings shuttled from owner to owner and from street to street. Gradually its scientific purpose was expanded to include performances of a sensational nature. In 1807, when John Savage was operating the museum out of a building on Greenwich Street, these included demonstrations of "Electric Fluid," a "Dance of Witches," and a "phantasmagoria" that promised the resurrection of the disembodied spirits of "departed and lamented Patriots."

From Savage the museum passed to John Scudder, who moved the collection first to Chatham Street, in 1810, and then, in 1815, to the New York Institution, a cultural hub housed in the city's old almshouse in City Hall Park. After Scudder died, in 1821, the museum continued under the management of his son John Jr., daughter Mercy, and a team of executors. But the museum faced stiff competition: Rubens Peale's Museum and Gallery of the Fine Arts opened in 1825 on Broadway, directly across the street from the American Museum, and Peale began drawing large crowds by supplementing his exhibitions with lectures, séances, and performances by dwarfs, automatons, ventriloquists, magicians, and mesmerists.

In 1830 the city revoked the American Museum's lease, and the Scudder family boxed up its collection and moved to the so-called Marble Building at the corner of Broadway and Ann Street, one block north of Fulton Street and directly across Broadway from St. Paul's Chapel. The Marble Building was five stories high, taller than almost every other building on Broadway, and featured a roof terrace that afforded, one 1834 guidebook noted, "some of the finest views in the City, and of the beautiful bay and surrounding country."

To attract business and compete with Peale, Scudder Jr. installed a brass band on a balcony overlooking Broadway, demonstrated an automated organ called the "American Apollonicon," and presented lectures by a "Dr. Collyer," who discoursed on animal magnetism. There was a "Grand Cosmorama" and a "Mammoth Sycamore Tree" on view, and Scudder soon acquired an anaconda and a boa constrictor and put them on display. The three blocks of Broadway between Scudder's and Peale's museums had become something of a sideshow well before P. T. Barnum entered the picture.

PHINEAS TAYLOR BARNUM was born in Bethel, Connecticut, in 1810 and moved to New York in the mid-1830s. He was a large man with generous jowls, thick eyebrows, cleft chin, tousled hair, and a mouth that turned up naturally into a quizzical smile. He wore vests, cravats, and frock coats in the style of the day, and a top hat made of felted rabbit fur.

To make ends meet, Barnum at first ran a boardinghouse and then a grocery, manufactured "bear grease," wrote ad copy for the Bowery Amphitheatre, and sold Bibles. Several times he left town for extended periods, traveling cross-country with a ragtag circus, and on occasion was pressed into service on the stage, where he sang "Zip Coon" in blackface.

His first sustained success in New York came in 1835, when as

P. T. Barnum, ca. 1865.

a twenty-five-year-old aspiring showman he put an elderly, blind black woman on display at Niblo's Garden, a pleasure garden at the corner of Broadway and Prince Street. Joice Heth had been touring the country in the guise of a 161-year-old former nurse of George Washington, and New York audiences bought the whole charade hook, line, and sinker. Within two weeks, Barnum claimed, he made back in ticket sales the $1,000 he had paid for custody of Heth. When Heth died suddenly in 1836, Barnum rented the City Saloon at 218 Broadway and turned her autopsy into a public spectacle, with tickets priced at 50 cents, twice the admission for Heth's show when she was still alive.

In 1841, Barnum bought the American Museum's collection from the Scudder family, assumed the Marble Building's lease, and changed the name on the façade from "Scudder" to "Barnum." Barnum added live snakes, bears, tigers, whales, and alligators to the museum's menagerie, and installed wax tableaux depicting various biblical scenes and allegorical vignettes that compared the advantages of temperance to the ravages of whiskey. But most of the museum's exhibitions and many of its performers, including the brass band that continued raising a ruckus on the balcony, were leftovers from the Scudder era. Barnum's genius was in advertising, and he reenergized the museum through witty, constant promotions that promised spectacular, unimaginable wonders but often turned out to be nothing more than examples of Barnum's trademark sideshow "humbug."

A typical afternoon in Barnum's "lecture hall," the museum's dingy theater that Henry James remembered so fondly, included performances by "Signor Blitz, the celebrated Magician and Ventriloquist," the "Industrious Fleas," and the "Gipsy Girl" and culminated in a hot-air balloon launch from the museum's roof. Then there was Barnum's famous "Feejee Mermaid," which turned out to be a pickled monkey corpse attached to the desiccated remains of a fish, and a replica of Niagara Falls that he promised was gigantic and awe-inspiring but proved to be nothing more than a tiny scale model. Scudder's dusty collections of minerals, fossils, and Indian artifacts were still on display, but many of Barnum's attractions were blatant rip-offs. His loyal customers didn't seem to mind, since the rip-off was part of the fun. The carefully straddled line between the real and the fake was what made Barnum so intriguing as a public figure, and his unapologetic humbug turned the American Museum into the country's foremost tourist attraction.

"The public appeared to be satisfied," Barnum shrugged, "but . . . some persons always *will* take things literally, and make no allowance for poetic license even in mermaids."

Barnum wasn't particularly original: Rubens Peale had found success displaying "Major Stevens, the American Dwarf" at his museum in the 1830s, and so Barnum followed suit by casting Charles Stratton, a four-year-old dwarf from Connecticut, as "General Tom Thumb." Stratton became a star, and in 1844, at the age of six, accompanied Barnum on an extended tour of Europe that culminated in two performances before Queen Victoria.

In 1850, Barnum orchestrated the American debut of Swedish soprano Jenny Lind with such precision that she was welcomed to town with a Broadway parade and something approaching mass hysteria. Barnum was by then world-famous and wealthy, with a palatial Moorish Revival-style estate called Iranistan in Bridgeport, Connecticut. In 1857, Barnum's mansion, in a sign of things to come, burned down.

BY 1865, TRIPLER HALL, Niblo's Garden, the City Assembly Rooms, and the Lafayette Circus had all been destroyed by fire; the Park Theatre and the National Theatre had both burned twice; the Bowery Theatre four times. Peale's Museum, the Broadway Tabernacle, and Contoit's Garden had all closed. But Barnum's American Museum had survived both the Draft Riots of 1863 and a firebombing by Confederate agents the following year, and as Broadway's places of amusement gradually shifted north to the Union Square area, Barnum's museum remained at the corner of Broadway and Ann Street, impervious to misfortune and time.

But on July 13, 1865, a mundane Thursday morning, museum employees on their lunch break smelled smoke. A fire had broken out on the museum's Ann Street side, quickly spread to adjacent offices and stores, and soon threatened the offices of the *New York Herald* around the corner. Firemen trained their hoses on the museum and rushed inside to save what they could, hurling melting wax effigies of George Washington, Patrick Henry, Franklin Pierce, Benjamin Franklin, and Lucrezia Borgia out the windows. A waxen Jefferson Davis was kicked and pummeled by a crowd of onlookers in the street and finally hung from the awning of a store.

The screams of panicked animals came from the museum's second-floor menagerie. Bears, lions, tigers, alligators, and a beluga whale all

The burning of Barnum's museum in the summer of 1865.

died in the fire, while monkeys, snakes, parrots, cockatoos, humming-birds, eagles, vultures, and a condor escaped through the museum's broken windows, much to the delight of the crowd of onlookers below. "Ned the Learned Seal," meanwhile, was rescued and temporarily sheltered at the Fulton Fish Market.

The museum's walls fell one by one, beginning with the Ann Street façade. Five minutes later the angled corner façade, which faced the diagonal of Chatham Street and bore the inscription "Founded in 1810," a remnant of John Scudder's proprietorship, came down in a "graceful sinking motion, not unlike the rolling down of an avalanche," the *New York Sun* reported. When the Broadway façade went, it didn't tumble inward or collapse straight down in the usual manner, but sprang suddenly forward into the street, injuring several bystanders.

The fire raged until three o'clock in the afternoon, died down, came briefly back to life at one o'clock the next morning, and finally settled to glowing embers. Nothing was left. Barnum sent a telegram from Bridgeport to his manager: "Don't fret a bit over the Museum," he wrote. "I can replace many of the curiosities, by look-

ing out sharp for them, and having agents in England and France
ready to buy them."

Less than two months after the museum was destroyed, Barnum
leased the former Chinese Museum on Broadway between Spring and
Prince streets, and on September 6, 1865, having joined forces with
famed animal trainer Isaac van Amburgh, reopened as Barnum's and
Van Amburgh's American Museum & Menagerie Company. The new
museum was larger but no more fireproof than the original one, and
on a frigid night in 1868 it was destroyed by fire. In 1872, Barnum
leased Lewis B. Lent's New York Circus on 14th Street, but after
only two months it, too, burned down. *Harper's Weekly* called him
"Phoenix T. Barnum."

CHAPTER 6

TRAFFIC

———

BARNUM'S ORIGINAL MUSEUM AT BROADWAY AND ANN STREET looked down on a perpetual quagmire of traffic, where Broadway and Chatham Street joined at the southern tip of City Hall Park and omnibuses, trucks, express wagons, coaches, carriages, cabs, and pushcarts converged and met more of the same coming up from ferry slips on Fulton and Wall streets. The resulting tangle was often stuck in one place for hours, creating a captive audience for Barnum's brass band and giving illustrators more than enough time to capture the scene. One drawing in *Harper's Weekly* in 1860 depicted the corner of Broadway and Fulton Street as a kind of Hieronymus Bosch maelstrom of tortured humanity, a tangled knot of careering sleighs, screaming omnibus drivers, rearing horses, sledding children, gesticulating police, and jostling pedestrians.

There were no rules, no lanes, no traffic signals. Traveling on Broadway was inevitably a "work of time and difficulty," English tourist Isabella Lucy Bird complained in 1856. "Pack the traffic of the Strand and Cheapside into Oxford Street, and still you will not have an idea of the crush in Broadway."

Not everyone minded the traffic: Walt Whitman loved the "tramp of the horses, the voices of the drivers, the rattle of wheels, the con-

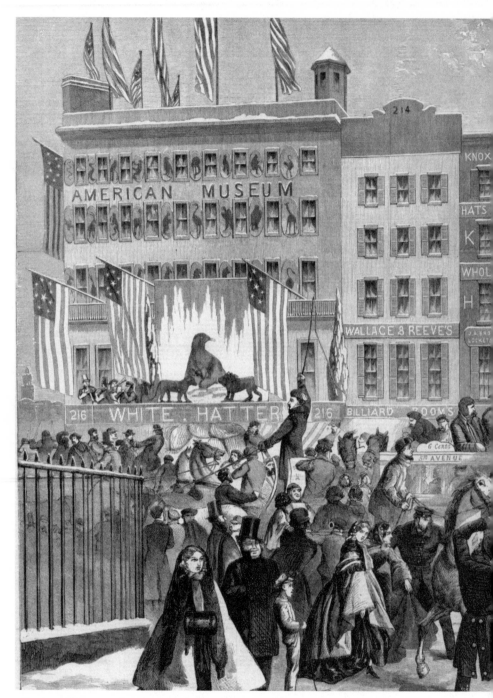

The corner of Broadway and Fulton Street, 1860.

fusion, stoppages, expletives, excitement, [which] are such as only Broadway can exhibit," and credited the declarations, insults, and retorts of Broadway's colorful omnibus drivers for the bold, aggressive rhythms he employed to such winning effect in *Leaves of Grass*. But most people found Broadway's traffic intolerable.

The "relief of Broadway" became a favorite topic of discussion, and plans were put forth over the years to widen the street, or to open new, parallel avenues to the east and west. One far-fetched proposal, published in *Harper's* in 1857, suggested that Broadway could be widened by moving its sidewalks to the *interior* of buildings along its edges, creating a continuous Parisian-style arcade 12 feet wide along both sides of the street. "It is true here and there a church may interfere," the plan's anonymous designer acknowledged. The idea was never implemented.

Pedestrians were run down on Broadway so often it barely registered with passersby. If a victim died, or was, at least, memorably mangled, the accident might get a brief line in the next day's newspapers. "Scarcely a day passes," the *Tribune* reported in 1859, "but some person—generally a female—is knocked down by some vehicle, and seriously, if not fatally wounded."

Footbridges seemed like obvious solutions, a way for pedestrians to pass safely over, rather than through, the relentless stream of oncoming vehicles, and in 1867 the cast-iron Loew Bridge was built over Broadway at Fulton Street. But the view of Broadway from the bridge was especially fine, and crowds began gathering at mid-span in such numbers that the bridge itself became perpetually jammed and, "laughed at and condemned," was torn down after only two years.

Broadway's traffic became such a problem the Metropolitan Police formed a special "Broadway Squad" to untangle vehicles and horses and guide pedestrians safely across the street. The men of the Broadway Squad were renowned for their bravery and pluck, wading fearlessly into heavy traffic, apprehending pickpockets, and heroically stopping runaway horses. And they were at least as well known for their fawning attention to female pedestrians, who they occasionally lifted tenderly from the curb over a puddle or snowdrift and onto a waiting omnibus.

"They are generally handsome," *Harper's Weekly* wrote approvingly of the squad's officers, "and they are always polite—to the ladies, especially to those who are young and pretty."

The officers weren't always so gallant, as slow-moving pedestrians found when officers shoved them gruffly from behind. ("Traffic had to be physically enforced in those days," retired squad captain Bernard Keleher recalled in 1922.) But the squad was comprised of strapping fellows—there was a height requirement of 6 feet—and the tall, manly officers were soon immortalized in songs and poems, taking their place alongside the Broadway Belle in the urban cosmos.

Tall and handsome fellow!
With his badge and star,
Standing by the gutter,
Watching near and far;
Watching for the women
All the bustling day—
Smiling and gallanting
The fair across Broadway.

Now he's in the gutter,
Now he's on the pave,
Now among the horses—
Don't you think him brave?
Boots outside his trowsers,
Through the miry clay
Wades the "star," gallanting
The fair across Broadway.

The Broadway Squad could help untangle the worst of Broadway's traffic, but couldn't prevent the omnibuses, carts, wagons, and horses from coagulating in the first place, and the problem of Broadway's traffic continued unabated.

A railroad running up and down Broadway, it was long thought, would fix Broadway's traffic once and for all, and proposals had been put forth as early as 1832, when inventor John Stevens urged an ele-

vated extension of the New York & Harlem Railroad, then under
construction, from City Hall down Broadway as far south as Trinity
Church. But nothing came of his plan, nor of an ingenious elevated
Broadway railroad designed in 1846 by John Randel Jr., the original
surveyor of the 1811 Commissioners' Plan.

In the 1850s, Second, Third, Sixth, Eighth, and Ninth avenues all
got surface railways, but omnibus companies and Broadway property
owners repeatedly foiled attempts by the Common Council to build a
railroad on Broadway. In 1852 twenty-one influential Broadway pro-
prietors including A. T. Stewart, who believed a noisy and sooty railroad running past his illustrious Marble Palace would hurt business,
banded together to oppose the project. The so-called Committee of

The manly
officers of the
Broadway
Squad were
known for
paying special
attention to
attractive young
women.

Twenty-One even took the novel position that Broadway's traffic, far from the ongoing civic crisis it was made out to be, was actually the very thing that made Broadway interesting and memorable.

"This din, this driving, this omnibus thunder, this squeezing, this jamming, crowding, and at times smashing, is the exhilarating music which charms the multitude and draws its thousands within the whirl," the committee members declared in a remonstrance submitted to the Common Council. "This *is* Broadway—this *makes* Broadway. Take from it these elements, the charm is gone, and it is no longer Broadway." Crowd it, the remonstrance continued, "and continue to crowd it until, like the mountain stream, it overflows its banks."

But the idea that Broadway should have a railroad wouldn't die, and in 1868 inventor Alfred Ely Beach, publisher of *Scientific American*, built a subway beneath Broadway—without asking permission and with hardly anyone knowing. The state legislature had granted Beach a charter to build an underground pneumatic mail delivery tube, not a railway, beneath Broadway, but Beach simply increased the diameter of the tube and began building what became the Beach Pneumatic Railway.

To build a subway underneath New York's busiest street, and *in secret*, was, to put it mildly, an audacious plan. Beach rented the basement of Devlin & Company, a well-known clothing store at the corner of Broadway and Warren Street, directly across Broadway from City Hall, and began tunneling at night, his workers removing dirt using horse-drawn wagons equipped with muffled wheels.

Beach built a subway station with frescoed walls, a fountain, a fish tank, and a grand piano beneath Devlin's basement. The station gave access to a 300-foot-long brick tube 20 feet below the surface of Broadway, extending one block south to Murray Street. The subway was powered by a single, gigantic fan at the Warren Street end of the tunnel, which blew a single railcar with a capacity of twenty-two passengers south to Murray Street, and then sucked it back in the opposite direction. It was, by all accounts, a brief but thrilling ride.

As soon as it opened, in February of 1870, a delighted public turned Beach's experimental subway into an instant tourist attraction. Beach ran the pneumatic car between ten o'clock in the morning and five

Alfred Ely Beach's improbable pneumatic subway.

o'clock in the evening at twenty-five cents a ticket and announced that he was ready to extend his tunnel south to Bowling Green and north to Central Park. But in digging his secret subway Beach had openly defied Tammany Hall and William M. "Boss" Tweed, who preferred handing out railway franchises to cronies. Governor John T. Hoffman, a Tweed ally, twice vetoed bills authorizing construction of Beach's pneumatic railway. When a new governor, John A. Dix, finally passed the bill, the Panic of 1873 killed Beach's subway for good. Beach ordered his tunnel walled up, with the train car left inside, and everyone forgot it had ever been there.

In 1893, Broadway finally got its railroad, a surface system of railcars pulled by an underground traction cable—the same type of system still used in San Francisco today—and between 1905 and 1918 two subway lines were built under the street. In 1912, workers digging the tunnel for the BMT-Broadway Line were surprised to discover a mysterious brick wall and, breaking through, Beach's long forgotten subway, its train car sitting silently on the tracks and rusting down.

Today, Broadway's first mile is still crowded with cars and trucks, but the traffic is generally orderly and nothing like the perpetual, hopeless tangle of the mid nineteenth century. Omnibuses and horses, and cable cars, too, are long gone. Broadway below 59th Street is now a one-way street, with traffic flowing south. There are stoplights at every cross street, and a subway ride beneath Broadway between Wall and Fulton streets takes all of twenty-five seconds.

MILE 2

CITY HALL PARK
TO HOUSTON STREET

CHAPTER 7

ACROSS THE MEADOWS

—

THE HEART OF BROADWAY'S SECOND MILE BISECTS A FORMER industrial precinct that was resuscitated in the 1970s as the SoHo–Cast Iron Historic District. It was in many ways an improbable transformation: Only ten years earlier the area had been so run-down and prone to fires it was called "Hell's Hundred Acres." SoHo's formerly dicey warehouses housed artists and then galleries and now expensive, tourist-jammed retail shops. What makes Broadway's second mile different from just any shopping mall is its wonderful iron buildings, but those didn't come until the mid nineteenth century, when the stores of Broadway's second mile were just part of a lively strip of theaters, hotels, and barrooms. Before that it was a sparsely populated semirural landscape of vacant lots, occasional dwellings, and constant floods.

Throughout the city's Dutch and British periods, Broadway was never longer than one mile in length, coming to a dead end at Anthony Rutgers's country estate a few hundred yards north of the Commons. Broadway didn't continue farther north because it was hemmed in by an expansive, primordial wetland called Lispenard's Meadows, which was fed by the freshwater Collect Pond just to the east of the present-day intersection of Broadway and Leonard Street. Water moved lazily back and forth across the Meadows, a 70-acre

**A sketch from 1800, looking west from Broadway,
showing children ice skating on Lispenard's Meadows.**

marsh flecked with tall grasses and shrubs that effectively cut off
lower Manhattan from the rest of the island.

Then, in the mid-1770s, the so-called Stone Bridge was built over
the Meadows, and Broadway was extended over the bridge all the
way up to the "two-mile stone" at the Sandy Hill Road, just east of
Greenwich Village. Broadway's Stone Bridge became a familiar landmark, a place, in winter, for children to meet, tie on skates, and glide
over the Meadows' frozen expanse. And it offered parents a convenient but wildly inaccurate story with which to scare their children
into staying close to home: "You must not cross the bridge or the
bears will catch you!"

For two hundred years the Dutch, then the British, and finally
the Americans tried in vain to channel the Meadows into a navigable canal, while failing to appreciate that Lispenard's Meadows was
a vitally important catch basin that held and absorbed the Collect's
fresh water, as well as brackish tidal backflow from the Hudson River
and runoff from storms and melting snow. From the perspective of
landowners and the city's Common Council, which at the time was
going to great lengths to build a new City Hall and develop the land
north of the city, Lispenard's Meadows represented a huge tract of

potentially lucrative real estate gone to waste, and so over the years the Meadows were flayed with ditches in the hope that the water might drain into the Hudson.

But because the land between the Collect Pond and the Hudson was flat, the water didn't behave as the city wished and, instead of flowing into the Hudson, pooled in streets, including Broadway, in vacant lots, and in the basements of new houses. The more the city fiddled with the Meadows, the more of a hydrological disaster the whole misguided project became. In 1807 alone the Common Council spent $13,000—$260,000 in today's dollars—on dirt, at five cents a cartload, and dumped it into the Collect and the low-lying areas surrounding it, in the process covering over what was then called the Negroes' Burying Ground, an eighteenth-century graveyard just north of City Hall Park that held the remains of slaves, free blacks, paupers, and Revolutionary War soldiers. (The burial ground wasn't rediscovered until construction of a federal court building in 1991 turned up broken coffins and human remains.)

By 1808 the once pristine Collect Pond had turned into what John Randel Jr. described as a "very offensive and irregular mound." In 1819 the city gave up the idea of a navigable canal and channeled what was left of Lispenard's Meadows into a subterranean culvert, covered it over, and called it Canal Street.

MOST OF THE LAND north of Canal Street had been part of the Bayard Family estate, which dated back to Dutch days. The estate had originally been granted to Nicholas Bayard, Peter Stuyvesant's brother-in-law, in 1638, and was subsequently enlarged by cobbling together eleven whole and partial tracts Bayard gradually acquired from small farmers and freed slaves. Between the 1730s and 1750s, Samuel Bayard, Nicholas Bayard's heir, built a mansion, plus a slaughterhouse and windmill, near a hill called Bayard's Mount. When Broadway was extended over Lispenard's Meadows, it bisected the estate, cutting it into two halves, with the Bayard mansion and Bayard's Mount just to the east of the new street.

(Bayard's Mount, known during the Revolutionary War as "Bunker's Hill" in honor of Bunker Hill in Boston, survived into the early nineteenth century, when it was leveled and pushed into the Collect Pond.)

Beginning as early as the 1780s another Nicholas Bayard, Samuel Bayard's son, subdivided the family estate into streets and building lots. The opening of Grand, Spring, Hevins (later Broome), Crosby, Clermont (Mercer), Union (Greene), Provoost (Wooster), and Concord (West Broadway) streets would, in time, provide the surrounding urban fabric for Broadway's second mile. In 1809, Broadway was paved, with sidewalks added on each side, from Canal Street to Art Street (Astor Place). It was beginning to resemble the thriving thoroughfare just to the south—all that was missing were buildings and people.

By 1812 there were still only forty buildings on Broadway between Canal and Houston streets. These included a few wood-frame houses and shops occupied by tanners, cartmen, carpenters, and laborers in the flood-prone vicinity of Broadway and Canal Street. Blackwell & McFarlan's Union Air Furnace, a smoky, wood-fired contraption used in the manufacture of cast-iron kettles, skillets, anvils, stoves, ploughs, and weights, sat just behind the houses at the corner of Broadway and Grand Street. The only other prominent landmark on that part of Broadway was Abraham Davis's tavern at the northeast corner of Broadway and Grand, across the street from the furnace. A few blocks to the north, near Spring and Prince streets, a coterie of prosperous downtown merchants built houses on what was referred to in real-estate circles as the "healthy part of Broadway," a section of high ground considered safe from flooding and the scourge of yellow fever. But other than those few houses, Broadway's second mile consisted of vacant lots.

Much of that vacant land was still owned by members of the Beekman, Bleecker, and Van Rensselaer families, descendants of the original owners of seventeenth-century Dutch land grants. Meanwhile, "merchant princes" of more recent wealth, including John Jacob Astor, were rapidly buying up lots along Broadway's second mile, guessing, correctly as it turned out, that the city would expand in that direction and their land would skyrocket in value.

They knew a good thing when they saw it. Even though Broadway's second mile was sparsely populated, Astor and other real-estate speculators fully expected Broadway to become the leading edge of development north of Canal Street, and in a clear sign that market forces were already at work, lots on Broadway in 1812 were worth three times as much as lots of the same size on Mercer, Crosby, Wooster, and other nearby streets.

Beginning about 1817, bricks and mortar arrived on Broadway's second mile by the cartload, and ranks of tidy brick houses appeared, so that by 1822 there were twice as many houses on Broadway between Canal and Houston Streets as there had been ten years earlier, while the total assessed value of the real estate on that stretch of the street increased from $154,250 in 1812 to a staggering $1,032,658 ten years later.

A boom in the production of Southern cotton, the establishment of regularly scheduled "packet" ships sailing between New York and Liverpool, and construction of the Erie Canal were the three main factors driving New York's newfound prosperity. In 1810 the city's population had been 96,373; by the time the Erie Canal opened in 1825 it had grown to 166,089 and was attracting more and more new residents every day. (New York's population would reach 242,278 by 1830—small by today's standards but at the time bigger than Philadelphia, Boston, and Baltimore *combined*.)

By 1825 the 8th Ward, the electoral district that encompassed Broadway's second mile, had been utterly transformed from a derelict landscape of flooded vacant lots to a densely populated, humming urban neighborhood with thirteen churches, four schools, two markets, an orphanage, a theater and a circus, mills and distilleries, and an average of two families packed into each of the ward's 2,300 houses.

As the city flowed northward into Broadway's second mile, artifacts from its rural past disappeared one by one. In 1798 the old Bayard mansion had been repurposed as the centerpiece of a pleasure garden called Vauxhall. Modeled after Vauxhall Gardens in London, it was a place of winding paths, discreet nooks and alcoves, benches and chairs and tables, and evening concerts, fireworks, and acrobatic demonstrations. But when Vauxhall moved in 1805, the Bayard mansion, stranded just east of Broadway near the intersection of Grand and Crosby streets like a ship that had missed the tide, stood in the way of progress and was finally put out of its misery in 1821.

CHAPTER 8

"A GLANCE AT NEW YORK"

———

ON THE EVENING OF FEBRUARY 15, 1848, AT THE OLYMPIC
Theatre, a small playhouse tucked mid-block on the shilling side of
Broadway's second mile, between Howard and Grand streets, one
block north of Canal Street, a strange, menacing figure with coat
slung over his arm, hat cocked insouciantly forward over one eye, and
hair plastered down in foppish "soap locks" over his temples, strode
to center stage. He took the stump of a cigar out of his mouth, spat
on the stage, and defiantly stared down the startled audience. "I ain't
a goin' to run wid dat mercheen no more!" he yelled.

It was midway through the first act of the premiere of a new "local
drama, in two acts" entitled *A Glance at New York in 1848*, and for a
moment or two there was dead silence. Accustomed to the polished
deliveries of English Shakespearean actors, the Olympic's patrons
didn't know what to think. Then it dawned on the audience that the
ruffian in their midst was the popular actor Frank Chanfrau, debut-
ing a new character called "Mose," and the playhouse erupted into
thunderous applause.

A Glance at New York was a theatrical insurrection and was
unveiled against the backdrop of the European revolutions of 1848.
There was no mistaking the political and social anarchy than ran
through the play: "Fellow citizens, of everywhere in particular, and

nowhere in general," one character shouts at one point, "I appear before you to say what I shall say; and I say, to begin, that I am opposed to all governments: I'm opposed to all laws!"

But the most revolutionary thing about the play, which was written as a lark by Olympic stagehand Benjamin A. Baker, was that its dialogue reproduced the local slang of its audience: "muss" for fight, "lam" for hit, "high" for funny, "crib" for place. And instead of stage sets of English drawing rooms and Scottish castles, the audience at the Olympic was treated to backdrops of familiar, Broadway-centric haunts: City Hall Park, the Astor House hotel, Barnum's American Museum, and Vauxhall Gardens (then located on Astor Place between Broadway and the Bowery). The cast included fast-talking thieves, con artists, newsboys, and Five Points "loafers," while the plot, such as it was, flattered New Yorkers by poking fun at naïve out-of-towners, including a wonderstruck girl from the sticks: "I declare," she exclaims, "I was never so delighted in my life! Such a never-ending display of silks, jewelry, and shawls as this Broadway boasts of! 'Tis enough to turn my brain!"

But it was Chanfrau's uncanny depiction of Mose that struck a nerve and made *A Glance at New York* a runaway hit, and before long the further adventures of Mose, his gal "Lize," and his sidekick "Syksey" were featured in an endless succession of dime novels and theatrical sequels. Chanfrau supposedly based the Mose character on Moses C. Humphreys, a printer who lived in the 1840s on Mulberry Street, and Mose became both a celebration and a spoof of the ultimate New York working-class hero.

Mose was a butcher by trade at a time when butchers, instantly recognizable for their checkered sleeves, were flamboyant public figures. They broke down hog carcasses on the sidewalks, marched as a body in Broadway parades, drank and brawled in barrooms and pleasure gardens, and held court in their stalls located in the city's open-air meat markets. Butchers represented all that was manly in mid-nineteenth-century New York, their position in the masculine pecking order rivaled only by the city's burly volunteer firemen—and Mose was one of those, too.

It was an era when the "fire laddies" were idolized, and often

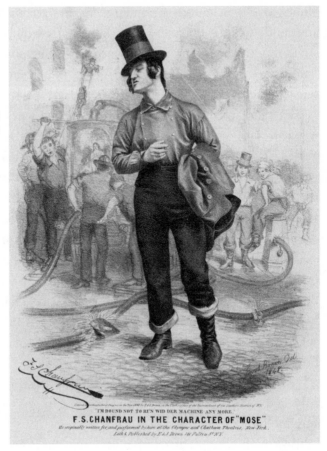

Frank Chanfrau as "Mose."

I'M BOUND NOT TO RUN WID DER MACHINE ANY MORE.
F.S.CHANFRAU IN THE CHARACTER OF "MOSE"

feared, for their bombast and brawling ways. They held "chowder parties" and annual balls, sang maudlin ballads, and marched in torchlight parades. Whenever a comrade was killed in a fire they donated generously to the grieving widow. But mostly, it seemed, firemen spent their time fighting each other, especially when rival companies met on the street. "[For] about four hours there was the biggest riot seen before the war," one retired volunteer recalled of a street fight between companies. "Bricks and stones were going around without owners, and half-a-dozen shots were fired. One fellow held his revolver in his coat-tail pocket, and fired her off at random."

Firemen insisted on pulling their ornately painted engines through the streets by hand, and boys and neighborhood toughs hung around the firehouses and vied for the honor of helping the laddies "run with the machine." Firemen were headstrong and opinionated, and quick to take offense, which is perhaps why Mose struck such a chord with the Olympic's audience when he vowed to never again "run wid dat merchenen." It was precisely the kind of overblown nonsense heard every day on the streets of New York.

But there was still another layer to Chanfrau's character: Mose was, through and through, a meticulously crafted send-up of New York's irreverent, flamboyant, and defiant "Bowery b'hoy" subculture.

Bowery b'hoys ("b'hoy" was Irish slang for "boy") had, by the 1840s, become bona fide New York archetypes, instantly recognizable by their distinctive clothing and bravado, and for their habit of standing on street corners with arms akimbo, as if they owned the city. They became so associated with New York that tourists sought them out, cautiously gawking at them as if they were anacondas in Barnum's museum. When William Makepeace Thackeray arrived in the city during a cross-country lecture tour in 1849, he reportedly approached a b'hoy standing at the corner of Canal Street and the Bowery and asked directions.

"My friend, I should like to go to Broadway," Thackeray supposedly said. "Well," the b'hoy replied, "you can go, sonny, if you won't stay too long."

Bowery b'hoys strutted up and down the Bowery, of course, but spent at least as much time on Broadway, where they rubbed shoulders with the city's wealthiest and most fashionable men and women. (For Mose, at least, Broadway was an acquired taste: "How comes it I find you in this part of the town?" one character in *A Glance at New York* asks him when they happen to meet on Broadway. "I heard that you held Broadway in such contempt, that you couldn't be persuaded even to cross it." "I've got over dat now," Mose replies.)

Night after night, audiences packed the Olympic to watch Mose do battle with the police and assorted lowlifes and feast on pork and beans and brandy at Vauxhall Gardens—or "waxhall," as Mose pronounced it. At one point Mose even takes in a foundling.

"The fire-boys may be a little rough on the outside, but they're all right here," Mose declares while clutching the crying infant and melodramatically touching his heart, "It never shall be said dat one of de New York boys deserted a baby in distress!"

IT WAS NO ACCIDENT that the Mose character was born at the Olympic. Only ten years earlier, the city's first real theater district had formed around City Hall Park, but by 1848 had moved north into Broadway's second mile. The Olympic was just one of at least a dozen theaters, circuses, museums, and halls between City Hall Park and Houston Street offering nightly plays, concerts, lectures, and exhibitions. Niblo's Garden, the Broadway Theatre, the Apollo Rooms, the Coliseum, and Wallack's Theatre all had their partisans, but it was the Olympic that best captured the riotous spirit of the 1840s, when the divide between rich and poor grew wider, immigrants battled nativists, and patriotic fervor carried the day.

The Olympic was small as playhouses went, and if not for a small marquee over the front door and an enormous American flag flying from a staff on the roof might have been mistaken for a house or commercial building. Tattersall's famous horse market was next door in a dilapidated wooden building that had once been a circus, and every day horses on the auction block were trotted back and forth in front of the Olympic. The theater was one block north of the low-lying intersection of Broadway and Canal Street, which only thirty years before had been nothing but a cluster of tradesmen's houses and shops. The area still maintained its working-class character, and nestled on either side of the Olympic were barrooms, billiard halls, restaurants, barbershops, daguerreotype studios, and "segar" stores frequented by the butchers, grocers, cabinetmakers, printers, and tanners who lived and worked in the neighborhood. The Olympic opened in 1837, but didn't become a success until John Mitchell took over as manager in 1839, and after that it was always called "Mitchell's Olympic."

"Mr. Mitchell has, with great tact, seized upon local incidents and prevailing follies, and moulded them into most amusing pieces," raved the editors of a guidebook published in 1846.

While the more expensive box seats were "nightly filled with the elite of the city," Mitchell lowered prices for pit seats from the traditional twenty-five cents to twelve-and-a-half cents, which led to an influx of "market boys, butcher boys, newsboys, big boys, small boys, of every age, shape, and size." On the occasions when his young audience became unmanageable, Mitchell would step from the wings and calmly announce: "Boys, if you misbehave yourselves I shall raise the prices."

As was the custom in theaters of that era, audiences applauded when they enjoyed a performance and groaned and hissed when they didn't. At the Olympic the audience threw all kinds of comestibles from the local markets onto the stage, much of it intended not as missiles but as tributes to favored actors. Stephen C. Massett, a member of Mitchell's company in the early 1840s, recalled "wreaths of onions, large-sized carrots, with turnips to match, a string of tallow-candles, [an] occasional 'red-herring,' and in one instance an immense codfish" hurled onto the Olympic's stage. One evening in the summer of 1843, Massett, who was known professionally as "Mr. Raymond," a stage name Mitchell gave him in 1842, entered, walked down middle stage, and broke into song, at which point a calf's head, "white as milk, beautifully clean-shaved, tied with blue ribbons, and a fine large lemon in its mouth," sailed onto the stage and landed at his feet, a surprise gift from an admiring butcher boy. The audience saved their spoiled eggs, fruit, and vegetables for actors they didn't like.

Despite its popularity, the Olympic couldn't withstand the tide of stores, offices, factories, and warehouses that were pushing up Broadway from the south. Rents skyrocketed, and theaters gradually shifted to the north and away from Broadway's second mile. In 1855 there were still twelve theaters operating on Broadway below Houston Street, but by 1865 only six were left; by 1875 there were only three.

The Olympic closed in 1852. Just before Christmas in 1854 it was destroyed, along with eight surrounding buildings, in a terrible fire that killed fireman James T. Laurie of Hose Company No. 7. The Olympic had been converted to artist's studios, and the painter Theodore Kaufman lost a series of eight canvases in the fire, each of them measuring 8 by 12 feet and representing "the development of the idea of God." He had been working on them for ten years.

MILLIONAIRES AND MURDERERS

———

T HE EARLY 1850S SAW A BOOM IN HOTEL CONSTRUCTION
along Broadway's second mile, driven in large part by a humming
economy and the prospect of an influx of tourists arriving for New
York's much-anticipated 1853 World's Fair, or "Exhibition of the
Industry of All Nations." The mammoth new Metropolitan Hotel
took up half a block at the northeast corner of Broadway and Prince
Street, relegating Niblo's Garden to an interior courtyard accessible
only through the hotel.

The Metropolitan, designed by the firm Trench & Snook and
owned by A. T. Stewart, who had branched out from the dry goods
trade to hotels and theaters, was gargantuan, an Italianate cliff of
brownstone five stories tall and extending 360 feet along Broadway.
For its time, it was incredibly modern, with four hundred rooms,
steam heat, and its own telegraph office, one of only six in the entire
city. The interior furnishings were unlike anything seen in the city
up to that time, with rosewood sofas and 120 mirrors imported from
Belgium—two of them reportedly the largest mirrors ever imported
into the country. Dances, called "hops," with music provided by Allen
Dodworth's band, were held in the ballroom every Wednesday evening before dinner.

Other hotels, including the Collamore House at Broadway and

Spring Street, and the Prescott House on the opposite corner, soon joined the Metropolitan along Broadway's second mile, their size and deluxe appointments the cause of constant astonishment. "Hotels capable of accommodating the population of a township rise in quick succession along the line of our great fashionable thoroughfare," the fledgling *New York Times* reported in 1852, two weeks after the Metropolitan opened to overflow crowds. But only a few months later a new entry into what had clearly become something of a competition opened on Broadway between Broome and Spring streets, and immediately vanquished all contenders in terms of its size and splendor.

The St. Nicholas Hotel, a marble-and-brownstone "monster," as the *Times* called it, was by a wide margin the largest hotel America had ever seen—bigger even than the Metropolitan. Before its opening in January of 1853 the St. Nicholas's owner, D. M. Haight, was already expanding in two directions along Broadway and west to Mercer Street, swallowing houses and shops in the process, until his hotel covered half the block. The *Tribune* called the St. Nicholas "the largest and most elegant hotel in the world," and it was probably exactly that.

Visitors entered from Broadway through a portico supported by four fluted white marble columns into a grand reception hall floored with marble and furnished with settees covered in wild animal skins, its windows hung in green brocade and damasks embroidered in gold. Off to the side was a "gentlemen's drawing-room" and, through a set of folding doors, a reading room lit by a large dome.

A monumental staircase of white oak, its first landing decorated with a large painting of Santa Claus stuffing presents into Christmas stockings, ascended from the reception hall to the upper floors, where there were four hundred guest rooms, many of them equipped with, wonder of wonders, their own water closets. The bridal chamber, its walls entirely covered with fluted white satin, went for $50 a night— $1,500 in today's currency.

A second-floor hall led to an 82-foot-long "Grand Dining Room" on the Mercer Street side of the building that was lit with three enormous chandeliers suspended from an ornately frescoed ceiling 22 feet high. The dining tables were of polished black walnut, the chairs of rosewood. Meals at the St. Nicholas were choreographed pageants, and patrons dressed to the nines when the dinner bell rang. "In a fashionable hotel, you *must* dress fashionably—of course," journalist Thomas Butler Gunn wrote in 1857 in his satirical travelogue *The Physiology of the New York Boarding-Houses.*

"Who could think of sitting down to a dinner at which two hundred guests assemble—where at a given signal, an equal number of carefully-drilled waiters remove the dish covers with a dexterous flourish of their white-gloved hands—where a band of music, in full blast, accompanies general mastication—in other than ball costume, or something very near it," Gunn wrote of the St. Nicholas.

Four hundred guests could sit down to dinner at once, and across the St. Nicholas's well-spread tables guests had ample opportunities to meet, or studiously ignore, dozens of people from far-flung corners of the globe. In a single, typical day visitors from Albany, Rochester, Buffalo, Bridgeport, New Haven, Hartford, Boston, Philadelphia, Baltimore, Washington, Detroit, Cincinnati, Toledo, Chicago, Charleston, Savannah, Nova Scotia, Tennessee, California, and Alabama, not to mention London, Liverpool, Manchester, Paris, and Brazil, might check into the St. Nicholas, each dipping a crow-quill pen into an inkwell and signing the pale blue pages of the thick, leather-bound guestbook at the reception desk.

New York had become a city of strangers. Who *was* that man sitting next to you and stabbing a fork into his squab?

"The man who sits beside you at dinner is as much a stranger as he who jostles you on Broadway," Gunn observed. "He may be either a senator or swindler, and you are as little surprised, three days hence, to learn that he is a millionaire, as that he's going to be hanged."

The anonymity of the St. Nicholas and other hotels reflected a loss of community in the wider city, which had gotten so big—the population had swelled from 391,114 in 1840 to 696,115 in 1850—that neither locals nor visitors knew many of the people around them. Millionaires and murderers alike passed up and down Broadway every day, and it was hard to tell one from the other.

It was an era when Dead Rabbits, Plug Uglies, and Roach Guards fought epic street battles; when thieves, con artists, and pickpockets lurked in the shadows; and when respectable citizens were targeted for regular muggings, beatings, or worse. Broadway, no less than the more notorious Bowery or the Five Points, was often the site of brutal crimes. It didn't help that Houston, Mercer, Crosby, and Greene streets had become Broadway's sordid backstage. Those streets had so many brothels, generally listed in city directories as "boardinghouses," that guidebooks were published to direct visitors to the most interesting ones. One brothel guide published in 1859 suggested visits to "Mrs. Hathaway" and "her fair Quakeresses," "Mrs. Everett" and her "beautiful senoritas," "Miss Lizzie Wright" and her "French belles," and "Miss Virginia Henriques," where "its lady, its boarders, its fixins and fashions" were of "the Creole order." Of the 105 brothels listed in the guide, 45 were within three blocks of the St. Nicholas, Metropolitan, Collamore House, and Prescott House hotels.

And all this extracurricular activity took place at a time when almost everyone, it seemed, carried concealed weapons.

"The practice of carrying concealed arms, in the shape of stilettos for attack, and swordsticks for defence, if illegal, is perfectly common," English visitor Isabella Lucy Bird wrote that year; "desperate reprobates, called 'Rowdies,' infest the lower part of town; and terrible outrages and murderous assaults are matters of such nightly occurrence as to be thought hardly worthy of notice."

Even the St. Nicholas Hotel, that gilded epicenter of elegance, couldn't escape the violence of the 1850s—how could it, when its guests were armed?

Just before dawn on August 2, 1854, one Dr. Robert M. Graham of New Orleans returned drunk and disorderly to his room at the St. Nicholas after a night spent carousing in dives on Mercer Street. Graham repeatedly rang a bell in the hallway, attempting to call a maid, and became enraged when none appeared. At this point Graham wore no pants. Colonel Charles Loring of California made the mistake of repeatedly coming out of his room to complain about the noise, and their arguments escalated to the point that Graham drew a concealed sword from his cane and ran Loring through the chest, killing him instantly.

Graham was tried and convicted of second-degree murder, and his high-profile trial did much to sully the St. Nicholas's image. One month after the Loring murder, a wary, self-described "greenhorn from the country" wrote to the *Tribune* for advice on where to stay during an upcoming agricultural fair. The *Tribune* cautiously recommended the famous St. Nicholas: "You need not be at all afraid to go there; the charges are moderate, and most of the guests plain, honest, country folk. The whole house is elegant and has but one fault—one common to nearly all the best hotels in the world—it has a bar-room."

Indeed, the St. Nicholas's well-appointed barroom had become an epicenter of alcohol-fueled violence. On June 30, 1854, one month before the Loring murder, Thomas R. White of Augusta, Georgia, stabbed Arthur Connor there, after a heated argument. One year later, on September 17, 1855, two estranged owners of a steamboat got into a spat in the barroom. Captain J. J. Wright attempted to strike Robert S. Dean, his erstwhile business partner, in the face with a cowhide, and Dean responded by stabbing Wright twice in the stomach and groin. In 1860 there was yet another stabbing in the barroom, by which time the reputation of the vaunted St. Nicholas had been taken down a peg or two.

THE *TRIBUNE* WAS RIGHT: Even the best hotels had barrooms, and since Broadway was lined with hotels, violence inevitably followed. On October 23, 1851, in the barroom of Florence's Hotel, at the corner of Broadway and Walker Street, bartender Charles Owens found himself held by his hair while two well-known boxers, William Poole and Thomas Hyer, "beat his face to a jelly," as the *Times* put it. Owens's tactical mistake had been in denying Poole and Hyer a third round of drinks. It was eight in the morning.

Poole, or "Pool" as it was often spelled in newspapers and city directories, was a less lovable, and very real, version of the "Mose" character, a tough butcher who liked to settle differences with his fists. But unlike Mose, Poole was also a politician, a Whig Party operative who often chaired Whig conventions at the Broadway

House, a tavern at the corner of Broadway and Grand Street, and was repeatedly accused of rigging primary elections. Poole fancied himself a stalwart patriot and was active in nativist societies like the Lundy's Lane Club and the Order of United Americans. Poole ran his own barroom at the corner of Broadway and Howard Street, where he routinely refused service to Irish Catholics.

Poole was one of the most notorious of the city's "sports," men who moved with a "fast" crowd and frequented brothels and gambling dens, drank until the wee hours, were known to carry concealed pistols and knives, and, in general, raised hell. One contemporary print depicted Poole as a dandy, a young blade with a devil-may-care grin and a jaunty, waxed mustache. But a photograph from the same period reveals a slack-jawed, street-hardened lout with a drooping mustache and the vacant gaze of a man who had been punched in the face too many times.

What ultimately did Poole in was a long-running public dispute with a younger, Irish-born boxer named John Morrissey, who ran a notorious barroom and gambling den on Leonard Street called the Belle of the Union. Morrissey, like many of the city's Irish, was

William Poole,
ca. 1854.

aligned with Tammany Hall Democrats, who were despised by nativists like Poole.

Both Poole and Morrissey were usually accompanied on their rounds by flocks of heavily armed acolytes, and on several occasions Poole and Morrissey had led their gangs into combat against each other. During the summer of 1854, Poole, age thirty-one, had severely beaten Morrissey, twenty-four, at the Amos Street dock on the Hudson River, and Morrissey and his backers had vowed revenge.

On the fateful night, February 24, 1855, Poole and Morrissey met by accident at Stanwix Hall, a newly-opened hotel, restaurant, and barroom at 579 Broadway, directly across the street from the Metropolitan Hotel. Morrissey and some of his goons were stuffing themselves in the rear dining room—Stanwix Hall specialized in terrapin soup and boiled sea bass—when Poole arrived with a few flunkies and began eating supper in the front barroom. Then Morrissey noticed Poole.

"Hallo, you here. You are a pretty fighting son of a bitch," Morrissey shouted. The two approached each other and Morrissey promised to best Poole in a match.

"You said that once before, down at the City Hotel, and, Honey, you tasted me and did not like it," Poole replied, before offering a few cutting remarks about Morrissey's Irish ancestry.

Morrissey: "I am as good an American as you are."

Poole: "You are a damned liar."

Morrissey aimed a pistol at Poole. One eyewitness claimed Poole remained calm, standing on a platform behind the counter with arms folded. Another witness said Poole held a revolver pointed at the floor, and still another claimed Poole pointed a gun at Morrissey. Then, with theatrical timing, the police arrived before any shots were fired. One cop took Morrissey outside onto Broadway, and then inexplicably let him go. Poole went to a nearby police station to make a complaint against Morrissey, and then unwisely returned to Stanwix Hall, where he and his friends ordered two more bottles of wine as the owners locked the doors for the night.

Around midnight four of Morrissey's associates—James Turner, Lewis Baker, Charles van Pelt, and an especially violent thug named

Patrick McLaughlin, alias "Paugene"—left John Lyng's barroom and gambling den at the corner of Broadway and Canal Street and marched up Broadway the five blocks to Stanwix Hall. When they found the restaurant closed and the front door locked, they burst in and surprised Poole and his gang, who were still drinking at the bar.

McLaughlin grabbed Poole by the lapels. Turner drew a pistol but, instead of shooting Poole, shot himself in the arm by mistake. Turner fell to the floor in agony, but managed, from a lying position, to shoot Poole in the thigh. Poole staggered and fell. Baker pinned Poole to the floor and, at point-blank range, shot him in the heart.

His assassins fled back down Broadway to Lyng's barroom, while Poole's cronies took him home. Amazingly, Poole could walk, and for a few weeks it looked as if he might make a full recovery. But he began to decline and finally died, probably of infection, early in the morning of March 8. The coroner found the fatal bullet wedged between the ventricles of Poole's heart.

POOLE'S CORPSE WAS laid out in the parlor of his home at 164 Christopher Street, a stone's throw from the Hudson River. The body was dressed in black broadcloth, and the badge of the Order of United Americans was laid across the breast. A Methodist minister read the 90th Psalm. The coffin was covered with a silk American flag and, borne on the shoulders of ten pallbearers, carried three blocks to Hudson Street. It was placed in an open hearse pulled by four white horses cloaked in black, with white plumes on their heads. A gilded eagle covered in black crepe was placed at the head of the coffin, while both sides of the hearse were decorated with black crepe, silver fringe, olive wreaths and, in silver letters on black velvet, the inscription "I die a true American"—supposedly Poole's dying words.

The funeral procession passed through Christopher and Bleecker streets and turned south onto Broadway, then proceeded down Broadway two miles to South Ferry. Buildings along the way, including the Metropolitan and St. Nicholas hotels, Wallack's Theatre, and the City Assembly Rooms, were draped in black.

One year earlier, Broadway had been the scene of a funeral proces-

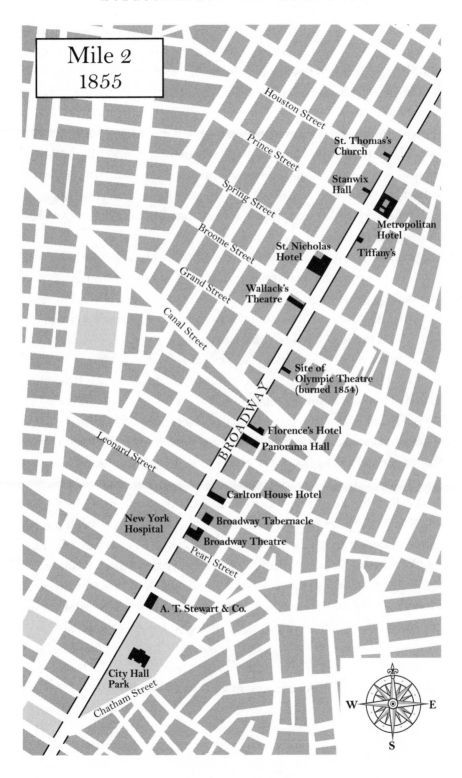

Mile 2
1855

Houston Street

Prince Street

St. Thomas's
Church

Spring Street

Stanwix
Hall

Broome Street

Metropolitan
Hotel

St. Nicholas
Hotel

Tiffany's

Grand Street

Wallack's
Theatre

Canal Street

Site of
Olympic Theatre
(burned 1854)

BROADWAY

Leonard Street

Florence's Hotel
Panorama Hall

Carlton House Hotel

New York
Hospital

Broadway Tabernacle

Broadway Theatre

Pearl Street

A. T. Stewart & Co.

City Hall
Park

Chatham Street

W   E
S

sion for ten firemen killed in a tragic fire that destroyed the William
T. Jennings & Company clothing store at 231 Broadway, opposite City
Hall Park. Three years earlier, Henry Clay and Daniel Webster, who
both died in 1852, had been honored with elaborate Broadway funeral
processions. But this time the street was lined with mourners paying tribute not to lamented firemen or senators, but to a decidedly
sketchy character. And yet, 4,000 people marched in William Poole's
funeral procession, while a crowd estimated at 100,000 watched from
sidewalks, rooftops, balconies, lampposts, and trees. The pageant
got underway at three in the afternoon and didn't reach South Ferry
until six o'clock.

Dodworth's band, its fifty-two members dressed in black, led the
way. Two companies of firemen were next, followed by the notorious nativist henchman Isaiah Rynders and members of the Order of
United Americans. Then came the hearse and *one hundred* carriages
filled with Poole's "friends and associates."

"It is generally conceded," the *Tribune* reported, "that the procession contained the largest representation of the sporting fraternity
which ever passed our streets."

And that was only the Manhattan segment of the procession.
Thousands more waited in Brooklyn, lining Atlantic Avenue and
Court Street, for a glimpse of the hearse as it made its way slowly
south to Green-Wood Cemetery.

What to make of 100,000 New Yorkers mourning the death of a
thug? The outpouring of sympathy for Poole may have been a misguided tangent in a larger search for a collective American identity.

"We are so young a People that we feel the want of Nationality, & delight in whatever asserts our national 'American' existence,"
George Templeton Strong had written the previous year, after nativist, anti-Catholic, anti-immigrant "Know-Nothing" candidates nearly
won campaigns for mayor and governor. "We have not, like England
& France, centuries of achievements & calamities to look back on—
we have no *record* of Americanism and we feel its want."

CHAPTER 10

"BROADWAY IS NEVER FINISHED"

——

Ow TO HAVE A TANGIBLE RECORD OF AMERICANISM, OR
a record of anything, really, on Broadway, when everything came
and went so quickly? A building boom in 1860 added thirty-three
new commercial buildings to the street—$5 million worth of bricks,
wood, stone, iron, and glass—and even beloved landmarks were sacri-
ficed in the name of progress. Thompson's Saloon, a once-fashionable
restaurant opposite Stewart's Marble Palace, was converted that year
to a wholesale warehouse, while the city's most renowned bookstore,
D. Appleton & Company, a wondrous Greek Revival emporium at
the corner of Broadway and Leonard Street, was altered into offices.
Broadway, the *Tribune* reported that summer, was "in the hands of
contractors, masons, carpenters, cellar-diggers, and hod-carriers,
and there is not the least hope to be entertained that building operations on this street will ever cease."

It was the heyday of iron construction, a happy coincidence of
materials and labor that to this day gives Broadway and surrounding blocks its unique character and defines SoHo. In its molten state,
iron could be cast into molds of wet sand and mass-produced into an
endless variety of cunningly designed components—columns, beams,
arches, consoles, brackets, pedestals, pediments, cornices, posts, and
railings—that were strong and durable, requiring only a coat of paint

now and then, and less expensive than marble or granite. They were hollow and easily bolted together, so that a façade could be erected in a matter of days instead of months, and were slim in profile, allowing builders and architects to flood the interiors of new stores, offices, and factories with sunlight. (Iron buildings were fireproof, too; at least when compared to wooden buildings, although the Great Chicago Fire of 1871 soon demonstrated that iron buildings tended to fail, and fail dramatically, when subjected to intense heat.)

Iron foundries proliferated in New York in the 1850s, part of a mid-century boom in local manufacturing, and Daniel D. Badger's Architectural Iron Works emerged as the foundry of choice for projects instigated by the likes of A. T. Stewart, William Backhouse Astor, Cornelius Vanderbilt, and Peter Cooper.

Badger had arrived in New York from Boston in the mid-1840s. He later claimed he was the first to erect an iron structure anywhere in the country, although it turned out he wasn't even the first to do it in New York—engineer James Bogardus was designing iron structures in the city four years before Badger arrived on the scene. But by mid-century Badger was dominating construction of iron buildings in the city, his horse-pulled wagons a ubiquitous sight as they ferried iron components from his foundry, at the corner of Avenue A and 13th Street, to building sites throughout the city.

Because his buildings were modular, Badger could ship them, in pieces, all over the world, and by the 1860s there were Badger-built stores in Halifax, sugar sheds in Havana, warehouses in Egypt, and a ferry terminal in Rio de Janeiro. Closer to home, Badger built stores, banks, and commercial buildings in Boston, Philadelphia, Providence, Rochester, Albany, Troy, Utica, Syracuse, Scranton, and dozens of other cities. In Washington, he contributed ironwork for the Library of Congress, the Treasury Building, and Ford's Theatre.

But it was in New York, and particularly on Broadway, that Badger made his deepest and most lasting impression. By 1865 Badger had built, or had helped to build, an astonishing 544 buildings in Manhattan—166 of them on Broadway—and his career was just getting going.

Badger's heyday came at a time when moving north along Broadway had become aspirational, an ongoing process of civic improvement. Stores, including Tiffany & Company, Ball, Black & Company, Strang, Adriance & Company, and Devlin & Company, found it expedient to abandon their stores on Broadway's first mile in pursuit of their customers, who were rapidly migrating north, colonizing the blocks surrounding Washington Square, Gramercy Park, Union Square, and Madison Square. Even A. T. Stewart joined the exodus, building an enormous cast-iron retail emporium in 1862 that covered the entire block of Broadway between 9th and 10th streets. (Stewart's storied Marble Palace at Broadway and Reade Street was converted to the wholesale and mail-order branches of his business.)

Badger wasn't involved in construction of Stewart's new "Iron Palace," but he did build the E. V. Haughwout & Company store, which had opened five years earlier at the northeast corner of Broadway and Broome Street. Haughwout's, a "fancy goods" store specializing in china, porcelain, chandeliers, statuary, clocks, and gas fixtures, was every bit as much of a palace as Stewart's, and was one of the few stores that actually moved down, instead of up, Broadway, vacating their old store on Broadway near Prince Street in order to move two blocks to the south.

Haughwout's new store was designed by architect John P. Gaynor—Badger's office may well have supplied the designs for the building's remarkable façades—in the prevailing Italianate style: The horizontality of its façade, enlivened by repeating modules of keystone arches set within rows of Corinthian columns, was reminiscent of the sixteenth-century Biblioteca Marciana in Venice, except for the large clock installed in the middle of the Broadway façade—a common flourish on a street where time was money. The new Haughwout's was five stories, with the upper two floors devoted to manufacturing. (Haughwout's, which maintained a branch store in Paris, imported unfinished china and porcelain and then did its own painting and gilding.)

Those in search of Haughwout's renowned china—customers included Mary Todd Lincoln, who ordered a set, in mauve, for the White House in 1861—entered from Broadway and proceeded to a dramatic stair at the rear of the store, or boarded a passenger elevator—a novelty and the first commercial use of Elisha Otis's new safety elevator, patented only three years before the store opened.

Haughwout's only serious rival in the fancy goods trade was Tiffany & Company, originally Tiffany, Young & Ellis, founded in 1837 and housed in three interconnected buildings at the corner of Broadway and Warren Street, opposite City Hall Park. Tiffany's sold china, bronzes, chairs, sofas, paintings, chess sets, tiles, and candlesticks, and in 1845 expanded into the jewelry line for which it is still famous.

In 1854, Tiffany's moved north, opening a new store at 550 Broadway, on the shilling side of the street between Spring and Prince streets. Designed by architect Robert G. Hatfield, the new Tiffany's was an Italianate palazzo gone mad, a frothy five stories of faux-Venetian stone. From a cast-iron storefront built by Badger the store rose to a second story featuring a portico of five grand arches and a Henry Frederick Metzler sculpture of Atlas bearing a giant clock on its shoulders. The roofline was a frilly, multilayered cornice. It was ridiculous, too gaudy for words, but Broadway's retail stores had long since shed any sense of architectural propriety, as architects held a no-holds-barred competition to see who could make their work stand out from the crowd.

Lord & Taylor, a venerable dry goods retailer and wholesaler that had been doing business at the corner of Grand and Catharine (present-day Mulberry) streets since 1826, approached Broadway not from the south but from the east, moving west along Grand Street to its intersection with Broadway. Lord & Taylor spent $180,000 on construction of its new Broadway store, which opened in the spring of 1860, plus another $200,000 for the land, an oversized lot that stretched 85 feet along Broadway and 100 feet along Grand Street.

The new store, designed by architect Griffith Thomas, was, like the new Tiffany's, exceedingly fussy—"Florentine," the *Tribune* called it. Thomas, who along with Hatfield had virtually cornered the market in store design, had dreamed up a five-story confection of Eastchester marble, with a large fanlight window arching over the Broadway entrance. Gaudy striped cloth canopies shaped like large hoop skirts shaded the display windows along the street, while the roof featured a dramatically cantilevered cornice.

The architectural gymnastics on the exterior only hinted at the merchandise within. Lord & Taylor's Broadway store (the company continued to operate its original Grand Street store until 1914) featured five floors of imported dry goods sold by the yard (dresses were still made by hand in those days), plus the "latest Paris novelties": gloves, shawls, scarves, ties, and handkerchiefs. In an era when women were weighed down by layer upon layer of clothing—a typical dress of the era might feature brocade adorned with small roses, a tight bodice, a bustle, a petticoat of corded silk trimmed in lace, plus skirts and hoops—Lord & Taylor offered fabrics "suitable for promenade, dinner, carriage, and evening dresses."

Broadway's second mile had become the mercantile center of New York, but it wasn't destined to remain that way for long. In 1869, Tiffany's moved north again, this time to Union Square, where it demolished, of all things, the Church of the Puritans and replaced it with an extravagant new store at the corner of Broadway and 15th Street that the press called the "Palace of Jewels."

The following year Lord & Taylor followed suit, building a vast new emporium at the corner of Broadway and 20th Street. And so it went. It was as if Broadway had become not a street but a notion—less a place than the very idea of movement and progress.

"Will Broadway ever be finished?" the editors of the *New York Tribune* had wondered in 1850. Journalist Junius Henri Browne answered the question in 1868: "Broadway is always being built, but it is never finished," he wrote. "The structures that were deemed stately and magnificent a few years ago are constantly disappearing, and new and more splendid ones are rising in their places."

MILE 3

HOUSTON STREET
TO UNION SQUARE

CHAPTER 11

THE BEND

———

W HEN VIEWED FROM THE SIDEWALK OPPOSITE CITY HALL
Park, or even from as far south as Trinity Church, Broadway's third
mile is plainly visible in the distance, owing to an intriguing optical
illusion: Grace Church, which stands out because of its soaring marble spire, looks as if it's moved into the middle of Broadway, a bishop
sliding diagonally between pawns. Walking north, the illusion isn't
dispelled until within fifty yards or so of the church's front steps,
where it is revealed that it isn't Grace that has moved, but Broadway,
which at 10th Street bends unexpectedly away from the orthogonal
streets and avenues around it.

That kink in Broadway has become a wellspring of urban myths
over the years, with countless variations involving a stubborn Dutch
farmer deflecting Broadway from its path or a team of surveyors
bending Broadway to avoid the demolition of a favorite tavern. The
myths are all captivating, hinting at a rural landscape not quite
destroyed by the modern city, but the real story about why Broadway bends at 10th Street is even more fascinating, since it originated
in a forgotten collision of two deeply ingrained American obsessions:
money and land.

———

WHEN BROADWAY was extended over Lispenard's Meadows and up to the Sandy Hill Road in the mid-1770s, the Bowery, just to the east, was the primary highway in and out of town, as it had been since Dutch settlers first laid out a series of farms, or "bouweries," along the road in the early seventeenth century. The Bowery's path, which remains unchanged today, curved to the northeast in order to avoid the Collect Pond, then curved gradually back to the center of the island. Broadway, meanwhile, was a straight line that came to a dead end at its junction with the Sandy Hill Road, which skirted around the base of an incline called Bowery Hill, part of a ridge of primordial dunes called the Sand Hills, or "Zandtberg" in Dutch, which ran from present-day Union Square to Greenwich Village. The Bowery was only accessible from Broadway by way of the Sandy Hill Road, which, since it skirted the bottom of Bowery Hill, was perpetually flooded. For travelers entering and leaving the city and with business on Broadway, it was all very muddy and inconvenient.

By the 1790s it had become clear that Broadway and the Bowery should meet in some way, but it was not a simple proposition. The geometry was difficult to resolve, and in the end the city decided that the two streets should simply crash into each other.

The first plan, conceived in 1797 by city surveyors Joseph-François Mangin (who went on to help design City Hall in 1802) and Casimir Goerck, called for Broadway to extend north in a straight line across the Bowery and continue until it met the Middle Road, a precursor of Fifth Avenue, near present-day 28th Street. That plan stalled when landowners refused to let the city cut Broadway through their properties. Surely it mattered that the landowners in question included a prominent judge, John Watts Jr., and the wealthy heirs of Nicholas Cruger, who, before his death in 1800, had been a well-respected local patriot, mentor to Alexander Hamilton, and perhaps New York's most powerful merchant, a trader of lumber, sugar, rice, and slaves. When approached by the three members of the city's road committee, Watts brushed them aside, declaring that he felt "no particular interest" in ceding even the rear portion of his land for a Broadway extension. Cruger's heirs just as quickly rejected the idea. Thus spurned, the Common Council began exploring an alternate route, and in 1804 proposed that Broadway should bend at a 22-degree angle—the origin of that mysterious 10th Street jog—and then continue due north until it joined the Bowery in an acutely angled fork at present-day 16th Street.

But in devising the new route, the city was forced to "treat"— negotiate—with a new set of landowners, most of whom owned property fronting on the west side of the Bowery and backing up to Minetta Water, a south-flowing freshwater creek that had its source near the present-day intersection of Sixth Avenue and 16th Street.

In those days, eminent domain—the taking of private land for public purposes—was a power wielded by the city only as a last resort. The dominion over one's land was a cherished, almost sacred right in those heady decades of Young America, and the city proceeded very cautiously when asking landowners to cede sections of their property for municipal use. The opening of new streets through Manhattan's tangled maze of existing property lines was a particularly difficult endeavor. It was often more trouble than it was worth, which is one reason why the city expanded so slowly prior to the passage, in 1807, of state legislation governing development patterns in Manhattan, which ultimately led to the Commissioners' Plan and its strict grid of streets and avenues. In the vexing matter of extending Broadway to the Bowery, the city came very close to giving up on the idea entirely, in which case the Bowery, not Broadway, may have ended up as Manhattan's fabled Great White Way.

New streets were considered improvements that generally increased property values, and so landowners were typically "assessed," or taxed, in order to help the city defray the costs of the roadwork. Conversely, if the opening of a new road caused injury to buildings, fences, or trees on private land, the city awarded "damages" to reimburse the affected landowners. In some cases the city simultaneously extracted assessments *and* awarded damages to the same landowner, but the dollar amounts of both assessments and damage awards typically varied landowner to landowner, a disparity that often led to resentment, then grievances and petitions, and finally litigation and lengthy construction delays.

The system of assessments and damages often had the effect of pitting neighbors against each other, but just as often brought them together as groups that collectively petitioned the Common Council for greater awards or alleviation of assessments. And so it happened that in the summer of 1804 a group of landowners headed by Henry Spingler came forward, petitioning the Common Council against running Broadway through their land. It was the beginning of a four-year-long legal stalemate.

IN JANUARY OF 1805, the Common Council appointed John S. Hunn as the city's new commissioner of streets. Hunn was assertive and opinionated, and within three months of taking office had obtained the consent of five of the nine landowners in Broadway's intended path. But Spingler and three of his neighbors, David Dunham and the brothers Thomas and Samuel Burling, still refused to sign deeds of cession. The following August the nine landowners received awards of damages totaling $7,021.50 ($140,420 in today's dollars) from the city, but Spingler, Dunham, and the Burlings still refused to budge.

By the summer of 1807, buildings, fences, and trees still stood in Broadway's intended path, and although Spingler had finally signed a deed of cession, both Dunham and the Burlings had neglected to remove various structures from the right-of-way, and Hunn's patience was at an end. "Mr. Dunham still occupies his house standing on the Street," Hunn fumed, "although long since paid for the ground and the expence [sic] of removal."

What to do when someone stands in the way of a street? The city did what it would probably do today: It called its lawyers. Richard Harison and Isaac A. van Hook, city counselors, advised the immediate removal of Dunham's house and other obstructions, although they thought one final request might be in order.

Then it was discovered that three of Spingler's tenants were also seeking damages from the city (they were eventually awarded $451) while Spingler himself petitioned against an assessment of $209, which the city had levied on him to help defray the expense of removing Dunham's and the Burlings' buildings. Then Rachel Arden, another of Spingler's neighbors, refused to sign a deed of cession unless the city released her from a $90 assessment. Hunn visited her house "three or four times . . ." he reported, "with the deeds for that purpose without finding her home." (It's easy to imagine Hunn pounding on the door while Arden hides behind the curtains.) It was beginning to look like the entire idea of extending Broadway was never going to happen.

Then, on June 21, 1807, off the Virginia coast, the British warship *Leopard*, on a search mission for British deserters, opened fire on the American frigate *Chesapeake*, killing three seamen. The United States had been trying to maintain its neutrality, and trade with both the British and French, adversaries in the ongoing Napoleonic Wars. But the British in particular had been preying on American shipping and, even worse, impressing American seamen. The "Chesapeake-Leopard Affair" enraged the American public and was one catalyst that ultimately led to the War of 1812, but in 1807, President Thomas Jefferson shied away from all-out war in favor of economic sanctions. On December 22 of that year Jefferson signed the Embargo Act, which forbade all American exports. It was a drastic measure meant to bring Britain to its knees; instead, it prostrated the American economy.

New York had never seen as prosperous a year as 1807, when its exports reached a record high of $26,300,000—$526,000,000 in today's dollars. But immediately upon passage of the Embargo Act, all port activity ground to a complete halt. Unemployed carpenters, shipwrights, sailmakers, caulkers, and cartmen wandered the streets, stranded seamen gathered in angry mobs in City Hall Park, and merchants, brokers, and auctioneers went bankrupt. And it was the dead of winter.

With thousands of destitute workers in danger of starvation, Hunn recommended pushing ahead immediately with the opening of Broadway between Art Street (the former Sandy Hill Road) and the Bowery, even if in only a "temporary manner." The extension of Broadway, which for so many years had been tied up in landowners' petitions, had suddenly become vitally important. The Common Council's road committee then consisted of Samuel Kip, Nicholas

Fish (a Revolutionary War veteran and father of the future governor Hamilton Fish), merchant John Slidell (father of future U.S. Senator John Slidell Jr., of Louisiana), and they recommended extending Broadway to the Bowery "with as many hands as can be usefully employed therein."

And so, in the freezing cold early months of 1808, work finally began on the opening of Broadway to the Bowery.

But even then, letters and petitions from angry landowners continued to arrive at City Hall. Spingler claimed that he had "misconceived" the terms of his deed of cession allowing Broadway to cut through his land, and requested that the deed be voided. And David Dunham's house was still in the way, its kitchen extending into Broadway's path. In February of 1808, Dunham came up with an alternative: Might the surveyors simply narrow Broadway as it approached his house, so that the kitchen could remain where it was? Fish, Slidell, and Kip confessed they were "at a loss" to even know how to respond, but a week later the Common Council ordered Dunham "to remove, forthwith, so much of his Kitchen as may encroach upon the public Street."

Then Spingler and six of his neighbors submitted a new petition to the city. This time they protested not the opening of Broadway—it was too late for that—but the amounts of their assessments. They were especially stung when they learned that the city planned to use their assessments to help pay for damages awarded to their neighbors, including Dunham and the Burlings, while ignoring damage done to *their* buildings, fences, and trees. The last of Spingler's neighbors to sign the petition was a local fixture named Henry Brevoort.

He was known as Henry Brevoort, Sr., to distinguish him from his son, the writer Henry Brevoort Jr. Brevoort Sr.'s father, who had died in 1798, had been known simply as Henry Brevoort and was the son of yet another Henry Brevoort, who had been known as "Henry Brevoort of the Bowery." Henry Brevoort of the Bowery was the son of the original landowner John Hendricks Brevoort, who, in 1701, had acquired the first 41 acres of the farm, which eventually swelled in size to 86 acres. In 1760 half of the farm was sold to Spingler and

Henry Brevoort was supposedly a country bumpkin who forced Broadway to change direction. In reality, he was a politically savvy landowner.

Henry Brevoort 1828,
Aetat. 81.

the Burlings, and by 1808, when Broadway was cut through it, only 11 acres remained.

Brevoort Sr. was sixty-one years old then and had become a well-known horticulturalist. "Brevoort's Purple Washington" plum was, according to Robert Manning's 1838 *Book of Fruits,* "of large size; form round, and nearly oval; skin dark blue, covered with a blue bloom; the flesh sweet and good," although landscape architect and horticulturist Andrew Jackson Downing, in his 1845 treatise *The Fruits and Fruit Trees of America,* offered a dissenting opinion: "[The Brevoort Purple Washington] is a handsome and most productive plum, but appears to us to have been overpraised as regards its flavor, which is of second quality." "Brevoort's Morris" peach, meanwhile, pleased Downing greatly: "One of the richest and most delicious of American peaches," he wrote, noting its "rich, sugary" taste.

Brevoort Sr. was also a politician, having served three consecutive terms, from 1771 to 1774, as an assistant alderman on the Common Council. He was elected to a fourth term in 1802 and was sitting on the council when the city first proposed extending Broadway to the Bowery. In 1806, Brevoort was named one of twenty-seven inspectors appointed by the city to monitor polling in the fall elections, a position given only to well-connected, politically savvy residents. Brevoort, in other words, was at the very center of political life in the rapidly developing city.

Yet somehow over the next century Brevoort became the lead character in the myth of the Broadway bend, an intransigent landowner standing up to the city and credited with causing the deflection of Broadway away from its straight-line path. The origins of the myth and all its variations arose from confusion over the nature of the 1808 Spingler petition that Brevoort signed and his later fight to stop the city from extending 11th Street from the Bowery to Broadway and through his house.

The tussle over 11th Street began in 1815, well after Broadway had been opened through the Brevoort farm. In letter upon letter and brief upon brief, Brevoort Sr. and Jr. protested the opening of the street, and the matter became a drawn-out legal contest between city and state that took the next thirty-four years to resolve, by which time both Brevoort Sr. and Jr. were dead. Grace Church took up the cause, since the extension of 11th Street would have grazed the back corner of the church, and 11th Street between the Bowery and Broadway never was opened and remains closed today. Over time, the Brevoort family's fight over 11th Street became confused with the origins of the Broadway bend at 10th Street.

But that doesn't fully explain how Brevoort, an astute politician and cultivator of fruit trees, should have become recast as the stubborn country bumpkin immortalized in Gideon J. Tucker's 1892 poem:

> *A merry old Dutchman was Uncle Brevoort,*
> *Who had not lived eighty odd years for naught;*
> *With abundant waist and laughing blue eye*
> *And nose of a color a trifle high,*
> *A gouty foot, and long silvery hair,*
> *And a forehead free as a child's from care . . .*

He fought all their maps, and he fought their reports,
Corporation, surveyors, commissioners, courts;
He hired his lawyers, well learned in the law;
The plans and the projects to fragments they tore.
But Uncle Brevoort, ere the law suit expires,
And calmly he sleeps at St. Mark's with his sires.

Washington Irving was on intimate terms with the Brevoort family, at one point lodging with Brevoort Jr. in a hotel on lower Broadway, and had made frequent visits to the Brevoort homestead during the time he was dreaming up Rip Van Winkle, an enduring archetype of old Dutch New York first introduced to the public in Irving's *The Sketchbook of Geoffrey Crayon*, published in 1819. Over time, it seems, Brevoort Sr. was remembered less and less as a real person and more like Rip, a man impervious to progress and lost in time.

In reality, Brevoort Sr. was a shrewd real-estate speculator who as early as 1807 had begun dividing his farm into building lots, in anticipation of Broadway's extension through his land, selling four of the lots to John Jacob Astor, who was related by marriage. (Brevoort's wife, Sarah Whetton, was the niece of Astor's wife Sarah Todd.)

Brevoort Sr. lived on what remained of the family farm for the rest of his life. Spry until the very end, he accompanied Brevoort Jr. on social rounds through the growing city, wondering, Brevoort Jr. wrote Irving, at the "novelties of the age." At eighty-nine, Brevoort Sr. was still energetic enough to walk the two miles from his home to Wall Street so that his solicitor, Peter Jay, could draft his will, which Brevoort signed with a shaky hand. In his longevity, Brevoort became emblematic of a lost, rural age, someone who had lived long enough to see the invention of the steamship and the telegraph, yet lived his entire life on a farm on Broadway.

In 1841, Brevoort stood on Broadway in a snowstorm to watch President William Henry Harrison's funeral procession pass by. He died four months later at the Rip Van Winkle–like age of ninety-four, and Brevoort Jr. gave his father's prized long gun to Irving. When Philip Hone heard that the old man had finally died, he immediately began calculating how much the Brevoort farm was worth—half a million, Hone reckoned.

Brevoort had left clear instructions in his will: The farm was to be divided among Brevoort Jr., his brother Elias, daughter Margaret, and Margaret's husband James Renwick, and cut into building lots. There was no hint of sentimentality in the will, nothing about preserving the old homestead. Brevoort, far from the stubborn farmer standing in the way of progress, encouraged his children to sell or trade the land for the best price they could get. Brevoort, it turns out, was a thoroughly modern man.

CHAPTER 12

GRACE

———

IN 1843, TWO YEARS AFTER HIS FATHER'S DEATH, HENRY Brevoort Jr. sold a large parcel of his father's farm to Grace Church, which wanted to sell its old church on Rector Street, next door to Trinity Church, and move north along Broadway to the corner of 10th Street. (Grace made a nice profit on the deal, selling the old church for $65,000 while paying only $35,000—$1,093,000 in today's dollars—for the Brevoort land.) Brevoort Jr.'s sister Margaret and her husband James Renwick, a well-known professor at Columbia College, had a twenty-four-year-old Columbia-educated son who was interested in engineering and architecture. Small wonder, then, that the commission for the new Grace Church went to James Renwick Jr.

He went on to design St. Patrick's Cathedral, Vassar College, and the Smithsonian Institution, among many other projects in a long and illustrious career, but in 1843, Renwick Jr. hadn't yet opened a proper architecture office. If Renwick was known at all, it was for the Bowling Green fountain, which he had designed the year before and which had been widely condemned—a "monstrosity," his former Columbia classmate George Templeton Strong called it.

But, like Richard Upjohn, Renwick had studied the treatises and pattern books of Gothic Revivalist Augustus Welby Northmore Pugin, and despite his inexperience, Renwick, no doubt with input from his father, dreamed up an architectural tour de force for what was then still called "upper Broadway." As construction progressed, the new Grace emerged as both rival and companion to Upjohn's Trinity Church then under construction at Broadway and Wall Street. By the spring of 1844 both Trinity and Grace were far enough along that one was clearly visible from the other. Exactly two miles apart, they became Broadway's Gothic bookends.

Grace was built in marble quarried by prisoners at Sing Sing, its delicate traceries, quoins, and bosses carved at Bird Bros., a marble yard conveniently located next door to the construction site. The off-white marble contrasted with Trinity's dark brownstone down the street and made Grace's spire glow in the morning sun. The spire, built initially in wood as a cost-saving measure, rose 220 feet from sidewalk to pinnacle, 60 feet shorter than Trinity's spire but still tall enough to tower over every other building in the area.

The church was cruciform in plan, with the central nave stretching 144 feet east from its front doors on Broadway, the rear façade butting up against the backyard fences of a row of brick houses on the Bowery that had replaced the old Brevoort homestead. Grace's stained-glass windows were modest compared to Trinity's, but the interior columns holding up the roof were remarkably thin, which lent a feeling of ethereal weightlessness to the whole enterprise. By the end of 1845 it was clear to most observers that Renwick had built a masterpiece.

"Have you seen the magnificent *kaleidoscope* at the top of Broadway?" the *Tribune* marveled as the church neared completion in early 1846. "You don't mean Grace Church?

"[We] were not prepared to find [Renwick] capable of exhibiting a degree of taste and ability in architecture which puts him at least upon a level with any one who has ever practised that art in the United States," the *Tribune*'s editors acknowledged. Commissions poured in, and before Grace was even finished, Renwick was busy designing Calvary Church, at the corner of Fourth Avenue and 21st Street, and the Church of the Puritans on Union Square.

But not everyone was convinced. George Templeton Strong, for one, thought Grace suffered from an "unhappy straining after cheap magnificence," and he didn't much care for Renwick, either, whom he found insufferably arrogant. (One evening Renwick ruined a stroll down Broadway by tormenting Strong with pontifications upon Grace's "points.") As the accolades for Renwick poured in, Strong could only scrawl vitriolic diary entries about "that most windy of all the bags of conceit & coxcombry that ever dubbed themselves Architect."

GRACE'S NEW CHURCH became a bastion of wealthy merchants, brokers, lawyers, and physicians. There were other fashionable churches nearby, including, just to the south, the Church of the Messiah at Broadway and Waverly Place, but the showy wealth of Grace's parishioners was of a different order.

Grace's flock included social climbers, those merchant princes and industrialists who lacked Dutch roots but had plenty of money; it was the old Dutch families, however, that gave Grace its fashionable luster. Grace's rotund sexton Isaac H. Brown, a former carpenter with a genius for organization, who kept the church furnace stoked and the parishioners sorted, bowing low to Livingstons, Stuyvesants, Remsens, and Schermerhorns while virtually ignoring the lesser strivers who had bought their way into the parish. (Brown, building on his renown, became Society's go-to event planner and social gatekeeper, the man to see when a ball, wedding, or funeral needed arranging, and was so well regarded as an arbiter of taste he even endorsed various products, including Mrs. Jervis's Cold Candy.)

"This is to be the fashionable church," diarist Philip Hone wrote of Grace as its consecration approached, "and already its aisles are filled . . . with gay parties of ladies in feathers and *mousseline-de-laine* dresses, and dandies with moustaches and high-heeled boots; the lofty arches resound with astute criticisms upon *Gothic architecture* from fair ladies who have had the advantage of foreign travel, and scientific remarks upon *acoustics* from elderly millionaires who do not hear quite as well as formerly."

In January of 1846, with the church nearing completion, Grace auctioned off its 212 black walnut pews, and old families and social climbers alike grappled to secure the best seats. "The bidding was quite lively and spirited," the *Tribune* reported. Two of the "choicest" pews were valued at $950 apiece, and many others went for as much as $400 above their assessed value.

The sturdy pews were private, with little doors opening from the aisles, and to dissuade trespassers the owners' names were stamped on brass plates firmly bolted to the wood—so firmly that many of the plates are still there today. Intrusions were not permitted, as became apparent at Grace's consecration, on March 7, 1846. The opening service was supposedly open to the public, or at least to those with tickets, but when one female reporter from the *Evening Post* twice sat down in private pews, she was twice ejected. The populist *Post* retaliated by refusing to cover the consecration, while the rival *Tribune* lost itself in the grandeur of New York's new cultural epicenter:

> The effect of the light through the many-colored windows falling upon the audience and illuminating with pictorial radiance the rich and gorgeous ornaments of the Church, was indescribably fine. Not the least impressive portion of the performances was the music of the choir, which gushed forth in symmetrical undulations, mingling with the harmonies of light so admirably created by the silent artists hid in the stained glass windowpanes, and completing to the satisfied soul a perfectly graceful and expressive picture, formed by music, light, the eloquent silence of architectural symmetry and the spirit of devotion which pervaded the audience.

Margaret Fuller, writing in the same newspaper a few days later, sounded a much different tone, chastising the church for its exclusivity while calling attention to the irony of wealthy Grace borrowing its architectural forms from the cathedrals of the medieval period. "[When] those cathedrals were consecrated it was for the use of all," Fuller wrote. "Rich and poor knelt together upon their marble pavements, and the imperial altar welcomed the obscurest artisan."

"This grace our Churches want," she went on, "the grace which belongs to all religions, but is peculiarly and solemnly enforced upon the followers of Jesus. The poor to whom he came to preach can have no share in the grace of Grace Church."

CHAPTER 13

UNION

—

G RACE CHURCH'S WELL-HEELED PARISHIONERS TENDED TO come from the immediate area surrounding the church, having moved with the general northward migration of families from downtown to uptown, where they settled in genteel Federal and Greek- and Gothic-Revival row houses along Washington Square, Bond Street, Gramercy Park, and the newly fashionable Union Square.

The land that became Union Square began not as a park but simply as the "Forks," the point where Broadway and the Bowery met at an acute angle, surrounded by a few taverns, clapboard dwellings, and open fields. It was the same junction that had, in its creation in 1808, pitted the city against landowners opposed to the extension of Broadway; David Dunham's house, the one that had protruded into Broadway's path when the street was cut through, had stood at the center of what would become Union Square.

Union Square appeared for the first time on city maps, as "Union Place," in 1811. It was a planned feature of the first version of the Commissioners' Plan issued that year, although it bore no resemblance to the urbane quadrangle it was to become. It wasn't yet rectangular or even in the same location, originating in an awkward trapezium of leftover land bounded east and west by the Bowery and Broadway, south and north by 10th and 17th streets. It was really an after-thought, the result of the three commissioners, with the assistance of their surveyor John Randel Jr., trying to resolve their rather strange idea that Broadway should straighten away from its bend at 10th Street and head north, crossing over the Bowery before terminating in a proposed "Parade," a 238-acre open space bounded on its southern edge by 23rd Street.

Its name came neither from the "Great Union Meeting" of 1861 nor from the many labor union meetings held there beginning in the 1880s. In 1864, looking back on the work he had done fifty years earlier, Randel remembered that the name came about because the Commissioners had badly mangled the intersection of Broadway and the Bowery, which "left so small an amount of ground for building purposes, that the Commissioners instructed me to lay out the ground, at the *union* of those streets and roads, for a public square, which, from that circumstance, they named *Union Place*."

When landowners around the Forks discovered the commissioners' proposal that Broadway be straightened and cut through their land, they petitioned the Common Council, and the council, as it so often did, sent the matter upriver to Albany. In 1815 the legislature, siding with landowners, passed an "Act making certain Alterations in the Map or Plan of the City of New York" that not only rejected the idea that Broadway should be straightened and "lost," as Randel put it, in the Parade, but also erased the first version of Union Place. For the next sixteen years Union Place disappeared from maps of the city, while the route of Broadway, including its bend at 10th Street, remained unchanged.

It wasn't until 1831 that the idea of Union Place was revived, and it came by way of another legislative act. The same argument used in 1803 to justify the expense of building City Hall—that civic monuments were vital to the city's image—was repeated as the rationale for Union Place. "It is worthy of remark," the city's Board of Assistants reported in November of 1831, "that almost every stranger who visits us, whether from our sister States or from Europe, speaks of the paucity of our Public Squares; and that in proportion to its size,

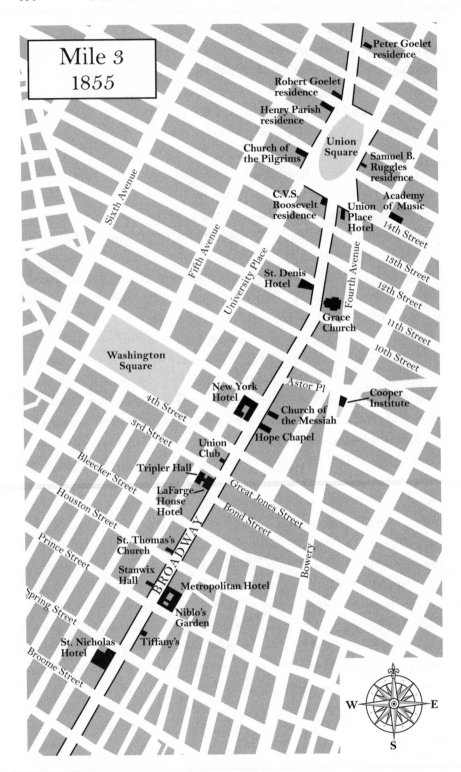

Mile 3
1855

Peter Goelet
residence

Robert Goelet
residence

Henry Parish
residence

Church of
the Pilgrims

Union
Square

Samuel B.
Ruggles
residence

C.V.S.
Roosevelt
residence

Union
Place
Hotel

Academy
of Music

Sixth Avenue

Fifth Avenue

University Place

Fourth Avenue

14th Street

13th Street

12th Street

11th Street

10th Street

St. Denis
Hotel

Grace
Church

Washington
Square

New York
Hotel

Astor Pl

Cooper
Institute

4th Street

3rd Street

Church of
the Messiah

Hope Chapel

Union
Club

Bleecker Street

Tripler Hall

LaFarge
House
Hotel

Great Jones Street

Bond Street

Bowery

Houston Street

St. Thomas's
Church

Prince Street

BROADWAY

Stanwix
Hall

Metropolitan Hotel

Spring Street

Niblo's
Garden

St. Nicholas
Hotel

Tiffany's

Broome Street

W   E

S

New York contains a smaller number, and those few of comparatively less extent than perhaps any other town of importance."

The new Union Place was nudged slightly to the north of the original site, squeezed between 14th and 17th streets and, curiously, wasn't conceived as a public park in the modern sense—as a place for contemplation, relaxation, and physical activity—but simply as a "ventilator," an open space supplying oxygen to a growing city beset by disastrous epidemics of yellow fever and cholera. That Union Place might also provide ample space for civic "festivities" was a secondary consideration.

At first, Union Place was only "a shapeless and ill-looking place, devoid of symmetry," and it took the intercession of local lawyer and real-estate developer Samuel B. Ruggles to turn the nondescript acres into a truly public park. After University Place was opened between 8th and 17th streets in 1833, Ruggles petitioned the Common Council to extend Fourth Avenue (present-day Park Avenue) south to meet the Bowery at 14th Street, giving the park crisply orthogonal east and west edges to match those of 14th and 17th streets to the south and north. Before long the park was laid out with gravel walks radiating from a central point, planted with shade trees and flowerbeds, and surrounded by a cast-iron fence.

Ruggles, inspired by the urbane squares of Bloomsbury in London, was an experienced developer. Two years earlier he had laid out Gramercy Park, six blocks to the northeast of Union Square, and was determined to repeat that success at Union Place. In 1839 he moved his family into a neat Greek Revival house at 24 Union Place, one in a row of houses he built facing the east side of the square between 15th and 16th streets, and lived there happily for the rest of his life. (It was in the parlor of No. 24 that George Templeton Strong wooed Ruggles's daughter Ellen, and upon their marriage in 1848, Ruggles helped the happy couple build a handsome new house on 21st Street, facing Gramercy Park.)

One by one, wealthy downtown merchants and financiers followed Ruggles's lead, and by the time the new Grace Church was consecrated in 1846, Union Square's perimeter was an almost unbroken rectangle of mansions. Cornelius van Schaack Roosevelt, an importer of plate glass, lived in a large house at the corner of Broadway and 14th Street, facing the southern edge of the square. (It was from a window on the second floor of that house that six-year-old Theodore Roosevelt, Cornelius's grandson, watched Abraham Lincoln's funeral procession pass slowly down Broadway in 1865.) James F. Penniman, a manufacturer of linseed oil, built a fabulously appointed brownstone mansion at 42 East 14th Street, just west of Roosevelt. Henry Parish, an importer of silk, built an opulent mansion, stuffed with Old Master paintings and featuring an oval stair ascending to a central dome, with an attached conservatory in the side yard, at the southwest corner of Broadway and 17th Street. Robert Goelet, heir to a family fortune made in hardware, lived directly across 17th Street from Parish, while, two blocks to the north, Goelet's brother Peter built a mysterious brick house set back from the street on one-third of an acre of lawn stocked with strutting peacocks. (Peter Goelet's house wasn't demolished until 1896.)

"This is now the *fashionable quarter*," the editors of the annual *New York Gazetteer* declared in 1842. But only five years later, Madison Square, six blocks to the north, opened and began luring residents northward once again. Moving had become a consuming passion in New York, an exaggerated version of the restless American desire for constant change.

"That's the way to live in New York—to move every three or four years," Arthur Townsend, a geographically ambitious young swain, pontificates in Henry James's novel *Washington Square*, in which its protagonist, Catherine, is doomed not only to an unmarried life, but an unmarried life below 14th Street. "Then you always get the last thing. It's because the city's growing so quick—you've got to keep up with it. It's going straight up town—that's where New York's going."

On the eve of the Civil War, Union Square was still a residential neighborhood but, because the city had grown so far to the north, was beginning to feel like the center of town.

AROUND MIDNIGHT on April 14, 1861, Walt Whitman was walking down Broadway on his way home to Brooklyn when he heard the shouts of newsboys announcing the surrender of Fort Sumter.

"I bought an extra and cross'd to the Metropolitan hotel (Niblo's) where the great lamps were still brightly blazing, and, with a crowd of others, who gather'd impromptu, read the news, which was evidently authentic. For the benefit of some who had no papers, one of us read the telegram aloud, while all listen'd silently and attentively. No remark was made by any of the crowd, which had increas'd to thirty or forty, but all stood a minute or two, I remember, before they dispers'd."

Within the week a recruiting office opened at 613 Broadway, just north of Houston Street, and dozens of volunteer regiments formed. George Templeton Strong arranged for an American flag to be hoisted up the spire of Trinity Church—an unprecedented political gesture on the part of the conservative parish. A huge crowd gathered at Broadway and Wall Street to cheer the raising of Trinity's flag, as the church's chimes played "Hail, Columbia" and "Yankee Doodle."

In those first hectic weeks of war, Broadway became less a street and more like a linear piazza full of milling crowds anxious to hear the latest news bulletins. Broadway's shops did a suddenly brisk business in patriotic goods. Spier & Company, 187 Broadway, was just one of dozens of shops selling badges, streamers, and "Union cockades." Up and down Broadway, the daily fashion promenade turned red, white, and blue: "A beautiful bonnet made by Miss A. M. Stuart in Broadway, and on which the red, white, and blue, with silver stars tastefully arranged, constituted the trimming, was worn on Broadway yesterday by a lady, and was much admired," the *Tribune* reported. "Thousands of rosettes were sold and worn, and in some instances the gentlemen placed them in their hats."

Broadway booksellers and publishers rushed out new military treatises and maps. The shelves at Van Nostrand's, 192 Broadway, included military engineer (and future real-estate developer of Manhattan's West Side) Egbert L. Viele's *Hand-Book for Active Service* ("At the command *forward*, the soldier will throw the weight of his body on the right leg, without bending the left knee"), Joseph Roberts's *The Hand-Book of Artillery*, and C. M. Wilcox's *Rifles and Rifle Practice*. D. Appleton & Company, 443-445 Broadway, sold not only "all the important textbooks for volunteers," but also, for 25 cents apiece, portraits of Major Robert Anderson, the "Hero of Fort Sumter." Two blocks to the north, Edward Anthony (501 Broadway), a supplier of photographic equipment, hawked portraits of Anderson alongside images of Abraham Lincoln, William H. Seward, Winfield Scott, and (no doubt to attract the business of the city's remaining Southern sympathizers) Jefferson Davis for the same price. Music publishers rushed out hastily printed, and apparently hastily written, patriotic songs:

> *A song for the Stripes and the Stars,*
> *A cheer for the land that bore us;*
> *And away to the camp*
> *With a soldier's tramp,*
> *And a rousing Union chorus.*

Early on the morning of April 19, 1861, the 8th Regiment of the Massachusetts Volunteers, 1,200 strong, arrived in the city by train, marched down Broadway, and bivouacked in style at the St. Nicholas, Astor House, and Lafarge House hotels before mustering in City Hall Park and departing by steamer for Washington. That afternoon thousands of spectators turned out to see the legendary 7th Regiment of the New York State Militia depart the city by way of Broadway, where "a heaving multitude . . . probably the largest crowd that ever thronged that thoroughfare," waved banners and handkerchiefs. The next day the 6th, 12th, and 71st New York militias marched down the street on their way to the Hudson River docks, where ships waited to take them off to war.

"The scene that burst upon the view in Broadway exceeded anything, perhaps, ever before witnessed in that thoroughfare of wonders," the *New York Herald* reported as the 6th Regiment marched down the street. "Every window, door, housetop, awning, was crowded. The street itself was thronged as though the populace were wedged together in one solid living mass . . . The Stars and Stripes waved everywhere, and one banner displayed the works 'Fort Sumter and its Band of 70 Heroes. No Surrender to Traitors.'"

By week's end thousands of additional troops from New England and New York had paraded down Broadway on their way to war, each departing regiment escorted by euphoric crowds lining both

**The 7th Regiment passing Broadway's magnificent St. Nicholas Hotel,
April 19, 1861, on its way to the front lines.**

sides of the street. Broadway stores raced to supply uniforms, boots,
cots, camp stools, pots and pans, and field glasses to the thousands
of departing troops that marched each day past their window displays. Joseph H. Semmons & Company, opticians, 669½ Broadway,
displayed a stock of military glasses, including "out-door double Perspective Glasses" for use on the field of battle. The furriers L. J. & I.
Phillips, 64-66 Broadway, guaranteed regiments "an enormous supply" of soldier's caps "at the shortest notice." Devlin, Hudson & Company offered "military clothing of all descriptions" from their two
Broadway locations (corner of Warren Street and corner of Grand),
promising rapid delivery of "large orders," while Brooks Brothers, at
Broadway and Grand Street, across from Devlin's and Lord & Taylor,
sold 12,000 uniforms to the New York volunteers, only to become
embroiled in a scandal when many of them fell apart.

Owing to its longstanding reliance on Southern cotton production, New York was, in many respects, a Southern city. New York
hotels, English tourist Isabella Lucy Bird had observed in 1854,

were filled with "southerners sighing for their sunny homes, smoking Havana cigars." Southern businessmen often brought their entire families for extended stays in the city, especially in summer, and hotels and restaurants that catered to them did good business. There was a Planters Hotel at Broadway and Spring Street, a Magnolia Hotel on West Street, and a Magnolia Lunch at Broadway and Chambers Street, while the New York Hotel at Broadway and Great Jones Street remained a hotspot for Southern-sympathizing "Copperheads" throughout the war. Broadway theaters, too, often pandered to Southern audiences: *The Seven Sisters*, a long-running production featuring bumbling black stereotypes and sniveling abolitionists, played at Laura Keene's Theater on Broadway even after the war began.

New York's alliance with the South vanished with the attack on Fort Sumter and, having suddenly lost access to lucrative Southern markets, the city turned to manufacturing as a way of shoring up its wartime economy—the beginning of the transformation of New York from a way station for goods produced elsewhere to a production center in its own right. B. F. Palmer & Company, manufacturer of artificial limbs, did such brisk business that it opened two Broadway stores catering to "mutilated soldiers." By 1863, Palmer had 3,000 prosthetic arms and legs in stock and was gearing up to produce 100 additional limbs per month.

UNION SQUARE HAD surpassed City Hall Park as the city's main public gathering place, and in the weeks following Fort Sumter became the epicenter of Unionist fervor. On Saturday afternoon, April 20, 1861, Union Square was the setting for an enormous "Great Union Meeting" that drew an immense crowd reported at 100,000—the largest public gathering in the city's, and possibly the nation's, history. By three o'clock a sea of people had pressed into the square from all sides and filled Broadway and surrounding streets. Dodworth's band was there, naturally, as well as a company of fifty schoolboys that marched around the perimeter of the park, cheered on by the crowd. A few foolhardy secessionist hecklers unwisely showed up; they were chased down and beaten.

Five stages were set up in various spots around the park, and in those premicrophone days, the crowd strained to hear the remarks of dozens of speakers representing a cross-section of the city's political, industrial, mercantile, and clerical elite. Archbishop John Hughes, too ill to attend, sent a warmly received letter pledging his fealty to the flag, but Major Anderson was the star attraction, and when he made his way laboriously through the crowd and mounted the first stage, on the 14th Street side of the square in front of an enormous 1856 equestrian bronze of George Washington, he was greeted by a deafening tidal wave of adulation. Anderson nodded appreciatively as an American flag that had flown over Fort Sumter, "stained with fire and bearing marks of the battle," fluttered overhead from Washington's outstretched arm.

Then Mayor Fernando Wood got up to speak, prompting both cheers and hisses. In a breathtakingly brazen about-face, Wood came out strongly for the Union, pledging the full support of his administration to the cause, only three months after publicly siding with "our grieved brethren of the slave states" and proposing that New York City secede from both state and country in order to protect its lucrative trade with the South.

By the time the scheduled speeches were over, it was growing dark, but the crowd, its energy barely dissipated, seemed in no hurry to go home. Spontaneous, unscheduled speakers continued rallying the crowd from the steps and balconies of buildings surrounding the park, and before long thousands were parading joyously up and down the streets. The *Sun* noted that in the whole crowd its reporters saw not one drunken man or heard one profane word. No doubt they weren't looking very hard.

IN 1870, TIFFANY'S DEMOLISHED the James Renwick–designed Church of the Puritans on the west side of Union Square and replaced it with a huge cast-iron store—the "Palace of Jewels." The following year C. V. S. Roosevelt died and his house at the corner of Broadway and 14th Street was demolished and replaced by the headquarters of the Domestic Sewing Machine Company. The blocks surround-

The "Great Union Meeting" at Union Square, April 20, 1861.

ing the formerly tranquil square hummed with commercial activity, with once-grand mansions converted to boardinghouses, stores, and offices rented to chiropodists, coal dealers, dressmakers, milliners, hairdressers, furriers, and cloak manufacturers.

In 1872 the city hired Calvert Vaux and Frederick Law Olmsted, designers of Central Park, to remake Union Square according to a more up-to-date, picturesque aesthetic. Four years later, Olmsted was put in charge of the culminating pageant of the city's 1876 "Centennial Celebration," the most ambitious public demonstration Union Square had seen since the 1861 Great Union Meeting. Coming in the wake of several years of sectarian violence between the city's Catholics and Protestants, the Centennial Celebration was choreographed to depict New York as a thriving city at peace, where everyone, rich and poor, black and white, Protestant and Catholic, native-born and immigrant, got along famously.

Just before midnight on July 3, following a torchlight parade up Broadway, its entire length decorated with flags and streamers and illuminated with gas jets, an estimated crowd of 40,000 to 50,000 squeezed into Union Square to await the midnight commencement of the Fourth of July and the nation's Centennial. Olmsted had made Union Square as festive as possible, adding red, white, and blue gaslight globes and hanging Japanese lanterns in the trees. The numerous brass bands that had marched in the parade were somehow combined into one group, forming an ungainly orchestra of 600 instruments that managed to play together, more or less, "The Star-Spangled Banner," "Hail the Atlantis," and Beethoven's "The Heavens Are Telling the Glory of God," accompanied by a chorus of 600 singers.

At the stroke of midnight, fireworks rocketed skyward from each corner of the park. Hats were thrown in the air and pistols fired (at least nine people were accidentally shot), church chimes pealed, and the immense crowd roared as Dodworth's band began "Hail, Columbia."

"There were men, women, and children of all nationalities in that enormous audience," the *Sun* reported. "Cosmopolitan New York, with her population gathered from all quarters of the globe, seemed to have emptied itself into this blazing square, with the one thought and purpose of celebrating the brotherhood that binds all races into one. The Irishman stood beside the Yankee and the Knickerbocker, and the German was shoulder to shoulder with the Frenchman, and the negro's right to be glad was not denied, and so all cheered and threw up their hats together."

People remained in Union Square all night, even as dawn broke and church bells struck the morning hours.

Amid the sea of changes that had enveloped Union Square, Samuel B. Ruggles still lived in his original row house facing the eastern edge of the park. (His son-in-law George Templeton Strong had died the previous summer.) On July 4, Ruggles, then seventy-six years old, joined a group of luminaries onstage at the Academy of Music for a patriotic program of speeches and songs. Poet William Cullen Bryant, eighty-one, contributed a special "Centennial Ode."

> *Oh! checkered train of years, farewell,*
> *With all thy strifes and hopes and fears;*
> *But with us let thy memories dwell,*
> *To warn and lead the coming years.*

CHAPTER 14

THE RIALTO

———

THE ACADEMY OF MUSIC, THE FIRST SUCCESSFUL OPERA HOUSE in the city, had opened at the corner of 14th Street and Irving Place, one block east of Union Square, in 1854. Its 4,600-seat auditorium was an acoustical masterpiece but included only eighteen private boxes, which were reserved for those in New York's social stratosphere. The Academy specialized in operas by Mozart, Bellini, Rossini, and, especially, Verdi, whose *La Traviata*, *Il Trovatore*, and *Rigoletto* were performed over and over, but also put on concerts by everyone from the great Norwegian violinist Ole Bull to Dodworth's band.

The Academy quickly became a secular version of Grace Church, a place to see and be seen, and who attended each season's opening night and who sat in whose box were reliable subjects of gossip on the society pages of newspapers. Other places of amusement and culture, including Wallack's Theatre, Irving Hall, Steinway Hall, and Lent's New York Circus, followed the Academy to Union Square, and by the mid-1860s the intersection of Broadway and 14th Street had become the new center of the city's theater district.

On any given evening, patrons could watch the immensely popular Wallacks—father James and son John, both with curly hair, mustaches, and extravagant muttonchops—in *The Rivals*, *The School for Scandal*, *The Road to Ruin*, or *Used Up* at their theater at Broadway and 13th Street; listen to Charles Dickens read from his latest works at Steinway Hall; or pack into Lent's Circus, across 14th Street from the Academy, for thrilling exhibitions of "unsurpassed riders, gymnasts, posture masters, & c."

In 1860 the *New York Times* satirically suggested that Broadway's impenetrable traffic might be alleviated by turning the street into a version of Venice's Grand Canal, complete with a Rialto Bridge spanning Broadway at 14th Street:

> Why not at once set about dyking the sidewalks of our great thoroughfare, and so convert its roadway into a complete canal? Canals are the order of the day just now in New-York, and we are even bent on taxing our railways to keep them prosperous. A canal stretching from Washington Heights to the Battery would be a magnificent job for the City contractors. It would perfectly attain the end now bunglingly aimed at by so many public-spirited builders of houses and shops, and render the street completely impassable for at least a year, thereby compelling us to open new avenues, to the east and to the west. And, when finished, how admirable its effects alike on the appearance of the metropolis, and upon the health and convenience of the population! We should rival Venice in our picturesque beauty, and New-Orleans in our interesting insalubrity. A noble Rialto might be thrown up at Union-square, and flat-bottomed steamboats, of the Western pattern, running anywhere where it is a "little damp," would deliver us from the plague of omnibuses forever.

Broadway was never turned into a canal and no Rialto bridge was ever built across it, but the entertainment district that grew up around Broadway and 14th Street did become known, undoubtedly because of the *Times* article, as New York's "Rialto."

The emergence of the Rialto coincided with a shift in how theaters were managed, away from the traditional stock company, where performers often worked for years for the same theater manager, to a "combination" system in which performers were hired for one production at a time and then let go. The combination system created a large population of temporarily unemployed performers, and the benches of Union Square and sidewalks, barrooms, and cafés along 14th Street soon filled with loitering actors, songwriters, and agents, and "What news on the Rialto?" a line from *The Merchant of Venice*, became their standard catch phrase.

"Hello, Granville," began one typical conversation between two out-of-work actors. "What are you with next season [meaning, which production company hired you]?"

"I'm still looking, old chap."

Theatrical side-industries flocked to Union Square, too: costumers, music teachers, sheet music publishers, sign painters, show card printers, and scenic artists all moved into nearby offices, while boardinghouses in the neighborhood filled with theatrical types. By the 1870s there were so many piano manufacturers—Sohmer, Arion, Louis Berge, Chickering, Lighte & Ernst, Lindeman, George Steck, Dunham, Steinway—on 14th Street it became known as Piano Row, with at least a dozen others on Broadway and surrounding Union Square. (The Rialto scene foreshadowed the rise of Tin Pan Alley a few years later and a dozen blocks to the north.)

The Rialto was in its heyday when Tony Pastor arrived on the scene. He was born in New York around 1837, the son of a Greenwich Street barber, and began his career singing at Barnum's museum. As an eight-year-old, he joined Raymond & Waring's menagerie, where he appeared in blackface and played tambourine in a minstrel band, and by the 1850s he was working as a clown in Nixon's Circus and at the Bowery Theatre.

In 1865, Pastor took over Hooley's Theatre, a vaudeville house on the Bowery, changed its name to Pastor's Opera House, and began offering inoffensive "family theater." Pastor was going against the grain of an era when vaudeville houses catered to an overwhelmingly male audience that demanded increasingly risqué performances, including the scandalous "Parisian Can-Can." He encouraged women to attend by banning smoking, drinking, and profanity, by giving away prizes—sewing machines, barrels of flour, and bouquets—and admitting women free on Fridays. It also didn't hurt that Pastor had a way with a song, performing such favorites as "Down in a Coal Mine" and "Sarah's Young Man" in evening dress, punctuating each line with casual gestures of a silk top hat he held in his hand, and became something of a heartthrob.

In 1875, Pastor jumped from the Bowery to Broadway, taking over the lease at the former Buckley's Hall, just north of Prince Street and opposite the Metropolitan Hotel, and there put on everything—melodramas, farces, minstrel shows, ballet, Gilbert & Sullivan operettas—and amid the hundreds of actors, singers, jugglers, acrobats, contortionists, comedians, magicians, clog dancers, animal trainers, and fire-eaters who tread his boards, Pastor discovered major new talents, including Lillian Russell, Nat Goodwin, May Irwin, and the comedy team of Harrigan & Hart.

Pastor wore diamond rings and stickpins, had a kind, open face, a wide, cantilevering mustache with waxed tips, and a generous midsection. He was a man-about-town: "[When] the weather's fine there's a bouquet for my buttonhole and I make some of the matinee idols look pretty pale when I stroll up Broadway," he told a *Tribune* reporter.

He became so famous that he had a winning thoroughbred racehorse named after him and endorsed the popular liniment St. Jacob's Oil: "Mr. Pastor . . . would not be without it," the ads went. Traveling by steamboat from New York to Albany in 1881, Pastor was mobbed and spent the trip banging away at a piano, the center of attention, while Vice President Chester A. Arthur and Senators Roscoe Conkling and Thomas C. Platt, then three of the most powerful and well-known men in America, sat unnoticed and in quiet conversation off to the side.

Pastor even fielded his own amateur baseball team called, naturally, the "Tony Pastors" and stocked with theatrical types. It was all in good fun apparently, even when the Tony Pastors unwisely challenged the Mutuals, a crack professional team, and were clobbered 39 to 2.

In 1881, Pastor took over Bryant's Minstrel Hall inside the Democratic Party headquarters, Tammany Hall, which was on 14th Street next door to the Academy of Music. There Pastor perfected his so-

**Tony Pastor
ruled the
Rialto.**

called "star combination" system, taking advantage of the glut of
performers hanging around Union Square, and soon bragged that he
had 160 actors, musicians, dancers, and novelty acts in his "Mammoth
Star Company." He was the toast of the town.

Pastor remained on 14th Street for the rest of his career, even as
the theater district moved north to, first, Madison and then Herald
and Times squares. Rival vaudeville houses undercut him by offering continuous all-day performances for one 50-cent ticket—half the
admission that Pastor charged for one show. For years he refused to
make changes to his theater, believing that his public liked it the way
it was, but eventually cut his prices and began offering continuous
shows himself to keep up with the competition. Finally, a few months
before his death in 1908, he was forced to give up his lease.

By that time Union Square was called the "lower" Rialto, to distinguish it from the glamorous theaters of the "upper" Rialto to the

north. Freak shows and dime museums, the lowlife descendants of Barnum's American Museum, moved in. Huber's Museum on 14th Street, opposite the Academy of Music—which by then had been converted to a vaudeville house—featured, in the Barnum tradition, both a vaudeville theater and a "curio hall" where audiences could view Krao the Missing Link, Young Sampson the Strong Man, Fedora the Snake Enchantress, the "wonderfully entertaining" Turtle Boy, the "jolly Chinaman" Sing Wah Foo, and the Zarros, sword artists who performed "the neatest, cleanest and most startling decapitation mystery ever witnessed." Two blocks to the west, at the northwest corner of Fifth Avenue and 14th Street, James Meade's Midget Hall featured performances by General Mite, whose specialty was an impression of Tony Pastor.

CHAPTER 15

INCENDIARY SPEECH

———

SAMUEL B. RUGGLES ONCE DESCRIBED UNION SQUARE AS A "theatre adequate to the utterance of the national voice," and when Calvert Vaux and Frederick Law Olmsted redesigned the park in 1872, they included a public piazza at the north end of the square that could accommodate crowds of 10,000 or more. The centerpiece of the piazza was a graceful pavilion similar to structures Vaux and Olmsted had designed for Central Park, with a wide porch that doubled as a stage for speeches and band concerts.

Vaux and Olmsted called the new structure the "Cottage" and envisioned it as a dais for orderly meetings of business associations, veterans groups, and cultural societies, and for patriotic pageants like the 1876 Centennial Celebration. But on September 5, 1882, the Central Labor Union and the Knights of Labor organized the first Labor Day, and when 10,000 people marched up Broadway to Union Square, Vaux and Olmsted's urbane park truly became *Union* Square, the outdoor headquarters of the city's labor movement.

The square, situated in the center of the growing Garment District and its many sweatshops, became the focal point of daily rallies, attracting vast throngs of the unemployed and dispossessed, many of them immigrants. Wagons were often set up around the square to serve as extra speaking platforms, where speeches were given in German, Yiddish, Polish, and Italian.

It was onto one of those wagons that twenty-two-year-old anarchist Emma Goldman climbed uninvited during a raucous May Day rally in 1892, a demonstration that at one point featured anarchists grabbing Central Labor Union secretary George K. Lloyd by the legs and hauling him off the stage onto the ground. From the wagon Goldman waved a red flag and harangued the crowd, refusing to stop speaking even as the owner of the wagon hitched up a horse and drove away. Her theatrical performance, the *New York Tribune* cheerfully reported, "was the chief incident of the evening."

GOLDMAN WAS BORN in Lithuania in 1869. In 1885 she immigrated with her Jewish family to the United States and for three years worked in a factory in Rochester. Inspired to political action by the 1886 Haymarket Affair, in which seven police officers and four demonstrators were killed at a labor rally in Chicago, Goldman moved to New York in 1889 and there joined a community of anarchists that included Johann Most and Alexander Berkman. Goldman became Berkman's lover, and in July 1892 helped him plan an unsuccessful assassination of Carnegie Steel chairman Henry Clay Frick in retribution for his part in the bloody Homestead Strike at a Carnegie mill outside Pittsburgh. Berkman was sentenced to twenty-two years (he served fourteen). Goldman was never charged, and continued speaking in union halls and before ever-larger crowds in Union Square.

On the evening of August 21, 1893, Goldman took the Cottage stage and, speaking in German to a crowd of 4,000 unemployed workers—the Panic of 1893 had caused unemployment in the city to skyrocket beyond 20 percent—suggested that if her listeners were hungry they should take bread by force. A police detective in the crowd took notes and a few days later arrested her for making public remarks of an "incendiary character" meant to incite a riot. The ensuing trial was a circus: The press universally condemned her, while taking great delight in calling attention to every detail of her appearance. "She is small," the *New York Evening World* wrote of Goldman, "has a smooth, clear complexion and a face full of intelligence. She talks fluently. When she speaks her face lights up and she is almost pretty in spite of a long, odd-shaped chin and lower jaw." (The *New York Sun*, meanwhile, described her as "distinctly pudgy.")

Goldman never had a chance. Grave doubts arose over the accuracy of the detective's field notes—it wasn't even clear if he understood German—but Goldman, despite ex-mayor A. Oakey Hall defending her in court, was convicted and sentenced to a year in prison on Black-well's Island (today's Roosevelt Island.) At the sentencing hearing the presiding judge called Goldman a "dangerous woman."

Released from prison eight months later, Goldman took up nursing and, much in demand on the lecture circuit, traveled throughout Europe and the United States. But in 1901, anarchist Leon Czolgosz assassinated President William McKinley in Buffalo, and claimed that Goldman's speeches had inspired him to action, Goldman was arrested and detained for two weeks. She was ultimately cleared, but was vilified after she refused to condemn Czolgosz.

In the wake of the McKinley assassination, Goldman disappeared from view for a couple of years, but returned to the fray after passage of the Anarchist Exclusion Act in 1903. Her style of public speaking—pacing back and forth, working herself up into a fury, and then unleashing a thunderous tirade—became the model for thousands of aspiring soapbox orators, Socialists, Communists, and members of the Industrial Workers of the World (the "Wobblies") among them, who each and every day took up positions on platforms scattered around the square and faced huge crowds laced with ever-increasing numbers of police.

On March 28, 1908, at a rally of the Socialist Conference of the Unemployed, twenty-two-year-old anarchist Selig Silverstein attempted to throw a homemade bomb at the police after they had clubbed demonstrators. The bomb exploded in Silverstein's hands, killing him and a passerby but leaving the police unharmed.

In the aftermath of the 1914 Ludlow Massacre in Colorado, in which National Guard troops murdered striking coal miners and their families, anarchists became more open in their calls for violence. After three hapless anarchists blew themselves up trying to make a bomb intended for Ludlow mine owner John D. Rockefeller, Berkman, who had been released from prison eight years earlier, staged a "funeral" for the would-be bombers in Union Square. Speakers, including anarchists Rebecca Edelsohn and Charles Plunkett and Wobblies Carlo Tresca and Elizabeth Gurley Flynn, held forth under the watchful eyes of Chief Inspector Max F. Schmittberger and a force of 1,000 police armed with clubs.

"I want to say it's about time the working class came out frankly and openly and said 'Yes, we believe in violence,'" Edelsohn, wearing a black dress and red stockings, told the crowd. "We will use violence whenever it is necessary to use it. We are not afraid of what your kept press says; and when we are murdered and cannonaded, when you train your machine guns on us, we will retaliate with dynamite."

"[I] am for violence," Charles Plunkett shouted. "Not only defensive violence, but offensive violence. I don't believe in waiting until we are attacked . . . [They] have guns, they have cannon, they have soldiers, they have discipline, they have armies—and we have dynamite. To oppression, to exploitation, to tyranny, to jails, clubs, guns, armies and navies, there is but one reply: dynamite!"

"[While] we are approaching the Social Revolution," Berkman declared, "there will always be individuals, more intelligent, more

The bodies of bomber Selig Silverstein and the passerby he killed, Union Square, March 28, 1908.

determined and daring than the rest, eager to pave the way by acts of individual devotion and sacrifice."

"That was pretty hot stuff," Schmittberger, a Broadway Squad veteran, remarked when Berkman finished. Schmittberger refrained from arresting Berkman or any of his cohorts that afternoon, but with each demonstration the police grew less tolerant of the Union Square gatherings.

"[The police] were always there; they always came around," Mary Sansone remembered. Her father, Rocco Crisalli, an Italian immigrant and IWW organizer, spoke in Union Square almost every day and in the evenings returned home to Brooklyn full of union fervor. In 1928, when she was twelve, Mary hugged her father "like glue" until he relented and took her along to Union Square, where he boosted her up onto his platform while he spoke to the crowds. "The place was mobbed," Sansone recalled.

She was hooked, and tagged along with her father to the square whenever she could. Before long she was giving speeches of her own, while the police lurked at the edges of the crowd, listening. "The police were bastards," she said. "If you spoke, and they didn't like your language, they'd take you away."

DURING THE DEPRESSION the IWW split into factions and its influence waned, while the Communist Party, its newspaper the *Daily Worker* published from a building overlooking the east side of Union Square, steadily gained in strength and numbers. On March 6, 1930, the Communist International called for global rallies in support of the unemployed, and riots broke out in Detroit, Cleveland, and Washington, in Germany, Spain, and Czechoslovakia. In New York, 35,000 protestors assembled in Union Square barely one week after police had brutally dispersed a union rally in City Hall Park.

At first the rally was tense but peaceful. Police Commissioner Grover Whalen, who had stationed thousands of police around the square's perimeter, stood on the Cottage porch and dared the Communists to make a false move. He had even forbidden newsreel crews from filming with sound movie cameras.

"I saw no reason for perpetuating treasonable utterances," he explained later.

William Z. Foster, chairman of the American Communist Party and a former IWW organizer, stepped onto the Cottage porch and encouraged the crowd to leave Union Square en masse, march down Broadway to City Hall, and demand an audience with Mayor Jimmy Walker. But the Communists had no parade permit, and Whalen ordered the police to stop them from entering Broadway.

"Any celebrities coming to town are allowed to use Broadway. When the workers want it they can't have it. Are we going to take 'no' for an answer?" Foster asked the vast throng.

"No!" came the reply.

"Then I advise you to fall in line and proceed," Foster shouted, pointing toward Broadway. But as the crowd tried to leave the square, 1,000 police blocked the way and then waded in, swinging clubs, blackjacks, and fists.

"From all parts of the scene of battle came the screams of women and cries of men with bloody heads and faces," the *New York Times* reported. "A score of men were sprawled over the square, with policemen pummeling them." One woman was "trampled into unconsciousness" by a patrolman and a detective. When a few police were knocked down by thrown bricks, Whalen retaliated by turning fire hoses on the crowd.

Foster, *Daily Worker* editor Robert Minor, and three others hopped in a taxi and sped away, but the police caught up with them. Convicted of inciting a riot, Foster served six months, and so was in jail when Communists convened at Union Square on May Day, two months later. This time, surrounded by police and with machine guns trained on them from surrounding rooftops, the Communists became docile and obedient and the rally ended without incident. Two months later, on August 1, a crowd of 5,000 Communists formed a phalanx in front of the *Daily Worker* offices and refused to disperse. The police moved in, someone threw a brick, and the police began clubbing everyone within reach, including a sixteen-year-old girl, bystanders, and an Associated Press reporter.

The 1930 riots were the worst New York had seen in years and for-

**Anarchist Alexander Berkman, center, speaking from
Union Square's Cottage, May Day, 1908.**

ever changed Union Square. Although it continued as a place of mass
meetings, the threat of violence from police gradually cowed demonstrators into submission, and speakers began to temper their language. Throughout the remainder of the Depression and World War
II, Communists, Socialists, labor unions, and other groups continued
to meet in Union Square, especially on May Day and Labor Day, but
their events were gradually upstaged by choreographed pageants
reminiscent of the 1876 Centennial Celebration. Beginning in 1947, a
patriotic "Loyalty Day" celebration replaced the usual May Day rallies in Union Square, and by the 1950s, with the rise of McCarthyism,
May Day in Union Square had become safe and sanitized. (One typical May Day, in 1958, featured red, white, and blue balloons sent aloft
bearing packets of "brotherhood seeds" and musical performances by
the United Nations Singers, the St. Francis Xavier High School Glee
Club, and the Department of Sanitation band.)

On Labor Day in 1960 a *New York Times* reporter went looking
for rabble-rousers in Union Square and found only a handful speak-

ing to a small gathering of hecklers and "impassive loungers." Union Square had become, the *Times* reported, "a graveyard of memories." There was a resurgence of protests in the square during the Vietnam War era—Catholic activist Dorothy Day gave a memorable anti-war speech there in 1965—but until very recently Union Square was known more for its drug dealers and large homeless population than as a bastion of free speech.

TODAY UNION SQUARE is shared by a cross-section of the city's richest and poorest citizens. It is a complicated common ground: Four days a week, a farmers' market catering to wealthy and upper-middle-class professionals takes over the northwest corner of the square, while a small but persistent community of homeless people and drug addicts colonize the benches and sleep on the grass along its eastern edge. Hip-hop dancers attract large audiences while, nearby, Hare Krishnas chant and bang on tambourines. People play chess, solicitors pester tourists with petitions and other come-ons, and commuters rush through in the morning and afternoon. Soap-box orators are rare, far outnumbered by lunch-hour idlers sitting on benches munching overpriced doughnuts and chatting quietly. Occasionally, Union Square still attracts protests, as on July 9, 2016, when Black Lives Matter activists marched there to demonstrate against police shootings in Minnesota and Louisiana. And there were more rallies in the square in the wake of Donald Trump's election to the presidency. But for the most part, Union Square has come full circle, reverting to Vaux and Olmsted's 1872 conception of the park as a pleasant, public node in the heart of the city, a verdant interruption in Broadway's relentless path.

MILE 4

UNION SQUARE TO
HERALD SQUARE

CHAPTER 16

LADIES' MILE

———

"WE ARE ALL SATISFIED THAT GENTLEMEN HAVE NO GENIUS for shopping," the editors of the *Emporia* (Kansas) *News* wrote in 1861. "Nature has left their facilities imperfect in that particular. They can write books and make speeches, and all that sort of thing, but they are not up to shopping. It takes the ladies for that. Men go to a store, select what they want, and buy it. But that is not shopping; that requires no genius."

Broadway had long been inseparable from its merchandise, and each new generation repeated the same rapturous descriptions of its shop windows. When *King's Handbook* of 1893 catalogued Broadway's "silks and velvets, laces and jewels, rich books and music, paintings and statuary, rifles and racquets, confections and amber-like bottles, *cloisonné* and cut-glass," it was only repeating Walt Whitman's description of thirty-seven years earlier, when he strode up Broadway past "pictures, jewelry, silks, furs, costly books, sculptures, bijouterie, plate, china, cut-glass, fine cloths, fabrics of linen, [and] curious importations from far-off Indian seas."

The opening, in 1846, of Stewart's Marble Palace, with its large plate-glass windows and spacious lounges, had consecrated shopping once and for all as a communal activity. The annual "opening of the spring fashions," when large wooden crates of dry goods from Europe arrived in stores, was a highlight on the city's social calendar on par with Christmas and New Year's Day. For women, a day spent shopping was a day out of the house, a chance to have lunch with friends and to *walk*, in an era when women didn't have many opportunities for exercise and recreation. Some observers admired their pursuits, as when William Henry Rideing wrote in *Harper's Weekly* that a "woman out of the house is always magnificent, and . . . never so elaborate in her toilet as when, with the plea of nakedness on her lips, she sallies out on a shopping expedition." But for others, shopping was not only a waste of time but an invitation to drift toward ennui, listlessness, and frivolous, sinful consumption.

"A woman who gets adrift on Broadway, without a clear and definite idea of what she wants to buy, is like a ship without a compass," the *American Phrenological Journal* warned in 1867.

There was something about legions of well-dressed women marching up and down Broadway that captured the popular imagination, and Broadway's shoppers were commemorated in poems and songs, as Broadway Belles had been a generation earlier.

> *On they go, on they go,*
> *The crowd rushes onward—*
> *All down Broadway they go,*
> *Ladies by hundreds.*
> *"What shall we do?" they said—*
> *The sky is blue o'er head:*
> *All down Broadway they go,*
> *Ladies by hundreds.*

But there were rules, beginning with a rather inflexible dress code: a dark silk dress, a merino shawl or possibly a fur, a bonnet, and kid gloves. Under no circumstances were fashionable women to appear on Broadway during the summer, as that would imply they had not the means, or the invitations, for trips to Saratoga or the White Mountains.

Shopping was further restricted to the hours between ten o'clock in the morning and two or three o'clock in the afternoon, hours that roughly coincided with the opening and closing gavels of the New York Stock Exchange. And there were geographical constraints, as well: Prior to the mid nineteenth century, the shopping and financial districts coexisted side by side, with substantial overlap, in the City Hall Park area. But as Broadway's commercial center stretched ever northward, an invisible, ever-shifting line formed, which separated the shopping district to the north from the financial district to the south, and women from men. By 1857 that line, at least according to *Harper's Weekly*, ran along Broome Street, where S. M. Peyser's dry goods store was located.

"Believe me, young ladies, let Peyser be your pillars of Hercules, beyond which no east wind should tempt you to wander," *Harper's* advised. "You may, of course, of a morning, when every Christian will respect your incog., steal down to the delightful bower of silk and lace, which Master Stewart has erected for the temptation of frail youth and the exasperation of moneyed age, but linger not in its alluring precincts after one. As two o'clock approaches, the film which covers the best-bred eyes is dispelled, and you may be recognized."

If southward excursions to Stewart's were condoned, it was considered social suicide for an unfettered woman to "wander" all the way down to the financial district. *Harper's* even provided a cautionary tale concerning one young woman who walked down Broadway all the way to Maiden Lane, only three blocks from the manly citadel of Wall Street. There, as fate would have it, she chanced to run into her fiancé, a territorial infraction so brazen that the embarrassed young swain turned and walked away. (The young woman, naturally offended, immediately returned his letters and a book of poems.)

The shopping district shifted gradually to the north as Broadway's stores closed or moved, subjected to the "vicissitudes of trade, the inroads of death and other antagonizing influences," as *The Economist* put it, but the mercantile world momentarily solidified enough that from the 1860s to the 1890s Broadway's shopping district was defined as the fourteen blocks between Stewart's "Iron Palace," on Broadway between 9th and 10th streets, and Madison Square. They called it "Ladies' Mile."

New York's greatest emporia were lined up one after another

along those blocks: There was Stewart's, of course, which remained financially robust and culturally prestigious until Stewart's death in 1876. (After his business was slowly but surely run into the ground by a hapless executor, the Iron Palace was taken over first by E. J. Denning & Company and eventually by Wanamaker's.) Diagonally across Broadway from Stewart's was F. A. O. Schwarz, a festive "toy bazaar" founded by a German immigrant. Two blocks up was James McCreery & Company, a dry goods house known for the quality of its imported silks. Then came Tiffany's, Brooks Brothers, Gorham's (at the time the largest American manufacturer of silverware), B. L. Solomon & Sons (furniture and household goods), W. & J. Sloane (carpets and furniture), Herter Brothers (cabinetmakers and decorators of opulent Fifth Avenue mansions), and, just south of Madison Square, two world-famous department stores: Lord & Taylor and Arnold, Constable.

ARNOLD, CONSTABLE & COMPANY—"Constable's" in the local shorthand—moved their retail branch from Canal Street to the corner of Broadway and 19th Street in the spring of 1869. New York had never seen anything like the new Constable's: It spanned 82 feet along Broadway and 172 feet along 19th Street, and although only five stories tall, it had high ceilings and towered over its shorter neighbors. The *Tribune* called it "a white house in the skies."

The architect was Griffith Thomas, who was awash in work in the 1850s and '60s and whose many other projects included the Astor Library and the Le Boutillier Brothers store. Thomas designed the new Constable's in the by-then-inevitable Italianate style, with a showy Broadway façade of marble and iron and a plainer 19th Street façade of brick. (Within a few years the store was extended along 19th Street to Fifth Avenue, an expansion that did much to open Fifth Avenue to trade. Two more floors and a jaunty mansard roof, edged with a frilly wrought-iron railing, were added, too.)

Customers swept into Constable's past a cloakroom and cafeteria— employees were given free lunch every day—and up a broad oaken stair to the immense salesroom on the second floor, a vast landscape of dry goods. Counters, 1,200 feet of them, filled the room. Each was staffed with knowledgeable, deferential clerks specializing in silks, muslins, flannels, blankets, linen, merinos, poplins, cashmeres, shawls, scarves, curtains, gloves, piano and table covers, handkerchiefs, embroidered collars, hosiery, towels, and napkins. At the back, out of sight, was a dimly lit "silk room" where customers could check the effect of crepuscular light on evening gowns before they bought them. Constable's was so vast, and so comprehensively opulent, that it practically defined the Gilded Age and may well have been the era's epicenter.

There were men's and boys' departments, too, but overwhelmingly Constable's, like the gargantuan new Lord & Taylor store that opened the following year at Broadway and 20th Street, one block to the north, was a place, a refuge even, for women. Certain men, already squeamish at the thought of women out of the house and exercising their independence on Broadway, were intimidated by the sheer size of the biggest of the Ladies' Mile stores. Women simply *disappeared* into Stewart's, McCreery's, Lord & Taylor, and Constable's. What exactly, many nervous men wondered, were they *doing* in there?

Brooklyn Eagle reporter George Ellington thought he knew, and the new Constable's had barely opened when he published *The Women of New York*. Ellington took its title from Marie Louise Hankins's *Women of New York*, published eight years earlier. Hankins's book was a collection of fictitious character sketches, and while she included an unflattering portrait of a Ladies' Mile regular trundling joylessly down Broadway by chauffeured carriage to Lord & Taylor, her other characters—widows, spiritualists, boardinghouse keepers, ballerinas, shop girls, philanthropists, and "adventuresses"—were often courageous. Hankins, writing for a young-adult audience, railed against "idleness" and urged women to learn skills and trades and join the workforce. Ellington's book, meanwhile, was subtitled *The Under-World of the Great City* and was a 650-page condemnation of a majority of the city's female population. Ellington thought women of the "faithless and sinning" variety far outnumbered those who were "true and noble" in the city, and didn't hesitate to lump the stores of

Ladies' Mile in with gambling dens, brothels, and barrooms as the worst sort of municipal temptations.

"The commerce of the world is here embodied in its most delicate and costly forms," Ellington wrote of Constable's. "Here is a room where two acres of ladies are shopping; it is a vast wilderness of elaborate pillars and counters for the display of goods. At night the electricity lights up five hundred chandeliers, and the great palace is illuminated. In this building there are employed nearly a thousand clerks, who do nothing but deal out dry goods to the women. A thousand pairs of gloves will be sold in one day; over a million dollars' worth of goods is disposed of in a week!"

Ellington attributed much of Constable's immorality to its many smooth-talking clerks, who, if his depiction is to be believed, twirled their mustaches all day long, awaiting their next seduction. It was most often in the gaslit, shadowy silk room, Ellington alleged, where Constable's retail Lotharios led women astray:

> The clerk from behind his moustaches smilingly tells her how well she would look in that 'moonlight-on-the-lake,' and asks her to walk into another room, where she can see it by gaslight. This gaslight is a sort of artificial moonlight, you know, and sometimes it produces the same effects. The clerk turns it down or up to produce the different effects, and being ever on the alert, he takes advantage of the first opportunity to steal a kiss. Stolen fruit is always the sweetest. The acquaintance thus commenced ripens into a more intimate one, and at last the fortunate clerk rides out in the lady's carriage, goes to the theatre with her, and draws all his supply of pocket-money from her well-filled purse. The husband of this susceptible creature may be in Europe, or off on an excursion to California, or yachting.

As long as there were yachting husbands to be jilted, some skittish observers thought it best for women to avoid shopping entirely, lest the devil come calling. "If you need exercise, go out and take a brisk walk around the block," the *American Phrenological Journal* advised. "If a sister woman comes and invites you to go [shopping] with her answer her (only in a more courteous form of words), 'Get thee behind me, Satan!'"

Perhaps a few women were seduced in the soft, amber light of Constable's silk room, and no doubt many more went there with the most frivolous of intentions. And at the height of the Gilded Age, when the divide between rich and poor had widened into a chasm of unbridgeable proportions, there was something unseemly about the private carriages standing four-deep along Ladies' Mile, each with a chauffeur waiting patiently and often an extra servant to mind the lap dog, while the destitute begged for food on the street corners. But undoubtedly most of the women who frequented Constable's and the other stores of Ladies' Mile went there for reasons of commerce, community, and the endless search for a place of their own.

CHAPTER 17

THE "MERRY CHAIR WAR"

———

ONSTABLE'S WAS SITUATED FOUR BLOCKS SOUTH OF THE crossing of Broadway and Fifth Avenue. There, on the north side of 23rd Street, lay a seven-acre park with gracious shade trees, a fountain at the center, lawns full of laughing children at play, and benches where young lovers, poor wretches, and wealthy businessmen alike sat and whiled away the hours.

Like Union Square to the south, Madison Square began as a fork in the road. It was a V-shaped junction where Manhattan's two principal upland highways, the Bloomingdale Road and the Eastern, or Boston, Post Road, began (or ended, depending on the direction of travel). In 1794 the land was appropriated by the city for use as a potters' field, a burial ground for the indigent and unclaimed. In 1807 a federal arsenal was added to the site and, a bit later, an orphanage called the House of Refuge. Still later it was used as the grounds for an exciting new local pastime—baseball.

The idea of turning the land into a public park dates to the 1811 Commissioners' Plan and the "Parade" that, had it been built, would have turned all the land bounded by present-day 23rd and 34th streets, from Third to Seventh Avenue, into an open space for the marshaling of troops. Subsequent versions of the Commissioners'

Plan cut the Parade down until there were only a few acres left, and this became Madison Square.

The park appeared in its present rectangular form on city maps as early as 1837. That year a terminal for the New York & Harlem Railroad was built at the corner of Madison Avenue and 26th Street, opposite the park's northeast corner, hastening the area's urban development. Madison Square opened as a public park in 1847, and by the 1850s the surrounding blocks had attracted wealthy families driven out of the Union Square area by intrusions of commerce and industry. Theodore Roosevelt was born three blocks south of the park, on 20th Street, in 1858; two of his uncles lived on the same street. Roosevelt's acquaintance Edith Wharton was born four years later on 23rd Street, just fifty yards away from the point where Broadway's diagonal path clips off Madison Square's southwest corner.

Madison Square soon eclipsed Union Square as the most fashionable spot in the city, a genteel oasis where birds trilled and nurses wheeled smartly dressed infants around the park's crushed-stone paths, singing to them from sheet music bought for a penny from vendors stationed at the park's main entrance at Broadway and Fifth Avenue. The park was surrounded by brownstone row houses in the inevitable Italianate mode, their monochromatic ranks punctuated by the soaring Gothic Revival spire of Madison Square Presbyterian Church, at the southeast corner of Madison Avenue and 24th Street, and the opulent Fifth Avenue Hotel opposite the park's southwest corner.

It was all exceptionally beautiful, a bit of Bloomsbury in New York, although Wharton, whose old-money family circle included Rhinelanders, Joneses, Schermerhorns, and Gallatins, never cared much for the local architecture. She considered brownstone a thoroughly monotonous building material, a layer of "cold chocolate sauce" poured over a city "without great churches or palaces, or any visible memorials of an historic past."

WHARTON AND ROOSEVELT were still pampered tots when hotels, offices, and stores began infiltrating their families' quiet brownstone blocks. It was a rapid transformation: By the 1870s, Madison Square had become the north end of Union Square's Rialto, which had stretched up Broadway like saltwater taffy. Madison Square Garden, Abbey's Park Theatre, the Madison Square Theatre, the Fifth Avenue Theatre, the San Francisco Minstrels Hall, the Eden Musée (a wax museum), and Wallack's Theatre all opened between 1873 and 1881 within four blocks or less of the park. The biggest draw was Madison Square Garden, built in 1879 on the site of the old New York & Harlem Railroad terminal at Madison Avenue and 26th Street.

Walking races, prizefights, fairs, bicycle races, and P. T. Barnum's circus—the "Greatest Show on Earth"—regularly attracted raucous crowds of 10,000 or more to the Garden, turning Madison Square into a place of spectacle. Boisterous civic demonstrations, mass meetings, political rallies, and other gatherings often spilled from the park into the pell-mell intersection of Broadway and Fifth Avenue, a wide-open triangular piazza between 23rd and 24th streets that was perpetually jammed with traffic and pedestrians. In the 1880s and '90s that intersection became the most vibrant place in the city and, for tourists and locals alike, seemed to present the best Broadway had to offer.

"This is the most interesting spot in the city to the stranger within our gates, and it is, after all, the Broadway that we know and like the best," Richard Harding Davis wrote in *Scribner's Magazine* in 1891. "It is so cosmopolitan, so alive, and so rich in color and movement, and so generous in its array of celebrities."

Those celebrities included prizefighters, speed walkers, and circus performers from the Garden, actors from adjacent theaters, and politicians who used the Fifth Avenue Hotel as their headquarters. A kind of Barnumesque theatricality ruled the place, and attracted all sorts of thrill-seekers, including, in the spring of 1903, one daredevil named Otto Peterson, who had just announced his intention to carry a man across Niagara Falls while hanging from a wire *by his teeth*. Peterson, age thirty-two, appeared one afternoon at the corner of Broadway and Fifth Avenue, chained himself to a streetcar, and pulled it a dozen feet, attracting a cheering crowd before cops arrested him for disorderly conduct and took him away.

Broadway's fourth mile in the 1890s meant endless, streaming crowds of cigar-puffing men in derby hats and dark suits, parasol-toting women in long silk dresses and cantilevering hats, and nannies minding children dressed in sailor suits and pinafores. It was noisy: There was the constant racket of horseshoes on pavement, the resonant, rhythmic rolling of wagon wheels over brick paving blocks, and the peculiar metallic, grating whine of the submerged cables that looped continuously through a conduit just below the street and pulled the cable cars that plied Broadway "up and down, up and down, in a mystic search," as Stephen Crane observed in 1896. (Cable cars lent a certain Harold Lloyd–like mayhem to Broadway: Conductors careered around the southwest corner of Union Square at such terrifying speeds, frequently running down pedestrians and throwing passengers onto the pavement, that the corner became known as "Dead Man's Curve.")

Broadway was colorful, too; a quality not captured in the black and white photographs of the era but depicted in all its brilliance in the vivid brushwork of Robert Henri, John Sloan, Everett Shinn, William Glackens, and other painters who set up studios in the blocks surrounding the crossing of Broadway and Fifth Avenue. Broadway's cable cars were painted bright yellow; office buildings of crimson brick and terra-cotta often had bright green roofs of verdigris copper and American flags flying from masts at the top. And everywhere were brightly painted billboards—not electric, yet—announcing the latest shows and the best deals. And in the middle of it all was the oasis of Madison Square.

It didn't have Central Park's endless glades and woods, but Madison Square remained, despite the constant commotion swirling around it, a prized public sanctuary, "the most charming of the smaller parks in the city," as *King's Handbook* put it in 1893. Those who weren't well off enough to summer in Narragansett or the Adirondacks felt a special sense of pride and ownership in the park. It was, as Davis described it in *Scribner's*, the "people's roof-garden, . . . their summer watering-place, their seashore and mountains."

But in the wake of the Panic of 1893, large numbers of unemployed men, and a few women, too, began monopolizing the park's benches and washing in the park's fountain, prompting complaints and angry letters to newspapers.

"[Only] on the rarest of occasions have I been able to find a bench which was not occupied by at least one dissolute loafer or extremely unkempt person of the tramp class," one grumpy citizen wrote to the *Sun*. The *Tribune* complained that it had become impossible to relax on a park bench without a "greasy, rum soaked tramp leaning against your shoulder."

By 1897 the city's economy was recovering, but Madison Square's "tramps" remained, taking over benches in the morning and often staying until late at night. Theodore Dreiser called the city parks of that era "a port of missing men."

Then, in the summer of 1901, during a horrendous heat wave that gripped much of the nation, an attempt by the city's Parks Department to provide more seating in Madison Square turned into a referendum on who exactly owned the city's public spaces. Were the parks for the rich or the poor? Did they belong to the city or to the people?

BROILING HEAT AND JUNGLE-LIKE humidity descended on New York during the last week of June. Sixteen people died of heat exhaustion on June 29—fifteen more the next day. Groups of boys defied the authorities and jumped into the fountain in City Hall Park for a swim. Thousands slept in the open air on the beach at Coney Island and thousands more in the city's parks. Charlie Poole, the mild-mannered son of William Poole, the thug who had been famously murdered on Broadway in 1855, stood each day in front of the Jefferson Market Courthouse with a hose, spraying water on each horse that passed him.

On Monday, July 1, a day when temperatures hit 98 degrees and killed sixty-six people, eighteen-year-old City College student Abraham Cohen decided to take a break between classes and amble over to Madison Square. (City College was located at the time at Lexington Avenue and 23rd Street, two blocks east of the park.) When Cohen entered the park, he noticed that the Parks Department had scattered seventy-six inviting armchairs, of the sturdy wooden type usually found on the porches of resort hotels, around the park. The chairs, painted a soothing shade of dark green, had cane backs and seats and straight runners on the bottom, to keep the legs from sinking into the grass. Cohen chose a chair pleasantly situated in the shade and settled in.

Immediately an attendant in a grey uniform appeared, demanding that Cohen fork over a nickel for the use of the chair. When Cohen refused to pay, he was ordered to move to a bench, most of which were in the full sun. Cohen refused to budge. A crowd gathered and attracted the attention of a patrolman, who ordered Cohen to pay up or move. Cohen refused and was arrested and dragged in front of magistrate John B. Mayo at the Jefferson Market Courthouse. Cohen remained defiant, calling the whole affair an "outrage."

"When the policeman told me to sit on the bench I told him to go bring me a bench and I would do so, but I did not propose to sit in the sun," he explained to Mayo.

Overwhelmingly, newspapers and even city officials took Cohen's side. The *Tribune* proclaimed that the city's parks were free and "for the people," while magistrate Lorenz Zeller declared in a personal, unofficial statement that the poor "should be allowed to enjoy [the parks] as fully and unreservedly and hampered as little by outlandish rules as possible." Police Commissioner Michael Cotter Murphy announced that the police would no longer arrest those who refused to pay their nickels. "The citizens of this community own the parks and they are the ones to be first served," he said. Still, park attendants continued trying to collect their nickels.

The unfolding drama came complete with two civically tone-deaf, made-to-order villains: George C. Clausen, the hapless Parks Department president, and Oscar F. Spate, a "thin, nervous, wiry little man," with whom Clausen had signed a five-year contract to place the chairs in all the city's parks, including Central Park, for an annual fee of $500.

Spate had been inspired, he said, by the use of rental chairs in European parks, and reckoned he could make a profit of $150 a day. He also made it clear that his chairs were for the "leisure class."

"I believe a certain class of people want [the chairs] ... that is, the people of means and refinement," he said. "They do not want to sit herded in with a lot of people whom they do not know, and with whom they do not wish to associate." As for the protestors, Spate thought they were nothing but "roughs" and "deadbeats."

None of Spate's remarks, which were eagerly jotted down by reporters and plastered across the pages of the *Times, World, Sun, Post, Tribune,* and *Journal,* went over well with the streams of people who, following Cohen's example, started turning up in droves in Madison Square just for the entertainment of sitting in Spate's chairs and then refusing to pay their nickels.

On July 2, temperatures reached 99 degrees and 280 people died of the heat; the next day another 317. Then the heat finally broke as thunderstorms swept in from the west, and the rain momentarily dampened what had become a full-fledged protest movement.

The Fourth of July dawned warm but breezy, with temperatures rising only to 80, and the chair protests went on momentary hiatus as everyone enjoyed the holiday and the clement weather. But on July 6, chair attendant Thomas Tully came to blows with a man who refused to move or pay his nickel, and a crowd of 300 to 400 people formed around him as the argument escalated. Six or seven men from the crowd began punching Tully and pelting him with brickbats, and a police officer standing at a discreet distance off to the side refused to intervene. His face gashed and bleeding, Tully ran from the park, crossed Broadway, and dashed into the lobby of the Fifth Avenue Hotel.

"Save me! They're going to lynch me!" he cried in terror to the hotel staff. Tully was taken to safety while the angry mob milled around outside the hotel for an hour before dispersing.

The next morning an estimated 1,500 people showed up in the park, took over all of Spate's chairs, and refused en masse to pay their nickels, as children heckled Spate's hapless attendants.

"What do you charge for looking at the fountain?" one boy yelled.

"Mister, will you sell me a couple of sunbeams?" another child called.

"Hey, there's a sparrow in your chair!" came another cry.

Spate's attendants—"bouncers," he called them—marched along

behind the chairs, tipping each one forward to dislodge the protestors, who would then immediately reseat themselves. Spate was clearly losing the battle, and his outnumbered attendants, the *Sun* reported, were treated to a barrage of insults "favoring the immediate extinction of aristocrats, pay chairs, and the Park Commissioner who had conveyed title to the parks to Mr. Spate."

The following day Commissioner Murphy ordered extra officers to the park, and with fistfights breaking out left and right—the protestors began targeting those few customers who *did* pay the attendants—they began making arrests. When two protestors were arrested and escorted up Broadway to the precinct house on West 30th Street, a crowd followed, pelting the police with rocks and sticks and chanting "Spate! Spate! Clausen and Spate!"

The next day, July 9, the "Merry Chair War," as the *Evening World* called it, escalated into a full-scale riot. As soon as a protestor sat in a chair, an attendant would flip it over, sending the occupant flying head-over-heels. They held on for dear life, even as their heads were pummeled against the ground; the *Sun* likened the spectacle to a violent game of beanbags. This routine continued for a full hour while a crowd estimated at 5,000 watched and cheered.

Then the dam broke. A youth seized a chair, carried it to Madison Avenue, and pitched it into the street. "Smash it! Break it up!" the crowd roared, as the chair was splintered beneath the wheels of an oncoming wagon. Others in the crowd joined in, and for the next hour chairs rained onto the street. Some drivers even reversed direction in order to run over the chairs twice.

The riot forced Clausen's hand, and he gave in. The following day he not only revoked Spate's contract but also announced that he would buy back the remaining chairs and donate them to the Parks Department for the exclusive use of women and children. Spate won a temporary injunction, but then several subsequent court rulings went against him, and that was the end of his short tenure as New York City's chair king.

The *New York Journal* organized a celebration for the evening following Clausen's announcement. The park filled with thousands of spectators for a program of songs, speeches, and fireworks. Spate, still defiant at that point, called a press conference in his office on the top floor of the St. James Building at the corner of Broadway and 26th Street, opposite the park. As Spate read a statement defending his actions, the reflections of fireworks played across his walls and the crowd in the park below cheered as speaker after speaker lambasted him.

CHAPTER 18

THE FREAK BUILDING

—

H AD SPATE POKED HIS HEAD OUT HIS WINDOW TO SNARL
at the crowd below, and had his eyes followed the line of a southbound
streetcar—an electric trolley by then, the last section of Broadway's
cable traction system having been removed a few months earlier—for
three blocks, he would have seen the mangled remains of an eight-
story apartment building called the Cumberland that was being
demolished on the south side of the intersection of Broadway, Fifth
Avenue, and 23rd Street. The building sat on a narrow wedge of a
block that because of its odd shape everyone called the Flatiron.

New York's economy was booming, the Panic of 1893 dimming
in the municipal memory, and Broadway was once again the leading
edge of a boom in construction. Even buildings still considered new
were coming down, and offices, hotels, and stores were rising in their
place. The city had seen its share of booms over the years, but unlike
in the past, when flurries of demolition and construction were universally acclaimed as evidence of civic virtue, the 1901 boom was largely
greeted with skepticism and something bordering on dread. Steelworkers, carpenters, plasterers, and other trades regularly walked
out on strike. Even some observers in the business world began to
question the pace of building and thought that perhaps the situation,
especially on Broadway, was getting a bit out of hand.

"At the present rate of improvement of real estate we may soon expect to leave our offices at night to find them the next morning hanging in midair, preparatory for lodgment in the tall steel skeleton of some skyscraper," one Broadway merchant scoffed.

The demolition of the Cumberland began in the spring of 1901, when the Flatiron site was sold at auction to a new development consortium known as the Cumberland Realty Company. One by one, the Cumberland's tenants vacated the building, until only Colonel Winfield Scott Proskey, a Floridian and veteran of the Spanish-American War, remained. Proskey refused to budge, and continued living in his sixth-floor bachelor flat even as the Cumberland was torn down around him. It was one month before the Madison Square chair protests unfolded in the park across the street, and in that summer of discontent Proskey became, for a few weeks, anyway, a local hero, held up by the *Tribune* as a "chivalric champion of tenants' rights."

By June, Proskey no longer had windows, running water, electricity, gas, or even a stair—he had rigged a ladder to get from the sidewalk to his apartment—but was adamant about staying until his lease expired the following October. Proskey went to court and won an injunction that compelled Cumberland Realty to leave his apartment intact and restore his gas and water, a decision that temporarily halted demolition.

Proskey rejected every offer to buy him out and seemed to enjoy the crusade tremendously. He gave tours of his shambles of a home, cheerfully escorting reporters up his ladder and through hallways filled with dust and smoke and occupied by crews hauling out chunks of marble flooring and broken sinks.

"Only five flights more," Proskey called down to one *Tribune* reporter who gingerly followed him up to his room. "Splendid exercise! Chance to fill out your chest. Ah, the air! None better. Blows right down Fifth Avenue. Look out for the broken glass on the floor."

The Proskey siege ended in early June, when a federal court ruling forced him to surrender his keys. Proskey moved to the Fifth Avenue Hotel across the street, and the remains of the Cumberland were in short order cleared from the site. What rose in the Cumberland's place was so startling the *Evening World* took to calling it the "Freak Building."

ARCHITECT DANIEL H. BURNHAM of Chicago was a burly fellow with a large brush of a mustache and hair carefully parted in the middle in the manner of Teddy Roosevelt. He had served as the acclaimed master planner of the 1893 World's Columbian Exposition in Chicago, the wildly successful "White City" built on the shores of Lake Michigan, and by 1901 was, at age fifty-five, the undisputed father figure of American architecture. He hadn't yet built anything in New York, but his influence was everywhere: The New York Public Library, the Metropolitan Museum of Art, Columbia University's Low Memorial Library, Hammerstein's Olympia Theatre, and dozens of other new monumental Neoclassical buildings in the city all reflected Burnham's aesthetic. Suddenly, the willful asymmetry and dark color palettes of the Romanesque and Queen Anne styles, so popular in the 1870s and '80s, seemed outmoded.

In 1901 the George A. Fuller Construction Company, owners of the Flatiron site, hired Burnham to design a futuristic skyscraper at the point where Broadway crosses Fifth Avenue.

Burnham was perhaps the busiest architect then working in America. As his associate Frederick S. Dinkelberg began work on what would become known as the Flatiron Building, Burnham was busy building Union Station in Washington, D.C., and updating Washington's master plan. But once the Cumberland was out of the way, construction sped along, and by the spring of 1902 an apparition of steel columns and girders towered over Madison Square.

There was something almost miraculous in the way the Flatiron Building rose into the sky. Architect Charles Follen McKim, of the celebrated firm McKim, Mead & White, watched the Flatiron Building's progress from his office in the Mohawk Building at the southwest corner of Fifth Avenue and 21st Street, one block south of the Flatiron site. In April of 1902, in a letter to Burnham, McKim marveled at how the Fuller Company's steelworkers seemed to add

The Flatiron
Building under
construction,
1902.

a new floor to the Flatiron nearly every day, and jokingly compared
the project to the Tower of Babel.

It wasn't the tallest building in the world, or even the tallest in
New York City—the Park Row, American Surety, World, Manhattan Life Insurance, and St. Paul buildings were all taller—but at 20
stories, and 307 feet, the Flatiron Building was still extremely tall
for its time: 23 feet taller than the spire of Trinity Church and only
84 feet shy of the Park Row Building, then the world's tallest.

Before the steel structure was completed, exterior walls were
attached to the frame, cloaking in the Revivalist forms of a bygone
era what was really a thoroughly modern building. Like an elongated
palazzo from the Italian Renaissance, the Flatiron was subdivided
into three horizontal sections: base, shaft, and capital. The first three
stories were of beige limestone, punctured on the Broadway and Fifth
Avenue sides by grand, arched entrances.

The middle section of the building, up to the sixteenth floor, was clad in cream-colored brick with white terra-cotta details. Floors seven through fourteen featured vertical rows of oriel windows that swelled gently from the Broadway and Fifth Avenue façades, like undulating sheets. Just beneath the cornice, so high up that they were hard to make out from the street below, were rows of lion's heads and Classical busts in terra-cotta. A majestic cantilevering cornice culminated in a sculpture of two full-length terra-cotta figures leaning almost casually against a shield high above the intersection of Broadway and Fifth Avenue, looking like two sailors on the bow of a ship.

The Flatiron Building's nautical allusions were hard to miss. It was the golden age of ocean liners, and ships of the Cunard and White Star lines were regularly breaking trans-Atlantic speed records. To many passersby, the Flatiron Building, especially during a rainstorm or pea soup fog, wasn't an office building so much as a seagoing vessel making its way steadily north along Broadway. Soon after the building was completed, photographer Alfred Stieglitz shot the Flatiron rising above a snow-covered Madison Square. "It appeared to be moving toward me," Stieglitz wrote, "like the bow of a monster ocean steamer—a picture of new America still in the making."

BUT WHEN THE FLATIRON BUILDING opened on October 1, 1902, critics unleashed a torrent of disapproval. Some newspaper editors were convinced the first windstorm would knock the building over, while critic Montgomery Schuyler, writing in the *Architectural Record*, even questioned the building's abundance of windows, likening a Flatiron tenant to a bird trapped in a cage: "As one looks through the bars of the cage, one pities the poor man," Schuyler wrote. "He can, perhaps, find wall space within for one roll-top desk without overlapping the windows, with light close in front of him and close behind him and close on one side of him. But suppose he needed a bookcase? Undoubtedly he has a highly eligible place from which to view processions. But for the transaction of business?"

"[It] is a great pity," Schuyler concluded, "that the architect should have chosen to build on this very odd site an ordinary tall building, 'built to the limit' in every direction, and thus have produced a very commonplace and conventional skyscraper."

Even the building's name provoked controversy: The Fuller Company intended to use the building as its headquarters, and insisted that everyone call it the Fuller Building. But the public kept calling it the Flatiron Building and, ignoring the critics, adopted it as a beloved landmark. Well before it was finished, the Flatiron Building had become a tourist attraction—even Chief Joseph, the exiled leader of the Nez Perce tribe, made a point of visiting the corner of Broadway and Fifth Avenue to gaze up at the Flatiron's improbable profile and seemingly endless rows of windows. The Flatiron was reproduced on countless postcards and stereoscopic views, while the cigar store in the "prow," the glassed-in storefront added to the building's narrowest point, quickly became one of the most popular rendezvous points in the city.

Painters and illustrators were drawn to the complexity of the Flatiron's dramatically thin profile, which, when viewed from farther up Broadway or Fifth Avenue, or from a bench in Madison Square, caught the light in unpredictable ways. At sunrise and sunset especially, the Flatiron became an abstract plane of light and shadow.

In 1906, John Sloan painted *Dust Storm, Fifth Avenue*, which depicted the Flatiron Building rising into the vortex of a storm that was bearing down on a group of windblown, terrified pedestrians. It was not an exaggeration: The Flatiron Building's triangular, vertical mass created unpredictable wind shears, downdrafts that rode down the Broadway and Fifth Avenue façades of the building to the sidewalk, where they gusted about and played havoc with pedestrians. The wind at the building's base even pushed one unfortunate lad into Fifth Avenue, where he was run over and killed by an oncoming bus. *Leslie's Weekly* called the sidewalk in front of the Flatiron Building "Hurricane Corner," and ran a cover illustration showing men's hats, women's scarves, and stacks of newspapers flying everywhere. The *Evening World* called it the "Home of the Winds."

"Winds not only blow from every point of the compass at this corner, but they have a way of blowing upward, lifting the clothing of

**The Flatiron
Building's
"Hurricane
Corner" wreaked
havoc with
dresses, hats,
and newspapers.**

the women in a most embarrassing way," the *World* reported. "Their
skirts wrap around their waists as if soaked in glue."

This was an unexpected and exciting development for the groups
of men that began coagulating in front of the Flatiron to watch
women attempt to round the building's prow. The wind affected men
too, sending their hats and umbrellas flying, but it was the "Flatiron
Girl," a latter-day version of the Broadway Belle, that became the
subject of countless news stories, popular songs, and comic strips.

Crowds gathered in such numbers that patrolmen from the Broadway Squad were stationed there to shoo them away. As the number
of Flatiron "rubberneckers" increased, and when they began to hoot
and holler whenever a woman lost control of her skirt, cops stepped
in and began making arrests.

In February of 1903, French tourist Julius Cesio was arrested in front of the Flatiron and hauled into the Jefferson Market Courthouse before magistrate John B. Mayo. Cesio made the highly original claim that he hadn't been watching the women at the Flatiron at all, but rather the spectacle of the men watching the women. Surprisingly, Mayo ruled in Cesio's favor, telling him it was fine to gawk, so long as he didn't gawk for too long.

"Now, two minutes is a reasonable time," Mayo admonished Cesio, "and you can use your eyes, but at the end of that time you must move on."

The *Evening World* interpreted Mayo's decision as a groundbreaking precedent: " 'Rubbering' at Flatiron Legal," screamed their headline. "Magistrate Mayo Holds that You Can't Prevent a Man from Using His Eyes When Wind Raises a Skirt." The next morning, legions of leering men showed up at the Flatiron.

Four years later they were still there: "Women's skirts flapped over their heads and ankles were to be seen," John Sloan wrote in his diary in April of 1907.

As always, the city gradually adapted: Women perfected the "flatiron grip," an improvised technique that involved pulling their skirts tightly around their legs with one hand while holding onto their hats with the other. As more tall buildings were built around the Flatiron, its wind shears were, to some extent, mitigated. It's still noticeably windy in front of the Flatiron today, although the gusts are rarely strong enough to lift a skirt. And with everyone's eyes glued on digital devices, no one would notice anyway.

CHAPTER 19

THE "LIGHT CURE"

———

B ROADWAY'S BRIGHT LIGHTS ARE AN ENDURING, UBIQUI-
tous American image that has been disseminated in countless musicals, books, magazines, posters, postcards, movies, and songs. The
street is bound irrevocably to its electricity, which has inspired in
people who tread Broadway a kind of yearning, the lights hinting at
something precious and ineffable, as if the key to America might lie
within that electrified path.

So how incongruous to contemplate that for most of its four-
hundred-year history Broadway was a very dark place. Shadows
closed in on the thoroughfare at sunset, ushering in an inky, unre-
lieved blackness that didn't recede until the sun came up again the
next morning. At night, Broadway was lit mainly by the stars overhead, and back when the street was still lined with houses, parents
could instruct their children on the positions of constellations and
planets by simply walking outside and pointing skyward.

"About 10 o'clock are now to be seen the Pleiades nearly on the
meridian, Aldebaran, Orion, and that splendid fellow which I have
gazed and gazed at with enthusiastic admiration, Sirius, about 15°
high in the east . . ." Michael Floy Jr., who lived on Broadway between
11th and 12th streets, wrote in his diary in December of 1836. "At 11
o'clock there is a beautiful view of Jupiter and Mars by his side."

Meteor showers were perfectly clear in the night sky above the city. During an especially impressive shower in August of 1855, even those who were too busy to ever consider celestial matters paused and craned their necks toward the heavens, watching the show. Children played in the streets beneath starlit skies riddled with careering bats, which they tried to catch by throwing their hats into the air while singing:

> *Bat, bat! Come under my hat!*
> *And I'll give you a pound of candle fat!*

Streetlights were first installed in November of 1697, when every resident was required to light their windows every night in the "Darke time of ye Moon." The city began using oil lamps in 1762, and by 1792 spermaceti—oil harvested from sperm whales—had become the fuel of choice for New York's streetlights. The city's oil lamps, housed in lanterns atop poles, provided only the faintest glimmer, and they were spaced so far apart—150 feet—that they were not much of an improvement over moonlight. They were so dim, in fact, that to save oil the city's lamplighters, who went out each evening armed with ladders, oilcans, and rags, painstakingly climbing and refilling each lamppost, didn't bother lighting the lamps when the moon was full.

Broadway was lighted above Canal Street for the first time in 1800, when Jacques M. J. Delacroix, proprietor of Vauxhall Gardens, placed whale-oil lamps along the street leading over the Stone Bridge and up to the old Bayard estate, where the gardens were then located, "to light up the dark road to his garden."

The Common Council first considered gas lighting in 1813, but the transition was a gradual one, and until the 1840s, gaslight was a novelty, used in only a few theaters and residences. As late as 1849 only 4,519 of the city's 11,239 streetlights, and only a few sections of Broadway, were lit with gas.

Gaslight was dim, flickered incessantly, and was responsible for several devastating theater fires, but it was one of the wonders of the age, and throughout the tenebrous gaslight era Broadway was widely considered a place of constant light, a playground of night-birds, an all-night bazaar where there was little difference between night and day.

"When all the rest of the city is asleep, Broadway is awake," William Henry Rideing wrote in *Harper's* in 1877, describing the street as a "vista between . . . two bead-like strings of lamps" where figures appeared at ungodly hours, "plodding along on various missions of crime, industry, pleasure, or charity."

ELECTRICITY CAME to Broadway in 1880, when the Brush Electric Light Company opened offices at 860 Broadway, one block north of Union Square. Charles Francis Brush, thirty-one, who wore the era's requisite handlebar mustache and an optimistic, steadfast expression, was an engineer and inventor of enormous intelligence, with a Barnum-like flare for theatrical self-promotion. Among Brush's patents were a more efficient electrical generator and an improved electric-arc lamp.

The "arc" in question was a current of electricity that jumped between two vertical burning pencil-shaped carbon rods, producing light that was intensely white in color. To this mechanism Brush added an ingenious device: As the lower carbon rod burned, the upper one moved slowly downward, maintaining the necessary spacing. Arc lamps flickered and were extremely hot, which limited their use in private homes. But they worked well in larger buildings and outdoors, and Brush used them successfully in theaters, stores, and factories, plus along Montreal's waterfront and in Monument Park in his native Cleveland. In Wabash, Indiana, Brush mounted four gigantic arc lamps on the courthouse roof and lit up the entire town, "backyards and all."

At the same moment, Thomas Edison was busy in Menlo Park, New Jersey, testing his own system for wiring cities with incandescent lamps. The competition between Brush and Edison, and between Brush and the United States Illuminating Company, which had developed its own version of the arc lamp, was as intense as the electric light they were producing. And in the fall of 1880, it seemed that Brush had the upper hand.

"While Edison has been busy with many funny things, the Brush Electric Light Company have [sic] been making preparations to put their lamps throughout New York," the *New York Sun* reported in October of 1880. "[Edison's] experiments at Menlo Park may soon be beaten by actual lamps in Madison square."

Brush built a power station at 133 West 25th Street, one and a half blocks west of Broadway and Madison Square, and installed three generators, their flywheels and drive-belts crisscrossing diagonally from floor to ceiling, that were powered by one Corliss steam engine. One week before Christmas, 1880, Brush's engineers placed twenty-two lamps, each mounted on a 20-foot cast-iron pole, twice the height of the existing gaslight poles, on alternating sides of Broadway between 14th and 34th streets, one lamp per block. After brief, mysterious tests on Saturday and Sunday, December 18 and 19, that had pedestrians doing double takes, company officials and newspaper reporters gathered in the powerhouse on the evening of December 20 to watch Brush light up the street.

Brush was counting on an outpouring of public support to sway members of the city's Common Council, many of whom were at that moment traveling to Menlo Park to attend a demonstration of Edison's incandescent lights. For maximum effect, Brush planned to test seventeen of the twenty-two lights situated along Broadway between Union Square and Madison Square, the street's busiest blocks and encompassing theaters, hotels, and the emporia of Ladies' Mile. The street was crowded with holiday shoppers going in and out of Lord & Taylor, Constable's, Brentano's bookstore, Delmonico's restaurant, and Tiffany's. By placing his lamps in the heart of the city, Brush was hoping for a repeat performance of his dramatic demonstration in Wabash, when men and women had fallen to their knees and wept when his lights were switched on. But this was no small town in the Midwest: It was Broadway, the big stage, and no one was sure how the public would react.

AT 5:27, THREE MINUTES ahead of schedule, Brush Company treasurer and secretary A. A. Hayes Jr. gave the signal to fire up the

steam engine, and current began to flow through 10,000 feet of wire
to the lamps along the street. Beginning with pinpoints of light,
the lamps began to glow all at once, growing in intensity until they
burned with what the *New York Times* called a "white, steady glare."

Startled pedestrians turned from Broadway's shop windows and
"exclamations of admiration and approval were heard on all sides."
Crowds of shoppers and theatergoers stood transfixed, shading their
eyes from the glare and taking in the strange transformation of the
city around them. Everything was suddenly crisper, clearer: Horses,
streetcars, building façades, and telegraph wires were picked out in
finely grained detail. Signs could be read clearly from great distances.

"The great white outlines of the marble stores, the mazes of wires
overhead, the throng of moving vehicles, were all brought out with
an accuracy and exactness that left little to be desired in the matter
of strength," the *Times* reported. Newspapers agreed that it was the
color of Brush's lights, their white intensity, that made them com-
pelling. Next to the Brush lamps, the *Sun* reported, the old gaslights
suddenly seemed "sickly yellow."

The demonstration was a clear and overwhelming success, and
gratified Brush Company officials returned to their headquarters at
Broadway and 18th Street for a celebration. From their office windows
they looked down on Broadway, uncorked bottles of champagne, and
spent the rest of the evening watching their lights blazing away.
Eventually, everyone went home, and Brush's lights burned on Broadway all night.

MORE TESTS FOLLOWED, and the following spring the Brush Company was awarded a city contract, for an annual fee of $7,400, to
install arc lamps along Broadway from 14th to 34th street and along
both 14th and 34th streets between Broadway and Fifth Avenue. In
Union and Madison squares, Brush mounted lights on 150-foot-tall
towers, illuminating the parks with harsh light that filtered through
the branches of trees, bathing everything in an unearthly green tint.
Suddenly, there was nowhere to hide. An 1882 illustration in *Harper's
Weekly* showed a well-dressed gentleman crossing Broadway to Mad-

The Brush Electric Light Company's powerful
arc lamps flooded Madison Square with light.

ison Square, his shadow crisply outlined behind him, staggering into the light like St. Paul at the moment of conversion.

Reformers noticed something else: Brush's lights illuminated every crevice of Broadway, every pickpocket and prostitute, every barroom and gambling hell. Within a month of Brush's demonstration the *Tribune* happily reported that doorways on Broadway were no longer "infested by drowsy tramps," and electric lights were seen as possible mechanisms for cleansing those marginal districts of the city that seemed beyond hope.

Broadway's west side had long concealed a red-light district that began with the eighteenth-century Holy Ground and over time moved north with the street as it developed, growing in size as it went. From Church Street in the 1820s to Greene and Mercer streets in the 1850s, Broadway's illicit shadow had metastasized by the 1880s into a vast swath that overlapped Ladies' Mile and the theater district and spanned both sides of the street. It was called the Tenderloin and was two and three-quarters of a mile long and one mile wide—more than half the size of Central Park—and encompassed everything from 14th to 42nd streets between Fourth and Seventh avenues and blurred into Hell's Kitchen, another notoriously sketchy area just to the west.

Most of the Tenderloin was within the boundaries of the Metropolitan Police Department's infamous 19th Precinct, where corrupt cops, protected by the Tammany Hall machine, shook down brothels, gambling hells, and illegal barrooms. The district's nickname came, at least according to local legend, from police officer Alexander S. Williams. A former shipbuilder who as a patrolman was nicknamed "Clubber" for his tendency to use his fists when making arrests—it was widely reported that he had once thrown two thugs through a plate-glass window—Williams was transferred to the 19th Precinct in 1876 and appointed captain. Shortly after he took over, the story goes, Williams was striding down Broadway when a friend overtook him and asked how he liked his new post.

"Great!" Williams supposedly answered, "I've come from a rump precinct to the Tenderloin."

Williams remained at his post until 1887, and during his tenure the Tenderloin's crime and corruption grew to epidemic proportions, with the most sordid blocks located just north of Madison Square. In 1881, property owners on 27th and 28th streets complained to the city's three-member Police Commission that their neighborhood was "infested with thieves and vagabonds" and described a nocturnal hellhole where men and women were regularly assaulted, windows were broken, cries for help went unheeded, and patrolmen went door to door, openly tapping the tills of disreputable businesses. The Tenderloin had descended, the residents wrote, into "pandemonium," and some people took to calling the district "Satan's Circus."

And yet the Tenderloin became a tourist attraction, a place "where the gay Bohemians dwell," as one popular song in 1897 put it. In certain dance halls and dives, whites and blacks mixed freely, while other establishments were strictly whites-only. It was illegal to deny service to blacks, but barroom owners got around the law by charging blacks as much as $1 for a single drink—about $28 in today's currency. In 1899 two black men who defied the bartender at former prizefighter James J. Corbett's barroom and ordered drinks anyway, saying they had plenty of money and didn't care what they cost, were hauled out onto the corner of Broadway and 33rd Street and beaten by 50 or 60 white men while a crowd estimated at 1,000 looked on.

Despite, or perhaps because of, such public displays of violence, out-of-towners kept venturing to the Tenderloin in search of tantalizing, voyeuristic adventures. Richard Harding Davis, describing the Tenderloin in *Scribner's Magazine* in 1891, assured his readers they could visit "the forbidden ground of Broadway" without compromising their virtue.

"There are some who will tell you that Broadway at this point should be as a howling wilderness to respectable men and women . . . [but it] is not essential that you should know that the smooth-faced, white-haired man who touched your shoulder as he brushed past keeps a gambling-house at Saratoga during the summer months, or that the woman at his side is not his wife," Davis advised. "They do you no harm, and you are not on Broadway to enlarge your visiting list, but only to enjoy the procession."

Reformers tried to stamp out the Tenderloin's depravity once and for all, but it refused to go away. In 1892 the Reverend Charles Henry Parkhurst, pastor of the Madison Square Presbyterian Church, accused Tammany Hall boss Richard Croker, Mayor Hugh J. Grant, and the entire police department of widespread corruption, which, Parkhurst claimed, allowed the Tenderloin's illegal activities to flourish in the open. Summoned to testify before a grand jury, Parkhurst was unable to substantiate his allegations and as a result was vilified in the press. In response, Parkhurst, in the company of a friend and a hired detective, went undercover and systematically visited gambling hells, brothels, and illegal barrooms in the Tenderloin and along the city's waterfront, "traversing the avenues of our municipal hell," as he put it, and gathering sworn affidavits that he then waved from the pulpit.

Parkhurst's crusade led to the formation of the Lexow Commission, which interrogated everyone from Grant to "Clubber" Williams and issued voluminous reports, but nothing much changed in the Tenderloin. Assaults and shakedowns continued, and in 1904 an estimated 50 percent of prisoners held in the 19th Precinct's dingy brick jail behind its station house on 30th Street were women arrested on charges of prostitution, confined as many as a dozen at a time in tiny 8-by-4-foot cells. Tourists wandered into the Tenderloin and never came back, and one particularly gruesome murder shocked a supposedly jaded city.

The victim was businessman James B. Craft of Glen Cove, Long Island, who spent the night of September 26, 1902, drinking heavily in dives along 29th Street. At the Bohemia and the Cairo he unwisely flashed a thick roll of bills, and by the time he reached the Empire Garden, near Broadway, it was four in the morning and he was in the company of three floozies named Grace, Stella, and Mamie—the Tenderloin's version of the three Fates.

Things went downhill from there, and when police alerted by the Empire's bartender arrived, they discovered Craft's nude, decapitated body beneath a pile of lumber in the barroom's basement. Poking around in the furnace, they soon retrieved what was left of his charred head. A bloody cleaver and wooden chopping block lay tellingly on the floor. The police arrested one Thomas Tobin, alias "Butch" or "Sewer Rat," whom they found hiding beneath a table in the barroom, and charged him with the crime. For the next two months newspapers recounted each new gory detail of Craft's demise, and the murder was even turned into a one-act play, *The Empire Garden Tragedy*, at the Oriental Music Hall, a Yiddish theater on Grand Street. (Tobin was convicted and sent to the electric chair at Sing Sing.)

The Craft murder was the fourth in the Tenderloin in less than two weeks, following on the heels of the killing of banker Nicholas Fish, scion of a prominent, old New York family and son of former secretary of state, United States senator, and New York governor Hamilton Fish, in a dive on 34th Street. The Craft murder caused yet another shakeup in the 19th Precinct, after it emerged that police had allowed the Empire Garden to operate with impunity, and in 1904 reformer William McAdoo was appointed police commissioner.

For McAdoo, much of the trouble in the Tenderloin could be traced to the district's black residents. "One of the most troublesome and dangerous characters with which the police have to deal is the Tenderloin type of negro," he wrote in 1906. "In the male species this is the over-dressed, flashy-bejewelled loafer, gambler, and, in many instances, general criminal. These fellows are a thorough disgrace to their race and have a very bad effect on decent colored people who come here from the South and other parts of the country." McAdoo was particularly troubled by Tenderloin barrooms and dance halls that catered to both whites and blacks. "All of these mixed-race places . . . have no redeeming quality, are breeding-places for crime, and present disgusting exhibitions of the degradation of one race and the worst vices of the other." McAdoo believed the mixing of races "produced violent quarrels."

It occurred to McAdoo that electric lights might help clean up the Tenderloin. Taken for a guided tour of the area's worst blocks, McAdoo noticed that the "vice-fostering gloom" of its side streets was "in sharp contrast to the radiance of Broadway."

"You can't have too much light on crime," he said, and ordered arc lamps placed in front of any house suspected of disorderly activities. The *Evening World* heralded the arrival of McAdoo's "light cure."

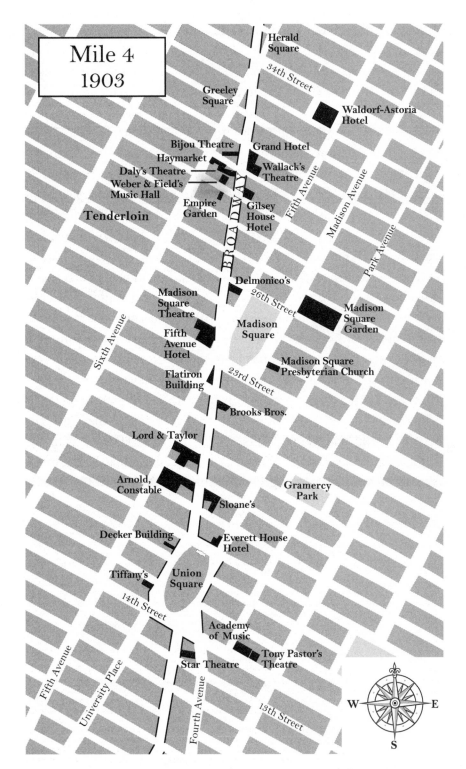

Mile 4
1903

Herald
Square

34th Street

Greeley
Square

Waldorf-Astoria
Hotel

Bijou Theatre   Grand Hotel
Haymarket
Daly's Theatre   Wallack's
Weber & Field's   Theatre
Music Hall
                  Empire   Gilsey
Tenderloin   Garden   House
                              Hotel

BROADWAY

Fifth Avenue

Madison Avenue

Park Avenue

Delmonico's

Madison   26th Street
Square
Theatre   Madison
              Madison   Square
Fifth   Square   Garden
Avenue   Square
Hotel

                                Madison Square
Flatiron   23rd Street   Presbyterian Church
Building

Sixth Avenue

              Brooks Bros.

Lord & Taylor

Arnold,   Gramercy
Constable   Park

              Sloane's

Decker Building   Everett House
                   Hotel

Tiffany's   Union
             Square

        14th Street

              Academy
              of Music
                              Tony Pastor's
Star Theatre   Theatre

Fifth Avenue

University Place

Fourth Avenue

13th Street

W   E
  S

But, illuminated or not, the Tenderloin was already undergoing a drastic transformation by then, as rents rose and commercial enterprises moved in from the south. "The Tenderloin isn't what it used to be," the *Evening World* lamented in 1903.

"Things have changed . . . I'm going to get out. I'm done here," muttered the thuggish Ed Corey, proprietor of the notorious Haymarket dance hall at the corner of Sixth Avenue and 30th Street.

In 1905 the *New York Times* announced that the Tenderloin had virtually disappeared, its brothels, gambling hells, and barrooms "broken up and scattered," pushed farther uptown by the migration into the area of businesses, restaurants, and barrooms frequented by wealthy, white patrons.

"The midnight throng on Broadway is now made up of respectable and responsible men who have worked hard downtown or elsewhere during the day, and who prowl around Sleeplessland at night in search of relaxation . . . ," the *Times* reported. "The modern midnight crowd consists of men with plenty of money to spend, and who are willing to spend it lavishly if they get their money's worth."

It wasn't that the city had been hit with a wave of virtue—so-called New Tenderloins took root in Hell's Kitchen, on the West Side between 42nd and 62nd streets, and in parts of Harlem—but the original Tenderloin was rebranded as a culturally palatable, dazzlingly bright funhouse that patrons began calling the "Great White Way."

MILE 5

HERALD SQUARE TO COLUMBUS CIRCLE

CHAPTER 20

GREAT WHITE WAY

———

W HAT WAS SO GREAT ABOUT THE GREAT WHITE WAY? FOR starters, it had no precedent in America as a public place. In an era of supposed White Greatness—the Great Houdini, Great White Fleet, Great White Hope—the Great White Way was a delirious exaggeration of American culture unspooled along the thirty-six blocks of Broadway between Madison Square and Columbus Circle, a two-mile stretch that included Herald and Times squares. People began calling that part of Broadway the Great White Way around 1900, and by 1910 it seemed like the center of the world.

The angled crossing of Broadway and Sixth Avenue produced two tiny wedges of land that in 1894 were christened Greeley and Herald squares. Greeley Square, between 32nd and 33rd streets, featured a bronze statue of *New York Tribune* founder Horace Greeley, slumped in a chair and looking exhausted, and was perpetually in the shadow cast by the Sixth Avenue Elevated tracks overhead and its station at 33rd Street. Herald Square, one block to the north, was flanked on the west side by the Herald Square Theatre and the era's three great department stores, Gimbel Brothers, Saks, and Macy's, plus, just behind Saks, the popular Childs restaurant, where coffee cost a nickel and a sandwich cost a dime.

The centerpiece of Herald Square was the Herald Building,

Looking up Broadway from Herald Square in 1903. The
Herald Building is on the right, next to the tracks of the
Sixth Avenue Elevated railroad. At the far left are two of
Broadway's great department stores, Saks and Macy's.

designed by the great architecture firm McKim, Mead & White as a
squat palazzo with a whimsical cornice crowned with a bronze goddess Minerva, two muscular bell ringers, and ranks of eagles and
owls. Across 36th Street from the Herald Building was the Sheridan
Building, where up-and-coming song-and-dance man George M.
Cohan wrote plays at a borrowed desk in the Miner Lithographing
Company. The Marlborough Hotel was on the west side of Broadway across from the Sheridan Building, followed on the next block
by the Hotel Normandie at the southeast corner of Broadway and
38th Street.

Then came Times Square, where Broadway crossed Seventh Avenue between 43rd and 47th streets and, at Broadway and 42nd Street,
its newspaper-headquarters centerpiece, the Times Building. Clus-

tered around Times Square were the Cadillac, Claridge, Astor, and Knickerbocker hotels, and the famous restaurants Shanley's and the deluxe Rector's, where lobster was prepared sixteen different ways at a dollar apiece. And holding it all together on those two miles of lights and people were the Great White Way's necklace of theaters—the Metropolitan Opera House; the Savoy, Empire, Casino, Broadway, Herald Square, Victoria, Majestic, Belasco, New Amsterdam, Lyric, Lyceum, Winter Garden, Criterion, Gaiety, Globe, and Circle—while above the fray huge electric billboards blinked on and off with animated kittens, waterfalls, raindrops, and chariots.

The Great White Way's closest corollary as an urban spectacle was the Midway Plaisance, the mile-long amusement strip at the center of Chicago's "White City," the 1893 World's Columbian Exposition. Like the Great White Way, the White City's Midway was a linear, nocturnal streetscape wired with electric lights and festooned with billboards. The Midway even strove for a taste of Tenderloin depravity—the "hootchy-kootchy" (belly dance) had its American debut there.

While the Midway was obviously fake, designed as a temporary installation, the Great White Way was very real, permanent and indelible, and solidly anchored in New York's past and future, a World's Fair that never ended. The Great White Way, or the "Gay White Way," as it was often called, grew organically, its form resulting more from the gradual but inexorable rise in the value of real estate along Broadway than from any overall, comprehensive design. Much of the Great White Way's appeal, in fact, came from its very lack of coherence, its stores, offices, theaters, hotels, clubs, and restaurants all thrown together, come what may.

In 1882, two years after Charles Francis Brush first brought electric streetlights to Broadway, Edison successfully wired the Financial District and began building power stations around the city. (Two years later, in a promotional tour de force, Edison mounted light bulbs on the heads of a contingent of employees and had them drag a steam engine and dynamo up Broadway during a parade for Republican presidential nominee James G. Blaine.)

Edison employees marching up Broadway.

Edison's incandescent bulb emitted a softer glow and lasted longer than Brush's glaring arc lamps, and it was Edison who built Broadway's first electric billboard.

Austin Corbin commissioned the sign in 1892. Corbin, listed in autobiographical directories of the day simply as "Capitalist," was a Harvard Law School graduate, banker, railroad magnate, and owner of an Arkansas plantation where convicts and Italian immigrants worked under harsh conditions. He was also the developer of Manhattan Beach, a resort on the eastern tip of Coney Island. Between 1877 and 1880, Corbin built two deluxe hotels there, the Oriental and the Manhattan Beach, and saturated newspapers with advertisements. He also owned the New York, Brooklyn, and Manhattan Beach Railroad that carried the guests back and forth from the sweltering city. (Those guests did not include Jews: Corbin, an outspoken anti-Semite, banned them from his resort.)

As part of the Manhattan Beach advertising campaign, Corbin hired Edison to install an immense electric sign, consisting of large sheet-metal letters lined with light bulbs, on the blank north wall of the Cumberland, overlooking the busy confluence of Broadway and Fifth Avenue. Corbin wanted people to read his billboard whether they wanted to or not, and it worked: The sign flashed incessantly on and off, over and over again, each line in a different color, first one line and then the next, and was impossible to ignore:

BUY HOMES ON
LONG ISLAND
SWEPT BY OCEAN BREEZES
MANHATTAN BEACH
ORIENTAL HOTEL
MANHATTAN HOTEL
GILMORES BAND
BROCKS FIREWORKS

Passersby were mesmerized. Theodore Dreiser noticed Corbin's sign within days of arriving in the city for the first time in 1894, and was overcome by an insatiable desire to visit Manhattan Beach. He and his brother, songwriter Paul Dresser (who had changed the spelling of his name) went that very weekend, following in the wake of an immense crowd that crossed the East River on the 34th Street ferry, boarded one of Corbin's suffocating trains at Long Island City, and chuffed over the hills and mudflats of Brooklyn to the beach.

Dreiser had grown up in Indiana and had never seen the ocean, let alone the festive band concerts (John Philip Sousa was holding sway that afternoon), fireworks displays, and fashionable crowds frolicking on the beach, boardwalk, and verandahs of Corbin's hotels. He was so wonderstruck by the whole scene he had trouble eating his lunch. Clearly, Corbin was on to something.

Corbin's billboard lasted only four years, and after Corbin's sudden death in 1896—he was thrown from a carriage—the Cumberland's coveted north wall was taken over by the H. J. Heinz Company, which hired O. J. Gude to design and install an enormous electric sign that featured a giant pickle in flashing green lights.

Gude was the first undisputed master of what people began calling "sky-signs," "fire-signs," or "spectaculars": oversized, animated displays that loomed over the street and bore into the minds of pedestrians—whether they liked it or not. Gude went on to build iconic sky-signs for Maxwell House Coffee, White Rock mineral water, Heatherbloom petticoats and Wrigley's Spearmint gum. His sprawling factory took up most of a block on the west side of Broadway between 68th and 69th streets, and Gude was largely responsible for turning Broadway into a festival, "brilliantly illuminated with electric lights in all the colors of the rainbow," as the *New York Times* put it.

Not everyone appreciated the new electric landscape. Civic groups, including the Municipal Art Society, the Women's Municipal League, and the Manhattan Central Improvement Association, banded together to try to curb sky-sign construction. "[Electric signs] have become so numerous, so big, and so blinding that people's attention has become deadened to them by their continual assault on the optic nerves," declared J. Horace McFarland of the American Civic Association in 1910, failing to fully appreciate that a continual assault on the optic nerves was precisely what Gude and his colleagues in the sign business had in mind.

That same year an entrepreneur named Elwood Rice upped the ante when he built a sky-sign on the roof of the eight-story Hotel Normandie at the intersection of Broadway and 38th Street. Rice's billboard was 72 feet high and 90 feet wide—much bigger than any sky-sign that had yet been built—and, inspired by the long-running Broadway hit *Ben-Hur*, featured a moving chariot race complete with galloping horses and cracking whips, animated by an ingenious sequencing of 20,000 incandescent bulbs that flashed on and off 2,500 times a minute. The names of corporate sponsors appeared in a space above the chariot race, which replayed every thirty seconds. It was so extraordinary that in the weeks after it was installed thousands of people stood gawking in the street, blocking traffic, their optic nerves delightfully assaulted.

By then, over twenty blocks on Broadway were lined with electric sky-signs and theater marquees. Black and white photographs and movies of the era couldn't capture the scene in all its full-color glory, but tourists who saw the Great White Way in person were stunned.

"This is the best day, but it will be better to-morrow," Methodist Bishop William A. Quayle, visiting from Oklahoma in 1910, declared after seeing Rice's billboard. "I was told New York was a bad town. It looks good to me at night, with all the lights, and the chariot race on top of a house, and doesn't it look good in the day, with its buildings climbing up into the sky!"

The news that New York possessed a nocturnal landscape where people anxiously crowded into department stores, theaters, and restaurants attracted the notice of every merchants association, chamber of commerce, real-estate company, and newspaper in America, and by the teens every town, no matter how small, had to have its own Great White Way. Chicago, Los Angeles, San Francisco, and Pittsburgh all built their own versions, as might be expected; but so did Pensacola, Topeka, Albuquerque, and even the tiny reservation town of Chickasha, Oklahoma.

"[Let us] get together and have a Great White Way as soon as possible," urged the editors of the *Daily Register*, a four-page newspaper in Richmond, Kentucky, population 5,000. "It is an indication of a prosperous condition, and a progressive spirit." One real-estate company in tiny Newberry, South Carolina, promised that with "a great white way in the near future, enhanced [real-estate] values are a dead certainty."

When El Paso turned its Texas Street into a Great White Way in 1920, El Pasoans heralded the event as the inauguration of a new era. "At the touch of a button to-night Texas Street, from Oregon to Campbell, will be transformed, as tho by magic," the *El Paso Herald* proclaimed, "into a great white-way of dazzling brilliance—the best-lit five blocks in El Paso and all Texas—and the city's show place."

In Omaha, the coming of the local Great White Way was described in biblical terms. "For many years Omaha has waged a war against the powers of darkness," the *Omaha Daily Bee* reported in 1911. The Omaha Electric Light & Power Company was spoken of in hushed tones; the all-powerful electric god that had turned Omaha's night into day. The Great White Way, the *Bee* predicted, would turn Omaha into the "Electric City" of the West. In Sinclair Lewis's 1920 novel *Main Street*, the leaders of fictitious Gopher Prairie, Minnesota, believed their new Great White Way would even make their little speck of a town the rival of Minneapolis–St. Paul.

It was inevitable that such unrealistic expectations led to profound disappointment. Electric lighting could extend business hours and bring in tourists, at least while the novelty lasted, but couldn't turn a small town into a metropolis. After a period of hoopla when the lights were first switched on, many small towns found that wiring their Main Street was one thing and paying the resulting electrical bills another.

"Less than a year ago Columbia installed a Great White Way," the exasperated editor of the *University Missourian* complained in 1913. "Yet, new as it is, the novelty has worn off and the expense is the one item of which the City Council thinks. The result is that only one of the three globes is ever lighted and the once Great White Way presents, to the stranger, a down-and-out face and to the resident a sickly, pale glance."

CHAPTER 21

EDEN

——

AS SMALL-TOWN AMERICANS WENT ABOUT WIRING THEIR downtowns in emulation of Broadway, the original Great White Way added more stores, hotels, and theaters, and with each passing year grew steadily northward past Herald Square. By 1900 it was approaching the awkwardly angled crossing of Broadway and Seventh Avenue. That hourglass-shaped intersection became Times Square, a place so ingrained in American culture as the epicenter of all things futuristic that it's shocking to consider that it began as a verdant, rolling farm of some 70 acres stretching westward from Broadway to the edge of the Hudson River. And had it not been for the machinations of two feuding descendants of a German-born fur trader and the dreams of a newspaper publisher whose parents were German immigrants, Times Square as we know it would never have existed.

The farm that would become Times Square began as a British colonial land grant in 1667. It passed through various estates over the next 130 years until, in 1798, it wound up in the hands of Medcef Eden Jr. Two years later Eden and his brother Joseph were sued for unpaid debts totaling over $53,000, and the courts issued writs of fieri facias, by which the sheriff, James Morris, was empowered to sell off the land in order to pay their creditors. Accordingly, in 1801 the

Eden tract was sold to Tunis Wortman. But Wortman, too, ran into financial problems, falling behind in mortgage payments to a group of mortgage holders that included John Jacob Astor.

Astor had arrived in New York from the village of Walldorf, Germany, in 1784 and began his career selling musical instruments imported from a brother in London. From there Astor got involved in the fur business, trading directly with Indians in the Hudson Valley and Canada. By 1800 he had moved into a mansion at 223 Broadway, opposite City Hall Park, and began financing trading voyages to China and South America. Astor's American Fur Company set him up for life, but it was his investments in New York real estate that made him the wealthiest man in America. Astor steadily acquired lots around Greenwich Village and here and there along Broadway's first three miles, but his first really big deal, the one that secured the fortunes of his descendants, was his finagling away of the Eden farm from Tunis Wortman.

In 1803, Wortman lost the farm when Astor and the various other holders of his mortgages foreclosed. Seized by the courts, the farm wound up in the hands of Astor and William Cutting for the consideration of only $25,000—$14,000 less than Wortman had paid for the farm only two years earlier. Cutting quickly, and unwisely as it would turn out, sold most of his share back to Astor, relinquishing for $4,346 a substantial swath of what would become Times Square.

The Astor real-estate empire—it was often simply called "the Estate" and everyone knew what that meant—accrued through the steady application of an almost fail-safe strategy: Astor and his son William Backhouse Astor bought up vacant lots, and entire farms when they could, and then signed tenants to leases of twenty years or more. The tenants paid all property taxes plus an annual rent, and any improvements (buildings) they added became the Astors' property when the leases expired. The Astors themselves rarely built anything and took few risks, preferring to sit back and watch their land gradually but steadily appreciate in value.

At the time of John Jacob Astor's death in 1848, the Estate was worth $20 million, then reached $100 million by the time William

Backhouse Astor died in 1876. At that point the Estate was divided between William's two sons, John Jacob III and William Backhouse Jr.

It wasn't until that third generation that the Astors really began acting the part of the richest family in America, cavorting on yachts, going to the races, and hosting fancy-dress balls in Newport. The first John Jacob Astor had been rough around the edges—paddling canoes, sleeping on the ground, and beating, baling, and loading his own furs onto ships—and had never cared much for "Polite Society." But his granddaughter-in-law Caroline Webster Schermerhorn Astor, wife of William Backhouse Jr., positively *lived* for Society, and from the 1870s to the 1890s considered herself *the* "Mrs. Astor," custodian of the fabled "Four Hundred," the jewel-encrusted descendants of New York's old Knickerbocker clans.

Upon the deaths of John Jacob III, in 1890, and William Backhouse Jr., two years later, the Estate was split between John Jacob III's son William Waldorf Astor, who inherited $150 million—almost $4 billion in today's currency—and William Backhouse Jr.'s son John Jacob Astor IV, who had to settle for *only* $65 million.

In photographs, William Waldorf, "Willie" to his friends and horses, often wore a quizzical expression, with hints of amusement

Cousins William Waldorf Astor (left) and John Jacob Astor IV (right).

around the edges, as if he were reminding himself of an off-color joke. In contrast, his younger cousin John Jacob IV, "Jack" to some and (inevitable, really) "Jack Ass" to others, appeared a bit bored in photos, drowsy, despairing even, as if submitting to the lens was an hour of yachting lost forever. Both Willie and Jack were tall and skinny, with angular scarecrow physiques.

They were not close. One very public feud, mocked in the press but taken very seriously by the participants, erupted in 1890 and centered on the question of who, Jack's mother Caroline or Willie's wife Mary, should be considered *the* Mrs. Astor and therefore the de facto head of Society. Willie's political career had already gone sour—he had twice lost elections for Congress—and his treatment by the press, never cordial to begin with, worsened. When newspapers began speculating on how much ransom kidnappers might get for Willie's son Waldorf, Willie, fed up, disavowed the United States entirely and moved his family lock, stock, and barrel to England.

Willie left the day-to-day operations of his portion of the Estate in the capable hands of a custodian, Charles A. Peabody Jr., and settled into Cliveden, a gigantic country house in Buckinghamshire. Jack remained in New York, the two branches of the family working out of a modest office with two separate entrances on 26th Street, near Broadway. Both Willie and Jack departed from the traditionally conservative Astor investment strategy, recognizing that a modern world of skyscrapers, railroads, steamships, and telephones called for a more aggressive approach to land development. After a century of their family playing it close to the chest, Willie and Jack began building with a vengeance.

In 1893, Willie ordered his parents' old mansion at Fifth Avenue and 33rd Street torn down and replaced with the gargantuan Waldorf Hotel, a project that greatly displeased his aunt Caroline, who lived next door at Fifth Avenue and 34th Street, as the hotel cut off all her southern light and overshadowed her garden. Jack responded by moving his mother farther up Fifth Avenue, tearing down her house, and building the even bigger Astoria Hotel, which opened in 1897, next to the Waldorf. An agreement between Willie and Jack combined the two hotels into the famous Waldorf-Astoria, a palace of a hotel with 1,000 rooms, a ballroom that could seat 1,500 for dinner, and, most crucially, corridors that could, at a moment's notice, be blocked off in the event Willie and Jack got into a spat.

Willie's Hotel Netherland at Fifth Avenue and 59th Street, and Jack's St. Regis Hotel at Fifth Avenue and 55th Street soon followed, and then Willie and Jack finally turned their attentions to the old Eden farm.

The farm had remained strangely underdeveloped, etched in city lore as an allegory of the vicissitudes of fortune and family. *If only your grandfather had been there in 1803,* the thinking went, *and if only he had bought even a few of those lots from John Jacob Astor himself, imagine how differently things would have turned out for you and your family.* "You wouldn't have to work, would you?" ran one bank's taunting advertisement.

As late as the 1860s much of the Eden farm was still a blank spot on city maps, terra incognita—a kind of secret garden of real estate encircled by the growing city. When the Astors did lease parcels of the Eden land, it was to unambitious builders of modest houses, churches, schools, breweries, coal yards, and so many horse-related industries—carriage factories, stables, and horse exchanges—that the blocks around Broadway and Seventh Avenue became known as Long Acre Square after London's Long Acre, a street just to the north of Covent Garden known for its many carriage manufacturers.

While Willie played lord-of-the-manor in England—he eventually gained a peerage and became "1st Viscount Astor"—Jack puttered at Ferncliff, the family estate in Rhinebeck, or at Beechwood, the family's cottage in Newport. He went sailing on his immense yacht *Nourmahal,* which cost $20,000 a year to operate, and in his spare time invented a bicycle brake and an engine that burned peat. In 1894, Jack tried his hand at writing, producing a science-fiction novel in the Jules Verne mode. *A Journey in Other Worlds: A Romance of the Future* follows the adventures of a group of intrepid New Yorkers involved in a utopian scheme for straightening the earth's axis, the idea being that an orthogonal rotation would bring on eternal springtime. The story is set in the year 2000, at which point, Jack predicted, wind power, air travel, intercontinental telephone communication, and color photography will have become realities. Jack's vision of New York in 2000 was revealing, considering that he owned so much of it: He foresaw an efficient, poverty-free, mechanized city with a park system linked by greenways, diagonal streets and public squares, and futuristic expressways where electric cars zipped along at speeds up to forty miles an hour.

Jack may have been wide of the mark in some of his predictions— he had New York's population as 14.5 million in 2000, about 6.5 million too many, and imagined that "twentieth-century stage-coaching" would still include plenty of horses, for "those that prefer them"— but his ideas about transportation were remarkably prescient. His expressways resembled the ones later built by Robert Moses, and Jack correctly predicted that a municipal subway system would revolutionize the city.

The subway was still a futuristic dream when Jack wrote *A Journey in Other Worlds.* Twenty years had passed since Alfred Ely Beach abandoned his experimental pneumatic subway beneath lower Broadway, and there had been many proposals but no progress in the meantime. Then, in 1900, construction commenced on the Interborough Rapid Transit system.

Construction of the IRT, coupled with the rebuilding and expansion of Grand Central Station on 42nd Street, led to a building boom in Long Acre Square that more closely resembled a frantic land rush. Overnight, real-estate prices in the vicinity of Broadway and 42nd Street rose by 30 to 35 percent, and theaters, offices, stores, restaurants, and hotels began flying up. With Broadway already dug up for subway construction, Long Acre Square became a catastrophe of open pits, debris, steam shovels, and broken water mains.

Willie and Jack found themselves perfectly positioned to cash in, and Willie engaged the architects Clinton & Russell to design a new hotel on a parcel of the old Eden farm at Broadway and 44th Street. The Hotel Astor was intended as the latest entry in the "Broadway hotel" tradition that over the previous century had produced the Astor House, Metropolitan, St. Nicholas, Fifth Avenue, and Gilsey

House hotels, swank clubhouses that catered to a clientele of young sports keen for the fast life and visiting businessmen looking for a bit of amusement on the side.

In the summer of 1903, with Willie's hotel well along in its construction, a wafer-thin skyscraper began rising at the south end of Long Acre Square. The Times Building's unlikely site was the product of the crossing of Seventh Avenue with Broadway's older meandering path, a collision that had resulted in an unpromising triangular wedge of land about the same size and shape as the Flatiron block twenty blocks to the south. The building was the pet project of newspaper publisher Adolph S. Ochs.

He was born in 1858 in Cincinnati to German-Jewish immigrants. After the Civil War the family moved to Knoxville, Tennessee, where Adolph, the oldest of six children, began working at the age of eleven as an office boy for the *Knoxville Chronicle*. He bought his first newspaper, the *Chattanooga Times*, at the age of twenty, and in 1896 took over the struggling *New York Times*. By the time the IRT began construction, Ochs had dramatically turned around the newspaper's fortunes—between 1896 and 1902 circulation jumped from 22,000 to 100,000—and decided to move the *Times* from its longtime Park Row headquarters to Long Acre Square. Ochs hired architects Cyrus L. W. Eidlitz and Andrew C. MacKenzie and asked them to duplicate the success of the Flatiron Building, which was then nearing completion.

Eidlitz and MacKenzie came close, and for a while the press even referred to the Times Building as a second Flatiron, but they couldn't quite achieve the vertical majesty of Daniel Burnham's masterpiece. They borrowed the Flatiron's materials (limestone, brick, and terracotta), structural system (a steel frame with extra bracing), and florid Renaissance Revival details, but tried to do too much in too little space, as architects are prone to do, and where the Flatiron's silhouette rose gracefully from the ground, the Times Building's seemed awkwardly stretched. Instead of extruding its triangular site to its full height, Eidlitz and MacKenzie stepped the Times Building back at the sixteenth floor, which made its top seem cramped. It was as if Giotto's campanile in Florence had been taken apart, shipped to

The Times Building, center, in 1908. Rector's restaurant is on the left, next to the Hotel Cadillac. The large building with the illuminated mansard roof is John Jacob Astor's Knickerbocker Hotel.

the middle of the Great White Way, and reassembled, but with the pieces in the wrong order.

Ochs bragged that his skyscraper was the tallest in the world. It wasn't, although it came within 16 feet of the mighty Park Row Building. But the Times Building was the first skyscraper in Long

Acre Square, and Ochs insisted on measuring its height not from the sidewalk but from the basement. And this made sense, since the really exciting thing about the Times Building wasn't its Renaissance Revival façade that towered into the sky but what was going on under the street. Ochs was fascinated with technology—he made early use of airplanes for taking photographs and delivering newspapers and in 1908 cosponsored, with the Paris daily *Le Matin*, an around-the-world automobile race from New York to Paris (by way of Siberia)—and the subway was for Ochs the coming of a futuristic transportation system that would completely remake the city.

The subway literally supported the Times Building, the two structures sharing steel columns and girders as the subway tunnel swept beneath the building from the southeast. Underground entrances led directly from the subway station to the building—a convenience later replicated with great fanfare in the Woolworth Building, Graybar Building, and, far in the future, World Trade Center—and commuters passed through a subterranean shopping arcade of barbershops, bootblack stands, florists, telegraph offices, drugstores, newsstands, haberdashers, confectioners, and soda water fountains. The station's most arresting feature was a huge electric sign mounted on the downtown platform, 4 feet high and 12 feet long, that read, simply TIMES. The sign was so bright it shone up through skylights placed in the Broadway sidewalk.

The newspaper's enormous printing presses were housed in a sub-basement beneath the station, 55 feet below street level. Ochs rented office space in his tower for up to $12,000 a year, and promised his tenants the "Highest Standard of 'Sky-Scraping' Architecture." But his most audacious move was in convincing the city's Board of Aldermen to change the name of Long Acre Square to Times Square.

Rival newspapers, naturally, hated the idea. The *Tribune* needed only one emphatic word—"DON'T"—to compose a headline condemning the proposal. "Long Acre Square" was a fine name, the *Tribune* complained, "a good one, intrinsically," and one "fixed in familiar usage." Then, clutching at straws, the *Tribune* argued that "Times Square" was impossible to pronounce: "The new name proposed is awkward because [since] the letter 's' is doubled in the middle of it, it cannot be correctly pronounced without an effort and even then it is not pleasing to the ear."

Albert Ulmann of the American Scenic and Historic Preservation Society also thought "Long Acre Square" was a "dignified, reputable, euphonious, and long established" name, and complained there had been no public debate over the change. And Ulmann worried that a worrisome precedent had been set.

"Why should not each of our other daily papers place its name on the people's lips through the medium of a similar change?" he protested, apparently imagining a city marred not only by Herald and Times squares but also by Tribune, American, Journal, Telegram, Post, World, Sun, and Evening Mail squares. To no avail: The resolution passed, on April 5, 1904, and Long Acre Square became Times Square. For years afterward the *Tribune* kept using the old name.

WILLIE'S HOTEL ASTOR opened the following September, with Willie himself on hand for the occasion, having sailed in the steamship *Majestic* from England. It was his first visit to America in five years, and the press had a field day, painting him as a rich snob who had renounced his country. *The Evening World* ran a series of unflattering cartoons depicting him as a fussy English lord bobbing up and down on his tippy-toes and uttering banal things like "it makes one dizzy to look at some of the tall buildings." The *Washington Times* suggested he wear an asbestos suit to shield him from the firestorm of criticism.

Willie's hotel had cost an unheard-of $9 million to build and was both enormous and opulent, a French Renaissance monolith with a façade of brick and limestone and a curved mansard roof of green slate and copper. The lobby was of cream-colored marble accented with gold leaf and decorated with panels depicting the history of New York. There were 600 rooms, a café, ballrooms, reading rooms, and lounges. Dining rooms were decorated in various themes: One was outfitted like the cabin of a yacht, with paintings on the walls meant to simulate a voyage up the Hudson River; another, the "college room," was lined with school insignia and photographs of athletes. Instead of the usual palm court on the ground floor, there was an orangery with ceilings two stories high, while, in the basement, a grillroom was decorated with American Indian artifacts loaned from the Smithsonian. Willie poked around and, satisfied that a small portion of his money had been wisely spent, sailed for home.

The IRT opened the following month. Excited riders kicked and shoved their way onto that first train—they haven't stopped since—and with Mayor George B. McClellan Jr. at the controls, hurtled north from City Hall Park to Grand Central Station. From there the train headed west under 42nd Street to Times Square and then careened into a hairpin turn beneath the Times Building, men, women, and children lurching from one side of the train to the other, and shot up Broadway all the way to 145th Street.

With the opening of the IRT, Times Square became the new center of town, the so-called Crossroads of the World. Even the ritual ringing in of the New Year shifted from lower Broadway, where for generations New Yorkers had gathered in front of Trinity Church to wait for the chimes to peal at midnight, to Times Square. With Barnum-like promotional precision, Ochs opened the Times Building on New Year's Eve, 1904, celebrating the countdown to 1905 with a fireworks display. (In 1907 a "time ball" that descended at midnight from a flagpole atop the tower was added to the festivities, the beginning of the "ball drop" tradition that we all know and avoid today.) Visitors flocked to Ochs's skyscraper, riding elevators to an observation deck on the roof, where they could see in its entirety the thrilling spectacle of the Great White Way.

"From there I could see the city as it slept," Prince Louis Alexander of Battenberg told reporters after a midnight ride to the roof, "but I discovered that New York does not sleep. I could see at that hour more lights in New York than are burning all over the world at 10 o'clock in the evening. Wonderful." He joked around with the elevator operator and asked if they were going to the moon.

MEANWHILE, JACK ASTOR's Knickerbocker Hotel, diagonally across Broadway from the Times Building, wasn't nearly finished. The project had been beset with problems from the very beginning: The architect—the great Bruce Price, whose many commissions included the American Surety Building on lower Broadway, Windsor Station in Montreal, and Osborn Hall at Yale—died of a stomach ailment in Paris in the spring of 1903, at which point the Knickerbocker was little more than a giant hole in the ground. There was a water main break in 1903, too, which flooded the site, and then labor strikes and a lengthy standoff with the hotel's lessee, James Regan, who demanded significant last-minute changes to the plans.

The Knickerbocker didn't open until the fall of 1906, but in every way it compared favorably with Willie's hotel two blocks to the north. The Knickerbocker's footprint wasn't as large as the Astor's, but the building was taller, fifteen stories compared to ten, and its curving mansard roof presented a festive profile of projecting dormer windows and jutting finials. It had 573 rooms, a library, and a Maxfield Parrish mural of Old King Cole in the barroom. Theatrical types gathered there so often they took to calling it the "42nd Street Country Club."

Jack went down with the *Titanic* in 1912. Seven years later, Willie died in England of a heart attack. But their hotels remained, coldly regarding each other across the chasm of Broadway, looming over a landscape that had once been called Eden.

CHAPTER 22

TIMES SQUARE TYPES

———

THE RIALTO, A "PARADE GROUND WITH ELASTIC BOUNDAR-
ies" as the *New York Sun* called it, gradually stretched up Broadway
from Union Square to Madison Square to Herald Square. As early as
the 1880s the Casino Theatre, the Metropolitan Opera House, and the
Broadway Theatre had opened even farther north, near the southern
end of Long Acre Square.

On October 21, 1882, Rudolph Aronson's Casino Theatre, a Moorish fantasy in brick and terra-cotta, opened at the southeast corner of
Broadway and 39th Street with a performance of the Johann Strauss
operetta *The Queen's Lace Handkerchief.* The building was far from
finished: Stairways didn't have balustrades, the boxes were missing
columns, draperies dragged on the floor, and tools, lumber, and saw-
dust littered the auditorium. There was no heat. Just before show
time the stage was cleared of debris and curtains were hastily thrown
up to hide unfinished woodwork. The theater, the *New York Sun*
reported the next day, was "in no fit state for occupancy." It closed
and reopened on December 30, and this time the building was ready.

The Casino was extraordinary, the theater as dreamscape, with
an "arabesque" auditorium with seating for 1,300, a roof supported
by columns that spread at the ceiling into sheaf-like capitals that ran
into Moorish arches, and a large chandelier hanging from the center

of the ceiling. The general color scheme was gold, with seats upholstered in dark blue.

The following summer Aronson opened a two-tiered "summer
garden" on the Casino's roof that included a concert stage and restaurant. For the price of one 50-cent ticket, patrons could watch the
main performance in the auditorium and then take elevators to the
roof to "promenade, sup, sip wine, flirt, laugh or grow sentimental,"
as the *New York Tribune* reported. The summer garden had sides that
could be opened in clement weather, introducing cool evening breezes
to the throngs listening to the orchestra.

When the Casino opened, the mammoth Metropolitan Opera
House was nearing completion just across the street, at the northwest corner of Broadway and 40th Street. The Metropolitan Opera
Company had been founded two years earlier by a group of wealthy
and powerful tycoons who hadn't been able to lease boxes at Union
Square's staid Academy of Music. Construction of the Metropolitan led to an "operatic war" between the two houses, and the Met's
seventy-nine private boxes were quickly leased, for $1,200 per season,
to a group of the city's most prominent financiers and industrialists.

Architect Josiah Cleaveland Cady's Romanesque exterior, in beige
brick, looked like an office building, but the interior was like no other
theater in America, with a 3,700-seat auditorium, walls in gold and
cream, and carpets and chairs upholstered in deep red. The *New York
Sun* called it the "Palace on Broadway."

The upstart Met opened on October 22, 1883, the same night the
Academy of Music opened its fall season, and newspaper reporters
gleefully flocked to both venues to see which house would attract
which members of Society. ("Where to go is this year quite as troublesome a question as what to wear," the *Tribune* fretted.) On that first
night the Brevoorts, Belmonts, Cuttings, Costers, Duers, Griswolds,
and Lorillards stayed loyal to the Academy, but plenty of other old-
money families, including the Rhinelanders, Ogdens, Suydams, and
Remsens, fled to the Met.

The Met's opening-night throng included John Jacob Astor III,
Cyrus W. Field, Russell Sage, Jay Gould, J. P. Morgan, William H.
Vanderbilt, Cornelius Vanderbilt II, William Rockefeller, and Austin

Corbin. It was a Gilded Age all-star team, and the tycoons, in full dress, their opera cloaks slung over the balconies, and their wives, in low-necked white dresses, spent much of the five-hour-long opera (Charles Gounod's *Faust)* visiting each other's boxes. "Diamonds glittered in all directions like crystals upon snow," the *Tribune* reported, while estimating the crowd's aggregate wealth at $450 million. (Caroline Astor outdid them all by leasing boxes at both houses and then, still in Newport, not bothering to show at either place.)

The opening of the Met was the death knell for the Academy, which gradually faded, doomed by its smaller size and a location that was rapidly becoming undesirable. Within three years it had changed management and stopped staging opera. (It survived as a vaudeville house and meeting hall and was finally demolished in 1926.)

Five years after the Met opened, and nine days before the Blizzard of 1888, the Broadway Theatre, its large auditorium decorated with Persian touches, opened just across 41st Street from the Met with a performance of Victorien Sardou's *La Tosca,* as the Rialto continued to stretch ever closer to Long Acre Square. But there were no theaters in Long Acre Square itself until 1895, when Oscar Hammerstein, grandfather of the great composer Oscar Hammerstein II, built the Olympia Theatre on Broadway between 44th and 45th streets.

Hammerstein envisioned the Olympia as a one-stop amusement mecca, with three theaters and a glass-enclosed roof garden (where the first version of the *Ziegfeld Follies* played to overflow crowds a few years later), plus a billiard hall and bowling alley. Hammerstein went bankrupt and lost the Olympia only three years after it opened, then made a dramatic recovery, and was solvent enough by 1899 to build the Victoria Theatre at the northwest corner of Broadway and 42nd Street and the smaller Theatre Republic behind it.

But it wasn't until the opening of the subway in 1904 that Long Acre Square, as Times Square, became the Rialto's epicenter. The building boom that produced the Times Building and the Knickerbocker and Astor hotels also brought theaters, so many that they no longer fit neatly on Broadway and began to colonize side streets. In 1903 alone the New Amsterdam, Lyric, Hudson, Comedy, and Lyceum theaters were built within a block or less of Times Square between 42nd and 45th streets; the next few years brought the Liberty, Lew M. Fields, Astor, Maxine Elliott, and Gaiety theaters.

"Is New-York to become 'the city of theatres'?" the *Tribune* fretted. "[The] number of theatres in Manhattan which are rising . . . is assuming truly alarming proportions."

But Times Square's theaters, though often grand and sometimes unbelievably seductive, with murals and inlaid cherubs and Art Nouveau swirls, were just the backdrops for a legion of characters whose foibles largely defined Broadway in the golden era leading up to World War I. They drank together beneath the Old King Cole mural at the Knickerbocker, dined together at Rector's, Maxim's, and Shanley's, joined the Friars, Players, and Lambs clubs, went to prizefights at Madison Square Garden, and sued each other often and dramatically. It was an era when eccentrics were not only tolerated but were often at the head of their class.

There was the coldly calculating, vindictive producer Abraham Lincoln Erlanger—"Dishonest Abe" they called him—who, with Marc Klaw, led the monopolistic Theatrical Syndicate, a consortium of six managers that owned theaters in New York, Chicago, Los Angeles, Washington, New Orleans, and other cities. The Syndicate formed in 1896 and by the early 1900s was so powerful that Klaw and Erlanger were able to largely dictate the schedules and terms of theater bookings across the country, at a time when the real money was in road productions of Broadway plays.

The Syndicate's main rivals were the brothers Lee, Sam, and Jacob Shubert, whom Erlanger called the "scum of the earth." Klaw and Erlanger didn't care for Oscar Hammerstein either, and 42nd Street became a kind of theatrical Maginot Line, with Klaw and Erlanger's New Amsterdam and Liberty theaters lined up on the south side of the street opposite the Shuberts' Lyric Theatre and Hammerstein's Victoria Theatre and Theatre Republic. Erlanger got so touchy about the 42nd Street divide he once chastised George M. Cohan for standing on the "wrong" side of the street.

In 1902, Hammerstein leased the Theatre Republic to David Belasco, a producer, actor, and writer who altered the Republic's façade and auditorium to suit his taste—he did much of the demoli-

Producer
David Belasco
in 1893.

tion work himself, at one point getting knocked unconscious by falling debris—and reopened as the Belasco Theatre. Like the Shuberts
and Hammerstein, Belasco refused to buckle to what he described
as the Syndicate's extortionist practices, and he waged a long legal
struggle against Klaw and Erlanger.

"[Erlanger] told me that if I refused his terms he would com-
pel me to go into the streets and blacken my face to earn a living,"
Belasco told theater critic William Winter. "I detest the man and
his methods."

Erlanger was in the habit of suing Belasco for plagiarism. In
one instance, Belasco defended himself by bringing the judge and
jury to his theater and staging the play he wrote back-to-back with
the play Erlanger claimed he stole. Winter watched this strange
double bill and condemned Erlanger's play as "impalliable trash."
The jury agreed.

Belasco was born in 1853 in San Francisco, and by the time he
moved to New York in 1882 had already found success as a playwright

and producer on the west coast. In New York he worked as the stage manager at the Madison Square and old Lyceum theaters, and then produced a string of hit plays, including *The Girl I Left Behind Me* at the Empire Theatre in 1892 and *Madame Butterfly* at the Herald Square Theatre in 1900. Belasco became a kind of theatrical sage, instantly recognizable for his shock of unruly hair and his improbable wardrobe: Although he was Jewish, Belasco always dressed in a black suit with a clerical collar, like a Catholic priest. Inevitably, people called him the "Bishop of Broadway."

Belasco was interested in "actuality" in theater, and went a good bit beyond the pale in establishing a sense of theatrical naturalism. For *The Governor's Lady* he built a convincing replica of a Childs restaurant on stage, with a working kitchen where his actors cooked and ate their own meals during the performance. If the script called for a character to make an entrance from an off-stage stair, Belasco built the entire staircase, even though it was out of sight of the audience. In *The Girl of the Golden West*, a runaway hit in 1905, Belasco simulated a sunset by slowly passing a succession of colored silks in front of a spotlight. In the play's climactic scene, he had telltale drops of stage blood fall from a loft above the stage onto a handkerchief.

In 1906, Belasco decided to build a new theater from scratch, according to his own exacting specifications. He found a lot on 44th Street, east of Broadway, hired architect George Keister, and broke ground that December. At the groundbreaking ceremony Belasco placed a copper box filled with souvenirs from his career (playbills, photographs) in a niche in the cornerstone. Blanche Bates, Belasco's favorite star—she played the lead in *The Girl of the Golden West*, and like Belasco was from San Francisco—troweled on a layer of mortar. Masons swung a stone cap into place, Belasco's two daughters broke bottles of champagne on it, and building commenced on one of the most remarkable theaters ever built on Broadway.

It was called the Stuyvesant Theatre at first to avoid confusion with the Belasco Theatre, which Belasco continued to operate. (In 1910 he renamed the Stuyvesant the Belasco and switched the old theater's name back to the Republic.) Belasco wanted his new theater to feel like a living room, and the auditorium was on the small side, with seating for 1,000. (By contrast, the New Amsterdam Theatre sat 1,750; the Broadway Theatre, 1,800; the Olympia Theatre, 2,800; the Metropolitan Opera House, 3,700.) Keister employed a California color palette of warm reds, ambers, and oranges, with softly glowing Tiffany lamps hanging from the ceiling and Everett Shinn murals on the walls and over the proscenium.

It was a mysterious, brooding, portentous performance space. But the strangest and most wonderful thing about Belasco's new theater wasn't the auditorium but the private studio and apartment he built on the roof.

Belasco wrote his plays there, conjuring characters and plots from thin air in a darkened room. Eventually he would emerge, call for a stenographer, and begin reciting dialogue, pacing back and forth. His desk was a rickety old sewing table covered in green baize, piled high with books and cluttered with pencils and figurines, surrounded by rough drafts of scripts scrawled on pieces of paper and pinned to boards. There was a small bedroom, decorated in a Japanese style, where Belasco took naps and reportedly seduced, or tried to seduce, many of his actresses.

The studio was stuffed with Belasco's vast collection of antiques, artifacts, mementos, and curios, a warren of seven Gothic Revival–style rooms connected by low, narrow doors (Belasco was 5 feet 3) and filled with glassware, paintings, books, suits of armor, shields, swords, cannon, lances, antlers, vases, statues, paperweights, cameos, necklaces, rosaries, reliquaries, crucifixes, urns, clocks, dueling pistols, snuff boxes, globes, candelabras, flags, tapestries, a mandolin, a bust of Shakespeare, a fireplace inlaid with tiles taken from the Alhambra, a crust of bread from the Siege of Paris, a lock of Napoleon's hair, and a swallowtail banner from the City Horse Guard of the New York State Militia. There was even a grotto with a gurgling fountain that emptied into a pool of violets, sweet peas, and roses.

Belasco knew precisely what was in his collection, where it came from, and where everything was, and hated it when some well-meaning person tried to clean up. When he died, in 1931, his studio was cleaned out and his collection put up for auction. The hammer fell for an entire week. Today, people swear Belasco's ghost still haunts his theater.

BELASCO WAS UNFORGETTABLE, but the strangest Broadway character of all might have been a self-described song-and-dance man who handed out spare change to struggling actors; dressed up in goofy costumes for charity baseball games; divorced his first wife and married one of his chorus girls; drank, heavily at times; had an explosive temper; talked out of the side of his mouth, his hat pulled low over his brow; and called everyone, even the feared Erlanger, "kid." A few old pals from vaudeville days could get away with calling him Georgie. Everyone else called him Mr. Cohan.

George M. Cohan combined in one performer the over-the-top patriotism of Tony Pastor, the Irish slapstick of Harrigan & Hart, the subtle, understated acting of Nat Goodwin, and the promotional genius of P. T. Barnum. He was a small whip of a man, 5 feet 6 inches tall and 135 pounds, with blue eyes and brown hair that began to turn silver at an early age and a jaw that jutted defiantly forward, turning

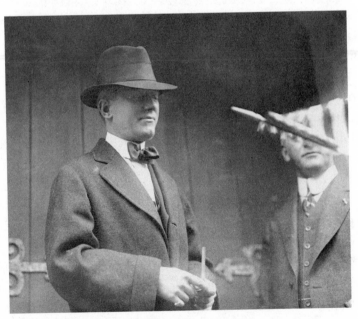

George M. Cohan in 1916.

his smile into a smirk. He formed a lucrative partnership with Sam H. Harris in 1904 and together they conquered Broadway, producing eighteen musicals before splitting up in 1919.

Cohan was by all accounts an astonishing dancer—the *Evening World* once described his legs moving in such a blur they seemed "kaleidoscopic"—and he could do more than dance: He was also a producer, director, singer, and actor, and such a prolific writer that in his spare time he dashed off sketches and songs as favors for friends. He wrote in epic, last-minute, all-night, coffee-fueled sessions, and was in such a perpetual hurry he frequently had shows in rehearsal before he had even begun considering what might happen in the second act.

He wasn't a groundbreaking technician like Belasco, or a theatrical revolutionary in the manner of George Bernard Shaw, Eugene O'Neill, Henrik Ibsen, or Clifford Odets. But the breakneck speed of Cohan's shows was fresh and exciting and perfectly in tune with an era of blinking electric billboards, all-night dance parties, and automobiles that coughed up and down Broadway in ever increasing numbers. His actors belted their lines in rapid fire, not waiting for applause, and hurled themselves on and off the stage. "Speed! Speed!" Cohan instructed his company, "and lots of it; that's my idea of the thing. Perpetual motion."

Cohan's productions usually featured dozens of bracing, emphatic, jackhammer anthems *("Over There! Over There! Send the word, send the word, over there!")* that thrilled audiences with their relentless American swagger. He insisted that his dressing room be decorated floor-to-ceiling with American flags—admirers told him he had put the red and the blue into the Great White Way.

COHAN WAS BORN in an Irish neighborhood in Providence in 1878, the child of traveling, penniless vaudeville performers, and at age seven was already part of the family show. He became a star with *Little Johnny Jones,* which opened November 7, 1904, at Klaw and Erlanger's Liberty Theatre. The show bombed, but after some fine-tuning on the road, it returned to Broadway the following spring and became a hit. Cohan wrote and directed and played the lead, a feisty character called "the Jockey" based on the real-life jockey Tod Sloan.

The play itself has faded into obscurity, but several of the songs from *Little Johnny Jones* have proven to be indestructible, especially the plaintive ditty Cohan sang at the end of the second act, as the Jockey watches a steamer sail from the docks of Southhampton, bound for America.

> *Give my regards to Broadway, remember me to Herald Square,*
> *Tell all the gang at Forty-Second Street, that I will soon be there;*
> *Whisper of how I'm yearning to mingle with the old time throng;*
> *Give my regards to old Broadway and say that I'll be there*
> *ere long.*

By 1905, "Give My Regards to Broadway" was "whistled everywhere" and its sheet music sat on virtually every piano in every parlor in America. Songs about Broadway were all the rage then ("The Indians Along Broadway," "I'm the Only Star That Twinkles on Broadway," "I'd Rather Be on Old Broadway with You," "That Broadway Glide," "It's Getting Dark on Old Broadway," "A Large Front Room on Broadway," "Dear Old Broadway," "I Wish I Was Back on Broadway," "King of the Great White Way"), but only "Give My Regards to Broadway," with that tenderly nostalgic phrase *"yearning* to mingle," revealed Broadway for what it really was: a rootless community of strangers.

But not even Cohan fully understood Broadway. He kept trying, putting Broadway itself in the starring role of play after play— *Forty-five Minutes from Broadway, Broadway Jones, The Man Who Owns Broadway, Hello, Broadway!*—while never quite articulating exactly what made Broadway so strange and wonderful. At one point, in *Broadway Jones,* two of Cohan's characters, Josie and Jones, try to pin it down.

> JOSIE: What is Broadway? . . . a street?
> JONES: Sure, it's the greatest street in the world.
> JOSIE: Some people say it's terrible.

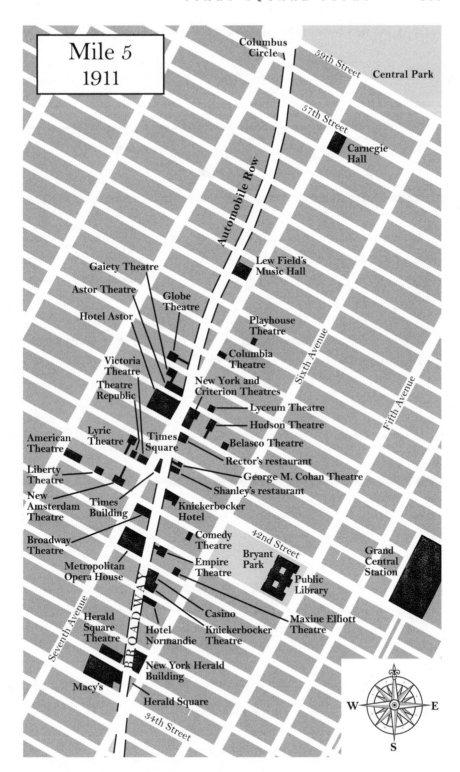

Mile 5
1911

Columbus Circle
59th Street
Central Park
57th Street
Carnegie Hall
Automobile Row
Lew Field's Music Hall
Gaiety Theatre
Astor Theatre
Globe Theatre
Hotel Astor
Playhouse Theatre
Sixth Avenue
Victoria Theatre
Columbia Theatre
Theatre Republic
New York and Criterion Theatres
Fifth Avenue
Lyceum Theatre
Hudson Theatre
American Theatre
Lyric Theatre
Times Square
Belasco Theatre
Liberty Theatre
Rector's restaurant
George M. Cohan Theatre
New Amsterdam Theatre
Times Building
Shanley's restaurant
Knickerbocker Hotel
Broadway Theatre
Comedy Theatre
42nd Street
Bryant Park
Grand Central Station
Metropolitan Opera House
Empire Theatre
Public Library
Seventh Avenue
Casino
Maxine Elliott Theatre
Herald Square Theatre
Hotel Normandie
Knickerbocker Theatre
BROADWAY
New York Herald Building
Macy's
Herald Square
34th Street

W E
S

JONES: Philadelphia people.

JOSIE: And some says it's wonderful.

JONES: That's just it. It's terribly wonderful.

JOSIE: I don't understand.

JONES: Nobody understands Broadway. People hate it and don't know why. People love it and don't know why. It's just because it's Broadway.

JOSIE: That's a mystery, isn't it?

JONES: That's just what it is, a mystery.

Cohan had spent his entire childhood on the road, never staying in one place for long. As an infant, he had been put down for naps in backstage trunks and boardinghouse bureaus, and no doubt romanticized Broadway because it was the closest he ever came to a real home.

"I guess Broadway, for me, was everything in life I've never had," he once said. "My education, and the friendships, games, adventures, and just plain fun of boyhood and growing up."

CHAPTER 23

BROADWAY GHOSTS

—

LITTLE *JOHNNY JONES*, FEATURING A CAST OF EIGHTY AND enough sets, props, and costumes to fill two baggage cars, traveled to Boston, Pittsburgh, Chicago, Los Angeles, and everywhere in between: Rock Island, Illinois; Clarksburg, West Virginia; Newport News, Virginia; Pensacola, Florida; Grand Forks, North Dakota; and countless other cities and towns, while its songs swept the country in the form of sheet music and the new-fangled phonograph records that were bringing the sounds of Broadway directly into the homes of small-town America.

"Do you like music? If you had one of these Talking Machines do you know what it would mean to you and your family?" read one advertisement in 1906. "Imagine yourself on Broadway; everybody is craning his neck to catch a sign of the procession about to pass. It's coming—hear that? That's the incomparable Sousa; see the drum major. Can you hear the trombone solo, and now the full band again?"

Broadway had become New York's chief cultural export. For many Americans it was less a place than a state of mind, a perpetual dream of success. Those seeking fame and fortune on the Broadway stage came by the thousands to New York, lining up for auditions in Shubert Alley, which ran between the Shubert and Booth theaters and the Hotel Astor, congregating in hallways outside the offices of agents, and pestering producers with pleading letters.

"I am a girl eighteen years old, of fairly good appearance, I should say, with brown eyes and hair," one letter to David Belasco began:

From the time I was a child I have loved the theatre. Nothing else has ever interested me nearly so much. I think I have some real talent for the stage—that is, my family and all my friends tell me I have. I have acted in several amateur plays in our city and have even had some of the most important parts. I have always received much applause.

After thinking it over carefully I am writing you to ask if you can find a chance for me in any of your companies. I can even come to New York to see you if you think there is any hope. I would prefer to act serious parts because I believe I have emotional ability. I would not expect to do very prominent work during the first year or two, so I would not ask very much pay at the start. Will you please consider my application, for it means so much to me?

Yours very truly,
Agnes Anderson

The percentages weren't in Agnes's favor. Belasco never replied to her letter, instead using it as a cautionary tale in his 1919 manifesto *The Theatre Through Its Stage Door.*

"Success," Belasco wrote, "or what seems to be success, in amateur theatricals . . . yields the theatre an abundant harvest—those who mistake the kindly applause of their friends as proof that they have the acting gift."

The *Daily Telegram* of Clarksburg, West Virginia, called Broadway the "Street of Broken Hearts."

But they kept coming. Young women who grew up reading *Photoplay* and *Variety* and memorizing every detail in the lives of Ethel Barrymore, Blanche Bates, Maude Adams, and Minnie Maddern Fiske came to Broadway determined to follow in the footsteps of those renowned dramatic actresses. Others were lured by tales of the glamorous world of producer Florenz Ziegfeld Jr., a smooth Lothario with a thin smile, lavender shirts, and pockets filled with diamonds and candy. Ziegfeld had turned Anna Held, Fanny Brice, and Billie Burke into stars, and each fall recruited fresh new faces for his wildly popular, mildly naughty *Follies*. Belasco, meanwhile, had discovered Mary Pickford. Was it so far-fetched that an unknown gal from Tucson or Tallahassee might make it on Broadway?

But when things didn't work out, many young women found themselves stranded in New York with few employment alternatives. After Alice Germaine didn't make it on the stage, she took a room near Times Square and began working as an escort.

"I do not ask whether they are married," she said of her clients. "It makes no difference to me. I take them to dinner, to a dance or a performance. I have a regular rate—$10 for one man, $15 for two and $20 for three, with dinner and other expenses."

Grace Le Gendre came to New York from a small New England village, but took to drink and wound up imprisoned in the Tombs, the city jail, for skimming $2,000 from the Hotel Gregorian, where she worked as a cashier.

"The lure of New York beckons a girl to ruin and the lights of the Great White Way only dazzle and blind her," she told a reporter who interviewed her in her prison cell.

Ida Brown, twenty, left her hometown of Cortland, New York, for Broadway in 1915 and found work as a chorus girl at the Winter Garden Theatre. But only a few days later she took a joyride with a group of pleasure seekers and was killed in a head-on collision on a foggy stretch of Pelham Parkway. A United Press account of her death and funeral drew contrasts between Broadway's frivolous fantasy world and the appalling reality of Brown's body coming home in a baggage car. The story ran in newspapers all over the country, with local editors adding their own cautionary headlines: "Broadway's Old Story Retold in Girl's Death," "Story of Ida Brown Typical of Numerous 'Careers' on Stage," "Broadway Lights Are Not for Her," "Dares City's Clamor, Goes Home in Coffin."

Other women simply disappeared. Another wire service story

labeled Broadway the "port of missing maidens," and recounted the sad tales of Ruth Cruger, Dorothy Arnold, Florence Whittier, Helen McCarthy, and Jessie McCann, women who vanished without a trace. Of the estimated 3,500 missing persons reported in New York every year, the story claimed, 800 were never found, and half of those gone "permanently missing" were young women.

"The glamour of the Gay White Way has been dimmed by the general knowledge of its sordid, paltry viciousness," the *Washington Herald* proclaimed in 1911. Five years later journalist Ida McGlone Gibson stated that the Broadway of George M. Cohan was no more.

THAT WASN'T TRUE, exactly: Both Broadway and Cohan were still thriving, but by the teens it was clear that the Great White Way was changing. World War I temporarily dimmed Broadway's bright lights, which were switched off to save electricity. Then a prolonged Actors' Equity Association strike in 1919 ruined much of the esprit de corps that had existed between theater types. And then Prohibition arrived and turned Broadway on its head.

When the Volstead Act took effect, at midnight on January 17, 1920, waiters circulated among the booths and tables of Broadway's lobster palaces and glumly informed patrons they could no longer order alcoholic drinks. Beloved institutions soon went by the wayside; even Rector's couldn't survive without selling alcohol. Bootleggers became Broadway's new heroes, and organized crime transformed the Great White Way into an illicit landscape of speakeasies, cabarets, and nightclubs.

Things got really sordid on Broadway then, the beginning of a long slide into nefariousness that has only been arrested in the last twenty years. But the early years of Prohibition, especially the nine years before the Great Depression, also marked Broadway's creative peak: In 1927 alone, 264 new shows opened, including the ground-breaking *Show Boat* at the new Ziegfeld Theatre. Times Square's new Paramount, RKO Palace, Rivoli, and Loew's State theaters featured combinations of movies, live music, and vaudeville, while a boom in the construction of traditional playhouses brought the Apollo, the

Earl Carroll, the John Golden, and other new theaters to the surrounding blocks.

On any given week, visitors to Broadway could see, live on
stage, Ethel Barrymore, Noel Coward, the Great Houdini, the
Marx Brothers, Eddie Cantor, George Gershwin, Ivor Novello,
Alfred Lunt and Lynn Fontanne, Paul Robeson, Mae West, Rudy
Vallee, and W. C. Fields. They could go to new plays by O'Neill,
Odets, Shaw, Ibsen, and Dreiser, and movies starring Charlie
Chaplin, Douglas Fairbanks, Mary Pickford, Lon Chaney, Harold
Lloyd, Norma Shearer, and Rin-Tin-Tin. After the shows, they
could descend on Lindy's, the Beaux-Arts Grill, or the Club Ana-
tole for dinner, then head to Roseland for dancing, and then, too
drunk or exhausted or elated to go home, to Texas Guinan's cab-
aret for the rest of the night.

MARY LOUISE GUINAN had been one of those unlucky women who
came to Broadway with stars in their eyes but never quite made it.
She was born and raised in Waco, Texas, and moved to New York in
1906 with dreams of a career on the stage, but found only bit roles in
road productions. She had a brief moment of fame playing cowgirls
in silent films, hence the nickname "Texas," but by 1922 was just one
of many has-beens floating around Times Square. Prohibition was a
godsend for Guinan, the thing that, along with grit and hard work,
finally brought her fame and fortune.

She began working in nightclubs as a performing hostess, where
she attracted the attention of Larry Fay, a racketeer and owner of
a lucrative fleet of taxis. Fay longed to mingle with the city's social
elite, and in 1922 he and Guinan opened the El Fey Club on 44th
Street, just east of Broadway. When federal agents padlocked the club
in 1925, Guinan momentarily moved her act—and her catchphrase,
"Hello, suckers!"—to vaudeville, and then opened a new club with
Fay a few blocks from the first one.

By 1927 Guinan, an angular woman with a blond bob and a fond-
ness for garish jewelry and red stockings, had detached herself from
Fay (who was later gunned down in another club) and was running

the 300 Club on 54th Street. Guinan had become the toast of Broadway's Prohibition netherworld, her regular patrons an improbable cross-section of the city: Society types from Fifth Avenue, Wall Street bankers, prominent judges, and Mayor Jimmy Walker, along with tourists, writers, baseball players, boxers, and assorted mobsters, leeches, and grifters.

Damon Runyon was often there doing research for the "Broadway stories" he began publishing in *Cosmopolitan* and *Collier's* in 1931. Brimming with allegorical "guys" and "dolls" with names like Regret, Sorrowful, Lola, Silk, and the Brain, all of whom spoke in vivid, present-tense prose peppered with Yiddish-inflected jazz-age slang—"scratch" for money, "chill" for relax, "equalizer" or "Roscoe" for gun—Runyon's stories were largely based on the 300 Club's crowd of nighthawks. Guinan herself appeared occasionally as "Miss Missouri Martin."

The 300 Club was small as cabarets went, with barely room for a kitchen, an orchestra in the corner, twenty to thirty tables, and a small dance floor. Chinese lanterns lent the place a soft, mysterious red glow. Guinan rarely arrived at the club before one in the morning, creating a nightly buzz of anticipation among her guests, who whiled away the hours before her grand entrance by listening to the orchestra, buying cigarettes from the cigarette girl, and eating sandwiches ordered from a battalion of waiters in red uniforms.

Guinan blew into her club, English writer Stephen Graham wrote after a visit in 1927, like an errant firework. Graham watched in fascination as Guinan circulated among the tables, kissing cheeks and caressing outstretched arms and calling everyone "darling," and then climbed onto a stool in front of the orchestra to preside over a *Ziegfeld Follies*–like revue that featured choruses of scantily clad women. Waiters hooted and hollered and encouraged the crowd to make as much noise as possible. The evening's entertainment culminated in an antic snowball fight, using "snowballs" of white felt.

Then came more dancing and drinking and a fistfight or two. Graham described patrons passing out on tables as night gave way to dawn, and three drunken women singing "Bye Bye Blackbird."

When Graham finally emerged from the club into the street, he was astonished to find the sun fully up and people striding purposefully to work. Guinan, following her morning routine, had a sandwich with her staff and a few friends and finally headed home to a house in Greenwich Village, where she had nailed four blankets over the bedroom window to keep out the sun and lived with a parrot that could only say "telephone" and "go to hell."

MILE 6

COLUMBUS CIRCLE
TO 79TH STREET

CHAPTER 24

THE BOULEVARD

—

ANYONE STAGGERING UP BROADWAY IN 1927 AFTER A LONG
night at the 300 Club would have passed through Automobile
Row, a strip of offices and showrooms for General Motors, Ford,
Buick, Cadillac, Studebaker, and Packard that had turned Broadway between Times Square and Columbus Circle into a futuristic
thoroughfare devoted to the wonders of the internal combustion
engine. At Columbus Circle, Broadway grazes the southwest corner
of Central Park and enters the expanse of the West Side. And once
past 59th Street, even an inebriated daybreak wanderer would have
noticed that Broadway had suddenly become an entirely different
street.

Broadway above Columbus Circle is wider, grander, and greener
than the street below it, and is a remnant of the Boulevard, or the
Grand Boulevard, the romantic vision of Andrew Haswell Green,
a well-connected mid-nineteenth-century lawyer and comptroller
of the powerful Central Park Commission. Green's Boulevard came
about because of an 1865 legislative act granting the Central Park
Commission absolute power in planning *all* of Manhattan above 155th
Street, the part of the island left unresolved by the 1811 Commissioners' Plan. In addition to coming up with a master plan for upper
Manhattan, the act also empowered the Central Park Commission to

lay out a "road or public drive" running up the West Side from 59th Street, "as far north . . . as the commissioners may determine," which ended up being all the way up to 168th Street. The act stipulated that the path of the new road should follow the old Bloomingdale Road between 59th and 106th streets; north of that point the commissioners could lay out the new drive wherever they wanted.

The Bloomingdale Road opened in 1703, beginning where the Bowery ended at present-day 23rd Street, and ran like a ribbon up the West Side. The road was about 65 feet wide, although its width was inconsistent and it was full of unexpected jogs and doglegs. It was never paved and throughout its history was often flooded. But the Bloomingdale Road was, by all accounts, a beautiful country thoroughfare lined with trees and fences and dotted on both sides with farms and estates, streams and ponds.

Well into the nineteenth century, Manhattan's West Side was called Bloomingdale, named by seventeenth-century Dutch settlers in honor of Bloemendaal, a city in northern Holland. Less a cohesive village than a wider district, Bloomingdale was a world apart from the big city to the south, and traveling up and down the Bloomingdale Road offered New Yorkers a chance to breathe fresh air and enjoy a few hours of solitude away from the daily grind of urban life. Horticulturalist Michael Floy Jr., for one, much preferred running errands on the Bloomingdale Road to selling camellias and dahlias from the family nursery on Broadway near 12th Street.

"I found today that 'labor was rest,' and coming down the Bloomingdale road I had a very good time," Floy wrote in his diary in the spring of 1834, adding that on his way back to town he had admired the trees, shrubbery, and "handsome little gardens" along the road and had been delighted by the sound of birds and frogs "tuning their voices."

Until 1811, when Eighth Avenue opened, the Bloomingdale Road was the only north-south route up the West Side. Eighth Avenue was straight as an arrow, topography be damned, one of twelve avenues laid out in the 1811 Commissioners' Plan that also called for the Bloomingdale Road's erasure. But somehow, perhaps through the intercession of the Astor family and other wealthy landowners who owned building lots along its path, the Bloomingdale Road wasn't closed, even as other highways and lanes superseded by the city grid gradually faded away. Legislative acts in 1838 and 1847 affirmed the Bloomingdale Road's continuation on city maps, and between 34th and 86th streets it was even widened to a uniform 75 feet. But when Green and the Central Park commissioners began plotting the Boulevard in 1865, the Bloomingdale Road north of 86th Street remained a muddy country lane, its very existence precarious: At any time it could have been closed by order of the city's Common Council.

The 1811 Commissioners' Plan was a product of the American Enlightenment, Cartesian in its insistence on straight lines. But by the time Green began considering construction of the Boulevard, Romanticism, with its allowance for ambiguity and approval of emotional responses to nature and art, and the Picturesque aesthetic, with its notion of idealized landscape as artistic composition—"scenery"—had become entrenched in the American consciousness. Calvert Vaux and Frederick Law Olmsted codified both ideas in Central Park, an 840-acre scenic tableaux built over the barren city-owned Common Lands in the middle of Manhattan.

If Central Park was nature as stage set, then Green's conception of the Boulevard was that of a verdant thread tugged loose from the park and stitched onto the West Side. Green speculated that the Bloomingdale Road's crookedness, which created oddly shaped building lots along its edges, gave it "peculiar value" in a city governed by the Commissioners' Plan grid. He was also astute enough to see that the leftover, triangular fragments of land created by the Bloomingdale Road's diagonal collision with the grid weren't throwaways but opportunities for creating public places along the lines of Bowling Green, City Hall Park, and Union and Madison squares; all of which had originated not by smoothing out spatial differences but by celebrating them. Where the Bloomingdale Road crossed Ninth and Tenth avenues, Green imagined urbane squares that might afford space "for monumental ornamentation" and would "add much to the variety and magnificence of the drive." (The two triangular fragments where Broadway crossed Ninth Avenue eventually became Lincoln Square and Dante Square; the wedges of land where Broadway crossed Tenth Avenue became Sherman Square and Verdi Square.)

Because of its extreme width—150 feet, much wider even than the 100-foot-wide avenues of the Commissioners' Plan—the Boulevard didn't so much preserve as obliterate the Bloomingdale Road. Although the extra width allowed for a 30-foot-wide "mall" running up its center, complete with a footpath shaded by elms, the Boulevard was a highway built for speed, a place where fast trotting horses and buggy teams might be given free rein.

"The law of the street is motion, not rest," Green declared, an insight that would have seemed perfectly obvious in any place other than traffic-clogged New York.

What Green was after were the wide boulevards that Georges-Eugène Haussmann, at the behest of Napoleon III, had begun plowing through the dense streets of Paris only a few years earlier, a vast public works project that left many New Yorkers feeling jealous.

"The boulevards and new avenues [of Paris] altogether are unequalled in extent and magnificence by anything of the kind in the world, and are a subject of pride, not only to Parisians, but to all France," the *New York Sun* raved in 1867. "Whether New York or Brooklyn will ever equal or surpass Paris in the elegance of their thoroughfares, depends entirely on the taste and enterprise of the people."

Green, not lacking in taste or enterprise, imagined the Boulevard running through a picturesque suburban landscape punctuated by monuments, civic institutions, and the opulent villas of wealthy merchants, bankers, and industrialists. In the 1860s the West Side was something of a blank slate, and it was still possible to project dreams onto its vacant lots, overgrown eighteenth-century country estates, and streets that had been surveyed but never opened.

The first piece of Green's project, a "Grand Circle" (today's Columbus Circle) where Broadway crossed Eighth Avenue at 59th Street, opened in 1867. Construction of the Boulevard began the following year, its crews of laborers drawn heavily from the city's burgeoning ranks of Irish immigrants. In 1870, Tammany Hall Democrats led by

William M. "Boss" Tweed rewrote the city's charter in the name of "home rule" and forced it through the state legislature. The Central Park Commission was absorbed into the city's new Parks Department under the direction of Tweed crony Peter B. Sweeny, and Tweed became director of public works. Green, an anti-Tammany Democrat, was temporarily relegated to the sidelines.

In July of 1871 the *New York Times* began printing long itemized lists of expenses that the city, under Tammany-backed mayor, A. Oakey Hall, had shelled out for various projects including, most egregiously, the new county courthouse behind City Hall, a seemingly bottomless pit of padded contracts and kickbacks. Tweed had pushed for the widening of Broadway between 34th and 59th streets, supposedly in order to pocket part of the assessments, and there were allegations that the Boulevard, too, was nothing more than a Tammany boondoggle. But work on the Boulevard did proceed under Tweed, even if progress was slow. Ironically, construction of the Boulevard led indirectly to Tweed's downfall.

THE CITY'S IRISH CATHOLICS were, in a general sense, supportive of Tammany Hall and tended to support Tammany Democrats in elections; Republicans and anti-Tammany Democrats, meanwhile, viewed the growing political power of Irish Catholics with alarm. In an era of widespread anti-Catholic bigotry, when *Harper's Weekly* cartoonist Thomas Nast depicted Irish Catholics as apes, Tweed fashioned himself as a protector of the rights of Irish Catholics to live and work in peace. But Irish Catholics were taking abuse from all sides: The mainstream press didn't like them; neither did wealthy Republicans or anti-Tammany Democrats. And the sectarian violence between Irish Catholics and Protestants had spread from Ireland to America.

Among Irish Protestants, July 12 was a day of celebration to commemorate William of Orange's 1690 victory over Catholic forces led by James II at the Battle of the Boyne. At the center of the annual celebration was a parade organized by the Protestant Orange Order, a fraternity established in Ireland in 1795. The Loyal Orange Institution of the United States of America was formed in 1869 and in short order there were thirteen lodges in New York City with some 1,300 members.

On July 12, 1869, Orangemen parading up the Boulevard met a crew of Irish Catholic laborers working on the road. Insults were hurled back and forth and the two groups traded gunfire near 115th Street. No one was killed, although fifteen were badly wounded. The following year, July 12, 1870, the Orangemen marched up the Boulevard again, and as they passed a group of Irish Catholic laborers swinging pickaxes and shoveling dirt at 69th Street broke into the anti-Catholic anthem "Croppies Lie Down":

> *Water, water,*
> *Holy water;*
> *Sprinkle the Catholics, every one;*
> *We'll cut them asunder,*
> *And make them lie under,*
> *The Protestant boys will carry the gun.*

Enraged, the laborers stopped working and followed the parade to Elm Park, a pleasure garden on the grounds of the old Charles Ward Apthorp estate at Tenth Avenue and 90th Street, where the Orangemen were holding a picnic. Taking up positions behind the garden's perimeter wall, the laborers attacked the crowd of 2,000 to 3,000 picnickers with pistols and rocks. Women and children fled in panic, Orangemen returned fire, and a full-scale riot erupted. Five people were killed.

The next year, July 12, 1871, the Orangemen, escorted by police and companies of the New York militia, marched south on Eighth Avenue through a neighborhood with a high concentration of Irish Catholics. Near 27th Street, skittish militiamen opened fire directly into the crowd standing on the sidewalks, killing at least forty-seven and injuring another fifty or so. The victims included women and children. The press, Republicans, and anti-Tammany Democrats blamed the fiasco on Catholics and praised the militia for upholding law and order.

"[I] have heard only one sentiment expressed to day—"diarist George Templeton Strong wrote, "viz. gratification that the Irish Roughs have had a rough lesson." Strong called the Irish "ferocious human pigs" and "gorillas."

The slaughter in Eighth Avenue—which didn't even stop the Orangemen, who continued marching past the dead and dying to the parade's planned terminus at Cooper Union—weakened Tammany Hall's grip on city politics. A chorus of detractors and reformers led by a newly organized "Committee of Seventy" was already taking back control of the city when, ten days after the parade, the *New York Times* printed its long lists of dubious Tammany expenditures. As part of the reforms that followed, Green was appointed as the city's comptroller, Tweed was convicted of embezzlement—he died in jail in 1878—and the Boulevard became, once again, Green's project.

But the Boulevard was a legal and topographical quagmire no matter who was in charge: There were complex assessments and awards to property owners along the route and flooding caused by complicated grading—it's not easy to level one street without forcing water into the streets around it—and through the 1890s the Boulevard resembled nothing so much as an unpaved, linear mud puddle.

CHAPTER 25

"DOWN THERE"

———

THE WEST SIDE SHANTYTOWNS OF THE IRISH LABORERS WHO built the Boulevard grew into Skinnersville, one of the largest Irish enclaves in the city. In 1867, Irish-American journalist Charles Dawson Shanly walked through the area and saw goats standing atop rock outcroppings and children in rags.

Then came row houses and, in the 1880s, four- and five-story tenements. Blacks began moving into the area in the early 1890s, having been displaced from the old Tenderloin and Hell's Kitchen to the south, and were soon joined by others migrating to the city from the American South and West Indies. White landlords did everything they could to discourage the influx, sometimes doubling the rent they would have charged to a white tenant and refusing to perform basic maintenance. But blacks kept coming, and by 1900 they outnumbered the neighborhood's Irish ten to one. People began calling the area Nigger Hill, a nickname, Jacob Riis wrote in 1902, that indicated the neighborhood's racial chasm "with unerring accuracy."

Despite its name, much of the enclave actually lay in a ravine, the remains of a creek that had once flowed west from the Bloomingdale Road to the Hudson River. Newspapers called the neighborhood the "declivity," locals called it the "dip," and cops referred to it simply as "down there." That the police, many of them of Irish descent, frequently beat up black bystanders for no apparent reason was a fact of everyday life, but unlike in the Tenderloin or Hell's Kitchen, blacks in the ravine began fighting back. It became the worst battleground in the city, and in the years following the Spanish-American War acquired yet another nickname: San Juan Hill.

Around seven in the evening of Friday July 14, 1905, an elderly white peddler of second-hand clothing, who had been menaced by Irish youths in the neighborhood in the past, asked a black customer and acquaintance, Henry W. Williams, to escort him as he made his rounds. At the corner of Tenth Avenue and 63rd Street seventeen-year-old Edward Connelly attacked the peddler; when Williams intervened, he was set upon. A passing patrolman arrested Connelly, but Connelly's friends pelted the cops with bricks and bottles. Black bystanders then attacked Connelly's gang, and by the time police reserves arrived on the scene, whites and blacks, both men and women, were fighting in the streets, firing pistols at one another, and hurling projectiles from windows and rooftops.

It became a full-scale riot that ranged from 57th to 68th streets, with the worst fighting in the ravine along 62nd and 63rd streets. Fleeing blacks tried to take refuge on Tenth Avenue streetcars, only to find the cars hemmed in and unable to move. Conductors and motormen hid under the seats as bricks shattered the car windows. Roosevelt Hospital was inundated with the wounded, most of them blacks. The police didn't gain control of the streets until after midnight.

In the tense days and nights that followed, hundreds of police stood guard on street corners. But just after midnight on July 18, four patrolmen were attacked by a group of blacks in front of George Foster's dance hall, a notorious dive on the first floor of a tenement at 236 West 62nd Street. Another riot erupted, with hundreds of blacks shooting at police and showering them with bricks.

In the aftermath it was noted that, even though both blacks and whites took part in the riots, police had arrested blacks in disproportionate numbers, just as they had during a 1900 riot in Hell's Kitchen. Rev. George H. Sims, a community leader and pastor of the Union Baptist Church on 63rd Street, met with Police Commissioner William McAdoo and stressed that the overwhelming majority of San Juan Hill's black population were hardworking, law-abiding, church-going citizens.

"If the police will only differentiate between the good and bad negroes, and not knock on the head every colored man they see in a riot, we shall be quite satisfied," Sims told a *Tribune* reporter. "As it is, there is no safety for any negro in this part of the city at any time."

McAdoo launched an investigation into police abuse of blacks and transferred John Cooney, captain of the 26th Precinct, the neighborhood's police station on 68th Street, out of the district. Still, McAdoo blamed the riots on the "lawless colored element" and his patrolmen tended to agree with him.

"They are without exception the worst lot of niggers in this town or any other . . . ," one cop told a *Sun* reporter after the riots had subsided. "They ought to be sent back to Africa, or to the Philippines, or off the earth."

EVENTUALLY THE "Naughty Negroes of San Juan Hill," as the *New York Sun* labeled them in 1905, were indeed "sent off the earth" or, at least, displaced. In 1955, San Juan Hill was designated for urban renewal under Title I of the Federal Housing Act of 1949, which allowed private developers to buy blighted properties from the city at steep discounts, with two-thirds of the resale write-down subsidized by the federal government and one-third by the city. The project was largely the vision of Robert Moses, chairman of the mayor's Committee on Slum Clearance Plans, and John D. Rockefeller Jr.

The Lincoln Square Urban Renewal Project demolished almost all of the neighborhood, displacing 7,000 families in the process, and replaced it with a sixteen-acre campus of housing projects, public high schools, new buildings for Fordham University, and the gleaming Modernist mecca of Lincoln Center for the Performing Arts, its theaters and concert halls perched above an immense subterranean parking lot.

The last glimpse of San Juan Hill came in 1961, when its deserted tenements were used as stage sets for the film *West Side Story*.

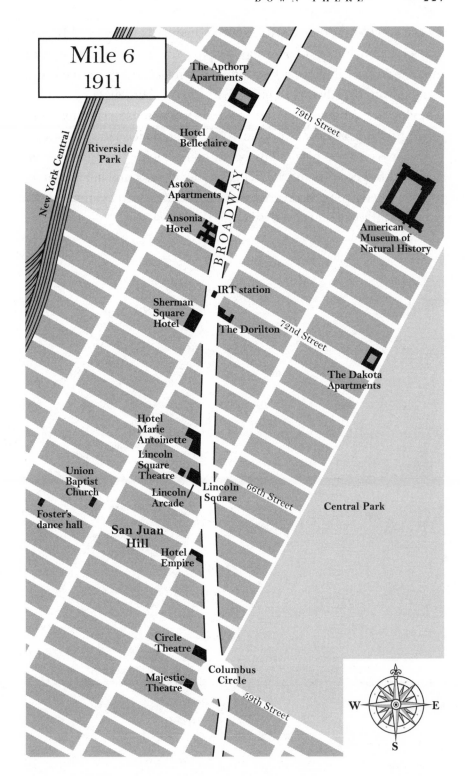

Mile 6
1911

The Apthorp
Apartments

79th Street

New York Central

Riverside
Park

Hotel
Belleclaire

Astor
Apartments

Ansonia
Hotel

BROADWAY

American
Museum of
Natural History

IRT station

Sherman
Square
Hotel

The Dorilton

72nd Street

The Dakota
Apartments

Hotel
Marie
Antoinette

Lincoln
Square
Theatre

Union
Baptist
Church

Lincoln/
Arcade

Lincoln
Square

66th Street

Central Park

Foster's
dance hall

San Juan
Hill

Hotel
Empire

Circle
Theatre

Columbus
Circle

Majestic
Theatre

59th Street

W   E

S

Lincoln Center didn't just erase San Juan Hill; it reversed Broadway's relationship to its own topography. You no longer walk *down* into San Juan Hill; you walk *up* into Lincoln Center, travertine stairs leading from Broadway to a plinth with a large fountain at the center. The chief attraction is the Metropolitan Opera House, relocated from its original site at Broadway and 40th Street, which faces Broadway from across a wide plaza. The opera house's lobby is a multi-level, hollowed-out core behind a soaring façade of glass, and during intermissions its patrons, always dressed to the nines, lean against velvet-covered railings and stare down into the abyss.

CHAPTER 26

CHICKENS ON THE ROOF

———

THE ANSONIA HOTEL BEGAN CONSTRUCTION IN 1899 ON THE west side of Broadway between 73rd and 74th streets and opened in 1904, the same year the subway began running beneath the street. It wasn't the only ambitious Parisian-inspired apartment building on Broadway: The Dorilton, an exuberant confection of mansard roofs and gamboling stone cherubs, was built simultaneously at the northeast corner of Broadway and 71st Street and featured all the latest gadgets: long-distance telephones and glass-lined refrigerators in each room, three elevators, and electricity "free at all hours."

But from the beginning the Ansonia was a world unto itself and might just be the most wonderful building on all of Broadway, a seventeen-story architectural cliff of nooks and crannies, quoins, brackets, scrolls, consoles, and laughing stone satyrs. French architect Paul E. M. Duboy designed the Ansonia in the Belle Époque mode, with swelling mansard roofs pierced by dormer windows and two *poivrières*—French for pepper pots—at the corners and castle-like turrets originally mounted with tall, open copper lanterns. The creamy tone of its limestone, brick, and terra-cotta façade allows the building, like the Flatiron Building further to the south, to transform dramatically depending on the light and weather, "black as slate in

The Ansonia Hotel was a world unto itself.

the fog, white as tufa in sunlight," as Saul Bellow described it in his 1956 novel *Seize the Day.*

In its heyday the Ansonia was the most deluxe of Broadway's "apartment hotels," which combined the comforts of home with the amenities of a swank hotel. Residents received fresh towels and linen every day, plus light bulbs, dishes, and free stationery; could order room service meals or dine in a restaurant featuring evening concerts and a menu of littleneck clams, turtle soup, shad, lamb, duck, and calf's head; and frolic in the building's palm court and billiard room. There was a barbershop in the basement, along with a Turkish bath and what was touted as the world's largest swimming pool. It was, one postcard proclaimed, the "Most Superbly Equipped House in The World."

Five recessed courts, one on Broadway and two each on 73rd and

74th streets, ran in shafts up to the roof, cutting the building into six monumental chunks that emphasized its verticality. Inside, off an ornate ground-floor lobby, a vertiginous marble stair with mahogany handrails climbed straight up the building through its center, culminating in a large skylight at the top. Apartments were organized along two 10-foot-wide corridors that intersected a third corridor 12 feet wide, forming an H-pattern and running like highways through the building.

The Ansonia was supposedly fireproof. It wasn't—there were fires—but its walls were an astounding 3 feet thick, closer to the dimensions of a fort than an apartment building. The thick walls soundproofed the apartments, an unintentional byproduct of its fireproofing, and the Ansonia quickly filled with singers, songwriters, voice teachers, and musicians. Metropolitan Opera conductor Arturo Toscanini lived there; Enrico Caruso is supposed to have lived there but didn't. Babe Ruth, never known for musical talent, moved in shortly after the Boston Red Sox sold him to the New York Yankees in 1919, and in 1927 made the unfortunate decision to take up the saxophone. The Ansonia's thick walls shielded his neighbors from the racket. (Ruth was often sighted in a bathrobe descending to the basement barbershop for a morning shave.)

The Ansonia's one- and two-bedroom apartments rented for as little as $900 per year—about $23,000, or $1,900 a month, in today's dollars—and so weren't out of reach of the writers, teachers, and actors who flocked to the neighborhood. But the Ansonia wasn't marketed as a refuge for the middle class; it was promoted as the height of opulent city living, a palace where a fully furnished, fifteen-room, four-bath apartment went for $6,000 a year in rent—about $12,500 a month in today's dollars. (Florenz Ziegfeld Jr.'s palatial apartment had more than enough space for him and his wife Billie Burke, but still not enough to include his mistress Lillian Lorraine, whom Ziegfeld set up in a separate apartment in the same building.)

The bigger, more expensive apartments unfolded like a dream, room after room after room. There always seemed to be another one waiting through the next aperture: parlors, bedrooms, round dining rooms, oval-shaped libraries, hidden servants' quarters—an urban fantasy of infinite space. It was like that dream many apartment dwellers have, in which they discover an entirely new set of rooms they didn't know they had. *This is mine, too?*

THE ANSONIA WAS the pet project of William Earle Dodge Stokes of the wealthy and socially prominent Stokes family. He had eyes set close together, a long nose, a handlebar mustache, and a decidedly eccentric personality: At age forty-three Stokes married nineteen-year-old Rita Hernandez de Alba Acosta, an American shipping heiress of Cuban and Spanish descent. The marriage, predictably, ended in divorce. In 1911 he was shot twice in the legs by vaudevillian Lillian Graham at the Varuna Hotel, Broadway and 80th Street, after he tried to retrieve a packet of compromising love letters. His second marriage, to Helen Ellwood, also ended in divorce, with the ugly details splashed across the front pages of newspapers. He was a wily misanthrope who dumped the Ansonia's waste, including hot ashes, in a heap on a vacant lot on 79th Street and then laughed it off when neighbors complained.

Stokes owned a stud farm in Kentucky and was the author of a vile tract, *The Right to Be Well Born; or, Horse Breeding in its Relation to Eugenics*, in which he urged the adoption of horse-breeding techniques in human procreation. Like other eugenicists, he characterized immigrants as "the diseased offscouring of Europe and the Orient" and recommended the sterilization of society's "defectives."

"Our pure healthy New England blood can no longer cross with or assimilate the rotten, foreign, diseased blood of ages, which the gates of our immigration laws now swing wide open and allow to flow in upon us," he fumed.

Stokes detested labor unions, their ranks swelled by recent immigrants, and reserved special scorn for the plasterers, metal lathers, and sheet-metal workers who continually walked out on strike and delayed the Ansonia's completion. In 1903, Stokes was hospitalized, due, he said, to stress induced by constant negotiations with unions.

But Stokes loved animals and, since he knew a thing or two about breeding, decided to try his hand at farming—on the Ansonia's roof.

Soon there were cows grazing high above Broadway, along with goats, geese, ducks, five hundred chickens, and a pig named Nanki-Poo. A bear cub had the run of the place. The Ansonia's freight elevators were sized for horses, so that Stokes's tenants could bring their mounts to the roof for exercise. The rooftop chickens were so productive—maybe it was the fresh air—that Stokes was soon inundated with eggs and began delivering them every morning to his tenants and selling them from a market in the basement. In 1907 the Board of Health finally got wind, perhaps literally, of Stokes's farm and ejected the entire menagerie.

STOKES DIED IN 1926, but the Ansonia remained in his family until it was finally sold in 1945. Three years later it was sold again, this time to a consortium called, ominously, the Ansonia Holding Corporation. Over the years the company lived up to its name, holding on to the Ansonia but doing little else while, bit by bit, the grandeur of the once-majestic building faded. Robert Reinhart, whose family moved into the Ansonia in 1913, when he was six years old, recalled a childhood spent bicycling and roller-skating down corridors that, with each passing year, grew grimier with age. By the time Reinhart moved out in 1954, much of the Ansonia's ornamental ironwork had been stripped from its façade, the corner lanterns were missing, the Broadway entry court had been blocked up, and the roof was festooned with television aerials. Gene Yellin, who grew up in the 1950s on 71st Street, near Broadway, remembers childhood afternoons spent exploring the Ansonia's dank corridors and stairwell with a gaggle of local kids. The building was still full of musicians then, but he never heard a single note escaping through the thick walls.

CHAPTER 27

HARSENVILLE

—

NEITHER YELLIN NOR ANY OF HIS CHILDHOOD PALS REAL-
ized their thriving neighborhood of bakeries, delicatessens, candy
stores, groceries, bookstores, automats, drugstores, movie theaters,
and dry cleaners clustered around the crossing of Broadway and
Tenth (Amsterdam) Avenue—like a stage set, really, with the Ansonia and the Sherman Square Hotel as the tattered props of a regal but
rundown backdrop—had once been a farm, part of a large tract that
had been in the Dyckman family since 1701. Five years after Nicholas
Dyckman died, in 1758, Jacob Harsen bought, for a price of £1,210,
94 prime acres of Dyckman's land. The Harsen farm stretched all
the way from the Common Lands at the center of the island west to
the Hudson River shore, with the Bloomingdale Road running right
through the middle.

Harsen took over Dyckman's old house, a Dutch-style manse on
a hill just west of present-day Tenth Avenue between 70th and 71st
streets, and the village that grew up around it eventually included a
church, tavern, military academy, grocery and post office, firehouse,
and assorted houses, stables, and artisans' shops straddling the
Bloomingdale Road from, approximately, present-day 68th Street
to 76th Street. In 1773, Harsen's nephew, also named Jacob Harsen,

inherited the southern half of his uncle's estate and moved into the old Dyckman house, where he continued his uncle's role as the de facto village leader.

The centerpiece of what became known as Harsenville was the Bloomingdale Dutch Reformed Church, a small, one-room frame building, painted white, on the west side of the Bloomingdale Road between present-day 69th and 70th streets. Harsen, with help from three other community stalwarts, had founded and built the church on his own land, some 300 feet southeast of his house, in 1805. Eleven years later, a bigger stone church, topped with a bell tower and surrounded by a graveyard within a picket fence, was built on a knoll at the northeast corner of the Bloomingdale Road and 68th Street, facing the river. Pew-holders in the church included lawyer Alexander Hamilton Jr., banker Nathaniel Prime, landowner William Rhinelander, merchants Archibald Gracie and John G. Coster, and Clement Clarke Moore, author of "A Visit from St. Nicholas."

Community and church were almost completely intertwined, with a small circle of families—Harsens, Hoppers, Havemeyers, Strikers, Beekmans, Somerindykes, Livingstons—serving as elders of both the village and the church. Harsenville was starkly divided by class and race: On Sundays, elders, deacons, and wealthy pew-holders took their places at the front of the church; tradespeople, artisans, and visitors crammed into the middle; and, crowded into six reserved pews and partially blocked from view by two wood-burning stoves, "colored" congregants, many of them the slaves of the church's most prominent families, sat at the back.

Well after Broadway's first mile had developed into a modern thoroughfare of shops, theaters, and museums, Harsenville remained a time warp where austere men named Jacob and Ichabod and women named Sarah and Hannah sang hymns to a tuning fork—musical instruments being considered the machines of the devil—and closely monitored their neighbors' "walk and conversation" for telltale signs of backsliding. (Even under constant surveillance, Harsenvillians were prone to occasional scandals, as when, in 1814, Philip Webbers, a church deacon and pillar of the community, was found to have surreptitiously joined a *Baptist* church in New York—the equivalent in Harsenville of falling in with pirates in Madagascar. He was excommunicated.)

By the time Jacob Harsen died, in 1835, Harsenville's population had grown to roughly 2,000 people. But the congregation of its Dutch Reformed Church had shrunk to just twenty-eight families, and the nature of the community was drastically changing. Assessors and street commissioners moved into the area like an invading army. The old farms were cut up into lots, and Irish immigrants soon had the village surrounded with shantytowns, the advance guard of an encroaching city that within a few decades would erase Harsenville from the map.

NO TRACES OF HARSENVILLE remain today, other than the land itself, which still rises and falls between Central Park and the Hudson River in much the same way it did one hundred years ago. And there is Broadway, which reveals in its curving trajectory at least an echo of the Bloomingdale Road that once ran through the middle of the village.

When Harsenville is remembered at all, it is because of an odd story that grew up around it concerning French royal fugitives using the village as a sanctuary after fleeing to America during the Reign of Terror in the 1790s. Harsenville historian Hopper Striker Mott, writing in 1908, described the center of this improbable circle as one "Mme. d'Auliffe, *dame d'honneur* to Marie Antoinette." "Mme. d'Auliffe" built a house, called "Chevilly" after a suburb of Paris, west of the Bloomingdale Road between 72nd and 73rd streets and just north of the Jacob Harsen farm.

In Mott's account, at Chevilly "Mme. d'Auliffe" surrounded herself with a memorable cast of French exiles that included Charles Maurice de Talleyrand-Périgord, Simon-Louis-Pierre, marquis de Cubiéres— whom Mott describes as dashing up the Bloomingdale Road on a horse named "Monarque"—and one Colonel August de Singeron. Talleyrand actually did stay three weeks at Chevilly; the others never did. And, as historian Margaret Oppenheimer has recently discovered, "Auliffe" was actually a mispronunciation of "Olive" and the

**A fanciful 1863 print depicting Louis-Philippe guiding his pupils
through their lessons in the Teunis Somerindyck house
along the Bloomingdale Road.**

Olive family patriarch, Nicholas Olive, was a wealthy merchant, not a courtier.

The most arresting detail of the story is the claim that none other than Louis-Philippe, duc d'Orléans and future king of the French, showed up in Harsenville with his two fugitive brothers and a valet in tow. Louis-Philippe is supposed to have lived in the Teunis Somerindyck house, on the west side of the Bloomingdale Road between 75th and 76th streets, and, even more improbably, was said to have taught school there.

Louis-Philippe—in paintings, his chubby cheeks, black pompadour, and expansive sideburns give him a passing resemblance to late-period Elvis—did indeed escape from France to America, in 1794, but his base of operations was Philadelphia and he passed only briefly through New York. Throughout his American sojourn Louis-Philippe retained his regal manners—he was once kicked out of an inn in Virginia for insisting that his dinner be served in a private room, away from the rabble—and it's difficult to imagine the future sovereign reigning over a classroom of pint-sized Harsenvillians.

But the persistent vision of Louis-Philippe at work, *struggling* like any immigrant, on a stretch of rural highway that was later to become part of Broadway, the most American of American streets, is too good a story to disregard entirely. It's a classic Broadway scenario—"French King Proves Mettle on Great White Way"—that is as perfect as it is unlikely.

MILE 7

79TH STREET TO 106TH STREET

CHAPTER 28

THE RAVEN OF SPECULATION

—

EDGAR ALLAN POE MOVED FROM PHILADELPHIA TO NEW York on April 6, 1844, arriving by steamboat amid a downpour. The boat docked at Pier 2, on the Hudson River, and Poe bought an umbrella and set off purposefully through the hectic streets of lower Manhattan while his tubercular young wife Virginia waited on board. Within thirty minutes Poe had rented a room in a boardinghouse on Greenwich Street and returned to the pier to fetch Virginia. Left momentarily behind in Philadelphia were Virginia's mother, Maria Clemm, whom Poe affectionately called "Muddy," and Catterina, or "Kate," the family cat. Poe wrote to Muddy the next morning: All was well, he assured her, the boardinghouse's coffee excellent.

Poe had tried to make a go of it in New York at least twice before. He had lived there for some fifteen months in 1837–38 and visited again in June of 1842, but it hadn't worked out either time. Through Baltimore, Philadelphia, Richmond, and Washington, Poe had consistently made a mess of things, wearing out his welcome, trying his friends' patience with nonstop begging for loans, starting petty feuds with other authors, alienating potential business partners and, especially, drinking too much. But in New York in the spring of 1844, it looked like the beleaguered Poe might make a fresh start. He had refrained from drink on the trip, he swore to Muddy, and Virginia's hacking cough had subsided.

Within a week of arriving in the city Poe sold a news story to the *New York Sun* about a supposed Atlantic Ocean crossing of a hot-air balloon from England to Charleston, South Carolina, in three days; news that, had it been true, would have been hailed as an astounding, unprecedented achievement. But the story wasn't true; it was a complete fabrication in the tradition of the *Sun's* famous "moon hoax" of 1835, when Richard Adams Locke made up a story about the eminent British astronomer Sir John Herschel discovering a race of bat-winged people on the moon using a telescope with a 30-foot-diameter lens. Poe's balloon hoax was supposed to be a literary calling card, an announcement of sorts that he was back in New York.

It backfired: *New York Herald* publisher James Gordon Bennett dismissed Poe's hoax as "ridiculously put together" and called *Sun* publisher Moses Yale Beach a "blundering blockhead." That same day Beach printed a retraction. Poe, unbowed, protested: "There is nothing put forth in the Balloon-Story which is not in full keeping with the known facts of æronautic experience—which might not really have occurred."

One month later, Poe told poet Nathaniel Parker Willis that he was feeling ill and depressed. His prospects dwindling, he cadged loans from friends and moved Virginia, along with his mother-in-law and cat, to a farm on the Bloomingdale Road between present-day 82nd and 85th streets, some six miles north of the city.

THE FARM BELONGED to Patrick and Mary Brennan and comprised some 200 acres. Poe and family rented rooms on the second floor of the farmhouse, which faced the Hudson River from atop a hill some 300 feet east of the road, on the line of the future 84th Street. The house had been built in two sections: The southern half was taller and had the front door; the northern half included the kitchen. The roof was pitched, and both sections of the house were of wood frame with wood siding; it was in all respects typical of farmhouses of that era and completely unremarkable.

Poe's room had a fireplace on the north end and a writing table—the Brennans' daughter Margaret remembered it scattered with books and letters—situated between the front windows. Poe's view as he worked at his desk consisted of two large shade trees and Brennan's Pond in the foreground, then the Bloomingdale Road and fields and outcroppings of bedrock beyond it, and, in the background, the Hudson River and the New Jersey Palisades. Margaret Brennan recalled Poe sitting on the ground at Brennan's Pond, writing, and wandering over to a large outcropping overlooking the Hudson—the broad, flat rock is still there today, near 83rd Street and Riverside Drive—where he sat for hours gazing out at the river.

To make ends meet Poe peddled stories to magazines and filed dispatches for an obscure weekly newspaper, the *Columbia Spy* of Columbia, Pennsylvania. In the first installment, published May 14, 1844, Poe described the landscape surrounding the Brennan farm, in the heart of what was to become Broadway's seventh mile.

"I have been roaming far and wide over this island of Manna-hatta," he wrote. "Some portions of its interior have a certain air of rocky sterility which may impress some imaginations as simply *dreary*—to me it conveys the sublime. Trees are few; but some of the shrubbery is exceedingly picturesque."

The Brennan farm was still far removed from town then, its solitude punctuated only by occasional horse-drawn wagons and stagecoaches rattling up and down the Bloomingdale Road. It might have made an idyllic writer's retreat, except that Poe was troubled. That summer he wandered the aisles of Tiffany, Young & Ellis in a daze, transfixed by the sheer volume and variety of the store's carved ebony furniture, chess sets, paintings, tiles, bronzes, fans, and candlesticks. "The perfumery department is especially rare," he marveled.

At one point Poe stopped in a tobacco store at the corner of Broadway and Prince Street, gave his name as Thaddeus K. Peasly, and, in exchange for tobacco, wrote a campaign song for a Democratic political organization called the White Eagle Club. He complained about the noise in downtown New York, the incessant "din of the vehicles" rolling over cobblestones, and whiled away the summer working in fits and starts. "I have . . . rambled and dreamed away whole months, and awake, at last, to a sort of mania for composition," he wrote James Russell Lowell in July. "Then I scribble all day, and read all night, so long as the disease endures."

By September, Poe had withdrawn so thoroughly he compared himself to a hermit and claimed he saw no one other than Virginia and Muddy and the Brennan family. But then came a break of sorts, when Willis hired Poe as an editorial assistant at his fledgling daily newspaper, the *Evening Mirror.* Stationed at a desk in the corner, Poe cheerfully answered correspondence and wrote unsigned filler, drudgework that made Willis admire Poe for his uncomplaining diligence.

To travel the six miles between the Brennan farm and the *Evening Mirror* offices at the corner of Nassau and Ann streets, Poe might have taken the Bloomingdale stage, which ran every forty minutes past the Brennan farm down to the corner of Eighth Avenue and 25th Street. Then, for a shilling, he could have transferred to an omnibus of the Knickerbocker Line running down Broadway to within a block of the *Mirror.* On days when Poe didn't have the fare, he must have set out on foot, a hike of about two hours assuming a steady, sober pace—and all along Broadway were tempting saloons and pleasure gardens.

BY EARLY 1845, Poe was writing lead articles for the *Mirror,* and on January 29 published a new poem of eighteen emphatic verses. It began:

> *Once upon a midnight dreary, while I pondered, weak and weary,*
> *Over many a quaint and curious volume of forgotten lore—*
> *While I nodded, nearly napping, suddenly there came a tapping,*
> *As of some one gently rapping, rapping at my chamber door.*
> *"'Tis some visitor," I muttered, "tapping at my chamber door—*
>   *Only this, and nothing more."*

Just how much the Brennan farm may have influenced "The Raven" isn't known. (Was the December Poe had just spent at the farm especially "bleak?" Did Poe consider the Brennan house a "home by horror haunted"?) He may have begun writing "The Raven" well before arriving in the city, although Margaret Brennan claimed she saw Poe working on the poem at his desk on the second floor of the Brennan house and heard him recite it to her family. Regardless, "The Raven," reprinted in the *New York Tribune* on February 4, 1845, turned Poe into a celebrity.

By then Poe had already decided to leave the Brennan farm and move back into the city, and with Virginia, Muddy, and Kate in tow, returned to Greenwich Street, taking up residence at No. 154, one block north of the boardinghouse where he and Virginia had stayed upon their arrival in the city the previous spring. Over the next year they moved to a boardinghouse on East Broadway, then to a house on Amity Street (present-day 3rd Street) in Greenwich Village.

His hermetic, rural existence temporarily at an end, Poe found himself invited to literary parties, where he was introduced as the celebrated author of "The Raven" and, finally, admitted to the inner circle of New York's artistic scene. He resigned from the *Evening Mirror* and became a partner in a new literary magazine called the *Broadway Journal*, published by John Bisco from offices at 153 Broadway. Poe was once more in the thick of urban life, working in a building three blocks north of Wall Street in a hectic row of bookstores, express offices, daguerreotypists' studios, and hotels.

The *Broadway Journal* was nothing if not ambitious, a literary magazine with an impressive list of contributors that included Lowell, Lydia Maria Child, Margaret Fuller, and Fitz-Greene Halleck. At first things went swimmingly, and the *Journal* moved to new offices in Clinton Hall, 135 Nassau Street, in the heart of the publishing district. But then subscriptions lagged and the *Journal* moved back to Broadway, not to the commercially fashionable blocks flanking Wall Street but to 308 Broadway, just north of City Hall Park and on the "shilling side" of the street. It was in those offices that a young journalist, Walt Whitman, visited, and meeting Poe found him cordial but subdued, "perhaps a little jaded."

In October, Bisco resigned and Poe became the *Journal's* sole owner. But Poe was drinking heavily and by January 1, 1846, had, as the *Tribune* put it, "disposed of his interest." The *Broadway Journal* became yet another of his failed projects.

By that summer, Poe and family had retreated to a cottage in Fordham, in the present-day Bronx. There, in January of 1847, Virginia died at the age of twenty-four. Poe, destitute and broken, slid steadily downhill. On October 3, 1849, his friend Joseph Evans Snodgrass found him in a tavern in Baltimore, insensible with drink and wearing someone else's clothes; he died four days later.

For the next forty years the Brennan farm remained on the Bloomingdale Road while the city grew steadily toward it from the south. In the late 1860s, construction of the Boulevard obliterated Brennan's Pond, and then the opening of 84th Street left the house stranded on an outcropping high above the street, accessible only by a winding wooden stair. Mary Brennan was listed in city directories as living in the house as late as 1879. Photographs from the period reveal a creaky house behind two towering elms.

By the mid-1880s the Brennan farm had been cut into building lots, and in 1888 the Brennan house was finally torn down. William Hemstreet, a retired Civil War colonel from Brooklyn, got there in time to rescue a mantelpiece upon which Poe had supposedly scratched his name. (Hemstreet took the mantel home to Brooklyn and in 1908 donated it to Columbia University, where it still resides.)

THE BRENNAN HOUSE was just one of the many dwellings demolished in the face of the advancing city grid. The Charles Ward Apthorp mansion, called Elmwood and built in 1764 some six present-day blocks to the north of the Brennan farm, was torn down in 1892. Once it had been among Manhattan's grandest estates, a Georgian villa on a knoll some 800 feet east of the Bloomingdale Road facing the river across sloping meadows dotted with elm, locust, buttonwood, and cherry trees.

When Tenth Avenue was opened in the 1830s, the Apthorp mansion was cut off from the Bloomingdale Road and, stranded in the middle of a block bounded by Ninth and Tenth Avenues, and 90th and 92nd streets, it languished. In 1860 impresario George Conrad

Nevermore: The Brennan farmhouse in 1879, with the
newly opened 84th Street running past it.

converted the house and what remained of its land into the picnic
ground Elm Park. When journalist Charles Dawson Shanly visited
Elm Park in 1867, he described the decrepit Apthorp mansion as
"debased," a place "where people congregate in the summer time to
smoke and drink beer."

One Sunday afternoon in 1891, one year before the house was
demolished, journalist John Flavel Mines, a retired Civil War colonel and ordained Episcopal minister who wrote under the pen name
"Felix Oldboy," rode the Ninth Avenue Elevated railroad up the West
Side and back in time, finding himself, after a short walk, in front
of the Apthorp mansion. It was a ruin, he wrote, "threatened on all
sides by the bewildering touch of improvement." He stood on the
porch, looked toward the river, and imagined himself as a Continental
Army soldier leaving a sweetheart at the house and racing off to join
Washington's troops as they retreated up the Bloomingdale Road just
ahead of the British in the fall of 1776.

"[The] air was thick with the shadows that trooped up from the
past," Mines wrote. "There had been nothing romantic in the ride

**The Charles Ward Apthorp mansion
just prior to its demolition in 1892.**

on the elevated train; there was no sentiment in the dilapidated surroundings; and the sunshine was the deadly foe of anything like
an apparition. Yet it seemed to me as I stood there as if I had lived
another life, in which the old mansion, not then weather-beaten as
now, but stately and untarnished, and set in a brilliant garland of
shrubs and flowers, had played a prominent part. I could hear close at
hand the rustle of silken dresses and the clank of swords—the merry
peal of laughter and the jingle of the wine-glass."

Edgar Allan Poe had seen it coming: "In some thirty years every
noble cliff will be a pier," Poe had written in 1844, "and the whole
island will be densely desecrated by buildings of brick, with portentous *facades* of brown-stone."

Almost fifty years later, Mines saw that Poe's raven hadn't been a
harbinger of romantic doom but a real-estate agent knocking on the
door, inquiring if the Brennans were ready to sell. "Going! Going!
Gone!" Mines lamented. "This has been the croak of the raven of
speculation over many an old colonial mansion that was stately even
in its decay, but lives now only in memory."

CHAPTER 29

BOOMTOWN

—

NORTH OF 78TH STREET, BROADWAY BEGINS TO STRAIGHTEN, and at 86th Street diverges from the path of the Bloomingdale Road and continues north between Tenth and West End avenues as if it were just another strand in the city's grid. Walking along Broadway's seventh mile is at times a dislocating experience, since the buildings are so much alike and the scene seems to repeat itself over and over: That grey-brick apartment building with the arched limestone doorway and the dry cleaners on the ground floor—*didn't you just pass that?*

It wasn't always like this: Through the 1890s, despite warnings from the likes of John Flavel Mines that speculators were running amok, Broadway above 79th Street was still mostly vacant lots. The subway changed everything, and most of the apartments along Broadway's seventh mile were built in the dramatic building boom that began when the Rapid Transit Subway Construction Company broke ground in 1900. Even for New York, a city defined by flux, what happened to the West Side was an astonishing act of transformation.

It came about largely because a group of wealthy and influential landowners kept up an insistent promotional drumbeat for decades before the subway finally arrived. Egbert L. Viele, a civil engineer,

Egbert L. Viele,
tireless promoter of
West Side real estate.

West Point graduate, and retired Civil War general, was among the many speculators who had bought land on the West Side and then grew impatient waiting for a return on his investment. In 1864, Viele, a rather severe-looking man with a balding pate, brush mustache and deeply set, penetrating eyes, and a group of landowners that included William R. Martin and Samuel B. Ruggles formed the West Side Association and began lobbying the city to make the necessary improvements that would attract homebuyers to the area.

Martin is credited with dreaming up the idea for Riverside Park; Viele was an expert in drainage. (In 1856, Viele had prepared the survey that Calvert Vaux and Frederick Law Olmsted used in designing Central Park, and during the Civil War he drafted the extraordinary "Sanitary and Topographical Map of the City and Island of New York," a map so detailed and accurate that city officials, engineers, and surveyors still use it today.) Viele, Martin, and the other members of the West Side Association pressured the city to install gas lines, water mains, sewers, and a system to carry off ground water through subterranean stone culverts. They pushed for completion of Riverside Drive (originally Riverside Avenue), started calling the West Side the more urbane-sounding "West End," and in 1880 convinced the city to change the name of Eleventh Avenue from 72nd to 106th Street to West End Avenue. Viele built a fine house for himself at Riverside Drive and 88th Street, and in a pamphlet urging residents to move to the West Side improbably compared the district to London, Paris, Berlin, Naples, Rome, and Vienna.

That was a stretch, a bit of speculator's stagecraft, since Riverside Drive and West End Avenue weren't much more than unpaved mud puddles, and the Boulevard was, as even Viele acknowledged, "in wretched condition." The West Side then was a denuded wasteland of shantytowns, bedrock outcroppings dotted with stray goats, and vacant lots filled with stagnant water. Buildings, the *New York Sun* reported, were "desultory and scattered." There was no post office on the entire West Side, and houses were so far apart the mail was still carried by a lone rider on horseback.

The West Side's obvious disadvantage was its lack of rapid transit, which made living there impractical to anyone working south of Union Square. What passed for public transportation on the West Side were horse-drawn streetcars moving slowly up the Boulevard and Eighth Avenue, and with no way to shuttle commuters quickly back and forth from downtown offices, the West Side was, from a real-estate standpoint, a bust.

When rapid transit finally came to the West Side, it came not to the Boulevard but to Ninth Avenue, two blocks to the east and a world away. In 1879, the New York Elevated Railroad Company, with Cyrus W. Field installed as its industrious director, extended its tracks north along Ninth Avenue from 53rd to 145th Street, building festive stations, each one like a little Swiss chalet, at 59th, 72nd, 81st, 93rd, and 104th streets. At first, nothing changed—Viele claimed that for the first two months the "El" was in operation, he was the only commuter disembarking at 93rd Street—but in that first year the number of passengers skyrocketed from 9 million to 46 million. The following year Edward Clark and Isaac Merritt Singer, wealthy co-founders of the Singer Sewing Machine Company, broke ground on the majestic Dakota apartments on Eighth Avenue (Central Park West) and 72nd Street.

The Dakota was completed in 1884 and for a while stood alone amid vacant fields, as if waiting for the city to catch up to it, but Clark also built rows of houses on cross streets near the 72nd Street El station, and other developers built tenements around the 93rd

Street station. Slowly but surely, banks and insurance companies took notice and began investing in West Side real estate—the Mutual Life Insurance Company lent to builders at less than 4 percent interest— and by 1889, Ninth Avenue was in the midst of a full-fledged boom.

Viele and other landowners were confident that development would soon spread west to the Boulevard, West End Avenue, and Riverside Drive. "They were mistaken," real-estate broker George S. Lespinasse commented. While Ninth Avenue and side streets between Eighth and Tenth avenues hummed with activity, blocks to the west remained empty. In 1889 a vacant lot on the Boulevard typically cost about $4,500; not much more than what they cost when the street was first laid out in the 1860s.

Part of the problem with the Boulevard was that cautious landowners, including the conservative Astors, still owned many of the lots along the street and were wealthy enough to pay property taxes year after year, holding out until prices were more attractive. As vacant lots between Eighth and Tenth avenues and south of 110th Street doubled in value between 1884 and 1889, prices west of Tenth Avenue stagnated. The Boulevard continued to languish through the 1890s, even as Ninth Avenue became the West Side's undisputed main street.

In 1890, in an effort to enhance the West Side's image, Ninth Avenue between 59th and 127th streets was renamed the more historic-sounding Columbus Avenue (and Tenth Avenue from 59th Street to Fort George Avenue was renamed Amsterdam Avenue). But Ninth, or Columbus, Avenue was already booming: By 1890 only 27 percent of the lots on Ninth Avenue between 59th and 110th streets were vacant, compared with 68 percent on the Boulevard. Above 84th Street, where 81 percent of the Boulevard's lots were vacant, the difference was even more glaring. Between 59th and 110th streets, 34 percent of the Boulevard's blocks didn't include a single building.

With so much land and so few homebuyers, architects and builders pulled out all the stops, competing with one another to see who could design the most exuberant, fanciful housing. Clarence F. True, Charles Buek, James A. Frame, and others bought up lots between the Boulevard, West End Avenue, and Riverside Drive and built rows of houses with whimsical, projecting façades of red or yellow brick or limestone festooned with quoins, urns, brackets, and swags. The drawing rooms and libraries had decorative floors of inlaid oak, cherry, and yellow pine; the stairs had railings of polished ash and oak. There were built-in fireplaces, porcelain sinks and toilets, and kitchens with the latest gadgetry.

New houses functioned as advertising billboards for architects, many of whom doubled as real-estate agents who floated low-interest loans to buyers and offered sales on installment plans. It wasn't simply the joy of invention that made them turn each new house into a showstopper: The West Side in those years was a buyers' market, and architects were forced to innovate in order to survive. "The demand is constantly for more elaborate buildings," Buek explained. Architects practicing on the West Side in the 1880s and '90s put in long hours at their drafting tables.

IN FEBRUARY OF 1899 the city issued a corrective of sorts when it renamed the Boulevard "Broadway." Everyone already called it by that name anyway, the editors of the *New York Tribune* pointed out, since it was obviously an extension of the same street that ran from Bowling Green to 59th Street. Besides, the *Tribune* added, "Boulevard" sounded too foreign, *too French*, and was an unpleasant reminder of the corrupt Boss Tweed era. The new name seemed to promise a new age of progress for "upper" Broadway: The street would finally be paved, landowners were told, and rapid transit, for so long a dream of West Side speculators, was finally coming to the street as well.

In November of 1898 the Third Avenue Railroad Company had begun replacing Broadway's antiquated horse-car line with electric trolleys. Since the conduits and wiring powering the trolleys were to be placed underground, the project involved ripping up all of Broadway clear up to 110th Street. "Hundreds of men, red-shirted and grimy, are digging trenches which are to form the channel for the new and mighty power by whose influence the torpor of years is to be converted into vigorous and active life," the *Tribune* reported

Broadway's electric trolley under construction, 1900.

in May of 1899. "Great piles of yellow clay are heaped on either side and the pick and shovel make music that must be sweet to those who are [financially] interested in the Boulevard."

Taking in the scene from his tenement on the west side of Broadway between 91st and 92nd Street, paperhanger Horatio Sweetser wrote to his little grandson Theodore, then five years old and in the throes of a childhood railroad obsession, and urged him to not delay a planned visit to New York from his home in Minneapolis. "They are making an underground trolley in the street in which we live," Sweetser wrote excitedly, "and if you do not wait too long, they will not have it finished, and you can see how it is done."

As it turned out, there was no hurry: By the following November the trolley project wasn't even close to completion, and newspapers leveled accusations that Broadway's long-awaited rapid transit system was just another Tammany Hall scam. With the horse cars gone and no trolleys in sight, Broadway had no transit at all that year, and shopkeepers complained about all the business they were losing to stores on Tenth Avenue. Builders hoping that the trolley would create an upswing in the real-estate market could do nothing but wait. The resourceful Charles Buek turned the delay into a sales pitch:

ATTENTION, BARGAIN HUNTERS.
SPLENDID NEW AMERICAN BASEMENT HOUSES
FROM 20 TO 30 FEET WIDE, CLOSE BY
RIVERSIDE [Drive], MUST POSITIVELY BE SOLD
BEFORE JANUARY 1st.
PAVING OF THE STREET HAS BEEN DELAYED,
TROLLEY LINE ON BROADWAY IS SLOW IN GETTING
TO RUN, AND I AM TIRED OF BEING TOLD SO.
THIS IS YOUR CHANCE.

But even with the delay in completion of the trolley, Broadway's real-estate market was steadily improving: In 1899 a small lot at the northeast corner of Broadway and 77th Street, which had sold in 1864 for $5,950, went for $37,000. Further to the north, a lot on the west side of the street between 112th and 113th streets that had sold for $45,050 in 1886 was resold at auction in 1899 for $147,600. Broadway's trolley line certainly enhanced the value of West Side real estate, but was almost immediately superseded by a far more ambitious transit system, one that would instantly transform Broadway, the West Side, and the entire city.

THE LONG-AWAITED Interborough Rapid Transit subway system was a project so vast in scope, the *Tribune* marveled, it was almost impossible to comprehend. The original route, announced in 1895, was supposed to have tunneled beneath lower Broadway up to Union Square, but influential merchants and landowners, afraid that construction would injure business and compromise building foundations, sued. When the courts ruled in their favor, the Rapid Transit Commission revised the subway's route so that trains would run from City Hall Park to 42st Street by way of Centre and Lafayette streets and Fourth Avenue, thereby avoiding lower Broadway altogether.

But north of 42nd Street the subway ran under Broadway up the West Side all the way to 145th Street, and the decision to dig the subway there, rather than on the East Side—which was provided only with a branch line running from Broadway and 103rd Street across the northern tip of Central Park and up Lenox Avenue to 145th Street—meant that the West Side was, after all those decades of waiting, almost instantly subsumed into the growing city. "Fifteen minutes to Harlem" became the catchphrase of commuters and real-estate speculators alike, and even though the reality was closer to "forty minutes to Harlem, if some idiot doesn't hold the doors," the perception that the subway would change the way West Siders worked and lived was enough to create as drastic and theatrical a building boom as any the city had ever seen.

The Subway Boom began in earnest as soon as the Rapid Transit Subway Construction Company, with the brilliant William Barclay Parsons as chief engineer and the hard-boiled John B. McDonald as contractor, began digging the line in March of 1900, the long-hoped-for development of the West Side suddenly coming all at once in a torrent of steel, brick, and limestone.

When the subway opened for service at seven o'clock in the evening of October 27, 1904, huge crowds gathered in front of every station along the way, pressing down the stairs into the netherworld below the street or simply watching, enjoying the strange sight of crowds of people emerging from underground. Church bells rang in celebration and people rode the trains back and forth just for the thrill of it. For the most part it all seemed natural, and many riders that first day didn't bother making the full round trip back to City Hall but instead got off at their local station and walked home, "as if they had been doing it all their lives," the *New York Times* reported.

The subway system provided the West Side with thirteen stations between 59th and 145th streets, an average of one station every six blocks. Broadway's seventh mile quickly became an unbroken line of apartment buildings (called "French flats") and apartment-hotels: There was the Forres, Saxony, Hotel Bretton Hall, Hotel Euclid Hall, Fife Arms, Versailles, St. James Court, Hotel Narragansett, Hotel Bonta, Tuileries, Wollaston, Wilmington, Powellton, William, Arragon, Navarre, La Riviera, Ben-Hur, Linlaugh, Darlington, Magnolia, Kent, Hotel Langham, Friesland, Ruremont, Elizabeth, Westbourne, Lancaster, Trouville, and, the supply of picturesque names apparently exhausted, simply "the Broadway."

The Bretton Hall, Narragansett, and Langham apartments were almost as tall as the magnificent Ansonia, then under construction at Broadway and 73rd Street, but most developers could afford to build only up to six or seven stories, and instead of height chose to put their money into lavish interiors. Apartments often came equipped with the latest technology and gadgetry: electric wiring, showers, washing machines, elevators, refrigerators, burglar and fire alarms, and telephones. Suites of six to ten rooms were common, and layouts typically included an entrance hall, parlor, dining room, library, four or five bedrooms, and a kitchen that was often as small as a closet. A tiny servant's bedroom was typically tucked behind the kitchen and sometimes included its own bathroom, an amenity that helped create a class division within the household and, since the apartments were marketed to the upper class and those aspiring to the upper class, was always mentioned in advertisements. (All those amenities didn't come cheap, and with the Subway Boom came soaring rents: In 1899, rents in Broadway's new apartment houses ranged from $100 to $200 a month—$3,000 to $5,000 in today's dollars—while ten years earlier "elegant" suites of six to ten rooms on Ninth Avenue could be had for as little as $30 to $80 a month.)

With so many buildings going up so fast, the prolific architecture firms of Janes & Leo, Neville & Bagge, Emery Roth, and others couldn't help repeating themselves. Real-estate agents Berry & Trenholm promoted the Magnolia as "a New Departure in Apartment Architecture," but, really, any differences were minor when compared to the similarities of the Darlington next door, the Ben-Hur and the Linlaugh down the block, and the Kent across the street. Inside and out, the development of Broadway's seventh mile amounted to an architectural cut-and-paste operation, which is why, since most of those Subway Boom apartments have survived, Broadway's seventh mile seems so homogenous today.

The Subway Boom finally convinced the Astors to play their hand,

and in 1906, William ("Willie") Waldorf Astor broke ground on the Apthorp Apartments. Its name an allusion to the vanished Apthorp estate, Willie's development was the largest apartment house yet built in the city, a square-footage monster that sprawled across an entire block along the west side of Broadway between 78th and 79th streets. The Apthorp's luxurious suites and duplex apartments were accessed not from the street but from a vast manicured garden in the middle of the block, a plan that was duplicated two years later in the Belnord, an even bigger building that filled a block on the east side of Broadway between 86th and 87th streets.

New Yorkers quickly adapted to living in apartments—"magnificent human hives," the *Tribune* called them—as the Subway Boom continued to resonate on the West Side long after the subway's opening. In 1900 there were still 189 vacant lots on Broadway between 59th and 110th streets. By 1910 there were only 53, and ten years later there were none, as whatever was left of the West Side's original terrain—the fields, outcroppings, creeks and ponds, and the Bloomingdale Road itself—disappeared beneath basements, subway tracks, and water mains.

CHAPTER 30

HOMETOWN

———

I N 1879, EGBERT L. VIELE HAD GAZED WITH ENVY ACROSS Central Park to the East Side. The New York & Harlem Railroad running up Fourth Avenue to the village of Yorkville ensured that the East Side developed at a much faster pace than the West Side. Yorkville in particular grew rapidly outward in all directions from the railway station at 86th Street, attracting Irish, Polish, Hungarian, Greek and, especially, German immigrants with the promise of cheap housing.

Lenox Hill, a gentle rise of ground along Fifth Avenue between, approximately, 60th and 78th streets, developed more slowly than Yorkville, but by the late 1870s was becoming a wealthy enclave that included the so-called Jewish Grand Dukes, German Jews who had immigrated to America between the 1830s and '60s and made fortunes in banking. The Grand Dukes not only had money but also large, rapidly expanding families—the investment banking house J. & W. Seligman & Company consisted of eight brothers who produced thirty-six sons—and Viele was keen on attracting their likes to the West Side.

Viele thought that north of Yorkville the East Side, which around 100th Street begins sloping down to the bottomlands of Harlem, was topographically flawed. Viele imagined that the Seligmans, as well as the Schiffs, Lehmans, Lewisohns, Goldmans, Sachses, Warburgs, and Strauses—"the large and opulent class of our Hebrew fellow-citizens," as he called them—would get bottled up on Lenox Hill and forsake low-lying Harlem for what Viele described as the "great west side plateau."

If the Jewish Grand Dukes didn't exactly flee the East Side *en masse*, a few key families did pull up stakes and head west across Central Park. In 1884, Isidor Straus, a wealthy importer of china and with his brother Nathan the eventual owner of Macy's, moved with his wife Ida and their five children (a sixth child was born two years later) from East 55th Street to a villa on an otherwise vacant block bounded by the Boulevard, West End Avenue, and West 105th and 106th streets. (Isidor and Ida went down with the *Titanic* in 1912; the following year Straus Park, the former Bloomingdale Square at the triangular junction of the Boulevard, West End Avenue, and 106th Street, was dedicated in their memory.) Various members of the Goldman and Sachs families moved into brownstones between West 70th and West 80th streets, and other wealthy Jewish families followed, so that by the 1890s Central Park West was called the "Jewish Fifth Avenue."

But the Grand Dukes weren't the only Jewish residents to colonize the West Side. Between 1882 and 1906, anti-Semitic laws and pogroms forced an estimated half-million Jewish immigrants to flee Russia and Eastern Europe for New York and the teeming tenements of the Lower East Side, where some 400,000 people were packed into every square mile. Newly arrived Jewish refugees were geographically, economically, and socially disconnected from the Grand Dukes, although many of the Dukes were instrumental in their immigration and resettlement: Banker Jacob H. Schiff, treasurer of the National Hebrew Relief Fund, urged the United States to keep its doors "wide open" to the refugees. "There is room for all of them," he declared in 1905.

By then 750,000 residents of New York were Jewish—one-half of the total Jewish population of the United States. But even after the subway opened in 1904, few recently arrived Jewish immigrants moved to the West Side; from the Lower East Side the more typical trajectory was to gravitate uptown to Harlem, the Bronx, or the Brooklyn neighborhoods of Williamsburg and Brownsville. It wasn't until after World War I that the Jewish influx of the West Side began in earnest. Harlem had by then become a largely Jewish neighborhood, but after the war blacks, lured by the promise of affordable housing, moved in and Jews moved out. That the Jewish migration from Harlem to the West Side was a product of matter-of-fact racism was abundantly clear to Jewish residents like Dorothy Greenwald: "The reason the Jews ran out of Harlem was because the blacks moved in," she remembered.

Greenwald was born in Harlem, in 1917. Her grandfather, a Jewish immigrant from Russia, moved their large extended family to the West Side in 1922 in order to be close to the synagogue where he worked as an assistant rabbi and that had relocated from Harlem to West 93rd Street. Dorothy's mother and uncles (her father had died when she was a toddler) ran a series of tennis courts on the West Side and did well enough to rent apartments of six rooms or more. If racism played a part in their removal from Harlem, so did the promise of the West Side's abundant new apartment buildings and row houses. With so much housing available, the Greenwalds switched apartments often, always sticking to the West Side between 92nd and 99th streets.

"[We] were upwardly mobile," Dorothy remembered. "If [we] could do a little better, [we] got a bigger apartment with a bigger kitchen or something."

But the biggest factor in the Jewish migration to the West Side wasn't racism or large apartments but mass transportation. In 1918 the subway was extended southward under Seventh Avenue to South Ferry, linking the West Side to the Garment District, which had enveloped Broadway between Union, Madison, and Herald squares and then spread west to Eighth Avenue and as far north as 42nd Street. The Garment District grew out of the city's old dry goods district, and for decades had been steadily pushing north from downtown, closely following the development and expansion of Broadway's Ladies' Mile and Sixth Avenue's Fashion Row. Many of the Garment District's suppliers, wholesalers, and manufacturers of clothing, furs, hooks, stays, and "notions" (buttons, ribbon, and thread) were Jewish, and the subway made commuting from the Garment District to the West Side considerably easier than traveling from the Garment District to the East Side, Harlem, or Brooklyn. By 1930, an estimated one-third of the West Side's population between 79th and 110th streets and from Broadway to the Hudson River was Jewish; a percentage that only increased once the Eighth Avenue line of the Independent Subway System began running in 1932.

Broadway became the centerline of a huge Jewish community, the so-called Gilded Ghetto, that spread south toward Columbus Circle and north toward Columbia University, with its epicenter at Broadway and 86th Street. Many West Side Jewish families were, like the Greenwalds, solidly middle-class, while others struggled and barely scraped by.

Lee Silver was born in 1921 and grew up in a tenement at 160 West 100th Street, next to his father's grocery store, which was the "focal point" of a threadbare childhood of cold floors and not enough warm clothes. "[My father] was too lenient for a grocery store," Silver remembered. "He was the good guy who wouldn't press a debtor."

"We were always, constantly, considering survival. We were teetering on the brink of survival because we didn't have resources. There wasn't anybody to give you a present. There wasn't anybody to give you a sweater. There wasn't anything but what you saw and what you could understand from what you saw on your own block."

Barely thirty years after the Jewish influx had begun, the neighborhood began to change: Between 1930 and 1954 the West Side's population increased by 160,000, but only 7,500 of those new residents were white. The West Side was nothing if not diverse—there were Jews, Irish, blacks, Greeks, Italians, and, by 1954, over 100,000 Puerto Ricans. All of those disparate ethnic groups didn't always get along, and the West Side's long-running turf war between white and Puerto Rican kids was immortalized in the 1957 Broadway musical *West Side Story.*

"To the Irish, the Italians were guineas and the Jews were kikes, and they were antagonistic and aggressive," Silver remembered of his Depression-era childhood, "so the Italians and the Jewish kids would coalesce against the Irish when the Irish would want to come and attack or want to break up a stickball game or want to break up a ring-a-levio game."

And other changes were afoot: After World War II, amid the "white flight" migration to the suburbs, sections of the West Side, especially the blocks surrounding Sherman Square and neighboring Verdi Square (nicknamed "Needle Park" for its role in the drug trade), began a long descent into crime and decay. But enough remained of the West Side's cultural fabric that residents tend to remember the 1950s as a golden era of Saturday matinees at the Beacon Theatre and afternoon games of stickball, stoopball, and ring-a-levio played on side streets while radio broadcasts of the Yankees and Giants blared from open windows. Gene Yellin recalled childhood hours whiled away at the counter of Harry Shalita's Alamac Rexall Drugs at the southeast corner of Broadway and 71st Street, just steps away from his house, swilling egg creams and cherry-lime rickeys and studiously watching drag queens congregating outside the Sherman Square Hotel on the opposite side of the street.

Shalita emigrated from Russia to Philadelphia in 1917 and made his way to Brooklyn, where he married Celia Levine. In 1943 he and Celia moved their growing family to 220 West 71st Street, just a few doors west of Broadway. Shalita took over the Sherman Square Pharmacy, on the ground floor of the Sherman Square Hotel at the southwest corner of Broadway and 71st Street, but within a few years bought the Alamac Rexall Drugs on the other side of the street. For several years he ran both stores, then sold the Sherman Square Pharmacy and devoted himself to the Alamac.

The Alamac was the quintessential Broadway drugstore: It had the distinctive orange and blue Rexall sign out front and a Formica-topped soda fountain running the full length of the store. Two soda jerks worked behind the counter dishing out a continuous stream of ham-and-cheese, egg-salad, and roast-beef sandwiches, eggs, sodas, egg creams, ice cream, and tall glasses of malted milk. Prescriptions were filled in the back of the store; Shalita made his own pills the

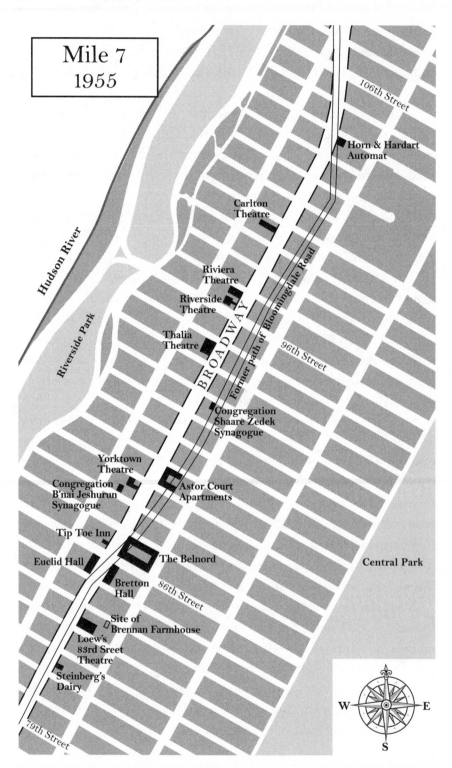

Mile 7
1955

Hudson River

106th Street

Horn & Hardart
Automat

Carlton
Theatre

Riviera
Theatre

BROADWAY

Former path of Bloomingdale Road

Riverside
Theatre

Riverside Park

Thalia
Theatre

96th Street

Congregation
Shaare Zedek
Synagogue

Yorktown
Theatre

Astor Court
Apartments

Congregation
B'nai Jeshurun
Synagogue

Tip Toe Inn

The Belnord

Central Park

Euclid Hall

Bretton
Hall

86th Street

Site of
Brennan Farmhouse

Loew's
83rd Sreet
Theatre

Steinberg's
Dairy

79th Street

W   E

S

old-fashioned way, using a mortar and pestle. He opened the store every morning at seven, didn't leave until midnight, and only stayed home on Yom Kippur.

Broadway unfurled north of the Alamac in a seemingly never-ending line of storefronts. "Mainly the West Side then was small shops, little mom-and-pop stores," Shalita's daughter Barbara remembered, calling to mind one candy store on Broadway between 75th and 76th streets where ice cream was displayed in big round tubs. "They'd scoop it and put it in a container like the ones you get from Chinese restaurants now, a little paper container," she recalled.

A few blocks north of Barbara's favorite candy store was Zabar's grocery, which Louis Zabar, a Jewish immigrant from the Ukraine, founded in 1941. Within a few blocks on either side of Zabar's were two other long-running West Side institutions, the C & L Restaurant, at Broadway and 75th Street, and the Tip Toe Inn, at Broadway and 86th Street. Aaron Chinitz, a Jewish immigrant from Russia, founded both restaurants in 1919. They featured almost identical menus heavy on mid-century American staples: chicken à la king and chicken-and-mushroom chow mein; crullers, turnovers, cherry cheesecake, sherbet, and blueberry pie; and Jewish fare like Nova Scotia salmon, lake sturgeon, schnitzel, and calf livers, plus a licentious-sounding sandwich called the "Tongue Temptation." And there were bagels, of course, which were so necessary to Jewish sustenance that by the early 1950s well over a million were consumed in the city in a typical weekend and a series of bakers' strikes and ensuing "bagel famines" were front-page news.

Midway between the C & L and the Tip Toe Inn was Steinberg's Dairy, a perpetually crowded lunchroom near the southeast corner of Broadway and 82nd Street, where locals stuffed themselves with chopped herring, smoked carp, cold fried flounder, baked whitefish, sandwiches piled high with cream cheese, smoked salmon, sardines, and tomatoes, blintzes, kasha varnishkes, latkes, and cold borscht soup. Steinberg's was decidedly unpretentious, a place where Walter Matthau used to get a rise out of the waiters by ordering in French.

Zabar's not only survived but expanded, in the 1970s, and now it stretches along two-thirds of the block on the west side of Broadway between 80th and 81st streets. But the C & L, the Tip Toe Inn, and Steinberg's are all long gone. Today Broadway on the West Side means glittering new stores and shiny condominiums that would have seemed, in the 1950s, like space ships from a distant planet. But occasionally, in that long line of storefronts, there's a holdout, like Murray's Sturgeon at Broadway and 89th Street, which recalls the Gilded Ghetto's heyday. And much of Broadway's past remains out of view, just below the surface: Near the southeast corner of Broadway and 82nd Street there is a brightly colored new sign for a lingerie store. Hidden beneath the new sign is an old sign that spells out in ten rusty vertical Art-Deco metal letters, like ancient hieroglyphics, STEINBERG'S.

MILE 8

106TH STREET TO
122ND STREET

CHAPTER 31

ASYLUM

——

NORTH OF 86TH STREET, THE HISTORY OF BROADWAY SPLITS into two strands, its story following both the nineteenth-century Boulevard, which grew more indelible with each passing year, and the eighteenth-century Bloomingdale Road, which, superseded, slowly faded away. The 1865 legislation that created the Boulevard required Andrew Haswell Green and the other commissioners of Central Park to follow the Bloomingdale Road only up to 86th Street. North of that line they could open the new avenue anywhere they pleased, and so they decided to plow straight north and abandon the Bloomingdale Road, which gradually fell into disuse.

But well-traveled highways like the Bloomingdale Road are remarkably difficult to erase, since they tend to double as boundaries for property lines, and the Bloomingdale Road, though officially banished from city maps, didn't disappear all at once. For decades after the Boulevard opened, the two streets existed simultaneously, not side-by-side but entangled, the meandering Bloomingdale Road crossing and recrossing the Boulevard like a drunk staggering home, veering first to the east and then to the west, coinciding with the Boulevard between 104th and 107th streets and then, as the Boulevard took over the roadbed of Eleventh (West End) Avenue, again crossing over the Boulevard until it came within a stone's throw of the Hudson River. Then, as if remembering itself, it jogged back inland, crossed the Boulevard at 126th Street, and continued north.

Today only a few barely discernible fragments of the Bloomingdale Road remain, in the form of short, orphaned streets, alleys, and oddly angled property lines that, when seen from above, form a ghostly image of the old road. By connecting those streets, alleys, and property lines, it is still possible to trace the path of the Bloomingdale Road through what is today Broadway's eighth mile, and imagine what it must have felt like to follow the road through the district of Bloomingdale and up a plateau of Manhattan schist between present-day 110th and 122nd streets that in the late eighteenth century was variously called Harlem Heights or Vandewater Heights, after a family that owned land there. (It was still called Harlem Heights into the late nineteenth century.) Until 1795, when it was extended to present-day 147th Street to form a V-shaped junction with the Kingsbridge Road (the main road connecting the village of Harlem to upper Manhattan), the Bloomingdale Road came to a dead end in front of Nicholas de Peyster's barn near present-day 115th Street.

At that time the Harlem Heights plateau consisted only of woods and fields and a few farmhouses, and in the Revolutionary War was the site of the Battle of Harlem Heights, where Lieutenant Colonel Thomas Knowlton and an outnumbered company of Connecticut Rangers valiantly repelled a contingent of redcoats in a buckwheat field near where the Bloomingdale Road ended.

Harlem Heights offered panoramic views of the Hudson River to the west, New York City to the south, the Harlem Plains and Long Island to the east, and Westchester (the present-day Bronx) to the north. It was an idyllic spot, perfect for taking the country air and recuperating from the stress and turmoil of the city.

In 1806, New York Hospital established a psychiatric wing at its downtown campus on Broadway between Anthony (present-day Worth) and Duane streets. In 1815 a letter from humanitarian Thomas Eddy inspired the hospital's board of governors to adopt a course of "moral treatment" for its patients based on the work of William Tuke, a Quaker and founder of the Retreat, a groundbreaking mental hospital in York, England, that had done away with beatings and restraints in favor of a benevolent program of exercise, prayer, and work. Eddy recommended that New York Hospital build a new Retreat-like ward for its mentally ill patients in the countryside north of town, and in 1818 construction of the Bloomingdale Asylum for the Insane began on 77 acres along the east side of the Bloomingdale Road at the summit of Harlem Heights.

The asylum's centerpiece was a three-story, 200-foot-long stone building completed in 1821 on the line of present-day 117th Street. Other structures, including a chapel, a superintendent's house, and wings for violent patients, were added over the years until the asylum, surrounded by landscaped grounds of ornamental trees and shrubs thoughtfully placed to "relieve the melancholy mind from its sad musings," as one guidebook put it in 1846, became the most prominent landmark on the West Side. Any concern that the streets of the Commissioners' Plan grid might interfere with the asylum's solitude was alleviated in 1838, when the state legislature passed an act prohibiting 115th through 120th streets from crossing through the grounds.

Situated 150 feet above the Hudson River, the asylum followed the Retreat model: Men worked the asylum's farm, women took in needlework, and all patients were allowed to make short trips in a car-

The bucolic Bloomingdale Asylum for the Insane was a model institution.

BLOOMINGDALE ASYLUM.

BLOOMINGDALE ASYLUM FOR THE INSANE.

riage provided for their use and encouraged to play games and read books and newspapers. The asylum was considered a notable medical achievement in a city ravaged by annual epidemics and shockingly high rates of infant mortality. Many city officials had active roles in the institution's work—ex-mayor Philip Hone was an asylum trustee for twenty-one years and dutifully inspected the asylum's grounds and wards once a week—and tabulations of patient statistics were printed annually in local newspapers. (Of the 4,182 patients admitted between May of 1821 and January of 1856, 1,911 were considered "cured" and 851 "improved" after their stay, although 471, or 11 percent, died.) The asylum became something of a tourist attraction and a must-see destination for social reformers.

"At Bloomingdale," Margaret Fuller wrote after a visit in 1845, "the shades of character and feeling were nicely kept up, decorum of manners preserved, and the insane showed in every way that they felt no violent separation betwixt them and the rest of the world, and might easily return to it. The eye, though bewildered, seemed lively, and the tongue prompt."

The asylum remained a point of pride as long as it was separated from the city by miles of open land. But by the 1870s the Boulevard had been opened through the asylum's grounds, severing the asylum from the Bloomingdale Road, which ran to the west, and it seemed that in short order the encroaching city would envelop the Harlem Heights plateau. In 1873 construction began on Morningside Park, designed by Calvert Vaux and Frederick Law Olmsted and situated along the craggy eastern cliff of the plateau between 110th and 123rd streets. Real-estate developers assumed Morningside Park would enhance land values, but even as the park took shape, vacant lots in the vicinity still weren't selling.

Lots on the plateau didn't appreciate because they weren't accessible by rapid transit: The Ninth Avenue Elevated station at 116th Street was at the bottom of Morningside Park, forcing commuters to walk up a steep flight of stairs to reach the top of the plateau, and the only other station in the area was at 104th Street, too far to the south. But it was far easier to blame the Bloomingdale Asylum than to build a subway, and led by lawyer Dwight H. Olmstead, one-time president of the West Side Association and president of the newly formed Morningside Park Association, a group of Harlem Heights landowners began a relentless campaign to force the asylum to move to a 300-acre farm in White Plains its board of governors had acquired in the 1860s. As soon as the asylum was gone, Olmstead predicted, land values in the area would skyrocket.

In 1879, Olmstead suggested that the Harlem Heights plateau, once cleared of the asylum, would make an ideal site for the upcoming 1883 United States International Exhibition. When nothing came of that idea—the Exhibition was never held—Olmstead argued that since the asylum charged some of its wealthier patients room and board, it no longer qualified as a public charity and therefore should be required to pay property taxes. When the city ruled in the asylum's favor, Olmstead took his complaints to the state legislature.

In February of 1888, Olmstead and lawyer Francis M. Bixby, a former state senator and owner of building lots on 119th and 120th streets, filed a grievance on behalf of the Morningside Park Association with the state Senate's five-member Committee on Taxation. Olmstead and Bixby demanded that the committee revoke the asylum's tax-exempt status, open 115th through 120th streets through the asylum's grounds, and force the removal of the asylum to White Plains within two years. In March the committee began weekly hearings, refusing to pause even for the Great Blizzard of 1888, which incapacitated the city that month.

On March 24, Olmstead and Bixby brought to the stand a string of witnesses to condemn the asylum. "The Bloomingdale Lunatic Asylum has damned the whole west side," Kiliaen van Rensselaer proclaimed. "People regard it with a perfect horror." John Brewer, who owned lots at Broadway and 108th Street, told the committee that the asylum was depressing property values all the way down to 59th Street, and predicted that its removal would double the value of lots.

"People won't live in the neighborhood of a madhouse," Frederick A. Conkling, brother of former United States senator Roscoe Conkling, declared. "The women and children are afraid."

A week later Charles Nichols, the asylum's superintendent, assured the committee that he would never refuse treatment to an indigent patient, and witnesses, including a surprising number of real-estate agents, lined up to speak on the asylum's behalf. Agent William Cruikshank testified that the asylum made Harlem Heights more, not less, desirable—"I have a sentimental love for the poor maniacs," he said—while Peter Meyers, another real-estate agent, testified that the asylum wasn't in any way preventing development, although, he admitted, he hadn't spent much time on the Harlem Heights plateau.

"Do you ever go up there?" Bixby asked him.

"No," Meyers replied. "Anyone who would climb up there must be insane."

On May 3 the senate committee, voting along party lines—three Republicans in favor, two Democrats against—ruled in the asylum's favor, rejecting Olmstead's claim that the asylum wasn't a charity. The committee found that the asylum wasn't operated for profit, that in the previous year 80 percent of the asylum's patients hadn't been charged a nickel, and further upheld the 1838 legislation prohibiting the opening of streets through the asylum's grounds.

But there was apparently a backroom deal in the works: Only two weeks after the ruling, the asylum's board of governors voted to move to White Plains after all, an about-face that the *New York Times* alleged was the result of a mysterious "tacit agreement" between the asylum and the legislature. Officially, the asylum had bowed to "public sentiment" but, as the *Times* reported, the prospect of auctioning off, at market value, the asylum's 558 lots along the Boulevard was too good to pass up. Once again, the allure of the real-estate market had triumphed over the desire to preserve open land.

As the asylum prepared to move, the *Sun* published a belated defense of an institution that had once been the pride of the city: "The lunatics in the asylum . . . are not of the howling, raving kind, but of the quiet, inoffensive variety. Were it not for the innate prejudice that people always have against living near an asylum, the place would be a grand one as it is."

With the asylum out of the way, Olmstead predicted, wealthy landowners would build huge mansions on its former grounds, and Harlem Heights would soon develop into a luxurious suburb of detached villas, just as Andrew Haswell Green had envisioned in the 1860s. But it didn't quite work out that way: Instead, something far more ambitious replaced the asylum at the top of the plateau.

CHAPTER 32

ACROPOLIS

———

K ING'S COLLEGE WAS CHARTERED IN 1754 AND HELD ITS first classes that summer in the vestry room of Trinity Church's schoolhouse. Two years later the cornerstone of the college's first building was laid on Church Street, between Barclay and Murray streets and one block west of Broadway, a festive occasion that involved much drinking but, the *New-York Gazette* assured its readers, was conducted "with the utmost Decency and Propriety."

For the next ninety-five years the college remained at the Church Street campus, its male student body translating Ovid, Cicero, and Virgil and studying writing, arithmetic, philosophy, surveying, navigation, geology, botany, and "Husbandry, Commerce, and Government." The college was officially connected not only to Trinity but also to the Church of England, and students were required to attend morning and evening services. (It would appear that many of the students were extremely active after services, too, as evidenced by Section IV of the college's "Laws and Orders," adopted in 1755, which included detailed prohibitions against drunkenness, fornication, frequenting "houses of ill Fame," vandalism, playing cards, throwing dice, and cockfighting; all occupational hazards of attending college next to the brothels and gambling dens of the adjacent Holy Ground red-light district.)

The college was nearly destroyed in the Great Fire of 1776 and was closed for the duration of the Revolutionary War, when the British occupied the city and used the college as a military hospital. After the war "King's College" didn't sound right to patriotic ears, and in 1784 it was renamed Columbia College.

In 1857, Columbia moved uptown into the former Deaf and Dumb Asylum at Madison Avenue and 49th Street. At first, Columbia's new campus was still several miles removed from the hustle and bustle of the city, but in 1871, Grand Central Depot opened only six blocks to the south, and by the 1880s the neighborhood surrounding Columbia was untenably noisy and crowded. In 1889, Seth Low became Columbia's new president and began laying the groundwork for the college's move to Harlem Heights.

Low, a confident, rather fleshy man with heavy dark eyebrows, large inquisitive eyes, and a thick mustache, had grown up in a brownstone mansion on Pierrepont Place in Brooklyn Heights. His father, Abiel Abbot Low, was a wealthy merchant who had made a fortune in shipping and foreign trade. Seth graduated from Columbia in 1870 and, forsaking the family business for a career in politics, was elected, at the age of thirty, mayor of Brooklyn.

Low transformed Columbia into a modern university, doing away with compulsory chapel service and fluency in Greek as a requirement for admission, while expanding course offerings and graduate programs. But his most daring maneuver came in 1892, when he engineered Columbia's purchase, for $2 million—about $52 million in today's dollars—of the main portion of the Bloomingdale Insane Asylum's grounds, 19 acres bounded by Broadway, Amsterdam (Tenth) Avenue, and 116th and 120th streets. The asylum's main building was demolished—some of the asylum's secondary buildings were later pressed into service as classrooms—and Low hired Charles Follen McKim of McKim, Mead & White to design the new campus.

McKim, the cerebral child of well-known abolitionists—McKim's parents had helped carry John Brown's body home for burial in 1859—had trained at Harvard and the École des Beaux-Arts in Paris. McKim's *bon vivant* partner Stanford White, a notorious rake who ended up shot to death, in 1906, by Harry Thaw,

Charles Follen
McKim.

the husband of White's one-time mistress Evelyn Nesbit, tended
to make the gossip sheets. But McKim was arguably the firm's real
talent, an expressive designer of houses, libraries, office buildings,
schools, and railroad stations whom a former employee remembered
as drawing equally well with either hand. (William Rutherford
Mead was the firm's nuts-and-bolts partner, the one who made
sure McKim and White's buildings had things like elevators, stairs,
closets, and steam plants.)

The Columbia commission came at a transitional moment for the
firm. Since the firm's founding in 1872, McKim, Mead & White had
practically cornered the market for Gilded Age casinos, clubhouses,
and mansions. But in the 1880s, with the commissions for the Villard
Houses in New York and the Boston Public Library, McKim, Mead
& White had begun to gradually turn away from the prevailing, picturesque "Shingle style" that had made the firm's reputation toward

an imposing, Neoclassical aesthetic drawn in equal parts from the monuments of the Renaissance and from ancient Greece and Rome. McKim's plan for Columbia, and White's simultaneous plan for New York University's new Bronx campus, ushered in the firm's golden era, which culminated, just before McKim's death in 1909, in the magnificent Penn Station on 33rd Street.

McKim's contribution to the firm was an uncompromising sense of permanence. His buildings were fortresses of stone, brick, and steel that possessed what critic Royal Cortissoz called "Roman weight"— they were built to last. So it's ironic that McKim's plan for Columbia was based in large part on a temporary structure that stood for less than a year before it was torn down.

In 1891, Daniel H. Burnham had invited McKim to join an all-star cast of architects in the design of the World's Columbian Exposition in Chicago, the so-called White City. Burnham, with substantial input from Frederick Law Olmsted, had planned the White City around two intersecting axes that created dramatic vistas and accentuated a sense of procession and ritual. The major axis was the Grand Basin, an artificial lagoon that began at the fair's railroad terminal and ended at the lakeshore and was crossed by the secondary axis, a canal that came complete with Venetian gondolas. And that was only part of the fairgrounds: On the periphery were pavilions showcasing foreign cultures and each of the forty-four United States, plus stockyards, islands, and the boisterous Midway Plaisance.

McKim designed the fair's New York State Building, but his main contribution was the Agricultural Building, a large exhibition hall crammed with everything from livestock and farm equipment to a 22,000-pound "monster cheese" and a map of the United States made entirely of pickles. The vast structure, which had a shallow dome cribbed from the Pantheon and a façade of columns like the Parthenon, stretched along the south edge of the Grand Basin. Bedecked with flags and statuary, the enormous Agricultural Building was only one of fourteen "Great Buildings" arranged along the Grand Basin and interconnected with colonnades, walkways and bridges, which helped turn the Chicago fair into an allegory of the new American imperialism, as if the Great White Fleet had been beached on the shores of Lake Michigan.

The Great Buildings weren't nearly as substantial as they appeared from afar. Burnham had to get them built quickly: Congress didn't award the fair to Chicago until 1890, and by the fall of that year the city still had not settled on a site, which left only two-and-a-half years to design and build the entire fair in time for its planned May 1, 1893, opening. Except for the Palace of Fine Arts (today's Museum of Science and Industry) the Great Buildings were intended only as temporary pavilions and so were constructed of lathe-and-plaster painted with white stucco. But the illusion was convincing, and the effect on the 27 million people who visited the fair that summer was immediate—*Why doesn't my hometown look like this?*—and over the following decade virtually every American city and town from Albany to Zanesville had a new bank, library, museum, or city hall inspired by the White City.

SETH LOW HAD BEEN among the streaming hordes of men, women, and ice-cream-gobbling children that visited the fair that summer, and only weeks after the fair's closing on October 30, Columbia hired McKim to design its new campus—a permanent simulation of a temporary World's Fair.

The White City had sprawled over 600 acres along Lake Michigan; McKim's plan for Columbia covered only 19. But his plan did manage to echo the fair's layout: It was arranged around a main south-to-north axis, which afforded views south to the growing city, flanked by classroom buildings and dominated by a concentric building at the center. In the White City, that center structure had been Hunt's Administration Building, a fanciful cribbing of Brunelleschi's dome in Florence; at Columbia it was a library.

Low paid for the library himself with a $1 million donation made in honor of his father. Although its basic building components were borrowed from Roman antiquity—its towering vaults borrowed from the Baths of Caracalla and its shallow dome copied from the

Columbia's imposing Low Library.

Pantheon—Low Library was first and foremost a souvenir of the White City, with one major difference: Instead of lathe and plaster, McKim built Low Library solidly in limestone, marble, and granite.

McKim situated the library atop a plinth on the site's highest point, and reaching the library from 116th Street required climbing fifty-seven granite steps—incoming students could be forgiven for wondering if their first visit to the library wasn't some sort of pass-fail test of academic resolve.

The front entrance was through tall, somber wooden doors behind a massive colonnade of Ionic columns. Inside was a high vestibule and, past two immense Connemara green-marble columns, the library's main reading room, a theatrically vertical rotunda as tall as a six-story building, with semicircular reading desks radiating from a circular bookcase at the center. Four massive stone piers, each labeled with one of the four points of knowledge—LAW, MEDICINE, PHILOSO-PHY, THEOLOGY—supported the rotunda roof. Statues of Roman and Greek philosophers looked down from a balcony, and more bookcases were crammed into the corners: Low Library had room for 600,000 volumes, making it the second-largest library in America at the time after the Library of Congress.

Sunlight poured in through four huge half-round windows

around the sides of the dome. At a time when electric lights were still something of a novelty, McKim proposed concealing eight powerful arc lamps around the balcony and directing their beams at a 7-foot-diameter wooden "moon" painted white and suspended from a ceiling painted a shade of deep blue, like the evening sky. It was a whimsical detail closer in spirit to a fantastical Arthur Rackham illustration than to the grave Baths of Caracalla. But McKim, Mead & White specialized in fantasy—the firm had festooned the Herald Building with mechanical bell ringers, mounted the spire of Madison Square Garden with an Augustus Saint-Gaudens sculpture of the goddess Diana, and a few years later would paint the ceiling of the Morgan Library with strange arabesque patterns— and McKim's moon was in keeping with those fairy tale inventions. Royal Cortissoz, who had once worked in McKim's office, described McKim as "enveloping serious ideas in garments of winning loveliness."

WHEN COLUMBIA OPENED for classes, on October 4, 1897, only Low Memorial Library and four other buildings were finished, and most of the lots along Broadway were still vacant. But other institutions, including Teachers College and Barnard College— both colleges for women affiliated with Columbia—were already building on adjacent blocks, joining the Cathedral of St. John the Divine, which had broken ground in 1892 on Amsterdam Avenue at 112th Street, and St. Luke's Hospital, its original building designed by the great architect Ernest Flagg, which opened on 114th Street in 1896. Grant's Tomb, a Neoclassical pavilion that could easily have been mistaken for one of the White City's Great Buildings, was completed in 1897 on Riverside Drive and 122nd Street. Those institutions had been drawn to a neighborhood that since the early 1890s was increasingly referred to as "Morningside Hill" or "Morningside Plateau" instead of Harlem Heights. Since 1895, Low had been calling it "Morningside Heights" and that's what it became, even though officials from St. John the Divine insisted it should be "Cathedral Heights."

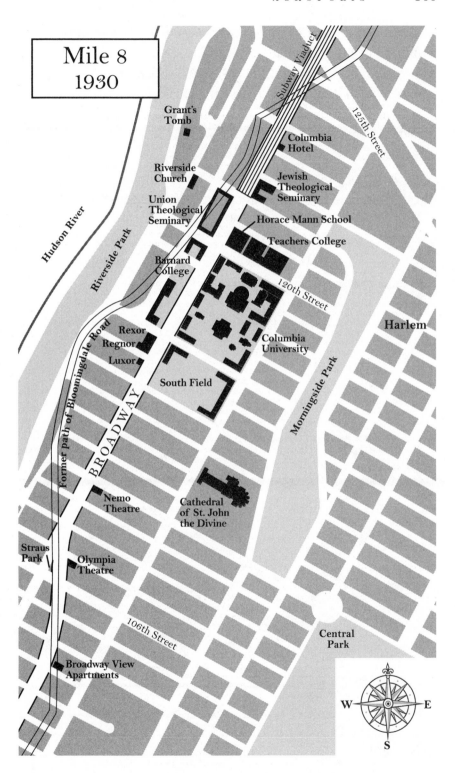

Mile 8
1930

Grant's Tomb

Columbia Hotel

Riverside Church

Jewish Theological Seminary

Union Theological Seminary

Horace Mann School

Teachers College

Barnard College

120th Street

125th Street

Hudson River

Riverside Park

Harlem

Rexor
Regnor
Luxor

Columbia University

South Field

Morningside Park

Former path of Bloomingdale Road

BROADWAY

Nemo Theatre

Cathedral of St. John the Divine

Straus Park

Olympia Theatre

106th Street

Central Park

Broadway View Apartments

W   E

S

More institutions opened on the plateau—the Jewish Theological Seminary in 1903, Woman's Hospital in 1906, and both the Union Theological Seminary and the Institute of Musical Art in 1910—as the press began referring to Morningside Heights as the "Acropolis." The *New York Tribune* called the glittering new buildings of Morningside Heights the "temples of the white man."

CHAPTER 33

GOD'S SKYSCRAPERS

———

I N 1901, SETH LOW RESIGNED AS COLUMBIA'S PRESIDENT IN
order to run for mayor of New York—he won, although he ended
up serving only a single two-year term—and under the long reign
of new president Nicholas Murray Butler, who didn't retire until
1945, Columbia grew in size and prestige. In 1903, Butler oversaw
the acquisition of two additional blocks south of 116th Street, which
became the university's South Field and marked the beginning of
Columbia's often-controversial and ongoing expansion beyond its
original campus and into the surrounding neighborhood.

By the 1920s the original campus north of 116th Street had grown
to sixteen buildings, including a twelve-story science facility, with
more going up across 116th Street around the perimeter of South
Field, which was then an athletic field where Lou Gehrig, then playing for Columbia, occasionally smacked a home run onto Broadway.
"Morningside Heights has entered a new era . . . ," the *Times Magazine* reported in 1926. "Here is to be found a veritable crossroads of
culture and education and religious life; a huge international power
station generating and absorbing mental currents."

Its enrollment grew steadily year-to-year, and while a few women
were admitted to graduate programs and professional schools and
allowed, with permission of the instructor, to take some undergrad-

uate courses, Columbia remained a male bastion of aspiring lawyers, historians, journalists, chemists, physicists, geologists, engineers, and architects.

Beyond Columbia's gates, Morningside Heights was growing, too: In 1890 there had been only four brick buildings on Broadway between 108th and 125th streets, plus some two-dozen diminutive wood-frame dwellings, barns, sheds, and shanties. Ten years later entire blocks of Broadway bordering Columbia remained vacant. But the coming of the subway in 1904, with stations placed at 110th and 116th streets, changed everything. Only two years after the subway's opening, both sides of Broadway's eighth mile were lined with apartment buildings—including the Regnor, Luxor, and Rexor—and on the entire stretch of the street from 108th to 125th Street only one vacant lot remained.

That last lot was at the northeast corner of Broadway and 122nd Street, just north of Teachers College, and consisted of an immense outcropping of bedrock thrusting 30 feet above street level. Throughout the Subway Boom the outcropping stood untouched and unused, a curious remnant of the island's primordial topography. Then, in the fall of 1925, Oscar E. Konkle, a Brooklyn real-estate developer and devout Baptist, decided to build the tallest building in the world there, a "skyscraper church" devoted to missionary work.

THE SEEDS OF Konkle's notion had been sown almost a century earlier, when the Broadway Tabernacle opened a few blocks north of City Hall Park, on the east side of Broadway between Worth Street and Catherine Lane. Built in 1836 for the fiery abolitionist preacher Charles Grandison Finney, the Tabernacle was sold in 1840 to a group of Congregationalists, who expanded the church's ministry until the Tabernacle became New York's foremost cultural center. Every week the Tabernacle hosted lectures, concerts, demonstrations, and meetings, and in the decades leading up to the Civil War became the main gathering place for the antislavery movement; William Lloyd Garrison, Wendell Phillips, Henry Ward Beecher, and Frederick Douglass were all frequent guests. In 1841, Philip Hone called the Broadway Tabernacle the *"omnium gatherum* and hold-all of the city."

The Tabernacle's programming was remarkably diverse: Renowned Norwegian violinist Ole Bull performed there, but so did choirs of Five Points orphans and newsboys. In 1854 an ambivalent Ralph Waldo Emerson lectured at the Tabernacle to a packed house. ("I saw the great audience with dismay . . . ," he wrote in his journal.) "I was most thankful to those who stayed at home." Demonstrations of mesmerism, telepathy, phrenology, or electricity might be followed the next evening by a meeting of Spiritualists. (In 1857, golden-curled teenage Spiritualist Cora Hatch so captivated her Tabernacle audience that hardened, cynical Tammany Hall operative Isaiah Rynders broke down in tears.)

In 1857 the Tabernacle sold its old building and built a new church at the intersection of Broadway, Sixth Avenue, and 34th Street, then on the outskirts of town. By 1903 the neighborhood around the second Tabernacle had become the heart of Herald Square, and the church cashed in and moved again, this time to the northeast corner of Broadway and 56th Street, in the midst of a commercial district that was about to become the city's Automobile Row. With each move the Tabernacle made a killing from the sale of its land, and with money to burn, pastor Charles Edward Jefferson, a social reformer in the Charles Henry Parkhurst mold, decided to build a deluxe church that was big enough to include spaces for all of the Tabernacle's varied cultural and social programs.

The *Tribune* called Jefferson "puritanical," but in the lead-up to World War I he was an outspoken peace advocate, and once the war began, he opened a canteen inside the Tabernacle to serve the city's swelling ranks of soldiers and sailors. He was both a charismatic preacher and an avid baseball fan, and in his conception of the role of churches in the twentieth century was a liberal and thoroughly modern theologian.

"The church may be dead," he declared, "but it is astounding how active the corpse is. It is doing a thousand more things dead than it ever tried to do in the days of its most abundant vitality."

Jefferson wanted the new Tabernacle to include not only a spacious auditorium for meetings but also lecture halls, theaters, offices, workshops, lounges, a Sunday school, and a museum. With no room to expand laterally, the only solution was to build vertically, and plans for the new Tabernacle soon grew to ten stories.

The Tabernacle inspired something of a craze in skyscraper churches: The same year the Tabernacle opened, John D. Rockefeller proposed a twelve-story church for the Euclid Avenue Baptist Church in Cleveland, which, though never built, would have included a gymnasium, library, Sunday school, and banquet halls. In 1908 the First United Evangelical Protestant German Church in Pittsburgh built a fourteen-story church encased by a secular office building, the first attempt by a parish to include commercial space in their plans as a way of making the church financially self-sustaining.

The strategy of raising funds by including office or residential space in church plans was followed in 1921 by the new Fifth Church of Christ, Scientist, on Madison Avenue and other cash-strapped parishes, although the practice was controversial: In 1922 a group of Episcopal Church officials led by William T. Manning, bishop of New York, threatened architect Alfred Granger with excommunication after he proposed a twenty-five-story skyscraper for the Diocese of Chicago's new cathedral.

"We should use in church buildings the aids and advantages science has conferred on the living generation," Granger protested. "It's not sinful to have an elevator in a church."

In 1923, Christian F. Reisner, pastor of the Chelsea Methodist Episcopal Church in Washington Heights, announced plans for a skyscraper church on Broadway between 173rd and 174th streets. Reisner, who saw little evidence of Christianity in New York's skyline, envisioned the Broadway Temple as an architectural sandwich of the liturgical and commercial: Twin twelve-story apartment buildings wrapping around a 725-foot skyscraper crowned with a lit cross that would be visible for one hundred miles and serve as a beacon for aviators. (Only the two apartment buildings were ever built.)

The following year Chicago's First Methodist Church opened a skyscraper church in the heart of the Loop. Designed in the Gothic

Revival style, the Chicago Temple included a gymnasium, class-rooms, meeting halls, and, at the top, an illuminated revolving cross. For the next six years it was the tallest building in Chicago.

In 1925, John D. Rockefeller Jr. swapped a parcel of land at 117th Street and Morningside Drive for one on the southeast corner of Riverside Drive and 122nd Street, one block west of Broadway, announced he would build a huge new ecumenical complex for his own Park Avenue Baptist Church, and convinced celebrity preacher and liberal theologian Harry Emerson Fosdick to take over as pastor. It was designed in the Gothic Revival mode but was actually a modern, steel skyscraper clad in limestone—more Woolworth Building than Chartres Cathedral—and though the press delighted in calling it the "Rockefeller Church" it was officially named the Riverside Church.

AS ROCKEFELLER WAS reviewing plans for Riverside Church, Oscar Konkle broke ground for the Christian Missionary Building one block to the east. The building's plans included a ground-floor church auditorium, a bank for missionaries, and a dining room that could seat 2,000. A swimming pool and gymnasium were planned for the basement, and a 4,500-room hotel would extend from the second to sixty-fourth floor, with twelve roof gardens and a hospital at the very top. When finished, the building would rise sixty-five stories and measure 800 feet from sidewalk to roof, 8 feet taller than the Woolworth Building, then the world's tallest structure. Konkle estimated the project's cost at $14 million.

But before any steel could begin rising into the stratosphere, 65,000 cubic yards of bedrock had to be removed from the site. Blasting began at the corner of Broadway and 122nd Street on February 25, 1926.

Konkle had tried this once before: In 1913 his six-year-old son Howard had contracted tetanus, and doctors held out little hope for his recovery. Konkle prayed, and when the boy made a miraculous recovery vowed to devote his life to raising funds for missionary work. In 1922 he found a site at the southeast corner of Broadway and

104th Street and hired architects Shreve, Lamb & Blake to design a seventeen-story building that would combine a new church for the Metropolitan Tabernacle, a Baptist congregation, with a hotel and bank for the use of Christian missionaries.

But for some reason Konkle altered the project, so that when completed it wasn't a skyscraper church at all but a secular hotel called the Broadway View. The Christian Missionary Building at Broadway and 122nd Street was intended as Konkle's fulfillment of the promise he had made twelve years before. Ten percent of the building's earnings would go toward the founding and maintenance of a medical mission in Africa, he announced, and smoking, drinking, and perhaps even Sunday newspapers would be banned from the premises.

Blasting continued at Broadway and 122nd Street through March. Contractor Gaetano Clemente, like many of his employees an Italian immigrant, directed the drilling and dynamiting of the rock, and with each detonation the jutting outcropping was whittled down until only one section remained at the edge and the rest of the site had turned into a deep pit. All was going well until just before noon on Tuesday, March 30, when, with no warning, the rock broke free and slid into the excavation, snapping the boom of a steam shovel on its way down and breaking into eight sections as it hit bottom. Five workers standing in the pit below were crushed to death.

Father Nicholas Fallotica of nearby Corpus Christi Church rushed to the scene and administered last rites as each mangled body was pulled from the debris. Positive identifications could be made on Anthony Ameno, Frank Cioffi, Joseph Como, Carlo Mazzulo, and Louis Toppi only by their clothing and the union cards they carried in their pockets.

CONSTRUCTION OF THE Christian Missionary Building was suspended in the wake of the accident, and then was further delayed by lawsuits filed against Clemente. In 1928, Konkle's dream of a modern-day Tower of Babel ended when he sold the property to the Jewish Theological Seminary, which built a new campus on the site. Completed in 1930, the new seminary was five stories of red brick with a squat tower at the corner—nice, but hardly the soaring skyscraper Konkle had vowed to build.

Riverside Church, one block to the west, was also completed in 1930, the bottomless Rockefeller money seeing the project through the 1929 stock market crash and ensuing Depression. The church seemed to fly up, especially when contrasted with the painstaking, barely discernible stone-by-stone progress at St. John the Divine seven blocks to the south. At 392 feet, Riverside Church remains the tallest church in America.

MILE 9

122ND STREET TO
143RD STREET

CHAPTER 34

"HONEST TO GOODNESS SLUM LAND"

———

ON OCTOBER 28, 1935, CHARLES-ÉDOUARD JEANNERET-GRIS, a forty-seven-year-old Swiss-born architect who called himself Le Corbusier, his mother's maiden name, lectured at Columbia's architecture school. It was his first visit to New York and his first stop on a planned national lecture tour. Whisked around the city, he turned up his nose at much of what he saw, famously proclaiming the new Empire State Building "too small." At Columbia, Le Corbusier spoke from a few sparse notes scrawled on index cards and drew feverish sketches of bridges, museums, and skyscrapers on long sheets of paper. Returning to Columbia on November 19 for another lecture, he arrived late, entering the auditorium in Havemeyer Hall casually munching on French bread, before enthralling his audience with "swift and nervous" drawings of towers marching across a park-like landscape.

Ten years earlier Le Corbusier had proposed demolishing the center of Paris and replacing it with a phalanx of cruciform towers set amid a grid of parks and highways. In *L'Architecture d'aujourd'hui*, a short film about his work produced in 1930 and shown during his 1935 American tour, Le Corbusier is seen on screen drawing a portentous black line across Paris and then blacking out the center of the city with a crayon. New York, Le Corbusier told his audience at Columbia, was the perfect laboratory for what he called *la Ville Radieuse*—the Radiant City. When Le Corbusier closed his eyes and imagined it, he saw a happy place.

THREE MONTHS BEFORE Le Corbusier appeared at Columbia, a woman sitting on a bench in Morningside Park was stabbed to death. Students were warned away from the park, but the blocks surrounding campus, where muggings and assaults had become commonplace, were dangerous enough. The fabled Acropolis, it seemed, was rapidly sliding toward desolation. Even its newer architecture faced withering criticism: "Columbia has lost conviction," Lewis Mumford wrote in 1938, "so that her latest buildings are neither studied Renaissance nor clear-cut expressions based upon modern engineering."

By the end of World War II much of Morningside Heights had devolved into a streetscape of rundown single-room-occupancy "hotels." As blacks, Puerto Ricans, and returning veterans in need of affordable housing began moving into the neighborhood, landlords, rather than renting entire six-to-twelve room Subway Boom–era apartments, cut them up and rented them by the room.

In 1947, Columbia, Barnard, Teachers College, St. Luke's, International House, Corpus Christi Church, Jewish Theological Seminary, Juilliard, Riverside Church, Union Theological Seminary, and St. John the Divine, alarmed at the changing demographics and deterioration of the area's housing, banded into a consortium called Morningside Heights, Inc. David Rockefeller, son of John D. Rockefeller Jr. and brother of future New York governor Nelson Rockefeller, served as president and city planner Lawrence M. Orton as executive director. Board members included Dwight D. Eisenhower, then president of Columbia, Barnard president Millicent C. McIntosh, Riverside Church pastor Harry Emerson Fosdick, and architect Wallace K. Harrison.

Orton blamed the neighborhood's decay on high density, poor maintenance, and "obsolete design." In October of 1948, Morningside Heights, Inc.'s Executive Committee, having analyzed data on housing and schools in the area, concluded that "nothing short of substantial rebuilding along the northern and southern border of Morningside Heights would assure the maintenance of a community in keeping with the interests of the local institutions." Rockefeller aggressively lobbied Robert Moses, chairman of the mayor's Committee on Slum Clearance Plans—Moses wore many hats: He was simultaneously the city's parks commissioner and construction coordinator, as well as chairman of the Triborough Bridge and Tunnel Authority—to help Morningside Heights, Inc., build housing for the faculty, employees, and graduate students of its member institutions.

Moses informed Rockefeller that he would support Morningside Heights, Inc., only if they built new housing on "honest to goodness slum land." That's when Morningside Heights, Inc., set its sights on Manhattanville.

MANHATTANVILLE, THE NEIGHBORHOOD directly north of Morningside Heights, is situated in a valley that runs in an easterly direction from the Hudson River to Harlem. The valley is a geological fault line, one of two faults underlying Manhattan (the second crosses under Broadway farther to the north, along Dyckman Street in Inwood). In Dutch times the valley was called Moertje David's Fly; in Revolutionary War days it was called the Hollow Way.

Manhattanville was founded around 1806 by drug merchants Jacob Schieffelin, his brother-in-law and business partner John B. Lawrence, and Thomas Buckley, a neighbor, and quickly grew into a bucolic village of tidy, working-class dwellings clustered around St. Mary's Episcopal Church, which was consecrated in 1826 on land donated by Schieffelin. Manhattan Avenue, present-day 125th Street, was the village's main street, a broad path connecting Harlem Cove, an inlet on the Hudson River, with the village of Harlem to the east.

In the 1830s the D. F. Tiemann & Company Paint and Color Works—owner Daniel F. Tiemann, whose father had founded the factory, served a term as New York's mayor from 1858 to 1860—

In 1860, Manhattanville was still a bucolic village along the Bloomingdale Road.

relocated from 23rd Street to Manhattanville and built a sprawling complex of buildings on the south side of Manhattan Avenue just west of the Bloomingdale Road. In 1851, Manhattanville became the Hudson River Railroad's first station north of New York, and the population exploded. Irish and German immigrants seeking work in Manhattanville's factories and mills moved in and the village grew into a factory town, although as late as the 1890s vacant lots were still plentiful.

The Subway Boom of 1900–1904 brought new tenements and apartment buildings and more people, and by 1909 the neighborhood's black population had doubled. By World War II the neighborhood was a dense urban landscape of tenements, breweries, garages, coal yards, and milk-pasteurizing-and-bottling facilities. Manhattanville wasn't very pretty, but it was hardly the slum that Morningside Heights, Inc., imagined. Morningside Heights, Inc.'s own survey of Manhattanville residents, undertaken in 1950 and funded by Rockefeller, revealed that over half of respondents weren't dissatisfied with their housing situation in the least and that there was "no exceptional incidence of [over]crowding" in the neighborhood.

THE LINK BETWEEN Morningside Heights and Manhattanville is Broadway, which, beginning at 122nd Street, descends into the valley while the subway continues in a straight line across a steel viaduct, the tracks disappearing into a tunnel again on the far side of the valley at 135th Street. Morningside Heights, Inc., homed in on two square blocks just north of the Jewish Theological Seminary, on the east side of Broadway between 123rd and La Salle streets, as the possible site for a middle-income housing project catering to the employees of its member institutions.

The site consisted of 71 buildings on about 10 acres. Sixty-four of the buildings were five-story "old law" tenements that predated the city's housing act of 1901. But there were newer buildings, too, including the seven-story Columbia Hotel at the corner of Broadway and 124th Street, which had a well-regarded Japanese restaurant, Chidori, on the ground floor. The two blocks were densely populated and down at the heels, but not necessarily beyond redemption. But Morningside Heights, Inc., anxious for the support of the Housing Authority and Moses, was more than ready to tear it all down.

Morningside Heights, Inc., formed its own real-estate arm, Remedco, and on October 1, 1951, Morningside Heights, Inc., and Moses's Committee on Slum Clearance Plans announced that the Manhattanville site would be demolished and a Title I middle-income cooperative housing project, called Morningside Gardens and sponsored by Morningside Heights, Inc., would rise in its place.

The announcement prompted an immediate outcry from Save Our Homes, a committee of residents formed to protest the forced displacement of residents from the Morningside Gardens footprint. In response, Bernard Weinberg of Morningside Heights, Inc., characterized the members of Save Our Homes as "hysterical."

"[The] aim of the redevelopment of the community is to decongest the area," he said. "Naturally, some people will be hurt, but it is for the good of the community."

Save Our Homes also agitated for low-income housing for the

neighborhood, and on November 12 the city announced plans to build a federally funded low-income housing project, called the General Ulysses S. Grant Houses, on a huge site extending from Broadway across Amsterdam Avenue to Morningside Avenue, just to the north of Morningside Gardens. To assuage Save Our Homes and other critics, Morningside Heights, Inc., promised that every displaced resident would get first preference for apartments in Morningside Gardens. Second preference would go to the employees and members of its nine sponsoring institutions, and those who couldn't afford Morningside Gardens would have places in the Grant Houses.

The city's Board of Estimate voted to approve Morningside Gardens on January 15, 1953, contingent on construction of the adjacent Grant Houses. That summer the Morningside Heights Housing Corporation, which consisted of nine of Morningside Heights, Inc.'s fourteen institutions, with Barnard president Millicent C. McIntosh acting as Chairman of the Board, purchased the Morningside Gardens site—10 acres in total—from the city for the "upset price" of $1,302,046.

ON JANUARY 11, 1954, in the midst of a driving blizzard, a "demolition ceremony" was held on the Morningside Gardens site. Rockefeller, McIntosh, Fosdick, Fr. George B. Ford of Corpus Christi Church, and Bernard Segal of the Jewish Theological Seminary were among the speakers. At the time the Morningside Heights Housing Corporation acquired the property there were 1,317 families and 68 commercial tenants on the site. A mass exodus was already underway when the bulldozers and dump trucks moved in. By the spring of 1955 only 305 families and 9 commercial tenants remained, and 42 buildings had been completely emptied and turned over to the demolition crews.

"After one or two futile attempts . . . the opposition disintegrated," Elizabeth R. Hepner crowed in a promotional booklet published in 1955 by Morningside Heights, Inc.

That summer Gertrude Samuels wrote a feature article about Morningside Gardens in the *New York Times Magazine*. Samuels

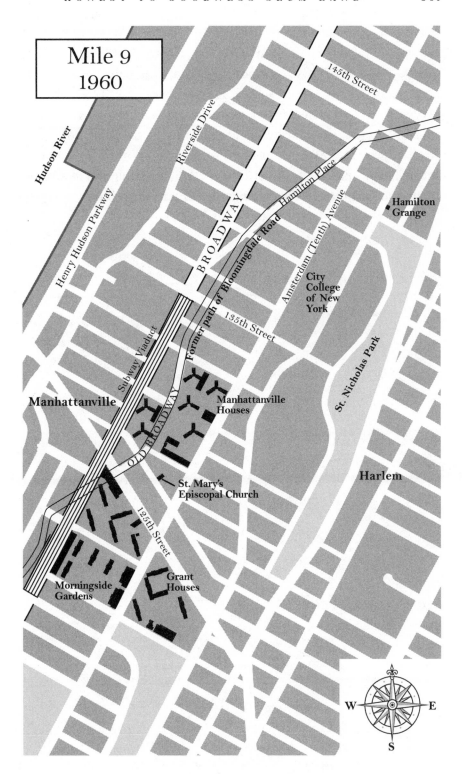

Mile 9
1960

Hudson River

Riverside Drive

145th Street

Henry Hudson Parkway

BROADWAY

Hamilton Place

Former path of Bloomingdale Road

Amsterdam (Tenth) Avenue

Hamilton
Grange

City
College
of New
York

135th Street

St. Nicholas Park

Subway Viaduct

Manhattanville

OLD BROADWAY

Manhattanville
Houses

Harlem

St. Mary's
Episcopal Church

125th Street

Morningside
Gardens

Grant
Houses

W   E

S

rejoiced as Manhattanville's "antiquated rat traps" were "wiped off the map," while dismissing Save Our Homes as an "extreme left-wing group." But Samuels also took note of a despairing public school principal, Anne Ruddy, whose school, P. S. 125 on 123rd Street, already overcrowded and underfunded, was about to be overrun by the children of Morningside Gardens' and the Grant Houses' new residents. Referring to the institutions of Morningside Heights, Inc., Ruddy said, "The people on the hill still have a long way to go to be sold on their responsibilities to the community and to the schools."

CHAPTER 35

MURDERVILLE

ROUND WAS BROKEN ON THE GENERAL ULYSSES S. GRANT Houses on July 14, 1954; demolition of the site's existing buildings, and relocation of its residents, had begun the previous summer. The project, designed by the architects Eggers & Higgins, consisted of 1,940 units in eight 20-story towers and one 14-story tower situated on 15 acres of land. The towers, unadorned red brick with swatches of beige set between small windows, were placed like chess pieces amid a vast greensward of playgrounds and lawns that erased sections of Moylan Place, Tiemann Place, La Salle Street, and 124th Street.

The following year, on September 16, 1955, amid mountains of rubble, Morningside Gardens broke ground on the south side of LaSalle Street. Mayor Robert F. Wagner, Robert Moses, David Rockefeller, and Millicent C. McIntosh all gave speeches. Seventy-five percent of the site's buildings had been demolished at that point, while five of the new towers had been completed up to the fourteenth floor.

The firm of Harrison & Abramovitz—that was Wallace Harrison, one-time Morningside Heights, Inc., board member—designed the project, which consisted of 980 units in half a dozen twenty-story towers arranged around a central garden. Like the Grant Houses, the towers of Morningside Gardens were reductively Modern, brick

**The Morningside Gardens and
General Ulysses S. Grant Houses projects, 1958.**

and rectangular, with little detail except for balconies cantilevered from the façades.

As construction continued on the Grant Houses and Morningside Gardens, another gargantuan housing project got underway two blocks to the north, on an L-shaped, 12-acre site on the east side of Broadway between 129th and 133rd streets.

Financed by New York State and originally intended for middle-income residents, the Manhattanville Houses ended up, like the Grant Houses, as a low-income project. The architect was William Lescaze, a Swiss-born, pipe-smoking Modernist at the forefront of a generation of European and American architects who, having cut their teeth on the English "Garden City" movement of social theorists Ebenezer Howard and Patrick Geddes, embraced a "towers-in-the-park" aesthetic that inflated scale and ignored existing street patterns in the name of "efficiency." The Manhattanville Houses was Le Corbusier's *la Ville Radieuse* imported to New York.

The project consisted of six twenty-story towers with a total of 1,272 units. Each tower had three sectors fanning out from a central elevator-and-stair core, a pinwheel arrangement that made the towers resemble the invading Martian tripods in H. G. Wells's *War of the Worlds*. Lescaze was a master stylist—his previous projects had included the streamlined Philadelphia Savings Fund Society skyscraper and the jazzy, ocean liner–like CBS Columbia Studios in Los Angeles—but, confined by the Housing Authority's budget and design restrictions, in the end all Lescaze could do to distinguish the Manhattanville Houses from every other public housing project in the country was to specify blue-glazed brick for the service cores and red-metal panels for the balconies. The towers had nothing to do with the older blocks around them, and not even much to do with one another. And all of them ignored Broadway.

BROADWAY'S COMMERCIAL, cultural, and social vitality came from its buildings—its department stores, shops, theaters, hotels, meeting halls, offices, and barrooms—crowding right up to the sidewalk. Land was expensive on Broadway, and only in a few instances—New York Hospital, City Hall, Peter Goelet's mansion just north of Union Square—had buildings been set back from the street. Both the east and west sides of Broadway had developed into almost unbroken walls of buildings, and the rare open spaces—City Hall Park and Union, Madison, Herald, and Times squares—were welcome aberrations from the pattern. The stretch of Broadway in Manhattanville wasn't exactly picturesque, but it didn't help matters that Morningside Gardens and the Grant and Manhattanville houses turned the east side of Broadway into a nebulous, undefined smear of garbage-strewn grass.

The elusive energy of neighborhoods that Jane Jacobs, in her groundbreaking 1961 treatise *The Death and Life of Great American Cities*, called "buoyancy" was largely absent from Manhattanville's three new projects, and much of what was missing was due to the architects' casual approach to the life of the street. A few concessions here and there—the Housing Authority added a supermarket at the corner of Broadway and 125th Street and preserved an existing branch library on 125th Street, while Harrison & Abramovitz

provided storefronts along the Amsterdam Avenue edge of Morningside Gardens—couldn't make up for a general lack of interest on
the part of the projects' designers for the complexities of what Jacobs
called our "complicated and ornery society." Harrison & Abramovitz's
acknowledgment that Broadway defined the western edge of Morningside Gardens was to build a windowless, brick parking garage
along its entire length between 123rd and LaSalle streets—hardly a
celebration of America's most famous street.

MORNINGSIDE GARDENS' first tenants moved in on June 24, 1957.
One-third of them came from the staffs of Columbia, Barnard, St.
John the Divine, and the other sponsoring institutions of Morningside Heights, Inc. Seventy-five percent of Morningside Gardens'
first residents were white, 20 percent black, 4 percent Asian, and 1
percent Puerto Rican—racial demographics that, at the time, were
considered ideal. Thurgood Marshall, then chief counsel of the
NAACP, was among the project's first residents, and over the next
decade, as the cash-strapped Housing Authority struggled to build
more projects, Morningside Gardens was held up as an aspirational
model. In 1982, twenty-five years after it opened, the buildings and
grounds of Morningside Gardens were still well maintained. Its
demographics hadn't changed much—by then, 60 to 65 percent
were white and 30 percent black—and residents felt generally safe
and content.

The Grant and Manhattanville houses didn't fare so well. The
Grant Houses opened on August 20, 1956, its first five families—two
white, two black, and one Puerto Rican—welcomed with speeches,
cookies and punch, and dancing. As night fell, the Housing Authority
spelled out HELLO by turning on lights in the windows of one of the
towers. Considering all that was to befall the Grant and Manhattanville houses in the coming decades, that final "O" might as well
have been left off.

Well-intentioned people had conceived the Grant and Manhattanville projects as bulwarks against urban decay, poverty, disease,
overcrowding, and "juvenile delinquency." But the 1950s image of

youths ditching school and battling over turf in vacant lots, Jets-and-Sharks-style, would come to seem quaint compared to the horrors that visited the Grant and Manhattanville projects beginning in the early 1960s.

Almost immediately, things went seriously wrong. Less than two years after the Manhattanville Houses opened, there had been so many robberies and rapes in the project that in September of 1962 battalions of tenants stayed up all night patrolling the lobbies of buildings that the Housing Authority hadn't equipped with locks. (The Housing Authority had only 612 police officers to cover 1,575 buildings in 105 projects across the city; only five had been assigned to the Manhattanville Houses.) Terror-stricken tenants at the Grant Houses organized themselves in similar fashion.

Only two days after tenants began pleading with the Housing Authority for more police protection, Anna Ayala, the twelve-year-old daughter of Puerto Rican immigrants, was stabbed to death in her apartment in the Manhattanville Houses. The Housing Authority's response was to assign six additional guards to the project and to install locks on the lobby doors.

For the next thirty years, as crime enveloped the Grant and Manhattanville projects, tenants continued to beseech the Housing Authority for more protection. "The tenants are afraid to leave their apartments at night, and they are not safe in the afternoon either," Janet Karlson, chair of the Manhattanville Improvement Association, told a reporter in 1968, after a resident was stabbed and robbed in an elevator in the Manhattanville Houses. "There is a pocketbook snatched, a person assaulted, or an apartment robbed virtually every day."

Still the violence continued: In 1980 twenty women reported being raped in the two projects. In 1994 the decomposed bodies of a mother and her three children were found stacked in a bathtub in the Manhattanville Houses. In 1997 a dispute between neighbors over noise resulted in a bombing that left a gaping hole in the façade of one of the Grant Houses' towers. Amid drug trafficking, muggings, and shootings, an ongoing turf war between residents of the Manhattanville and Grant projects resulted, in 2011, in the senseless murder of eighteen-year-old Tayshana Murphy, a charismatic young basketball star nicknamed "Chicken." Not for nothing did locals begin calling Manhattanville "Murderville."

In the meantime, Columbia was steadily taking over the opposite side of the street. In 2006 the university announced plans for a $7 billion expansion into Manhattanville along the west side of Broadway between 125th and 135th streets. Old warehouses and factories were leveled, and new buildings, including the Italian architect Renzo Piano's sleek Jerome L. Greene Science Center, rose in their place. It was wholesale demolition, although no one called it "slum clearance."

TODAY, WALKING NORTH on Broadway as it dips in and out of Manhattanville is a disorienting experience. Morningside Gardens and the Manhattanville and Grant houses tower over the east side of the street, while the west side is lined with tenements, gas stations, warehouses, billboards, industrial buildings, and, at the southwest corner of Broadway and 125th Street, a McDonald's sitting in the middle of a parking lot. The subway rattles back and forth overhead. The Boulevard-era mall running down the center of Broadway north of 59th Street doesn't continue through the valley of Manhattanville, its shrubs, trees, and benches replaced by parked cars jammed chaotically into the spaces between the subway viaduct's massive steel supports. The Henry Hudson Parkway is only a block to the west, and the intersection of Broadway and 125th Street is a catch basin of honking livery cabs, careering delivery trucks, and rumbling eighteen-wheelers.

Almost nothing remains of the original village of Manhattanville except for a short surviving fragment of the Bloomingdale Road running between 125th and 133rd street, one block east of Broadway. Now known as "Old Broadway," the narrow road isn't much to see, its middle portion erased by construction of the Manhattanville Houses. Between 125th and 126th streets, Old Broadway cuts across a strip of neighborhood—tenements, churches, a synagogue, nail salons, botanicas, a police station, delicatessens, liquor stores—that somehow escaped the slum clearances of the 1950s. Just on the other side of 126th Street, squeezed between a playground and a swimming pool, is St. Mary's Episcopal Church.

A handsome Gothic Revival stone building designed by the firm of Carrère & Hastings, architects of the New York Public Library, the current St. Mary's replaced the original church that Jacob Schieffelin built in 1826. Next to the church, set back from the street in a courtyard shaded by enormous trees, is a modest building of yellow clapboard, the church's one-time rectory, which was built in 1851 and is the oldest building in the neighborhood.

St. Mary's remains a neighborhood anchor, a vibrant parish whose members pack lunches for the homeless, run a thrift store, organize concerts and movie nights, and cultivate an urban farm. On Sundays the church is crowded. Schieffelin himself is there, too. He and his wife Hannah and brother Jonathan are buried in a vault in an alcove near the church's front door.

MILE 10

143RD STREET
TO 165TH STREET

CHAPTER 36

THE HOUSE ON THE HILL

—

T 135TH STREET THE SUBWAY DISAPPEARS BACK INTO ITS
tunnel beneath Broadway and the street climbs out of the valley
of Manhattanville and becomes the Boulevard once more. Bisecting Hamilton Heights, a neighborhood that since the 1960s has had
a large Dominican population, Broadway reasserts itself, drawing
crowds of neighbors, men mostly, to benches along its central mall,
which reappears between 135th and 169th streets, for games of check-
ers and dominoes. Students from the City College of New York nod
to the men and trudge uphill from the subway station at Broadway
and 137th Street on their way to the campus one block to the east,
passing delis and bodegas and lunch spots crammed with neighborhood types. It is a hectic, vibrant community, and full of life.

At the northeast corner of Broadway and 136th Street, just past
a ramshackle fruit-and-vegetable stand where oranges, plantains,
yams, and yucca roots are stacked up in piles and occasionally bounce
into Broadway, a diagonal street—it was once actually called Diagonal Street—angles away from Broadway and continues north uphill
to 144th Street. Today the street is called Hamilton Place and it is
the longest surviving fragment of the Bloomingdale Road.

If you were to travel back in time to 1800 and land near the
Bloomingdale Road, a walk up its narrow, rutted path would have

revealed farms and woods and then, at the crest of a hill, Jacob Schief-felin's estate sweeping down to the Hudson River, his house facing the Bloomingdale Road on the line of present-day 143rd Street. It was an idyllic spot that was much admired by travelers passing along the road on their way between New York and Albany, and in 1800 Alexander Hamilton asked Schieffelin if he could buy it. Schieffelin said no, but offered Hamilton 15 adjoining acres on the other side of the road. Hamilton took it, and with his wife Elizabeth set about building what Hamilton called their "little retreat."

ELIZABETH, OR ELIZA, Schuyler was born in 1757 into a prominent New York family. Her father was Philip Schuyler, a Revolutionary War general, one-time commander of the Northern Army, and member of the Continental Congress. Both the Schuylers and the Van Cortlandts on Eliza's paternal grandmother's side were descendants of some of the first settlers of New Amsterdam. Even more impressive, her mother was Catherine van Rensselaer, and the Rensselaers were *the* New York family, tracing their origins back to Kiliaen van Rensselaer and the patroonship—a kind of Dutch fiefdom—that had been granted him by the Dutch West India Company in the 1620s and included most of what later became Albany. Eliza was also related to the Rensselaers by marriage: Her sister Peggy married Stephen van Rensselaer, the wealthy "last Patroon" and one of the largest landowners in the state.

In 1779, in the thick of the war, Eliza, then twenty-three, visited relatives in New Jersey and there met Hamilton, a twenty-five-year-old aide to General George Washington and former King's College student. They fell in love; Hamilton affectionately called her Betsey.

Their backgrounds could not have been more different: Hamilton was an immigrant from the West Indies, the illegitimate son of a Scottish-born merchant. Eliza, meanwhile, grew up on 80 acres just south of Albany, in a brick Georgian-style mansion overlooking the Hudson River. Eliza and Hamilton were married in that house, in 1780, Hamilton having obtained a hasty furlough from the battlefield.

Following the Continental Army's victory at Yorktown, where Hamilton led a brigade in the capture of a key redoubt, Hamilton retired from the army and rode to Albany and the Schuyler mansion, where Eliza and their new baby, Philip, awaited his return. After the eight-year-long war finally ended in 1783 with the evacuation of the British from New York, the Hamiltons settled in a house on Wall Street, within sight of Broadway and the burned-out shell of the first Trinity Church. Hamilton, who had been admitted to the New York bar while living in Albany, set up a flourishing legal practice specializing in the defense of Loyalists systemically abused in the wake of the British evacuation.

In 1789, Hamilton was nominated as the nation's first secretary of the treasury, and the following year the Hamiltons moved to Philadelphia, which had replaced New York as the temporary capital. In Philadelphia, Hamilton, while engaged in a brutal political feud with Secretary of State Thomas Jefferson, carried on an affair with one Maria Reynolds. Eliza's good name was dragged through the mud, but somehow the marriage survived.

In 1795, Hamilton resigned as treasury secretary, and he and Eliza returned to New York with their children. They lived first at 26 Broadway, on the curving east side of the street adjacent to Bowling Green—the huge Standard Oil Building covers the site today—then at 107 Liberty Street, a few blocks to the north, and later at 54 Cedar Street. As Hamilton toiled at his law practice, Eliza raised the children and shuttled between New York and her parents' estate in Albany.

In 1800, Hamilton turned forty-five and his nemesis Thomas Jefferson was elected president. His political influence fading, Hamilton decided, at long last, to build a permanent home for his family.

SOON AFTER HAMILTON bought Schieffelin's 15 acres on the Bloomingdale Road, he added adjacent parcels of 3 and 17 acres, enlarging the estate to 35 acres. The land extended from about present-day 140th Street to 146th Street, with the northern boundary at the junction of the Bloomingdale Road and the Kingsbridge

Road, which connected the village of Harlem with upper Manhattan and the present-day Bronx. It was a convenient place to live for a lawyer with business and family in both New York, to the south, and Albany, to the north.

Hamilton hired architect John McComb Jr. to design a house he nicknamed the Grange after his uncle's plantation on the island of St. Croix and his grandfather's ancestral home in Scotland. McComb, thirty-nine, was two years away from designing New York's City Hall and was well known for his work designing "country seats" in the area, including, in 1799, the Archibald Gracie mansion overlooking the East River near present-day 88th Street. (Since 1942 the Gracie mansion, one of only three country houses from that period remaining in Manhattan, has been used as the city's official mayoral residence.)

Hamilton had been acquainted with McComb since at least as far back as the 1790s, when Hamilton, as treasury secretary, had hired McComb to design several lighthouses along the eastern seaboard. For the Grange, McComb furnished Hamilton with plans for a symmetrical house with restrained Classical details.

Hamilton's father-in-law, Philip Schuyler, weighed in from Albany on every facet of the project. "You have forgot to send me the plans of your intended house," he chided Hamilton in the summer of 1800, before dispensing detailed advice on how to treat the house's lumber: Soak and dry it carefully, Schuyler recommended, lest it shrink. Construction began in 1801, with Ezra Weeks serving as contractor.

The house faced southwest, the Bloomingdale Road in the foreground and the Hudson River and the Palisades of New Jersey beyond. From the road, a driveway lined with boxwood hedges led to the house. The backyard, etched with creeks, had a barn, root house, henhouse, icehouse, milk house, and shed, and offered stunning views of the Harlem Plains and, in the distance, the turbulent waters of Hell Gate.

McComb designed a house of two stories, painted yellow, with an ornate balustrade running around a low hip roof from which four chimneys, two of them fake to preserve the symmetry, protruded. The Grange's second floor had three bedrooms that somehow accommodated Hamilton, Eliza, and their seven children. The kitchen, in the manner of the day, was in the basement. McComb designed the house's first floor around two "Octagon Rooms," as he called them, one a parlor and the other a formal dining room, that could be joined by opening three intervening doors. The Octagon Rooms had floor-to-ceiling triple-hung windows that flooded the interior with light, and pushed beyond the box-like envelope of the house, creating a sense of expansion. In summer, the top sashes of the windows could be pulled down to encourage cross-ventilation; alternatively, the two lower sashes could be raised, turning the windows into doors that provided access to verandahs on either side of the house.

Hamilton indulged in agrarian fantasies and became obsessed with the placement of the Grange's every tree, vine, and flower bed. He planted a circle of thirteen American sweet gum trees, meant to symbolize the thirteen states, in the front yard just outside his first-floor study, so he could enjoy their distinctive star-shaped leaves and brilliant red autumn foliage while he was toiling away on voluminous legal briefs.

A few days after Christmas 1802, Hamilton wrote a letter to Philadelphia lawyer Richard Peters. "A disappointed politician you know is very apt to take refuge in a Garden," he began. "Accordingly I have purchased about thirty acres nine miles from Town, have built a house, planted a garden, and entered upon some other simple improvements." That part of the letter is famous and has been often quoted; lesser known is the heart of the letter, in which Hamilton hits up Peters for a couple of bushels of his best grass seed.

Whenever Hamilton was away on business, he sent Eliza obsessive messages detailing tasks around the Grange that required her immediate attention. "Don't forget to visit the *Grange*," he wrote her in January of 1801. "From what I saw there it is very important the drains should be better regulated."

More instructions followed: Eliza must see to a new roof for the icehouse, Hamilton wrote, and oversee the planting of hemlocks along the garden fence ("I mean the side nearest the house," he clarified). There were ditches to be dug, he reminded her, and cow dung (one wagonload) and black mold (two wagonloads) that must be spread immediately in the garden's compost. "You see, I do not forget the Grange," he joked.

Once the Grange was finished, in 1802, Hamilton and Eliza finally had a home of their own, and Hamilton enjoyed a brief two years playing the part of the country squire. From his office on Stone Street to the Grange was a round trip of three hours by stagecoach, but he gamely made the trek four or five days a week. The hilltop Grange was exposed to the full force of wind and rain coming off the Hudson, and during thunderstorms the house "rocked like a cradle," James Kent, chief justice of the New York Supreme Court, wrote after a visit in April of 1804. But Kent also wrote that he had never seen the mercurial Hamilton so "friendly and amiable."

ONLY THREE MONTHS after Kent's visit, Hamilton was famously killed by Vice President Aaron Burr in a duel in Weehawken, New Jersey. Hamilton was $50,000 to $60,000 in debt at the time of his death. Ten days before his fateful meeting with Burr, Hamilton drew up a summary of the woeful state of his finances and appealed to the generosity of his wealthy father-in-law to provide for Eliza and the children. "[Schuyler] knows well all the nicety of my past conduct,"

**Alexander and Eliza Hamilton's Grange in its original
bucolic location along the Bloomingdale Road.**

he wrote, conveniently forgetting his past marital infidelity. But Schuyler, as it turned out, wasn't as wealthy as he appeared—he was, like Hamilton, in debt—and died only four months after Hamilton.

Hamilton had made out a will two days before he died. Rather than transfer the Grange's title to Eliza, Hamilton left the house to three executors, Nathaniel Pendleton, Nicholas Fish, and Hamilton's brother-in-law John B. Church, instructing them to auction off the house to cover his debts. "I pray God that something may remain for the maintenance and education of my dear wife and children," he wrote.

Hamilton figured the Grange was worth about $25,000. On April 8, 1805, it fetched $30,500 at auction, and Pendleton, Fish, Church bought it back and sold it to Eliza at half price. Even so, she had been left deeply in debt, and Hamilton's friend and eulogist Gouverneur Morris solicited subscriptions for a fund to help her make ends meet. In 1816, Congress passed "An Act for the relief of Elizabeth Hamilton," restoring to Eliza the military pension that Hamilton, as a Revolutionary War veteran, was entitled to but had turned down.

Eliza wore widow's black for the rest of her life and outlived her husband by fifty years. She devoted her life to charitable pursuits— she was the founder of the New York Orphan Society—and managed to hold onto the Grange until 1848, when she sold it and moved to Washington D.C. Although her stature grew over time, she never mingled in Washington's fashionable circles. She died in 1854, at age ninety-seven, and was laid beside Hamilton in Trinity Churchyard. A grandson, Alexander Hamilton III, born a decade after Hamilton's death, credited Eliza with teaching him to be a man and a citizen.

ELIZA WAS GONE, but the Grange was just beginning a long and tortuous second act. After Eliza's death her land was rented out as pasture for horses and then wound up in the hands of William H. De Forest, a real-estate speculator and importer of French silk. In 1887, De Forest subdivided what real-estate agents called the "Hamilton Grange" into 300 lots and put them up for auction. But when the hammer began falling, De Forest declared he was unhappy with the sales prices and abruptly halted the proceedings. Three months later De Forest went bankrupt, and the estate was divided among his creditors. Wall Street broker Amos Cotting became the owner of Hamilton and Eliza's house on the hill.

The eighty-five-year-old house was nothing if not forlorn, a curious remnant from another era adrift in a sea of vacant lots. In the 1880s it was painted a shade of olive green and rented to a family named Foley. A reporter from the *Evening World* noticed a goat roaming the yard, a clothesline hung with undergarments, and the sound of a piano coming through the open windows. The original carriage drive lined with boxwood hedges still wound around the house, and all thirteen of Hamilton's sweet gum trees, enclosed in a brown picket fence, remained in the front yard outside the room that had once been Hamilton's study. The trees were tall but spindly; Hamilton, not much of a horticulturalist as it turned out, had planted them too close together.

The Grange, stranded on a fragment of its original grounds, sat at a 30-degree angle to 143rd Street, which was scheduled to open through the property that fall. The back corner of the house intruded slightly into the path of the planned street, and its foundations had been compromised by the roadwork. The Grange, it seemed, faced certain demolition.

Then St. Luke's Episcopal Church moved from Hudson Street, in Greenwich Village, to Harlem. Isaac H. Tuthill, St. Luke's pastor, came upon the Grange while scouting for building sites and contacted Cotting about donating the house to the church for use as a temporary chapel. Cotting agreed, on the condition that Tuthill build the new St. Luke's in the neighborhood. (Cotting no doubt figured that the presence of a fine new church like St. Luke's would increase property values in the area.) In early 1889 the Grange was gingerly picked up, moved 400 feet south to the corner of Convent Avenue and 141st Street, swiveled so that one of its sides faced Convent Avenue, and placed on a new basement next to the site where the new St. Luke's would be built. (The new church, a magnificent Romanesque brownstone building, was completed in 1892.)

The Grange's original basement stayed behind on 143rd Street, along with Hamilton's sweet gum trees. Marooned in the middle

Two police officers and a dog pose next to Hamilton's prized sweet gum trees, ca. 1890. In the background is the Grange, on a new foundation, and St. Luke's Episcopal Church, then under construction.

of the block between 142nd and 143rd streets, the trees languished, and by 1904, when three generations of Hamilton's descendants—his grandsons Colonel John C. L. Hamilton and Major General Alexander Hamilton III, great-grandson Rev. Alexander Hamilton IV, and, looking bored out of his mind, great-great-grandson Alexander Hamilton V—gathered on 143rd Street to observe the 200th anniversary of Hamilton's death, only seven dead trunks remained. The last trunk was cut down in December of 1908.

In 1924, a six-story brick apartment block was built right up to the property line on the Grange's north side, originally the house's rear façade. With St. Luke's front portico projecting just slightly in front of the Grange along Convent Avenue, the old house was effectively trapped. That same year the American Scenic and Historic Preservation Society, through a $100,000 gift from J. P. Morgan and George F. Baker Jr., took over the Grange, and beginning in 1933 operated the house as a museum. But it gradually went to seed.

THROUGH LONG YEARS of degradation there remained a persistent idea that the Grange should be moved to a more appropriate location. In 1950 the American Scenic and Historic Preservation Society, apparently believing that New York landmarks were interchangeable, suggested to Robert Moses that the Grange might be moved to Riverside Drive near 125th Street as a replacement for the historic Claremont Inn, which was slated for demolition. Nothing came of that idea, or of a plan in 1955 to move the Grange a few blocks south to St. Nicholas Terrace and 130th Street, on the campus of City College.

In 1962, President John F. Kennedy signed a congressional act designating the house as the Hamilton Grange National Monument and placing it, at least in theory, under the supervision of the National Park Service. But the law stipulated that the house could only be restored if it was moved to a better site, and when that didn't happen, the house continued to decay.

Landscape painter and author Eric Sloane, who had grown up around the corner from the Grange but hadn't been aware of its history, rediscovered the house in 1967 and became friends with its caretaker, Raleigh Henry Daniels, who had become an expert on Hamiltoniana, always referred politely to Hamilton as "the General," and by the time Sloane came on the scene was desperately driving nails into the Grange's rotting planks and beams in an ongoing effort to keep it upright. The Grange was in miserable condition. During thunderstorms, Daniels, who lived in the basement, listened to the house creaking, snapping, and groaning, just as James Kent had 163 years earlier.

"The Grange is a sad house," Daniels told Sloane. "The sadness seems to have a special meaning; perhaps I am the only one aware of that. It is as if the General wants to say something across the years, and there is no one else to listen."

FOR THE NEXT forty years the Grange remained wedged between St. Luke's on its south side and the apartment building on its north side. The house had been fixed up to a degree, and staffed by courteous park rangers giving tours to school groups and occasional history buffs. There were periodic rumors that the Grange might be moved to a more appropriate site but, as before, nothing happened. Finally, in 2006, the National Park Service announced that the Grange would be hoisted up and repositioned around the corner in St. Nicholas Park, on land that had once encompassed the southernmost corner of Hamilton's estate.

Moving the Grange was decidedly tricky: Since St. Luke's portico jutted in front of the house, and the apartment building squeezed it on the other side, there was no room to maneuver, and it had long been assumed that if the house was ever moved it would have to be sawed in half. Enter the Wolfe House and Building Movers of Bernville, Pennsylvania, experts in moving historic buildings. Led by Jamin, Mark, Nathan, and Nevin Buckingham, four brothers who dressed in the modest clothing of the German Baptist Brethren, the Wolfe movers used hydraulic jacks to lift the 298-ton Grange inch-by-inch, like a Buick getting an oil change, while inserting small, rectangular wood cribbing—7,000 blocks by project's end—beneath the house's foundation. Slowly but surely, over a period of weeks, the house rose high above the street, as the cribwork below it got taller. Soon it resembled a house atop a giant Lincoln Logs set.

Once the Grange had cleared the church portico, a second wood-block tower was built in the middle of Convent Avenue. Steel beams were laid from one tower to the other, like a bridge, and on May 26, 2008, the Grange was pushed on rollers along the beams from the first to the second tower. There it perched for another week or so, 35 feet above Convent Avenue, its forgotten front façade, hidden since 1889 behind the church, revealed to all. Then, block-by-block, the tower was taken down from beneath the house until the Grange rested on rubber-tired dollies in the middle of the street. The house was braced on the inside and two miles of chains were wrapped around it.

Early in the morning of Saturday, June 7, the Buckingham brothers commandeered a remote control device mounted to the dollies and drove the Grange, ever so slowly and gingerly, down the hillside of 141st Street to St. Nicholas Park, where a new foundation and basement awaited. It was a journey of only 500 feet but took over three hours—journalist David W. Dunlap, covering the story for the *New York Times*, calculated the Grange's speed at .04 miles an hour.

The Grange having safely arrived in the park, locals from the neighborhood, along with the house movers and their children, City College students and professors, preservationists, reporters, and politicians enjoyed a picnic on the woody hillside behind the house's new basement. There was a profound sense of accomplishment, that the right thing had been done, and done well, and that the Grange had finally found a home.

IT IS THE NATURE of things in New York that very little lasts. In 1926 the *New York Times*, in speculating on the city's tendency toward perpetual change, predicted that while City Hall, the New York Public Library, Grand Central Station, and Penn Station (wrong about that one) were sure to survive the test of time, everything else in town "may be regarded as fluid."

Even some of the things that do last don't necessarily remain fixed in the same location. The Grange, built securely on a hilltop nine miles north of the city, moved not once but twice, each time leaving its basement behind, like a hermit crab trading in its old shell. Even the Bloomingdale Road, once so critical to New York's commerce and social networks, disappeared, leaving only a few short fragments and barely discernible traces behind.

Today the Grange has been restored to the tune of $8 million. Knowledgeable, friendly park rangers, besieged on occasion by fans of the Broadway musical *Hamilton*, guide visitors through the Grange's first-floor rooms. (There were 682 visitors in February of 2015, the month *Hamilton* opened quietly at the Public Theater. During the following October, by which time the show had moved to Broadway and become the most talked-about musical in years, 6,735 visitors filed through the once-lonely house.)

The Grange, neglected for so many years, now seems rooted in its new site and reassuringly permanent, but it's unwise to bet against change. If it was improbable that Eliza Hamilton should have outlived her husband by fifty years, or that the Grange, a fragile wooden house, should have outlasted the World Trade Center, it's equally unlikely that the positions of both the Grange and Broadway will remain fixed for eternity. Two hundred years from now, Broadway itself might have shifted course once again or even disappeared altogether. The row houses, tenements, and churches that rose up around Hamilton's former estate might be gone too, and the Grange might have moved again. Maybe someday it will even be returned to its original hilltop overlooking the Hudson, and eventually surrounded by nothing but fields and woods.

CHAPTER 37

NECROPOLIS

ALEXANDER HAMILTON'S DEATH—SHOT TO DEATH BY THE
sitting vice president of the United States!—was nothing if not
unique. Most New Yorkers in Hamilton's day died more commonplace
deaths: of "dropsy" (edema), colic, dyspepsia, croup, measles, small
pox, yellow fever, scarlet fever, typhoid fever, cholera, pneumonia,
heart disease, cancer, consumption (tuberculosis), or whooping cough.
They drowned, fell down wells or off roofs, were kicked by horses,
run over by wagons, drays, and carts, were killed in fires, killed each
other, or killed themselves. Thousands upon thousands of children
never made it past their first year.

Hamilton was buried in Trinity Churchyard, in a grave just inside
the south fence. Burials had begun there in 1681, seventeen years
before the first version of Trinity Church was built, and when Hamilton went into the ground in 1804, the cemetery was already stuffed
with thousands upon thousands of Sarahs, Samuels, Deborahs, Ruths,
Ezekiels, Hannahs, and Isaacs. In 1808, tourist John Lambert noted
that the churchyard was already "crowded with the dead."

"One would think there was a scarcity of land in America, by seeing such large pieces of ground in one of the finest streets of New
York occupied by the dead," he wrote. "[The] continual view of such
a crowd of white and brown tomb-stones and monuments which is

exhibited in the Broadway, must at the sickly season of the year tend very much to depress the spirits."

The "sickly season" was in the late summer and fall, when annual epidemics visited the city and carried off men, women, and children. Yellow fever killed over 4,000 New Yorkers in seasonal epidemics between 1702 and 1805—2,086 died in the particularly dreadful 1798 epidemic—but its causes were poorly understood. Medical experts blamed noxious air ("miasmas") and figured the disease came from swamps, dirty streets and buildings, immigrants—the Irish were often blamed for the scourge—and cemeteries. (It wasn't until 1900 that physician Walter Reed discovered that mosquitoes, not bad air or the Irish, spread the virus.) In January of 1806, two years before Lambert's visit and a few months after yet another yellow fever epidemic befell the city in the fall of 1805, the city's Board of Health recommended prohibiting all burials in the city.

That rather drastic recommendation wasn't followed, and by the 1820s Trinity Churchyard, though it encompassed less than 2 acres, held thousands of corpses. Another yellow fever epidemic arrived in the fall of 1822, and in 1823 the Common Council voted to ban the digging of new graves south of Grand Street. (Existing family vaults were exempted, which meant that the wealthy continued to be buried in the lower sections of the city while many of the city's poor went into potters' fields north of town—Washington Square, Madison Square, and Bryant Park all began as potters' fields. Subsequent laws extended the line northward until by 1859 no burials were allowed below 86th Street.)

In 1838 Green-Wood Cemetery, 300 acres of rolling hills with stunning views, was founded in Brooklyn, inspiring Trinity to begin planning its own rural cemetery. In 1842, Trinity purchased 24 acres of hilly, rocky land along the Hudson River from box manufacturer Richard F. Carman, who was then developing a village called Carmansville along Tenth Avenue between 142nd and 158th streets. The new Trinity Cemetery spanned from Tenth Avenue to the river between 153rd and 155th streets, which hadn't yet opened. James Renwick Jr., then just embarking on the design of Grace Church on lower Broadway, was hired to design the grounds. The first burials took place in 1843.

The views from Trinity Cemetery of the Hudson River and New Jersey Palisades beyond were breathtaking, and as soon as the cemetery opened, steamboat companies began offering daily trips upriver to see it. "A more desirable excursion for schools cannot be found than a visit to the Cemetery," noted one 1845 advertisement in the *New York Herald*.

It was an idyllic, quiet, contemplative spot, but in 1871, less than thirty years after it was laid out, Trinity Cemetery was cut in two by the opening of the Boulevard, which divided the cemetery into east and west sections of roughly equal proportions and left outcroppings of sparkling grey schist jutting high above the street on either side. As soon as the road was opened, Trinity hired Calvert Vaux to design a pedestrian suspension bridge across the breach, linking the cemetery's two sections. Vaux's jaunty little span, like a Brooklyn Bridge in miniature, didn't last: It was torn down in 1911 to make way for the new Church of the Intercession at the southeast corner of Broadway and 155th Street, and ever since then visitors interested in seeing both parts of the cemetery have had to leave and cross over Broadway at street level.

TIME HAS NOT HEALED the incision. Winding, bucolic pathways still end abruptly at the cut, the edges of which remain fresh and jagged above streams of traffic below. But the cemetery, especially its hilly western section, is dotted with maples, oaks, and honey locusts of girths not usually associated with present-day Manhattan. The wide Hudson seemingly within spitting distance, the cemetery is one of the very few remaining places in Manhattan where it is still possible to visualize a time when most of the island was rural.

Trinity Cemetery also presents a kind of reunion of prominent nineteenth-century New Yorkers; an ingathering of long-dead merchants, politicians, real-estate developers, physicians, lawyers, actors, poets, painters, and their wives and children, all huddled together and minding their own business in a village of granite vaults and worn grave markers. You almost want to interrogate them a bit, now that they're all stuck in one place and unlikely to run away; to ask

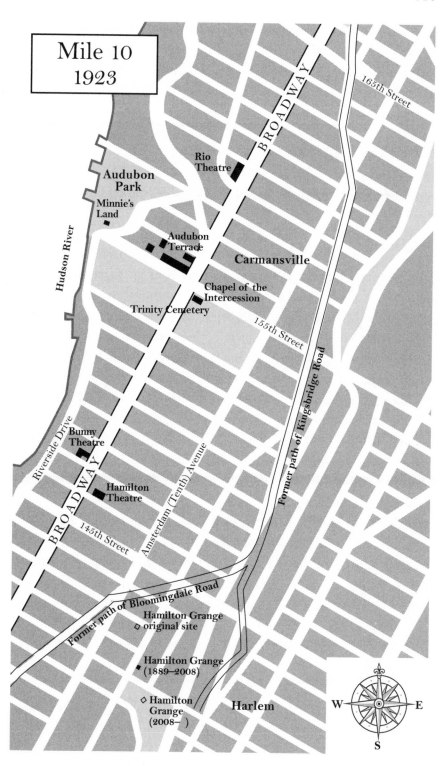

Mile 10
1923

165th Street

BROADWAY

Rio
Theatre

Audubon
Park

Minnie's
Land

Hudson River

Audubon
Terrace

Carmansville

Chapel of the
Intercession

Trinity Cemetery

155th Street

Former path of Kingsbridge Road

Riverside Drive

Bunny
Theatre

BROADWAY

Hamilton
Theatre

Amsterdam (Tenth) Avenue

145th Street

Former path of Bloomingdale Road

Hamilton Grange
◇ original site

Hamilton Grange
(1889–2008)

◇ Hamilton
Grange
(2008–)

Harlem

W   E

S

shipbuilder Robert Bowne Minturn how it felt to watch the *Flying Cloud* unfurl its sails for the first time in 1851; to get a sense from Eliza Jumel of what it was like to be married to the likes of Aaron Burr; to ask John Augustus Shea, an Irish immigrant who died in 1845, to recite a few lines from his poem "The Ocean."

> *How humbling to one with a heart and a soul,*
> *To look on thy greatness and list to thy roll,*
> *And to think how that heart in cold ashes shall be,*
> *While the voice of eternity rises from thee.*

Clement Clarke Moore would no doubt be interested to know that people still recite his poem "A Visit from St. Nicholas." Samuel B. Ruggles, his marker faded to illegibility, would probably be astonished to find that Union Square is populated by everyone from hip-hop dancers and Hare Krishnas to hedge-fund managers. Richard F. Carman would probably be dismayed to learn that only the nerdiest of New York historians can still locate Carmansville on a city map.

There are thirty-seven members of the Astor family buried in vaults along the westernmost hillside of Trinity Cemetery. They include the original John Jacob Astor, who died in 1848 and was temporarily interred at St. Thomas's Church, at Broadway and Houston Street, before his remains were moved uptown, and his great-grandson John Jacob Astor IV, the science-fiction-writing "Jack," whose frozen body was fished out of the Atlantic after the *Titanic* disappeared beneath him in 1912. Two questions for the Astors: What do you think of the view? And isn't it strange to have spent your lifetimes buying and selling land, only to have become land yourselves?

CHAPTER 38

MINNIE'S LAND

———

THE REMAINS OF JOHN JAMES AUDUBON LIE IN TRINITY Cemetery beneath an ornate stone crucifix carved with birds (including a vulture), cougars, bison, deer, and bears, along a winding path to the rear of the Church of the Intercession. A relief of Audubon's ruggedly handsome face encircled with long, flowing locks—he was always vain about his hair—protrudes from the monument's base.

Audubon was born in 1785 on his wealthy father's plantation in Saint-Domingue (present-day Haiti), the bastard son of his father's mistress. He immigrated to New York in 1803 in the midst of that year's yellow fever epidemic, fell ill, and was nursed back to health by Quakers, who also taught him English. He traveled to a farm his father owned in Pennsylvania, and there fell in love with seventeen-year-old Lucy Bakewell. He was nineteen.

Audubon had always loved birds and had always loved drawing, and in Pennsylvania he experimented with drawing birds from life, procuring his specimens by shooting them. He devised armatures to hold their limp bodies, piercing their lifeless carcasses with sharpened wires fixed to a wooden plank. At the time, almost none of the thousands of American bird species had been documented, and when ornithologists did find new specimens, they stuffed them into rigid, lifeless poses. Audubon, a romantic through and through, wanted to capture the spirit and movement of birds, the exuberance of the mockingbird "pour[ing] forth his melody, full of exultation," the "ethereal motions" of the hummingbird, "so rapid and so light," and the silent flight of the great horned owl, "gliding on extended pinions across the river, sailing over one hill and then another, or suddenly sweeping downwards, and again rising in the air like a moving shadow, now distinctly seen, and again mingling with the somber shades of the surrounding woods, fading into obscurity." Audubon was positively Byronic when it came to owls.

For the rest of his life Audubon traveled back and forth to Europe, through the American South and West, up into the wilds of Canada, and down to Central and South America in search of birds and business. As his renown grew, he glossed over the particulars of his French upbringing, and despite his French accent was esteemed as more authentically American than just about anyone else—Daniel Boone with a gun in one hand and pencils and paper in the other. When the *New York Herald* asked him to describe his nationality, Audubon deflected the question with a joke: "I am part Frenchman, part American, part Spanish, and a bit of the Louisiana alligator."

AUDUBON AND LUCY married in 1808 and moved first to Louisville, Kentucky, and then to Cincinnati, where Audubon worked for a while as a taxidermist, and then to New Orleans. Around 1820, Audubon conceived of a gigantic project that was to consume much of the rest of his life, force lengthy separations from Lucy, and expend all the energy of his two sons. In 1826, Audubon took a portfolio of drawings to a printer in Edinburgh, who etched and colored the first plates of what was to become Audubon's life's work, *The Birds of America.*

It is among the most astounding books ever published. Printed in installments between 1826 and 1839 and sold by subscription, *The Birds of America* was published as an oversized "double elephant" folio measuring almost 40 by 30 inches. The book was expensive, issued as "numbers" of five unbound prints and ultimately bound into four volumes of one hundred plates each, which ended up costing a total

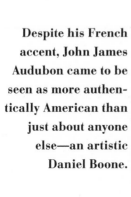

Despite his French accent, John James Audubon came to be seen as more authentically American than just about anyone else—an artistic Daniel Boone.

of almost $1,000—about $25,000 in today's dollars—and Audubon had some difficulty in securing subscribers. But those who saw the pages as they were produced were enthralled. Today it's difficult to understand, in this era of telephoto lenses and *National Geographic*, what it must have been like to see for the first time, in life-size prints colored by hand, a golden eagle, an ivory-billed woodpecker, an auk, a flamingo, or a painted bunting.

Audubon's birds were fully realized characters, and so vividly rendered they seemed about to fly off the page. Audubon often captured his subjects in mid-song, or mid-kill—there are a lot of bloody rabbit carcasses in his work—and there was something of Audubon himself in the wood thrushes, phoebes, kingfishers, whooping cranes, and herons that posed on each page. "His bird pictures reflect his own temperament, not to say his nationality," John Burroughs wrote in a 1902 biography, "the birds are very demonstrative, even theatrical and melodramatic at times." Philip Hone inspected *The Birds of Amer-*

ica in the Library of Congress and pronounced it the "most splendid book ever published."

Hone entertained Audubon in his Broadway mansion in the spring of 1833 and found him "an interesting man . . . modest in his deportment, possessing general intelligence, an acute mind, and great enthusiasm." Audubon became a celebrity in New York, where he was treated as a wonder of nature. "Audubon, the great naturalist . . . is one of the finest looking middle-aged men we ever saw," the *New York Herald* raved in 1837. "He has a large half Roman, half Grecian nose— a fine high forehead—a beautifully turned chin—and a profusion of iron grey hair, 'Streaming like a meteor in the troubled sky.' . . . His head is a study—his broad muscular shoulders like Apollo's—and his eye as bright as an eagle's."

The press found in the gregarious naturalist an irresistible subject, and Audubon, a tireless and constant promoter of himself and his work, was more than happy to give interviews. When, in 1837, *Herald* publisher James Gordon Bennett ran into Audubon on a steamship delivering passengers to the Liverpool-bound packet ship *England* anchored at Sandy Hook, Audubon offered Bennett a drink while cheerfully promoting *The Birds of America*, which, Audubon made sure to mention, was available for sale at William A. Colman's bookstore at 205 Broadway.

Audubon also told Bennett that he felt most at home in the woods, and New York City might seem like a strange choice of residence for such a restless outdoorsman. But New York had people with deep pockets, and it had fast packet ships, and so was much closer to his business contacts in England and France than was Louisiana or Kentucky, and Audubon became a familiar sight in Broadway's shops, museums, lecture halls, and bookstores.

A smaller "imperial octavo" edition of *The Birds of America* was published between 1839 and 1844 and was immensely popular— volunteer firemen presented a copy to Jenny Lind, the "Swedish Nightingale," upon her much-anticipated arrival in New York in 1850—and the edition earned $36,000 for Audubon and family, enough to buy 15 acres of land north of town near Carmansville.

He called the rural retreat Minnie's Land in Lucy's honor—

Children playing baseball at Minnie's Land, 1865.

"Minnie" being a Scottish term of endearment for "mother"—and built a wood-frame, two-story clapboard house with porches across the front and back. Completed in 1842, Audubon's house, which bore a striking resemblance to Alexander Hamilton's Grange just a mile to the south, faced east, its back to the river, near what is today the intersection of 155th Street and Riverside Drive.

Audubon's two sons, Victor and John Woodhouse, built houses for their own families close to the river on either side of their parents' house, and for a while the Audubon family lived in a kind of naturalist's Noah's Ark overrun with the otters, martens, muskrats, elk, and buffalo that, improbably, Audubon kept as pets. Minnie's Land was remote—the only way to get there was by stagecoach from the city or by walking or riding up the Kingsbridge Road—but the Audubons never lacked for visitors. Samuel F. B. Morse visited sometime in the 1840s and hooked up New York's first telegraph in Audubon's basement laundry room, the wires snaking out a window and running across the Hudson to New Jersey.

Around 1845 journalist Parke Godwin hiked up to Minnie's Land for a visit. Turning onto a "rustic road" that ran west to the river between woods and fields of grain, Godwin passed loitering cattle eating grass along the roadside and heard only the buzz of insects and songs of birds. His walk soon brought him to a "secluded house . . . unpretending in its architecture, and beautifully embowered amid elms and oaks. Several graceful fawns, and a noble elk, were stalking in the shade of the trees, apparently unconscious of the presence of a few dogs, and not caring for the numerous turkeys, geese, and other domestic animals that gabbled and screamed around them."

Shown into a ground-floor studio crammed with easels, drawing supplies, stuffed birds, the skin of a panther, and "promiscuously" scattered drawings of mice, orioles, and woodpeckers, Godwin waited for the great man to make his entrance.

"How kind it is [of you] to come see me; and how wise, too, to leave that crazy city!" Audubon announced, striding into the room and warmly shaking Godwin's hand. "Do you know how I wonder that men can consent to swelter and fret their lives away amid those hot bricks and pestilent vapors, when the woods and fields are all so near? It would kill me soon to be confined in such a prison-house; and when I am forced to make an occasional visit there, it fills me with loathing and sadness. Ah! How often when I have been abroad on the mountains has my heart risen in grateful praise to God that it was not my destiny to waste and pine among those noisome congregations of the city."

AUDUBON'S FIRST YEARS at Minnie's Land were full of vigorous activity: In 1843 he went on an expedition up the Missouri River, hunting for specimens for *The Viviparous Quadrupeds of America*, the rather awkward follow-up to *The Birds of America*—somehow Audubon's depictions of badgers, squirrels, otters, and prairie dogs didn't have the verve of his paintings of birds—then returned to Minnie's Land full of energy. But dementia gradually took over. Unable to remember family members or friends, eating as many as eleven meals a day because he couldn't keep track of when he had last eaten, Audubon sat in troubled silence, his mind, a friend wrote after a visit, "all in ruins." He died, at age sixty-five, on January 27,

1851, and was laid to rest in Trinity Cemetery, just a few minutes' walk from his house.

AUDUBON'S DEATH LEFT Lucy heavily in debt. To make ends meet, she sold off parcels of the estate and started a small school in her second-floor bedroom. In 1851, the Hudson River Railroad began running along the river edge from New York to Peekskill. A station, the second stop on the way out of town, was built at 152nd Street, only 600 feet south of Minnie's Land. The station was a godsend for the Audubons, who reconstituted Minnie's Land as a suburb called Audubon Park and sold building lots to a small coterie of wealthy merchants who commuted on the railroad to downtown offices. Audubon Park grew into a small community of perhaps a dozen rambling Victorian houses scattered in the woods around Minnie's Land, united by a winding dirt road and closed to the public by a large wooden gate, painted white, near the present-day intersection of Broadway and 156th Street.

At first, the residents of Audubon Park happily subscribed to the Audubon ethos, living in seclusion among the hemlocks, hickories, oaks, chestnuts, dogwoods, and pines, with no lawns or fences between their houses. It was a tightly knit community. George Bird Grinnell, son of a prominent downtown merchant and later one of the founders of the Audubon Society, recalled evenings when John Woodhouse Audubon would step off his porch and holler over to the Grinnell house, about a hundred yards away, "If you have nothing to do," he'd yell, "I'll come up and play you a game of billiards."

Grinnell remembered sylvan days of fishing for eels and catching crabs in the tidal pond between the river edge and a causeway over which the railroad ran, watching the sky darken with flocks of migrating passenger pigeons, and playing among wooden boxes of bird skins and unsold stacks of Audubon's *Ornithological Biography* stored in the loft of John's barn. He recalled Aubudon's house as "worn and shabby from the tramping and play of a multitude of children," a magical house full of paintings and antlers of elk and deer festooned with guns, shot pouches, and powder flasks.

Eventually fences went up between Audubon Park's houses, and lawns and flower beds replaced the brambles. Victor died in 1860, after an accident; John followed two years later. Their father's house was offered for rent: An 1861 advertisement in the *Herald* mentioned that the house enjoyed 230 feet of river frontage and was free of mosquitos and "fever and ague." Lucy, always in financial straits, sold Audubon's prints to the New-York Historical Society and his original copper engraving plates for scrap. She moved back to Louisville in 1873 and died there the following year.

WHEN THE SUBWAY was extended to 157th Street in the fall of 1904, it effectively destroyed Audubon Park. By 1909, Grinnell's father, who had earlier acquired title to most of Audubon Park—except for the three surviving Audubon houses—had sold the land to developers, who built apartment houses on new streets that were cut through the property.

Shortly after the subway opened, wealthy scholar and philanthropist Archer Milton Huntington bought part of Audubon Park and began building Audubon Terrace, an Acropolis-like, interconnected campus of institutions designed in the Beaux-Arts style on the west side of Broadway between 155th and 156th streets, just steps away from Audubon's house. In 1905, Huntington broke ground on the Hispanic Society of America, which was followed over the next two decades by the American Numismatic Society, the American Geographical Society, the Museum of the American Indian, the Church of Nuestra Señora de la Esperanza, and the American Academy of Arts and Letters.

The three Audubon houses hung on for years afterward, even as every other trace of Audubon Park disappeared. In 1897, Riverside Drive was extended north from 125th Street, dooming the remaining houses along the river. Even then, somehow, Audubon's house survived, abandoned on a fragment of land between the New York Central railroad tracks and Riverside Drive's high stone abutment where it curved inland at 155th Street.

"If there is such a thing as communication between this and the spirit world it must be a trial of trials for Audubon to see his former estate shorn, first, of its beauty, then of its size, and now hemmed in by a fortlike buttress at the back, the only six-track railroad in America on the front, and a row of garages in the small remaining strip not already occupied," the *New York Tribune* reported in 1917. "A more forlorn, desolate and dispiriting section is not to be found in the city, nor within a day's walk of the city, than the old home in which the greatest ornithologist of all time lived during the zenith of his career."

The house disappeared without ceremony in 1931.

MILE 11

165TH STREET
TO 179TH STREET

CHAPTER 39

THE HEIGHTS

———

OR SOMEONE WHO SPENT LESS THAN TWO MONTHS THERE, George Washington cast a long shadow on upper Manhattan. Washington Heights, Fort Washington Avenue, the George Washington Bridge, Fort Washington Presbyterian Church, Washington Car Service: Walking along Broadway's eleventh mile, there's no escaping the old guy.

Washington arrived in upper Manhattan on September 14, 1776, having evacuated New York following the disastrous Battle of Brooklyn, and set up headquarters in Roger Morris's mansion on a hill 120 yards east of the Kingsbridge Road. (Today the house, lovingly restored, overlooks present-day Edgecombe Avenue between 160th and 161st streets, a couple of blocks east of Broadway.) It was from the Morris house that Washington watched the Great Fire of 1776 engulf the city on September 21.

Washington's troops took up defensive positions south and north of Fort Washington, a pentagonal earthwork built the previous month on Manhattan's highest hill, some 265 feet above the Hudson River, near the present-day intersection of Fort Washington Avenue and 183rd Street.

All the effort put into building the fort, plus Fort Lee across the river in New Jersey, was for naught: On November 16, 1776, Fort Washington fell to an overwhelming force of British regulars and Hessian mercenaries, who renamed it Fort Knyphausen in honor of Hessian commander Wilhelm von Knyphausen. Washington had already fled across the river to New Jersey. The British occupied Manhattan for the duration of the war, and after the war Fort Washington and the various trenches, breastworks, and redoubts that surrounded it were left to gradually decay. As John Randel Jr. hiked through upper Manhattan some forty years later, surveying the island for the Commissioners' Plan, he stumbled across their remnants.

"All the redoubts and forts . . . consisted of embankments of earth," Randel wrote in 1864, "some of which remained standing, from 6 to 8 feet in height, and the outlines of the ruins of others remained pretty well defined upon the ground, when I surveyed them in the years 1819, 1820." The forts appear in Randel's "Farm Maps" as ghostly forms amid fields and woods. In 1881, the *Magazine of American History* reported that the ruins of Fort Washington were still there, though "hardly visible."

Randel was a meticulous surveyor, and realized the strictly orthogonal Commissioners' Plan grid he marked out below 155th Street wouldn't work in the hills and valleys of upper Manhattan. Two-dimensional grids simply don't fit cleanly onto three-dimensional forms unless they're allowed to bend and warp, but Randel's employers, commissioners Gouverneur Morris, Simeon De Witt, and John Rutherfurd, made it plain that they weren't interested in continuing the street grid past 155th Street anyway. They thought it "improbable" that the land north of 155th Street would be developed for "centuries to come."

They had a point: Upper Manhattan is an extremely narrow spit of land, barely three-quarters of a mile across at 166th Street, and steep, the land west of Broadway falling away drastically toward the Hudson River. But that didn't stop city and state officials and real-estate speculators from trying to continue the grid into upper Manhattan. An attempt in 1851 came to nothing, but in 1860 the state legislature appointed a commission to study the matter, even as it acknowledged that the whole idea of trying to continue the grid was probably "impracticable . . . ruinous to land owners, and injurious to the interests of the city."

The 1860 commissioners—president James C. Willett, vice president Henry H. Elliott, John A. Haven, Isaac P. Martin, Isaac Dyckman, Charles M. Connolly, and John F. Seaman—were all owners of real estate in Washington Heights who had built ostentatious mansions there and stood to profit from the area's further development. They envisioned "Fort Washington Park" as a planned community along the lines of Audubon Park, only much larger and wealthier, with a winding boulevard following the natural contours of the land between the Kingsbridge Road and the river. There would be no attempt to level the ground or superimpose a grid, and the Kingsbridge Road would be widened and planted with trees. Newspaper publisher James Gordon Bennett, who had just built an opulent mansion practically on top of the remains of Fort Washington, actively promoted the commission's work in the *New York Herald*.

"We trust that the Commissioners, having once entertained this excellent idea, will not abandon it, but will carry it out in the same refined taste in which it has been conceived," Bennett wrote. "Let them do so, and in a few years New York will be able to point a Parisian to a Champs-Élysées and Boulevards more exquisite than his own."

Calvert Vaux and Frederick Law Olmsted, then engaged in the design of Central Park, were brought in as consultants. Olmsted detested the Commissioners' Plan's Cartesian uniformity, its intentional lack of hierarchy. "[Some] two thousand blocks were provided, each theoretically 200 feet wide, no more, no less," Olmsted wrote, "and ever since, if a building site is wanted, whether with a view to a church or a blast furnace, an opera house or a toy shop, there is, of intention, no better a place in one of these blocks than in another."

Olmsted was a romantically inclined designer of picturesque scenes. He saw in Washington Heights a chance to counteract the inherently democratic proportions of the Commissioners' Plan grid, by laying out winding streets that would follow the natural topography of the region's hills and allow ample space for wealthy landowners to build mansions overlooking the river. Olmsted was himself from a wealthy background, and in an 1860 letter to Elliott of the Washington Heights commission revealed his vision of that enclave as a private sanctuary for the "rich and cultivated," a place for "pleasure driving," where residents could enjoy "the frequent recognition of friends of their own class." Unless its streets were designed as circuitous secluded drives, with villas arranged in discreet clusters, Olmsted warned Elliott, within ten years Washington Heights would be overrun by "brewers & grocers and coal merchants," and Irish and "Dutch" (German) squatters.

But then the Civil War intervened and the plan for Washington Heights was put on hold. Olmsted was appointed director of the United States Sanitary Commission and moved to Washington, D.C. Vaux maintained his office at 110 Broadway, briefly forming a partnership with Lewis W. Leeds before reuniting with Frederick Withers, his original partner. In 1863, Olmsted resigned his position at the Sanitary Commission and unwisely took a position in California overseeing the operation of a gold mine in the Sierra Nevada Mountains. When the venture failed, Olmsted suffered a nervous breakdown and sank into a deep depression.

In April of 1865, as part of the act authorizing construction of the Boulevard, the legislature put Andrew Haswell Green and the Commissioners of Central Park in charge of laying out a system of streets for upper Manhattan. On May 12, 1865, barely a month after the war ended, Vaux wrote to Olmsted urging his return to New York. There was work to do: That spring Vaux had begun designing Prospect Park, in Brooklyn, and wanted to take another stab at upper Manhattan. Vaux imagined Olmsted and himself as city planners on a grand scale.

"Our right unquestionably is to control matters from Washington Heights to the other end of Brooklyn," he told Olmsted.

Olmsted did return to New York to work on Prospect Park and lay the groundwork for his and Vaux's conquest of the city. In 1866 they proposed a new boulevard extending from Prospect Park to the harbor, then turning north and passing through Brooklyn to Ravenswood, in Queens. From there, they imagined the road carrying across the East River on a bridge to the East Side of Manhattan, where it would connect through Central Park to Green's planned West Side Boulevard and then proceed north to Washington Heights. Travelers could take in Prospect Park, the ocean, the East and Hudson rivers, Central Park, and Washington Heights all in one day, returning to Prospect Park by a different route, the plan forming a vast, citywide circuit.

In the end, for better or worse, Vaux and Olmsted's "grand municipal promenade," as they called it, wasn't built, and they remained park designers, not urban planners. But Washington Heights, at least the hilly part to the west of Broadway, did develop into a suburb of detached villas, just as Vaux and Olmsted and Green had envisioned, and the area wasn't subsumed into the city until well after the subway was completed to the northernmost tip of the island in 1906.

"This is the most picturesque route to the city from the land side," journalist Charles Dawson Shanly wrote of Washington Heights in 1868. "It winds past villas that stand on sloping lawns, or, like amateur Rhenish castles, frown from lofty peaks down upon the unresenting river. Evidences of wealth and culture meet the eye everywhere. Gate lodges give an air of European aristocracy to the locality. There is a feudal atmosphere about the place; one can, with due confusion of associations, almost fancy the curfew tolling here at nightfall, from the *campanile* that crowns yon lofty knoll."

CHAPTER 40

HILLTOPPERS

———

AT 169TH STREET, BROADWAY AND ST. NICHOLAS AVENUE cross over each other and switch names, with Broadway angling away from St. Nicholas Avenue and continuing through a densely packed neighborhood with a large Dominican population and dominated by the sprawling complex of Columbia-Presbyterian Medical Center, on the west side of Broadway between 165th and 168th streets. Broadway is the neighborhood's main street, lined with apartment buildings with cell phone stores, restaurants—La Dinastia, at the corner of Broadway and 171st Street, offers *comidas China Griolla*—delis, fruit stands, coffee shops, nail spas, bagel joints, and dry cleaners in their ground-floor storefronts. Broadway is also a cultural dividing line between the affluent white neighborhood to the west and the working-class Dominican neighborhood to the east.

Mitchel Square and Duarte Square (named in honor of Juan Pablo Duarte, one of the founders of the Dominican Republic) mark the spot where Broadway and St. Nicholas Avenue converge. Both squares are, like Herald Square and Times Square to the south, not squares at all but narrow, triangular islands amid a sea of traffic. Mitchel Square was originally called Audubon Square but was renamed in 1919 in honor of mayor John Purroy Mitchel, a World War I pilot who died while training to go overseas. Mitchel Square is punctuated by an outcropping of schist that breaks through its surface, a preserved fragment of the neighborhood's once-rural landscape. If you sit in the park and gaze to the west across Broadway, it's possible to edit out the hustle and bustle, the thousands of people going in and coming out of Columbia-Presbyterian across the street, and call to mind what the street must have been like around 1900, before the subway came and apartment buildings overran the street; when the Deaf and Dumb Asylum on Fort Washington Avenue, one block west of Broadway, was the only large building in the neighborhood and Broadway consisted mostly of vacant lots. Stare at Columbia-Presbyterian long enough, and it might just dissolve in the mind's eye, replaced by the wooden grandstand of a baseball field called Hilltop Park.

THE GROUNDWORK FOR bringing professional baseball to Broadway's eleventh mile began in 1901, when sportswriter-turned-executive Byron Bancroft "Ban" Johnson declared that his upstart American League would compete on equal footing with the established National League. When the American League's Baltimore team went bankrupt, saloon and casino owner Frank J. Farrell and former chief of police and one-time Tammany Hall thug William S. Devery, two decidedly sketchy New York characters, bought the team and, in January of 1903, moved it to New York.

New York already had a team, the National League's Giants, which played in the Polo Grounds, a strange, oval-shaped ballpark at the base of Coogan's Bluff on the East River shore between 157th and 159th streets. Giants' owner John T. Brush tried to block the American League's intrusion into his market, but Farrell and Devery found a large piece of undeveloped land on the west side of Broadway between 165th and 168th streets, and in only two months, as if by magic, a new ballpark had risen on the site.

The new field was officially called American League Park but was soon dubbed Hilltop Park, since it enjoyed majestic views of the Hudson River and was only fifteen blocks south of the island's highest point at Fort Washington. It was large as ballparks went, a vast yard of 9 acres with the diamond near the center of the site and the third-base bleachers stretching along Fort Washington Avenue. The distance from home plate to the far corner of the outfield, at the southwest corner of Broadway and 168th Street, was almost 600 feet. The outfield fence along Broadway was plastered with advertisements, mostly for whiskey, and punctuated by a ticket office, a simple two-story shed with GREATER NEW YORK BASEBALL CLUB OF THE AMERICAN LEAGUE painted in big block letters on the roof and walls. The whole affair was built entirely of wood and looked a bit like a child's summer play fort.

Getting to Hilltop Park wasn't easy: It was a thirteen-block walk from the Hudson River Railroad station at 152nd Street, even longer from the station at Fort Washington Park, and the only other way to get there was by electric trolley or horse-and-buggy (almost no one had a car yet). But somehow 15,000 fans—the men in derbies, the women in big hats and full skirts, the boys in knickers, neckties, and caps, the girls in pinafores—showed up on opening day, April 30, 1903, to see the New York Americans take on the visiting Washington Senators.

The grandstand roof wasn't finished and there was no grass in the outfield. There was a large pond behind first base—any balls hit into

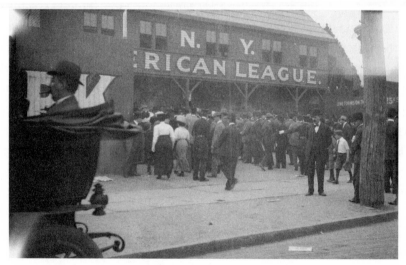

Fans lining up at Hilltop Park's ticket windows, ca. 1912.

the water were ground-rule doubles—and because a clubhouse hadn't been built yet, players had to change at their hotels. But the atmosphere was festive: Vendors circulated through the crowd hawking sandwiches and lemonade and, the *New York Tribune* reported, there were "enough diamonds in the shirt fronts of the politicians to start a fair sized jewelry store." Fans blew horns and whistles and waved small American flags as the 69th Regiment Band escorted the players onto the field "to the tune of a patriotic song." Ban Johnson, who, it must be said, resembled a torpedo with a face painted on, threw out the ceremonial first ball.

In the tradition of the day, New York batted first. After Lefty Davis grounded out to Washington shortstop Rabbit Robinson to start the game, Wee Willie Keeler came up to bat. Keeler, an ex-Giant and the source of that immortal piece of advice "hit 'em where they ain't," was the team's star, a 5-foot-4, 140-pound ball of energy with a prominent nose and large, protruding ears. Batting from the left side, Keeler promptly cracked a pitch into left field and alertly moved up to second base when Senators leftfielder Jimmy Ryan bobbled the ball. Jimmy Williams hit a double, scoring Keeler with Hilltop Park's very first run, and the Americans went on to win 6 to 2.

"Lefty," "Wee Willie," "Rabbit": It was the golden era of great baseball nicknames. The Senators had not only Rabbit Robinson but also a pitcher named Highball Wilson and a first baseman named Boileryard Clarke. Detroit had Kid Elberfeld, Sport McAllister, and Doc Gessler; Chicago had Ducky Holmes, Cozy Dolan, Pep Clark, and Patsy Flaherty; Philadelphia had Chief Bender (an American Indian), Rube Waddell, Socks Seybold, and Topsy Hartsel; St. Louis had Pinky Swander.

Teams—the St. Louis Browns, Boston Beaneaters, Brooklyn Superbas (or Trolley Dodgers), Philadelphia Phillies (or Quakers)—had great nicknames too, and at first sportswriters called New York's new team the Invaders, since they had infiltrated the Giants' turf and raided the Giants' roster for players, or the Highlanders, a possible reference not only to the high elevation of the new ballpark but also to the Scottish Highlanders who were among the invading forces of the British Army in the Battle of Fort Washington in 1776. Over the twelve years the team played at Hilltop Park, there was never a consensus about what they should be called, and sportswriters also referred to them as the Hilltoppers, Hilltops, Hillmen, Hillers, and even the Harlemites.

The name that eventually stuck was first suggested by an anonymous fan from Paterson, New Jersey, in a letter to the editors of the *New York Sun* dated May 4, 1903, barely a week into the team's inaugural home stand. "If the new baseball team is to have a name that is in keeping with the 'Giants,'" the fan wrote, "does it not seem reasonable that if they are 'New York Americans' they might be called the 'Yankees' or 'Yanks'?"

THE TEAM GOT a boost in 1906, when the subway was extended from 157th to 221st Street, with the 168th Street station located right outside the outfield fence. The station made it much easier for fans to reach the ballpark, and on opening day, April 14, 1906, when Cy Young and the Boston Americans came to town, attendance was well over 20,000.

With the subway came the requisite boom in construction of apartment buildings, and soon the residents of the Alfred, Wilton, Carrollton, Courtwood, Medford, Hamlet Court, Richmond Court, Charleston Court, Princess Court, Balmoral Court, Rosbert Hall, and Carolyn Court could peak down on the Yankees from their living rooms. With new apartments came all the things that people require of a neighborhood: theaters, schools, stores, and churches. Only two years after opening, Hilltop Park was in the middle of a thriving neighborhood of skyrocketing land prices.

The Yankees were disappointing: In nine seasons at Hilltop Park they never finished higher than second place, while the Giants, led by fiery manager John McGraw, took National League pennants in 1904, 1905, 1911, 1912, and 1913. But in the end it wasn't the mediocre team but the escalating value of its playing field that forced the team to abandon Broadway.

In 1912 the Yankees moved into the Polo Grounds, where for the next decade they played second fiddle to the Giants. In 1915, Farrell and Devery sold the team to brewer Jacob Ruppert and the unfor-gettably named Tillinghast L'Hommedieu Huston, and the rest—the fateful purchase of Babe Ruth from the Red Sox in 1919, the building of Yankee Stadium in the Bronx in 1923, and the twenty World Series championships between 1923 and 1962—is well-trod history.

Hilltop Park was long gone and forgotten well before Ruth began launching moonshots in the Bronx. The charmingly ramshackle park was demolished in 1914—with all of that exposed wood, it should have burned down but never did—and the site was subdivided into six square blocks, with three new streets (apparently never opened) mapped through it. The land sat empty until 1925, when ground was broken for the new Columbia-Presbyterian medical complex. Colum-bia's College of Physicians and Surgeons was built where Hilltop Park's outfield had been, Presbyterian Hospital (Sloane Hospital) rose near home plate, and Babies Hospital went up along the Broadway side, close to the spot where crowds used to flock to the ballpark's ticket-office windows.

In 1993, the Yankees donated a bronze plaque in the shape of home plate and installed it in the garden between the hospital's old and new wings. The plaque, which was removed in 2011, was positioned where Hilltop Park's home plate had been, but when you crouched beside it, raised your arms in a batting stance, and looked east toward Broad-way, you saw endless rows of hospital windows where Wee Willie Keeler once saw only acres of open space.

CHAPTER 41

THE FOURTH REICH

I N 1912, THE SAME YEAR THE YANKEES LEFT HILLTOP PARK
for the Polo Grounds, theater impresario William Fox built the Audubon Theatre and Ballroom on the east side of Broadway between
165th and 166th streets, just across from the outfield fence. The Audubon had a theater for movies and vaudeville acts and a separate ballroom for meetings and dancing. (Much later, in 1965, Malcolm X was
assassinated there, a tragedy which has since lent the Audubon an
aura of doom.) At the time of the Audubon's opening, the irrepressible
Fox owned sixteen theaters in Manhattan and Brooklyn and was at
the height of his power, but responded melodramatically when asked
what the Audubon might mean for his career.

"Ruination," he cried. "Utter ruination!"

"The Audubon is a much larger theatre than the Washington Heights
section needs, and I don't expect to make any money at the start," he
explained. "I'm depending on the future of Washington Heights."

FOX WAS RIGHT: Washington Heights had a bright future. Within
a decade it had become as full of people and life as any neighborhood
in the city, and Broadway was its main drag. By the Depression,
Rian James wrote in 1931 in *All About New York: An Intimate Guide,*

Broadway's eleventh mile was a "long, unending monotone . . . of low, squat, colorless buildings, baby-carriage laden sidewalks, and neighborhood hausfraus."

Hausfrau: Washington Heights already had a pronounced German flavor by the time James visited, but after Hitler came to power in 1933, Jewish refugees from Germany flooded into the neighborhood, drawn by plentiful, cheap housing. By 1940 there were so many German immigrants in Washington Heights the "Place of Birth" column of that year's Federal Census forms repeated "Germany" so often it resembled an abstract pattern, and locals were calling the neighborhood *das vierte Reich*—the Fourth Reich.

Most Jewish refugees had left family members behind in Germany; many arrived at Ellis Island with nothing but the clothes on their backs; and entry into America, New York, and Washington Heights was, to say the very least, profoundly dislocating. But those who gravitated to Broadway found a vibrant mix of American and German culture. German was spoken in many of Broadway's stores, and Broadway had theaters—six of them just in the twenty blocks between 160th and 181st streets—where refugees could watch war footage on newsreels and then lose themselves for a while in the latest Cary Grant picture. (These weren't little neighborhood theaters but huge, opulent dream worlds: Loew's 175th Street Theatre was perhaps the most intricately designed movie house ever built in the United States, a fantasyland designed by Thomas W. Lamb in a quirky style that journalist David W. Dunlap has characterized as "Byzantine-Romanesque-Indo-Hindu-Sino-Moorish-Persian-Eclectic-Rococo-Deco.")

Jewish refugees from Germany packed into city blocks already overflowing with Russian and Eastern European Jews, blacks, Irish, Italians, Puerto Ricans, Poles, Romanians, French, and Hungarians. Inevitably, there were racial, ethnic, and religious tensions. "Negro-white antagonism [is] sharp," the *New York Times* reported in 1945, "and there [is evidence] of growing anti-Semitism." Administrators at P.S. 169, on Audubon Avenue and 168th Street, a school with a student body represented by forty-two nationalities, took fifth-graders and members of the PTA on field trips to the Jewish Theological

Seminary and to the New York Public Library's Schomburg Collection of Negro History and Literature on 135th Street, hoping the
experiences would build mutual understanding.

Adina Bernstein, of Hungarian Jewish descent, moved to Washington Heights as a sixteen-year-old in 1936, and remembered the
neighborhood's Irish youths as especially brutal. "I was walking
along Dyckman [Street] with one of the guys from Yeshiva [Uni-
versity]," she told journalist Jeff Kisseloff in 1986. "Two [Irish kids]
got on either side of him and shoved him from side to side. 'The Jew
Boy! The Christ Killer!' It was an ugly time. Kikes, sheenies, whatever. It was a constant problem."

Richard Arnstein arrived in Washington Heights in 1938 with
$4 in his pocket and without his family, who had been left behind in
Stuttgart. He rented an apartment, for $4 a week, at 62 Wadsworth
Terrace, one block east of Broadway, and got a job, at $12 a week, as
a shipping clerk for a garment wholesaler on Broadway, near Times
Square. The wholesaler's office building included a Horn & Hardart
automat on the ground floor, where almost everything from soup
to pie to coffee cost just a nickel. This, along with another Horn &
Hardart on 181st Street in Washington Heights, kept Arnstein afloat
in those difficult first years. "[The automat] was really a blessing,"
he recalled.

Arnstein's wife, Charlotte, and their two children soon made
their way from Stuttgart to Washington Heights, and the family
moved into a two-room apartment at 96 Wadsworth Terrace, next
door to the first one. The rent was $38 a month. Charlotte liked
the neighborhood; the hills reminded her of Stuttgart. "We had a
marvelous view—we could see the Cloisters from our window," she
remembered. "We were thrilled." By 1940, Arnstein had been promoted to salesman and his income had risen to $624 a year—about
$10,000 in today's dollars.

Robert L. Lehman also arrived in 1938, at the age of eleven, his
family having escaped the Nazis by way of Romania. They graduated from a rooming house on 90th Street to an apartment on 140th
Street, and then to a six-room apartment on 157th Street near Broadway, where his parents lived rent-free by subletting the extra rooms

to other refugees—a common practice in that era. In Germany his father had been a banker and the family middle-class, but in New York both his parents had to find whatever work was available. His father washed dishes and toiled long hours in a fountain-pen factory before being hired as a Fuller Brush man; his mother cleaned houses and then got a job in a hairnet factory.

At first, Lehman felt utterly alone in New York.

"My problem was that I didn't speak English." he remembered. "[When] I got to school I knew that I was different." Enrolled in a school with a heavily Irish population, he felt ostracized for his different clothes and interests. "I remember that I had no friends."

Lehman didn't understand baseball or the comic books his classmates read, but quickly learned English and before long was glued to the family radio and addicted to *Jack Benny, The Lone Ranger,* and *The Shadow.* He joined the Boy Scouts, went on camping trips, and learned to love New York. "I liked the excitement," he recalled. "I liked the speed of it, I liked the diversity of it, I went everywhere by myself. I really had a good time growing up there."

Lehman remembered Washington Heights as a "self-contained" German-Jewish community where families promenaded up and down Broadway on the weekends. "I could spot a German Jew three blocks away, by the way they walked [and] by the way they dressed," Lehman recalled. "Men came first, always, with their hands behind their backs. Women came behind, dressed in a suit . . . [that] by the cut you could tell wasn't from Lord & Taylor. And children [followed] behind."

Lehman, who stayed in the neighborhood, eventually becoming a rabbi at the Hebrew Tabernacle Synagogue, remembered Broadway as a solidly German avenue of grocers and butchers, who sold potato salad, sauerkraut, beef salami, and sausage without pork, and *Konditoreien,* pastry shops where people sat and talked over cake and coffee.

"This is the way people used to do it [in Germany]," he said. "They would go in the afternoon to this pastry shop and they would buy a piece of cake and they would have coffee and they would sit a couple hours and they would talk and then they'd go about their business. This they did here, too."

"There was a great deal of European ambience in Washington Heights in those years," he remembered. In those days before air-conditioning, people sat and visited on Broadway. "Everything was still intact. There were trees. There was no graffiti. There were no beer bottles. There was nothing of that nature. There were no loud radios."

"It was a genteel kind of neighborhood for a long time."

CHAPTER 42

THE BRIDGE

———

BETWEEN 178TH AND 179TH STREETS BROADWAY PASSES over Interstate 95 and beside one of the world's great suspension bridges. The expressway and the bridge's long approach plow through Washington Heights and the bridge's central span soars across the Hudson River to New Jersey, a dramatic arc of steel that makes Broadway seem narrow and inconsequential. The bridge so dominates the landscape surrounding Broadway's eleventh mile it's worth briefly exploring how it was designed and built.

The Hudson is wide, narrowing in places but generally about a mile across, and although a series of tunnels were dug beneath the river—the earliest, the twin "Hudson Tubes" connecting lower Manhattan and Jersey City, were completed in 1906—no bridge had ever been built across the river. But there had been many attempts: One of the earliest was in 1807, when John Stevens, the steamboat and locomotive inventor, petitioned the New York legislature to allow him to build floating bridges of his own design across the Hudson and East rivers. The legislature seemed vaguely interested, but when Stevens's scheme was announced to the public, it was coldly received. The economy of the city and state depended in large measure on the free passage of goods up and down the rivers, and merchants feared Stevens's bridges would obstruct navigation.

"The scheme of building on the North [Hudson] River I conceive to be entirely chimerical," one anonymous "Merchant" complained in a letter to the *American Citizen*, "and if attempted, it would be proper that the constituted authorities should enquire whether it is not a plan of foreign projection, to aid in injuring the welfare of the city by obstructing the navigation at a certain period."

The concern that bridges might obstruct river traffic remained a sticking point for years afterward, even after the Brooklyn Bridge opened in 1883 and did not prove a hindrance to East River shipping. Even railroads, with all their political influence and money, couldn't bridge the great divide between New Jersey and Manhattan. In 1871 the Pennsylvania Railroad had extended its main line to Jersey City, just across the Hudson from Manhattan, but had to send its passengers across by ferry and its freight by barge, a cumbersome means of transport that was slow on a good day and incapacitated in bad weather. The Penn wanted to extend its line directly into Manhattan, the better to compete with its archrival, the New York Central, which enjoyed a direct link into Manhattan by way of the Bronx. In 1884, the Penn hired engineer Gustav Lindenthal to design a bridge over the Hudson to bring its trains directly into Manhattan, and in 1890 the federal government chartered the North River Bridge Company, with Lindenthal as president and future Penn president Samuel Rea serving on the board of directors.

Lindenthal proposed a bridge spanning from Hoboken, New Jersey, to 23rd Street in Manhattan, and ground was broken on the Hoboken side, but the Panic of 1893 killed the project. In 1902 the Penn began tunneling beneath the Hudson from Jersey City to 33rd Street in Manhattan, and by 1910 had opened Penn Station. But with the railroad's freight still brought across the river by barge, Lindenthal and Rea continued to advocate for a Hudson River bridge.

In 1910, the newly formed Interstate Bridge Commission recommended building a bridge from Washington Heights to Fort Lee in Bergen County, New Jersey, an announcement that set off a mania of speculation on both sides of the river. Real-estate agents accosted passersby with free round-trip tickets for steamboat "excursions" across the Hudson to inspect suburbs like Gilpin Park, a proposed development in Dumont, New Jersey.

As the Washington Heights–to–Fort Lee bridge began to gain favor, Lindenthal continued working on his bridge, and in 1920 envisioned spanning the river from Weehawken, New Jersey, to 57th Street in Manhattan. It was much larger than any suspension bridge ever contemplated, its twin 825-foot-high support towers taller even than the Woolworth Building, then the world's tallest building. Its central span was an unheard-of 3,240 feet, nearly three times as long as the Brooklyn Bridge's central span. Lindenthal's bridge was so massive and out-of-scale with everything around it that a proposed skyscraper atop the Manhattan anchorage looked like a toy. Designed to carry sixteen lanes of automobile traffic and transit lines, plus twelve sets of railroad tracks on a lower level, the bridge was virtually a city unto itself, a colossus that the *Tribune* called "the dream of every New York motorist."

For a while it looked like both the Washington Heights-to-Fort Lee and Weehawken-to-57th Street bridges would be built, but as the size and price tag of Lindenthal's bridge spiraled out of control, ballooning to a preposterous half a billion dollars, Othmar Ammann, Lindenthal's assistant engineer and protégé, began designing his own bridge—in secret.

ONE REASON NO ENGINEER had yet succeeded in spanning the Hudson was that the various boards and commissions created by the governments of New York and New Jersey could never agree and follow through on a strategy. The creation, in 1921, of the Port of New York Authority (much later renamed, more equitably, the Port Authority of New York and New Jersey), an interstate agency with wide-ranging power to condemn property and float bonds on the open market, changed everything. Ammann, frustrated at Lindenthal's unwillingness to make his bridge lighter and less expensive, went behind his employer's back and presented his own bridge to the Port Authority, and in 1925 was appointed chief engineer of the Washington Heights–to–Fort Lee bridge.

Lindenthal felt betrayed, naturally, but Ammann's graceful design was both lighter and cheaper than Lindenthal's behemoth and had none of its clunky gravitas. On September 27, 1927, ground was broken on Ammann's bridge simultaneously in Washington Heights and Fort Lee, and construction proceeded with few delays. It was the Port Authority's first start-to-finish project.

(Undeterred, Lindenthal continued to advocate for the 57th Street bridge, but the War Department held final approval on all bridges constructed over navigable waters, and on May 29, 1929, Secretary of War James William Good, concerned that the new class of ocean liners might not be able to pass under Lindenthal's bridge, ruled that the height of the center span, 175 feet above water level, was *25 feet* too short. Lindenthal was outraged, but the 57th Street bridge was dead.)

AMMANN'S BRIDGE WASN'T as massive as Lindenthal's, but it was still much larger than any suspension bridge that had ever been built anywhere in the world. The bridge's two support towers—one on the New York side that was built on Jeffrey's Hook, a spit of land below Riverside Drive, and one on the New Jersey side that was built in the river itself—were 635 feet high. The clear span from tower to tower was 3,500 feet, nearly twice as long as the previous record holder, the Ambassador Bridge connecting Detroit and Windsor, Ontario, across the Detroit River.

Construction began in August of 1928 and progressed so rapidly, with teams of steelworkers and riveters scrambling about the girders like acrobats, that the towers were finished by the following spring. Cass Gilbert, the renowned architect of the Woolworth Building, designed a concrete-and-stone façade to hide the steel, but in the end the towers were left as they were, each a latticework of steel columns, beams, and braces that seemed as lightweight as airplane struts, even though they weighed 73,000 tons.

Once the towers were complete, four immense cables, each 36 inches in diameter and made up of 26,474 steel wires, were threaded through saddles at the apex of the towers and hung in great parabolas that supported a roadbed suspended 253 feet above the river. The cables were secured on the New Jersey side by drilling into the cliff face of the Palisades, while on the New York side they were buried in an immense concrete anchorage built against the bluffs of Washington Heights.

IN JANUARY OF 1931, with the bridge nearing completion, the Port Authority decided the bridge needed an official name. It had generally been referred to as the "Hudson River" or "Fort Lee" bridge, but the Port Authority announced it would be called the George Washington Memorial Bridge, since the bridge's path between Washington Heights and Fort Lee was the same path Washington had crossed and recrossed by boat in 1776, as the Battle of Washington Heights unfolded. Strangely, the name didn't go over well—critics claimed it would be constantly confused with the nearby Washington Bridge over the Harlem River—and the Port Authority decided to go back to the drawing board and solicit suggestions from the public.

Letters flooded into the Authority's offices: Among the hundreds of suggestions were the Alexander Hamilton Bridge, Ulysses S. Grant Bridge, Pieter Minuit Bridge, Thomas Edison Bridge, Washington Irving Bridge, Woodrow Wilson Bridge, Bridge of Progress, People's Bridge, Prosperity Bridge (a bit of optimism in the midst of the Depression), and Half Moon Bridge, an idea inspired by the name of Henry Hudson's ship.

Some suggestions were underwhelming (the Bergen Bridge, New York Bridge, Public Bridge) or puzzling (the Mothers' Bridge), and some were downright strange (the Heflin-Hellespont Bridge, which must have been a joke). One person, curiously, suggested the Verrazano Bridge. Women's clubs in New Jersey agitated for the Palisades Bridge, but groups of school children pleaded Washington's cause and the Port Authority agreed, sticking with the name it had originally proposed four months earlier and thus avoiding a showdown with a bunch of aggrieved fourth-graders.

ON OCTOBER 24, 1931, only four years after the project began, the bridge was finished. Ammann had organized the project so efficiently it was completed eight months ahead of schedule and considerably under the expected $60 million budget.

The bridge was dedicated with a ceremony in the middle of the span, at the point where New York and New Jersey meet. A grandstand was set up for 5,000 spectators, who listened to New York governor Franklin D. Roosevelt and New Jersey governor Morgan F. Larson extoll the wonders of Ammann's bridge. A crowd estimated at 20,000 watched from Washington Heights, while a smaller crowd gathered in Fort Lee. Airplanes flew in formation up and down the Hudson; one, to the delight of the crowds, even flew *under* the bridge.

Former New York governor Alfred E. Smith, who had been a driving force behind the bridge's construction, was in attendance, but Mayor Jimmy Walker skipped the dedication to go to a football game at Yankee Stadium. The loudest applause, the *Times* reported, was reserved for Ammann.

When the bridge opened to pedestrians that evening, Fred Ammerman, age fourteen, and Leonard Moiseyeff, eleven, two Bronx kids, were the first across. They went on roller skates.

Ammann went on to design the Bayonne, Triborough, Whitestone, Throgs Neck, and Verrazano-Narrows bridges, and was a key consultant on the Golden Gate Bridge, but the George Washington was always his favorite. It remains the busiest bridge in the world. Le Corbusier saw it for the first time in 1935, and thought it the most beautiful bridge in the world. "It is blessed," he wrote in *When the Cathedrals Were White*. "It is the only seat of grace in the disordered city."

CHAPTER 43

THE CUT

—

THE WASHINGTON HEIGHTS TAXPAYERS ASSOCIATION HAD been opposed to construction of the George Washington Bridge from the beginning, fearing that it would displace residents and fill local streets with traffic. In 1925, Port Authority chairman Julian A. Gregory had brushed aside those concerns, claiming that the bridge would allow "access to the great outdoors."

Construction of the bridge's approach necessitated razing four city blocks along a corridor between 178th and 179th streets from Broadway to Riverside Drive. The Port Authority had begun buying up the properties in May of 1927, and by the fall of 1929 about half of the residents had moved out. The twenty-eight demolished buildings on those blocks were mostly new apartment buildings, including the rather opulent ten-story Donald Court at the southwest corner of Broadway and 179th Street. Two churches with large, active congregations, the Fourth Church of Christ, Scientist, and Chelsea Methodist Church, were also torn down. The work displaced 3,000 people, but that was nothing compared to what was coming.

Ammann had designed the George Washington Bridge so that a second, lower deck with an additional six lanes could be added at some point in the future. By the time work began on the lower deck, in 1957, the alteration had become part of a gargantuan collaboration between the Triborough Bridge and Tunnel Authority, led by the indefatigable Robert Moses, and the Port of New York Authority.

The project was a key point in the two agencies' ambitious joint "arterial program" of bridges, tunnels, and expressways, announced in 1955, that included not only the George Washington Bridge improvements but also construction of the Verrazano-Narrows and Throgs Neck bridges and the Long Island, Bruckner, Lower Manhattan, Mid-Manhattan, Cross-Harlem, and Trans-Manhattan expressways. The following year, Congress passed the Federal Aid Highway Act, which authorized construction of the Interstate Highway System. By linking the Triborough and Port authorities' "joint program" to the Interstate system, and by making the George Washington Bridge and its new approach part of Interstate 95, Moses was able to tap into federal funding—and the federal government was slated to pay for 90 percent of the Interstate system.

The highway act was a windfall, and Moses was ready: He had been planning for the moment since the 1940s, when he mapped out a system of arterial roads that he hoped would facilitate "the free flow of traffic without stoplights, congestion, lost time and frayed tempers." The Lower Manhattan, Mid-Manhattan, Cross-Harlem, and Trans-Manhattan expressways were each planned to cut east-to-west across Manhattan, but in the end only the short (less than a mile long), twelve-lane Trans-Manhattan Expressway was built.

The Trans-Manhattan Expressway, designed as the link between the George Washington Bridge and the Cross-Bronx Expressway, was depressed into a block-wide trench that cut through Washington Heights. The project looked enticing on maps—the clean lines of the roadways and bridges, the loops and curls of the bridge approaches—but up close, at jackhammer level, it wasn't about flow and continuity; it was about disruption and displacement.

In all, the project involved demolition of eighty apartment buildings, a post office, and the Congregation Mount Sinai Anshe Emeth synagogue, and forced the relocation of 1,855 families. When the city's Board of Estimate met to consider approval of the project, on May 15, 1957, tenants from Washington Heights showed up to denounce the project but received almost no mention from the pro-Moses *New York Times.*

Moses could be astonishingly caustic when it came to the social upheavals his projects often caused. He was only interested in the "guts" of projects, he said, the often-tricky construction of bridges, ramps, and approaches: "The rest is battling obstructionists and paper workers, moving people and dirt, paving, planting, veneering and painting the lily, and slicking up the job for the dedication ceremonies, the raising of the flag and the playing of 'The Star-Spangled Banner,'" he had written in 1945, as if forcing a family out of its home was no different than emptying debris from a dump truck.

Moses scoffed at the people he called "eagle[s] with vision" and compared himself to a mole methodically burrowing his way beneath the city.

THE GEORGE WASHINGTON BRIDGE's lower deck, which increased the volume of bridge traffic by 75 percent, opened on August 29, 1962, the occasion marked by a reenactment of the 1931 ceremonies that had originally opened the bridge. New York governor Nelson Rockefeller and New Jersey governor Richard J. Hughes, playing the parts of their predecessors Franklin D. Roosevelt and Morgan F. Larson, arrived at mid-span in touring cars from 1931. Again there were speeches, and Rockefeller and Hughes unveiled a bust of Othmar Ammann destined for the lobby of the new George Washington Bridge Bus Station, which was under construction and hovered above the Washington Heights end of the bridge like a lunar landing module, its soaring concrete fins right out of *The Jetsons.*

Ammann, eighty-three, was in the crowd, but it took a few minutes to find him; he was standing in the back.

THE BUS TERMINAL, designed by the great Italian structural engineer and architect Pier Luigi Nervi, pioneer of thin-shell concrete structures, opened on January 17, 1963, along with the Trans-Manhattan Expressway and the Alexander Hamilton Bridge, which connected the expressway over the Harlem River to the Cross-Bronx Expressway. The following year the Bridge Apartments, four thirty-four-story towers of middle-income housing perched on immense columns over the expressway, were completed.

The whole bridge-bus terminal-expressway-housing project looked futuristic, but the conceptual cracks began to show almost immediately. Even the most meticulously considered bus stations aren't places so much as transitional nodes, and by the 1970s, after Trailways and other bus companies decided to leave, the Washington Bridge Bus Station had become a grim gateway echoing with the despair of the forlorn and homeless. A recent renovation has helped matters, but the blocks surrounding the station and expressway are nevertheless grim. Those living in the Bridge Apartments, meanwhile, are subjected to noise, fumes, and grit rising out of the expressway below.

From 178th to 179th Street, Broadway threads its way over the expressway and under the bus station. It is a decidedly dreary block, with none of the grandeur associated with the Great White Way or the West Side's Boulevard farther to the south. But the road that really matters at that particular spot isn't Broadway but the roaring expressway underneath it: I-95, that relentless American strand that begins in Maine and ends, 2,000 miles later, in Miami.

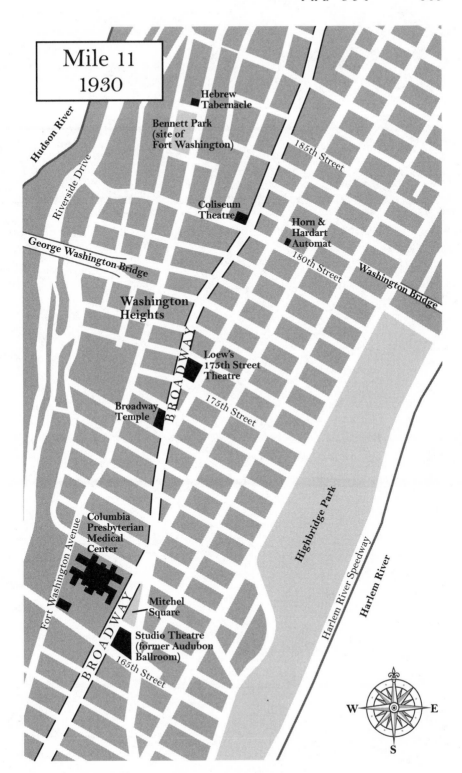

Mile 11
1930

Hudson River

Hebrew
Tabernacle

Bennett Park
(site of
Fort Washington)

185th Street

Riverside Drive

Coliseum
Theatre

Horn &
Hardart
Automat

George Washington Bridge

180th Street

Washington Bridge

Washington
Heights

BROADWAY

Loew's
175th Street
Theatre

175th Street

Broadway
Temple

Columbia
Presbyterian
Medical
Center

Highbridge Park

Harlem River Speedway

Harlem River

Fort Washington Avenue

BROADWAY

Mitchel
Square

Studio Theatre
(former Audubon
Ballroom)

165th Street

W E

S

MILE 12

179TH STREET TO DYCKMAN STREET

CHAPTER 44

MR. BILLINGS

———

Norte of robert moses's expressway, broadway is also called Route 9. It follows the path of the old Kingsbridge Road through the northern half of Washington Heights, or "Hudson Heights," as real-estate agents have recently taken to calling it, on its way to Inwood. Broadway between 179th and 187th streets is a decidedly unremarkable stretch of asphalt lined with brick-and-limestone apartment buildings, banks, bodegas, liquor stores, gas stations, pizza-by-the-slice joints, funeral parlors, clinics, 99-cent stores, and, at the northwest corner of 181st Street, the abused shell of the once-magnificent Coliseum Theater.

But just beyond 187th Street, Broadway passes Gorman Park, a steep, woody hillside leading up to Wadsworth Terrace just to the east, and begins to shake itself loose from the city. Over its final two miles in Manhattan, before it reaches the Bronx, Broadway is defined not only by the Deal$ discount store, Rita's Style Beauty Salon, Broadway Automotive, and No. 1 Chinese & Tex-Mex Express, but also by vertiginous hills, grassy slopes, woods, and outcroppings of bedrock.

Once Broadway crosses Bennett Avenue, the landscape changes entirely: Broadway curls in a wide arc back to the *east*, of all things, as the entire west side of the street rises abruptly in an Appalachian eminence called Fort Tryon Park.

ON NOVEMBER 16, 1776, British and Hessian forces overran Fort Tryon, which had been built as an "outwork" of the ill-fated Fort Washington. It was in the midst of that battle that Margaret Corbin, wife of a Continental Army soldier, took over her husband's cannon after he was killed and blasted away until she was shot through the shoulder and taken out of action. (Corbin, disabled, survived the war and became the first American woman to receive a soldier's pension.)

Like Fort Washington, Fort Tryon's traces lingered long after the war ended, and telltale ridges and swales in the earth could still be detected in the early twentieth century. During the Revolution, the fort's situation high above the Hudson River was purely strategic; that it was also the most heavenly spot on the island was a secondary concern. Fort Tryon Hill remained untouched, an oasis just ahead of the city's northward development, until the last dying flickers of the Gilded Age, when it wound up in the hands of a singularly memorable tycoon.

CORNELIUS KINGSLEY GARRISON BILLINGS was raised in Chicago, the son of Albert Merritt Billings, president of the Peoples Gas Light & Coke Company. After graduating from Racine College in 1879, Cornelius (friends called him "Ben") joined his father's business and in 1887 became the company's president.

Though its customers were in Illinois, Peoples Gas was really a New York company—all but two of its directors were New Yorkers—and Billings spent much of his time in the city attending to business. Like his father, he loved horses—"Mr. Billings's connection with the turf is too well known to need any special mention at this late hour," read one notice in the *New York Times* society pages—and when the Harlem Speedway, a race course snaking along the Harlem River between 155th and Dyckman streets, opened in the summer of 1898, Billings was there. He began bringing his impressive stable of trotters and pacers to the Speedway for the spring and fall racing seasons, taking on all challengers in timed trials and impromptu "brushes." Billings's exploits helped the Speedway become so popular that weekend crowds of 15,000 were common, gambling being the chief attraction, and New York became the center of a national trotting craze.

In 1901, unable to tear himself away from the Speedway, Billings stepped down as president of Peoples Gas and was installed as chairman of the board, a position that didn't require residency in Chicago. He and wife Blanche (half-sister of poet Archibald MacLeish), moved to New York, settling into a mansion on Fifth Avenue among the Astors, Belmonts, Vanderbilts, Carnegies, Guggenheims, and Fricks. But the Fifth Avenue mansion wasn't nearly close enough to the Speedway, and so Billings bought, from the estate of recently deceased industrialist Hugh N. Camp, 25 undeveloped hilltop acres next to the remains of Fort Tryon. The property, bisected north-and-south by Fort Washington Avenue, commanded majestic views of the Hudson River to the west and, even better as far as Billings was concerned, the Speedway to the east.

Billings hired Boston architect Guy Lowell to design a large stable on the east side of Fort Washington Avenue and, on the other side of the street, an octagonal observation tower that doubled as a weekend house. The stable cost $200,000 to build and was 250 feet long by 125 feet wide and two stories high, the roof sweeping up into pointed cupolas. It was divided into two wings, horses on the right, automobiles on the left, and arranged around a courtyard exercise ring. Billings moved in his prized trotters (Lucille, Doctor Book, Ellert, Mabel Onward, Aggie Medium, Jimmie Hague, Major Greer, Franker, and Rightwood) and pacers (Free Bond, Sunland Belle, and Hontas Crooke) and got down to the business of living in style among the halters and horseshit.

IN THE SPRING of 1903, seventeen mills in Lowell, Massachusetts, temporarily shut down, locking out 17,000 workers; cooks and waiters went on strike in Denver; a trolley conductors' strike in Waterbury,

Connecticut, turned violent; six steelworkers were burned to death in a furnace accident at Carnegie Steel in Pittsburgh; the Indiana Supreme Court struck down as unconstitutional a minimum wage law; and Billings celebrated the completion of his stables at the top of Fort Tryon Hill.

On Saturday evening, March 28, Billings invited thirty-six members of the Equestrian Club, including ex-mayor Hugh J. Grant, to Fort Tryon Hill to view his palatial new stables. The plan was to have the guests picked up at the Hotel Netherland, on Fifth Avenue, and driven up to the stables in touring cars, where they would be served dinner while seated on wooden hobbyhorses in the stables' carriage hall, a cavernous space measuring 50 by 90 feet and decorated for the occasion as a forest dell. But when details of the festivities were leaked to the press—"Guests to Ride Wooden Horses," a headline in the *Evening World* announced—Billings, to avoid the embarrassment of gawking crowds at his gates, switched the venue at the last minute to Sherry's, a fashionable restaurant at Fifth Avenue and 44th Street.

Then came the bait-and-switch: Billings substituted real horses for the wooden variety, renting thirty-six well-behaved mounts from a riding academy and ferrying them up the restaurant's freight elevator to the banquet room, where they were tethered in a circle. Dinner was served on specially designed tables attached to the saddle pommels; champagne was available by sucking on a tube running into bottles concealed in each saddlebag; servants were dressed as grooms. Billings reportedly spent $50,000 on the soiree—over $1 million in today's currency. The horses ate too, from feeding troughs "filled with oats," the *Times* reported, "so that the animals dined with their riders."

ALL WAS WELL with Mr. Billings: Peoples Gas was trading at over $100 a share, which made its stock more valuable than even Union Pacific or U.S. Steel, and Billings, flush with cash, had Lowell expand the observation tower atop Fort Tryon Hill into a full-fledged château. Billings called it "Fort Tryon Hall" in honor of the patriots who fell there in 1776, a rather shallow gesture considering that, to the

C. K. G. Billings's famous dinner on horseback, 1903.

dismay of the American Scenic and Historic Preservation Society, construction of the mansion destroyed a well-preserved section of the fort.

Built of brick covered in grey stucco with white trim, Fort Tryon Hall cost $2 million, and while architect and client had in mind the grandeur of the sixteenth-century Château de Chenonceau in the Loire Valley, the mansion's style might best have been described as "High Capitalist" or even "Tycoonesque." The list of architectural crimes perpetrated by Lowell and interior decorator P. W. French at Fort Tryon Hall were long and varied: For starters there was the reckless use of marble, of both the creamy and more expensive green kind; the profusion of wrought-iron bannisters, oak floors, and mahogany wall paneling; the wild animal skins strewn on the floors; the vast oceans of oriental rugs and sixteenth-century Flemish tapestries; the flamboyant Louis XVI–style furniture; and the ancient Chinese vases, antique fans, and rather bland nineteenth-century French and Dutch landscapes that cluttered up the place.

The house enveloped the observation tower and under Lowell's

The Billings estate, looking north.

sure hand became a festival of turrets, oriels, and mansard roofs. The plan was organized around a central "patio," a double-height space with a glass roof and a fountain featuring a copy of Andrea del Verrocchio's sculpture *Putto with Dolphin* from the Palazzo Vecchio in Florence. The living room looked out over a lawn on Fort Washington Avenue and featured French walnut wainscoting, a gilded pipe organ and the outstretched skin of a lion, its glass eyes staring into oblivion in front of a sofa. The dining room, paneled in mahogany, and the drawing room, decorated like Versailles, both overlooked the river.

Down one hallway was the billiard room, paneled in walnut and lined with shelves displaying Billings's various trotting trophies. The wall above the fireplace was reserved for portraits of his favorite horses, including the famous Lou Dillon, the first horse to trot a mile in less than two minutes. Bedrooms for Billings, Blanche, and children Pauline and Albert were upstairs. There was a reception room, "Lavender Room," "Blue Room," "Rose Room," and, behind the scenes, quarters for the servants (generally English, Scottish,

Austrian, Danish, Norwegian, and Swedish immigrants), a kitchen, pantry, servants' dining room, storerooms, scullery, pastry room, housekeeper's office, laundry, trunk room, coal cellar, and wood room.

A separate building to the north of the house included a 75-by-30-foot swimming pool, plus a bowling alley and squash court. Nearby were tennis courts, gardens, greenhouses, and a small farm that provided the house with fresh produce. A mechanical building had two immense boilers that heated the house and pool, plus two 40-horse-power Alberger centrifugal pumps that in case of fire could (supposedly) deliver water to hose outlets on each floor of the house and to hydrants stationed around the grounds.

Billings soon added a dramatic back entrance to his estate off Riverside Drive, a double switchback that passed through a towering arched gallery right out of a Piranesi etching. Billings's yacht, the *Vanadis*, was moored on the river below, excursion-ready. It was all impossibly grand, but on Broadway, far down Fort Tryon's precipitous eastern slope, life unfolded along a very different path. As Billings settled into his new mansion, a man looked up the hill from the other side of the street and cursed his luck.

CHAPTER 45

MR. MOLENAOR

—

IN THE SPRING OF 1913 A SEVENTY-FIVE-YEAR-OLD GENT WITH a chip on his shoulder took up residence in a 13-by-12-foot squatter's shack on the opposite side of Broadway from Fort Tryon Hill and loudly proclaimed that he owned 17 acres of the Billings estate, plus 7 acres on the east side of the street, including the land beneath the shack, and 47 acres between 120th and 129th streets spanning from Harlem to Manhattanville—all told, some 71 acres of prime Manhattan real estate. He figured the value of the three parcels at somewhere between $300 million and $500 million.

The shack had low ceilings, a wooden floor and sides, and a canvas roof. It was equipped with a stove, chairs, table, and bunk. A smoky kerosene lamp provided light; neighbors let him draw water from their taps. "I expect to stay here quite some time," the man announced.

Martin Montrose Molenaor's quixotic campaign to reclaim much of upper Manhattan as his own had begun thirty-five years earlier, when on January 30, 1878, he served notices to some two hundred tenants of houses, stores, and churches occupying buildings in the three parcels in question, demanding that they either pay him rent or vacate the premises.

"You are hereby notified that the heirs of David W. Molenaor are the owners of the premises now occupied by you," the notice read, "and that you are required to pay the rent of the said premises to the undersigned, or, in default thereof, to surrender the same to him. Martin M. Molenaor."

A Catholic priest who received Molenaor's notice tore it up. But Molenaor was just getting started. A few days later, he made the rounds again, this time painstakingly gluing large FOR SALE signs on all the buildings. Enraged occupants just as quickly removed them. "I was not long in getting that notice off my building," William H. Higgins, owner of a hotel at the corner of Eighth Avenue and 125th Street, said, "although it had been stuck very fast with good paste."

In pressing his claim, Molenaor was taking on a group of extremely wealthy, influential landowners, which included not only Billings and Higgins but also Vincent Astor, James Gordon Bennett, and the Mutual Insurance Company. Observers didn't give him much of a chance.

"The Molenaors are poor," one resident said, "and a lack of funds to carry on actions at law will be a disadvantage to them; while on the occupants' side there is plenty of money to employ capable lawyers."

Sure enough, Molenaor's adversaries sent what he later recalled as "an army of lawyers" after him, and by 1882 he was bankrupt. He moved to Colorado and took up ranching, then went to Flagstaff, Arizona, where he worked as an architect and builder. By 1913 he and wife Evalina had saved enough money to return east and resume the fight. In New York, Molenaor founded the Molenaor Recovery Company, with an office at 50 Church Street, and he and Evalina, along with son Wilfred, thirty-eight, and daughter Evalina, or Evelyn, forty, moved into the shack below the Billings estate. Evelyn, a nurse, became the family's breadwinner, while Wilfred, a carpenter, assisted his father by reading up on property law.

MARTIN M. MOLENAOR was born in 1838 in his grandfather's homestead at Eighth Avenue and 125th Street. By the time he was fourteen he had lived in Manhattan on Bleecker and Elizabeth streets and First Avenue; in Astoria, Queens; in Camptown, New Jersey; in West-chester; and in Kingston, Jamaica. During the Civil War he moved to the Bahamas, where he married Evalina and where their first two children, Montrose and Evelyn, were born. Then the family moved to St. Augustine, Florida, and had three more children, including Wilfred, born in 1871.

In 1872, Molenaor's brother Andrew visited him in Florida and told him their grandfather's will had been discovered in a "secret drawer." In 1878, Molenaor returned to New York with Evalina and the five children, opened a jewelry business on Fulton Street in Brooklyn, and laid plans for the reclamation of his grandfather's land.

The grandfather, William M. Molenaor, had died in 1812 and his estate, including his land, "good horse and chaise," "black girl Sarah," and "black boy Isaac," was divided between his wife Mercy, a daugh-ter, and three sons. The oldest son was David William Molenaor, Martin's father, who in the 1820s invested heavily in the Harlem Canal Company. His land had been put up as security to cover the canal company's debts, and when the company failed much of David's considerable inheritance disappeared. By 1850, David had lost every-thing, his occupation on that year's federal census listed as "None." (Under "Real Estate" the census enumerator had simply entered a question mark.) He died in 1858.

The gist of Martin M. Molenaor's claim hinged on the wording of a single clause in his grandfather's will: "To my eldest son, David William Molenaor, the legitimate heirs of his body or the nearest heirs of his body, I do give and bequeath all my homestead . . ."

Molenaor interpreted that line as meaning that his grandfather had intended to pass on his estate not only to his son but also to his son's children and their children, the "heirs" of David's "body." To Molenaor's way of thinking, that meant that his father had been granted only a "life interest" in the land, not a clear title, and there-fore had had no legal right to sell it. And if he had had no right to sell it, Molenaor figured, then all of his father's transactions and all sub-sequent transactions pertaining to the land in question were invalid, and the land must still belong to the rightful heir—none other than Martin Montrose Molenaor.

He was tilting at windmills, of course. The great tragedy of Manhattan's development in the nineteenth century was how very unfair its division of land had been, the old land grants somehow remaining intact to the benefit of a few wealthy families—the Astors, the Harsens, the Brevoorts, the Rensselaers—who cashed in while the less fortunate majority had to make due with cramped tenements and squatter's shacks. Periodically someone would materialize to claim ownership of a prime swath of the island, usually part of the Astor estate and usually in the middle of Midtown or the West Side or whichever section of town was booming that year, but they usually gave up after a few thrusts of the lance, their cases remaining in the courts just long enough to remind everyone that *their* grandfathers hadn't left them anything, either. But Martin Montrose Molenaor was unusual among the Quixotes of real estate—he simply wouldn't give up.

In 1916, the Kiowa Realty Company and its president, Emil Fried, owner of five vacant lots at the southeast corner of Broadway and Hillside Avenue, where Molenaor was squatting, sued for eviction. This was precisely what Molenaor wanted—a day in court. *Kiowa Realty Company v. Martin M. Molenaor et al.* became a test case that was watched carefully by many landowners in Washington Heights, Harlem, and Manhattanville who wished that Molenaor would go away, since his endless claims against their property were beginning to muck up the clear transfer of titles.

The case went all the way to New York State's Supreme Court, First Judicial District, where Molenaor faced off against Kiowa Realty's lawyer, Louis Franklin Levy of Eisman, Levy, Corn & Lewine. Legal opinions don't make for the spiciest reading, but every line of Justice Nathan Bijur's opinion seethed with exasperation—no doubt he had better things to do with his time—and he quickly swatted down the heart of Molenaor's argument as if it were a fly buzzing about the courtroom.

"[The defendants], as I understand it, do not contest the general proposition of law," Bijur wrote, "but hold it inapplicable because, as they construe the will, no estate was devised to David William Molenaor, but . . . only 'to the legitimate heirs of his body, etc.' From the standpoint of grammar, they urge that the language should be construed as in the phrase 'John Jones, his mark,' and that the devise [the land] should be read as one to the legitimate heirs of the body of David William Molenaor."

"To this extraordinary construction I cannot give my assent," Bijur continued, slamming the door shut once and for all. "Altogether, apart from the violence which I think it does to the rule of grammatical construction prevalent at the time of execution and probate of this will, the last will itself is replete with persuasive suggestions of the meaning of the testator to the contrary."

Bijur then dutifully cited dozens of precedents to back up his opinion that in 1812 William M. Molenaor surely had meant to give his property to his son David William Molenaor, come what may; that the son, as owner, had been entitled to sell it; and that, therefore, Martin M. Molenaor had no claim to the land beneath his shack, nor to the Billings estate across the street or the lots in Harlem and Manhattanville. Bijur ruled in favor of Kiowa Realty.

That should have been the final blow, but still Molenaor held out, his shack sitting undisturbed on its vacant lot. "He sits at evening in the door of his cabin," Henry Edward Smith wrote in the *Pittsburg Press* in 1917, "with the shadows of the big apartment houses lengthening toward him, with the hum of the Broadway cars making an inspiring song in his old ears—dreaming his great dream all undismayed."

IN THE SPRING OF 1921, Molenaor was eighty-four and nearly blind. William F. Norton, a contractor and the new owner of the lot upon which the Molenaors squatted, appeared at the shack's door and told the family to clear out; he wanted to put up a commercial building on the lot. The Molenaors refused to budge. Norton began excavating anyway, each day coming closer to the shack and each day making the Molenaors angrier and more determined to stay.

**Martin Montrose Molenaor's approximate view of Fort Tryon Hill
and the Billings estate (at far left).**

"Undermine our home, will you?" Evelyn shouted at the steam
shovel operator. "Still, we can only die once and we might as well die
defending our home."

Norton stopped digging just short of the shack, spooked by the
possibility that he might injure, or even kill, the Molenaors, who
crowed that he had been bluffing all along. But the stress of being
threatened with a steam shovel had been too much for Molenaor,
Evelyn told *New York Herald* reporter Eleanor Booth Simmons. He
died shortly afterward.

Simmons had visited the shack before, and had glimpsed Molenaor
gazing longingly through the shack's small windows at Fort Tryon
Hall across Broadway. "All that . . . is mine," he told her. "Some day
the courts will decide that it is mine, and I shall be one of the richest
men in America, richer than John D. Rockefeller Jr., who fancies that
he owns that Washington Heights property."

CHAPTER 46

MR. BARNARD

———

T HE TROUBLE WAS, ROCKEFELLER *DID* OWN FORT TRYON HALL: He had bought it in 1917 from Billings, who, bored with New York, moved first to Oyster Bay, Long Island, and then to Santa Barbara, California, where he and Blanche died on the same day in 1937. Rockefeller wanted to tear down the Billings mansion and turn the grounds into a public park, but when a group of architects protested, Rockefeller rented out the house to N. C. Partos, a drug manufacturer.

In 1926 the château burned down. The fire started at three in the afternoon, March 6, and burned far into the night. Because of its prominence atop Fort Tryon Hill, the fire was visible for miles: The *New York Times* estimated that 100,000 people watched it from Washington Heights, University Heights in the Bronx, and the New Jersey Palisades. Billings's elaborate system of fire hydrants and pumps failed miserably, its volume and pressure far too low to get water up the hill.

Landscape painter Eric Sloane, who grew up in the neighborhood, remembered exploring Fort Tryon Hall's roofless ruins, its charred stair ending in open sky. Bicycling around the wooded hills south of Fort Tryon, Sloane befriended sculptor George Grey Barnard, whose studio was on Fort Washington Avenue just south of the Billings estate. At the time, Barnard, a stocky, eccentric character with a shock of unruly dark hair, jutting jaw, and matching ego, was perhaps America's most preeminent sculptor; the *New York Times* called him a "human dynamo" and even compared him favorably to Michelangelo.

BARNARD WAS A preacher's son from Pennsylvania. He was educated at the Art Institute of Chicago and in 1883 went to Paris to study at the École des Beaux-Arts. Barnard's big break came when Alfred Corning Clark, the wealthy heir of Edward Cabot Clark, cofounder of the Singer Sewing Machine Company and developer of the Dakota Apartments, commissioned an allegorical sculpture entitled *The Struggle of the Two Natures of Man*. Included in 1894's prestigious annual Salon du Champ-de-Mars, the nightmarish *Struggle*, which depicts one nude Greek figure stepping on another while ferocious, fanged bats materialize between the lower figure's limbs, put Barnard on the map.

His career seemingly taking off, Barnard married Edna Monroe of Boston in 1895 and moved to New York, where he opened the Washington Heights studio and began teaching courses at the Art Students League. But Barnard struggled and, in dire financial straits, considered quitting his chosen profession. He was saved by an enormous $700,000 commission to complete the sculptures, thirty-three figures in all, for the new Pennsylvania State Capitol building in Harrisburg. He decided to work on the project in France, and in 1903 moved his family to the village of Moret-sur-Loing near Fontainebleau, some two hours southeast of Paris.

"I was getting $2,000 a week," he remembered ten years later, "and I and my stone cutters and models were encamped in a French village giving over our lives to art completely. Then one week the money didn't come."

A month later he was $10,000 in debt. It came out that cost overruns in Harrisburg had gotten out of control, and amid the political firestorm that ensued, Pennsylvania governor Samuel W. Pennypacker cabled Barnard to "come home." Instead, Barnard stayed in France and continued working on the sculptures. (The Capitol's architect, Joseph Miller Huston, and four others were ultimately convicted of graft; private donors ultimately financed the statues, which were finally completed in 1911.)

To make ends meet, Barnard bought and sold medieval antiquities, beginning an obsession that would define his life and career. He began by bicycling around the French countryside asking locals if they had ever seen any "old carvings" lying about. As it turned out, they had: For centuries farmers had been repurposing parts of ruined medieval churches and cloisters, including magnificent statuary, for use as scarecrows, pigsty walls, grape arbors, and stones to dam up creeks.

"I went into every cellar and would surprise the peasants by getting on my hands and knees with a candle to look under wine vats," Barnard recalled. "I found some of my very best Virgins under wine vats."

Barnard gradually amassed an unsurpassable collection of some seven hundred Romanesque and Gothic antiquities. He sold some of the pieces to support his family and spirited others back to New York, a practice that so angered French authorities one accused him of "stealing the soul of France." But others praised Barnard for rescuing forgotten artifacts and rekindling interest in France's extraordinary medieval art.

Returning to New York with his sizable collection of icons, friezes, crucifixes, architectural components (including parts of four cloisters), tapestries, and stained glass, Barnard built a large barnlike brick museum across 190th Street from his Washington Heights studio and put his collection on display. He called the museum the Cloisters and opened it to the public in December of 1914, charging $2 on weekends and $5 during the week. The proceeds, he declared, would benefit the widows and children of French sculptors killed in World War I.

Barnard had become an outspoken peace advocate during the war, and began agitating for the creation of a vast "Acropolis" on Fort Tryon Hill, a sprawling "National Peace Memorial" with its centerpiece a monumental 100-foot-tall and 60-foot-wide "Rainbow Arch" that in Barnard's conception was to include sculptures of four hundred figures. The peace memorial, Barnard said, would be an "intellectual Coney Island."

The *New York Times* once called sculptor George Grey Barnard a "human dynamo."

Rockefeller, who had commissioned three sculptures from Barnard for his Pocantico Hills estate, was supportive and let Barnard take over the old Billings stable as a studio to begin work on the Rainbow Arch. Rockefeller even offered to underwrite the entire project, but Barnard refused the offer on moral grounds, romantically insisting that funding should come in nickels and dimes from the public. To raise money Barnard put the Cloisters up for sale, and in 1925 agreed to sell his entire collection of medieval art to Rockefeller for $600,000. Rockefeller donated the collection to the Metropolitan Museum of Art, and the reconstituted Cloisters opened on May 3, 1926, in its original building next to Barnard's studio. Barnard was there, greeting guests in a velvet jacket and bow tie.

IN 1930, ROCKEFELLER donated the Billings estate and some adjacent parcels, 56 acres in all, to the city for a public park. The old Billings stables were slated for demolition, and Barnard, evicted, set up a new studio in a nearby abandoned power station and kept working on the peace memorial, which by then had become a quixotic scheme and was never finished. The stables were torn down and Frederick Law Olmsted Jr. began designing Fort Tryon Park, which opened in October of 1935.

Rockefeller reserved 4 acres on the north edge of the park, almost exactly on the spot where Margaret Corbin had fought so valiantly in 1776, as the site for a new, larger version of the Cloisters. Intent on re-creating a French monastery, Rockefeller even bought 700 undeveloped, wooded acres on the opposite side of the Hudson and donated them to New Jersey as part of Palisades Interstate Park, so that visitors to the Cloisters could enjoy a view unobstructed by buildings.

Designed by Boston architect Charles Collens, Rockefeller's Cloisters was built in granite with roofs of red tile. Rockefeller had scoured France for new pieces to augment Barnard's original collection, although he hadn't searched in farmyards or knelt in grimy basements the way Barnard had, and his acquisitions, including the magnificent chapter house from the twelfth-century Notre-Dame-de-Pontaut abbey, significantly expanded the scope of Barnard's original vision.

The original Cloisters at Fort Washington Avenue and 190th Street closed on February 9, 1936, and its title reverted to Barnard. In the ten years since selling his collection to Rockefeller, Barnard had amassed an entirely new stockpile of medieval art, and in October of 1937 he reopened the museum as the Abbaye.

On April 24, 1938, only weeks before Rockefeller's new Cloisters opened to the public, Barnard died of a heart attack at age seventy-four. His funeral was held in the Abbaye, his coffin surrounded by the statues and crucifixes he had collected in France. Among those paying tribute was Mathilda Burling, president of the Gold Star Mothers, which had made Barnard an honorary member for his peace advocacy. When Rockefeller's Cloisters opened to the public on a wet Saturday, May 10, 1938, a long line of people waited in the rain to get in. By closing time, well over 4,000 had filed through.

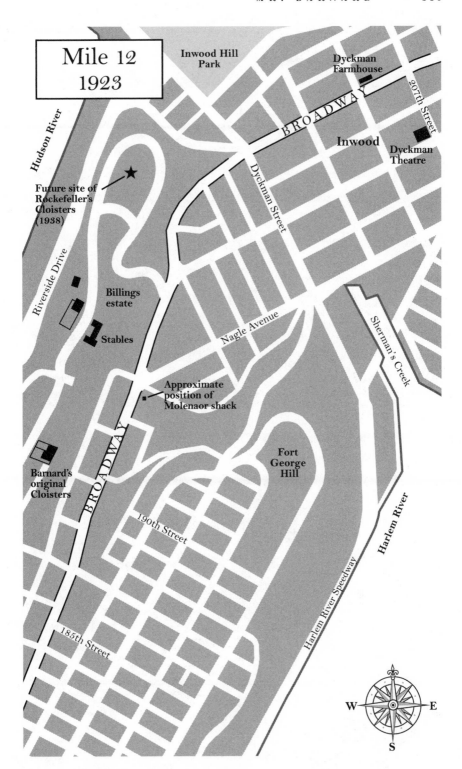

Mile 12
1923

Inwood Hill
Park

Dyckman
Farmhouse

207th Street

Inwood

Dyckman
Theatre

Hudson River

BROADWAY

Dyckman Street

Future site of
Rockefeller's
Cloisters
(1938)

Riverside Drive

Billings
estate

Stables

Nagle Avenue

Sherman's Creek

Approximate
position of
Molenaor shack

Fort
George
Hill

BROADWAY

Barnard's
original
Cloisters

190th Street

Harlem River

185th Street

Harlem River Speedway

W E

S

MILE 13

DYCKMAN STREET TO 228TH STREET

CHAPTER 47

LIFE AND DEATH IN INWOOD

——

JUST PAST THE CLOISTERS, BROADWAY CURLS IN A LAZY ARC to the east-northeast as it begins its initial approach into the Bronx by way of the Broadway Bridge over the Harlem River Ship Canal. Crossing Dyckman Street, which traverses the island along a seismic fault line, Broadway skirts the base of Inwood Hill, where streets turn into staircases—215th Street between Broadway and Seaman Avenue is like Montmartre in New York. Seaman, Vermilyea, Sherman, Post, and Nagle avenues bend along with Broadway, so that the entire neighborhood of Inwood doesn't align with the rest of the city grid and seems in many ways like a separate village.

Well into the nineteenth century the area that became Inwood was virtually uninhabited, and no streets or lanes other than the Kingsbridge Road passed through it. The Dyckman family and a few others farmed the rich bottomland along the Harlem River, where land was so cheap, and in such poor demand, that they practically gave it away. (One tenant's rent consisted only of one hen per year for seven years.) In 1820, when John Randel Jr. surveyed the area for the Commissioners' Plan, he catalogued fields, orchards, outcroppings, swamps, and the outlines of Revolutionary War–era redoubts but almost no buildings other than a few small farmhouses, barns, stables, and fishermen's shacks.

The area began to change after 1851, when the new Hudson River Railroad built a station at Tubby Hook, a knuckle of land protruding into the river at the end of present-day Dyckman Street. Only a thirty-minute ride from the railroad's terminal at 30th Street and Tenth Avenue, Tubby Hook developed into a suburb of wealthy downtown commuters that in prestige and beauty rivaled Audubon Park and Washington Heights to the south.

In those early years Tubby Hook was remote, sleepy, and informal enough that in the morning the railroad conductor would patiently wait for his regular "Tubby Hookers" to arrive on the platform before departing for the city. Tubby Hook's residents included cartoonist Joseph Ferdinand Keppler, one of the founders of *Puck*, Samuel Lord and George Washington Taylor of Lord & Taylor, and James McCreery, founder of the famous Ladies' Mile department store at Broadway and 11th Street. (McCreery didn't take the train to work, choosing instead to drive his team of bay horses to his store downtown.) McCreery's house wasn't ostentatious, but some of his neighbors' villas were comically opulent: John F. Seaman's elaborate "Marble House," built in 1855, featured twenty-five rooms plus an observatory, swimming pool, solarium, and manicured grounds punctuated with eighteenth-century statuary. Its approach was from the Kingsbridge Road through a gatehouse that was a scaled-down replica of the Arc de Triomphe.

Tubby Hook's isolation from the rest of the island made it desirable and mysterious, an idyllic pastoral retreat of mansions with large porches, barns, stables, and gardens tucked into the woods along unpaved tracks. "Among the rocks and forest trees of this primitive region," T. Addison Richards wrote in *Harper's New Monthly Magazine* in the summer of 1861, "one may be as secluded as in the farthest mountain wilds."

In 1864, William B. Isham, a prosperous downtown leather merchant, bought an Italianate villa, cruciform in plan, with wings projecting from a huge circular hall at the center, next door to the Seaman estate, and for the next forty-five years lived in apparent contentment with his wife Julia and their six children, surrounded by 24 acres of woods and lawn that looked out over the Hudson and Spuyten Duyvil Creek at the island's northern tip. Around the time Isham moved in, local real-estate agents began to take notice of Tubby Hook and decided it needed a more marketable name. Tubby Hook became Inwood, a designation, the *Tribune* complained, that was "utterly without salt and savor." One defiant Hudson River Railroad conductor continued to announce "Tubby Hook!" when his train pulled into the station, always following in mock apology with "Inwood!"

By 1867 the Hudson River Railroad was running eight daily trains between Inwood and 30th Street, and, with the imminent sale of the 400-acre "Dyckman Tract" and the instigation of the Central Park Commission's new street plan for upper Manhattan, it looked as though an Inwood boom was inevitable.

"Inwood seems, by its beautiful situation on the river, to be the spot where the finest . . . residences will ultimately be located," the *Tribune* reported in 1868. "Its convenience of access by the many avenues and drives, as well as by water and rail from the city, will render it accessible from every side."

But in 1869 the Hudson River Railroad merged with Cornelius Vanderbilt's New York Central, and in 1871 many of the trains that had run between Inwood and the city were diverted to the opposite side of the Harlem River, in the Bronx, where a bridge at Fourth Avenue provided direct access to Manhattan and Grand Central Depot. With fewer trains stopping at Inwood, the expected building boom never materialized, and the houses on the hill began to disappear even further into the woods.

On the other side of the Kingsbridge Road from the hill, there were still virtually no buildings of any kind. In 1881, historian Wilson Cary Smith, writing in the *Magazine of American History*, described the area as "unchanged by the march of improvement." About the only people who lived east of the Kingsbridge Road were Irish, German, and Italian immigrants, who threw up shanties around the base of Fort George Hill, next to the Harlem River.

A fresh-water creek that locals called the "Run" flowed from

Inwood Hill under the Kingsbridge Road to Sherman's Creek, a brackish tidal marsh that cut in from the Harlem River just to the north of Fort George Hill. Dyckman's Meadows ran from the creek along the Harlem River edge, and at low tide became a boggy, treacherous warren of reeds and hidden mud holes. The terrain on the flat side of the Kingsbridge Road was so forbidding that in 1887 Magdalena Zorn, a ten-year-old child of German immigrants, lost her way during a school picnic on Fort George Hill and wandered into the meadows. Her body, mysteriously mangled—an arm and leg were missing—wasn't found for a full week. The police assumed she had been murdered, but the city's coroner, Ferdinand Eidman, concluded that she had drowned and chastised the school for holding a picnic in such a desolate place.

"The teachers had no business to go into such a dangerous neighborhood with so many little ones, and so few to look after them," he said. "Why, I have been there several times and I wouldn't be sure of not getting lost myself."

Inwood was such a backwater even the subway couldn't domesticate it. By 1910, four years after IRT stations opened at Dyckman, 207th, 215th, and 221st streets, only a few tenements had been built in the neighborhood, and much of the land between was still given over to farming. By World War I, Inwood had more houses, schools, churches, and the Dyckman Theatre, but at least half of the lots in the area were still vacant. Not until the 1930s did Inwood really fill in and begin to resemble an urban landscape, and even then vacant lots weren't hard to find.

ON THE WEST SIDE of Broadway, Inwood Hill's landed gentry died off one by one. Following Isham's death in 1909, his daughter Julia donated the family estate to the city for Isham Park, which runs from Broadway up and over the hill to Spuyten Duyvil Creek. The Isham mansion was preserved as the park's centerpiece and served as Parks Department offices and the headquarters of the Daughters of the American Revolution until Robert Moses tore it down in the 1940s.

In the 1890s, Andrew Haswell Green promoted an ambitious idea of turning the entirety of Inwood Hill into a park, but nothing came of the plan. Following Green's death in 1903—he was murdered by an intruder—civic-minded landowners and the American Scenic and Historic Preservation Society took up the cause, and in 1916 the city began acquiring land for what was to become the city's second-largest park after Central Park.

By then the once-bucolic hillside was an increasingly dangerous place: In the summer of 1913 the mutilated body of a pregnant Italian woman, her skull fractured and her head nearly decapitated from multiple knife wounds, was found on an isolated park trail cutting through what had once been the McCreery estate.

As the park's trees were allowed to infiltrate what had been lawns and gardens, the old mansions on the hill were abandoned. For years the Joseph Keppler house stood vacant, decaying furniture visible through the windows, its front porch lattices covered with wild roses. *Tribune* reporter Eleanor Booth Simmons, rambling over Inwood Hill in 1921, found overgrown box hedges, "quaint houses with cupolas and pillars," and the foundations of old stables that had turned into grassy terraces.

In the fall of 1933 writer Helen Worden visited the old Seaman estate while researching her book *Round Manhattan's Rim*, which documented her rambles around the perimeter of the island. She reached the mansion after trampling through tangled weeds, only to find the doors locked and the place deserted except for a suspicious caretaker. Directed to the estate's Arc de Triomphe entrance gate on Broadway, Worden found the estate's then-owner, James Dwyer, a contractor, sitting behind a walnut table in an office at the top of a spiral staircase. "And what do ye be after?" he demanded.

After some prodding, Dwyer let Worden inside the old mansion, and her brief tour revealed great halls, an ornate drawing room, a library, a large kitchen, and furniture of walnut and mahogany, but also broken windows, wide cracks in the front doors and dust on the balustrades. The house was torn down shortly after her visit.

Today almost nothing is left of what had once been perhaps the most sought-after enclave in Gilded Age New York. There are outlines of foundations deep in the woods, covered with earth and brambles, and along Broadway, tucked behind an auto body shop on the west side of the street between 215th and 218th streets, Seaman's Arc de Triomphe still peers out at the street, covered with graffiti and gradually succumbing to the weight of time.

CHAPTER 48

THE LAST FARM

———

A<small>T THE NORTHWEST CORNER OF BROADWAY AND 204TH</small> Street, across the street from a gas station, there is, of all things, a farmhouse sitting incongruously atop a knoll above a stone retaining wall. From a wide front porch beneath a swooping Dutch gambrel roof, visitors enter through double "Dutch" doors that open in upper and lower halves. The parlor and dining room on the ground floor and the five bedrooms upstairs are filled with family mementos: a Dutch clock, a family Bible from 1702, an eight-legged mahogany table from 1740. There is a summer kitchen in a small south wing that includes two stone ovens recessed into the wall and a winter kitchen in the basement, its fireplace hung with antiquated implements: bellows, tongs, tinderboxes, trammels, skillets, and skimmers.

The Dyckman Farmhouse Museum is a time machine, the last surviving remnant of a time when most of Manhattan consisted of plowed fields.

The first Dyckman in the New World was Jan Dyckman, a Westphalian immigrant who arrived in New Amsterdam in 1660. Dyckman built a farmhouse just southwest of the present-day intersection of Ninth Avenue and 209th Street, and when he died, in 1715, the land and house passed to his son Jacobus. When Jacobus died in 1773, the estate passed to Jacobus's son William, whose house was near what is now the north side of 210th Street, some 350 feet east of present-day Ninth Avenue.

William Dyckman sided with the Americans during the Revolution. Four of his sons served in the Continental Army, two of them in the "Westchester Guides" that spied on the British and passed along intelligence to General Washington. The Dyckman family waited out the war in Peekskill, thirty-six miles up the Hudson, and when they returned to Manhattan at war's end, in 1783, they found that their house had been burned by British and Hessian troops in retribution for the family's revolutionary activities. Starting over, William began building a new house on the west side of the Kingsbridge Road, and it is that house that survives today at the corner of Broadway and 204th Street.

William died in 1787, and his estate passed to his son Jacobus and then, after Jacobus's death in 1837, to Jacobus's sons Isaac and Michael, who remained lifelong bachelors. In 1820, Isaac took charge of his sister Hannah's seven-year-old son, James Frederick Dyckman Smith, who was raised in the farmhouse overlooking the Kingsbridge Road.

By the 1860s the "Dyckman Tract" had grown to about 400 acres, making it one of the largest private tracts ever assembled in Manhattan, rivaled in size only by the eighteenth-century estates of Peter Stuyvesant, James de Lancey, and Teunis Eidesse van Huyse. The Dyckmans' land extended from Fort George Hill north to Spuyten Duyvil Creek and included large parcels on both sides of the Kingsbridge Road and on Inwood Hill, and almost all of the fertile bottomlands stretching along the Harlem River shore. Isaac and Michael let drovers making the trek from Westchester down to the city's slaughterhouses pasture their cattle in the fields surrounding their house, and the influx of noisy livestock along the Kingsbridge Road was perhaps one reason the brothers abandoned the family homestead and built a new house near the present-day intersection of Broadway and 225th Street.

Isaac outlived his brother and, with no children of his own, designated his nephew James as heir. But James's last name was Smith, not Dyckman. Isaac couldn't bear the dissolution of the family name, and so he added a provision in his will that required James to change his name to Isaac Michael Dyckman. (James's response must have been something along the lines of "You're giving me *four hundred acres of Manhattan?* You can call me anything you want.")

James, or rather Isaac Michael, wasn't sentimental when it came to real estate, and upon his uncle's death in 1868 he immediately partitioned his inheritance into building lots and put them up for sale. Seventeen hundred lots were auctioned off in 1869, five hundred more in 1871. The dispersal of the Dyckman Tract was probably the largest land sale in Manhattan's history, part of a frantic auctioning of farmland following the Civil War that didn't abate until the Panic of 1873.

Isaac Michael, suddenly wealthy beyond all reckoning, turned his back on the soil—he was listed in the 1880 Federal Census as a "retired farmer"—and lived out his days in a new, bigger house he had built in the 1850s near the corner of what is now Broadway and 218th Street.

The old Dyckman farmhouse was sold, although the land around it continued to be farmed into the early twentieth century. Hugh and Mary Drennan, who had arrived in New York from Ireland in 1864 with four children in tow—they had five more in New York—operated a dairy farm next to the old Dyckman homestead. In the 1880s and '90s the Drennans' second-oldest daughter, Elizabeth, operated a general store and post office there, and for many years was the neighborhood's postmaster. The Dyckman farmhouse, meanwhile, fell into disrepair, and by 1916 was almost a ruin, a "hovel," Sarah Comstock reported in the *New York Times*, "with an unkempt yard and slovenly surroundings."

ISAAC MICHAEL, who died in 1899, had two daughters, Mary Alice and Fannie, and although they had never lived in the old farmhouse—they grew up in the mansion at Broadway and 218th Street—they were sentimentally attached to the place and decided to buy it back and donate it to the city as a museum. Mary Alice's husband, Bashford Dean, a curator at the Metropolitan Museum of Art, and Fannie's husband, architect Alexander McWilliam Welch, took charge of the restoration.

Welch, a Columbia graduate, did meticulous work, even replacing rotten beams with hand-sawn duplicates of the same approximate vintage. The original house had been extraordinarily well built, and many features, including its distinctive Dutch doors, remained intact despite the wear and tear of 133 years. Welch demolished one wing of the house added in the 1830s, removed later finishes from the interior, rebuilt the missing back porch, and replicated period details.

That Dean and Welch and the Dyckman sisters were going against the grain of progress was precisely what had stirred them to action. "There is, perhaps, not a city in the world one-tenth of [New York's] size which has less average interest in its own past," they wrote in a booklet explaining the project. "It grows quickly, takes its population from everywhere, and tears down its buildings and rebuilds them at a furious rate."

The house opened to the public in the summer of 1916 as the Dyckman House Park and Museum. "You will probably come upon it with a start," Comstock reported in the *Times*, "a flawless little old Dutch house, surrounded by trim brick paths, immaculate in its new paint, looking down primly upon the procession of automobiles that constantly flows past its door."

The Dyckman house remains much the same today, an unlikely oasis from the unceasing business of the city. WE ARE OPEN! PLEASE KNOCK! ESTAMOS ABIERTOS! POR FAVOR TOQUEN! a sign on the front door announces. An annual fall festival attracts local stroller-pushing parents and their charges for an afternoon of stories, pumpkin carving, cider press demonstrations, and even Dutch language lessons, which, once you're inside the Dyckman house, all seem like perfectly normal things to do on a weekend in twenty-first century New York. That's the thing about cities: one's perspective can shift slightly and suddenly everything appears altered. When viewed from Broadway, the Dyckman house doesn't seem real; when seen from the Dyckman house, Broadway doesn't seem real.

BY THE TIME the Dyckman house was resuscitated and opened as a museum, Inwood's remaining farms had been plowed under by new

apartment buildings. Then, in 1924, a large Italian family began till-
ing the soil on Broadway and so became Manhattan's last farmers.

Vincenzo and Mary Benedetto were both born in Italy and immigrated to New York in 1900. Their four boys (Patrick, or "Patsy,"
Vito, Carlo, and George) and five girls (Marie, Martha, Marietta,
Josephine, and Diana) were all born in the city. Vincenzo delivered ice
to apartment buildings from a horse-drawn wagon. The Benedetto
farm, four blocks north of the Dyckman farmhouse, was situated on a
little less than 2 acres of land encompassing a small block bounded by
Broadway, Tenth Avenue, and 213th and 214th streets. The land came
with an existing, decidedly humble two-story red brick house that
peered out at Tenth Avenue from beneath the elevated IRT tracks.
Mary, who unlike her husband could read and write, managed the
farm, and Vincenzo, Patsy, Vito, and Carlo, with help from an uncle
or two, did the planting and plowing. The landlord, Leo Fellman of
New Orleans, rented the spread to the Benedettos for $30 a month.

The farm had good soil and produced "delicious" vegetables and
fruit, according to Josephine Benedetto, who was three years old when
her family moved there. They grew tomatoes, corn, string beans,
carrots, beets, broccoli, radishes, and lettuce; peaches, cherries, pears,
pumpkins, and squash; and raised chickens that laid both brown and
white eggs priced at fifteen cents a dozen. Josephine was spared from
heavy farm labor but helped sell produce from a stand next to the
house. She didn't like the chickens and stayed away from them.

The Depression hit only five years after the Benedettos plowed
their first furrow. When Federal Census enumerator Clarice Kagan
stopped by the farm on April 17, 1930, she was apparently so under-
whelmed by the scale of the Benedettos' operation that she left column 10 of the census questionnaire ("Does this family live on a
farm?") blank. Kagan listed Vincenzo's occupation as "iceman," not
farmer, and Mary as a "worker" in what Kagan characterized not as
a farm but only as a "vegetable garden." Later that fall, Mary told
Time magazine that 1930 had been an especially hard year.

Despite the Depression, Inwood had become a humming, working
community of clerks, dressmakers, taxi drivers, contractors, accoun-
tants, printers, salesmen, stenographers, waiters, laborers, plumbers,

The Benedetto
farm as seen from
Broadway, 1933.

steelworkers, butchers, seamstresses, and electricians. The Benedetto farm was an anomaly, the surrounding blocks filling up with people, some 300 of them in just two apartment buildings on Broadway on the other side of 213th Street.

The Benedetto family became perennial subjects for newspapers and magazines, and in time came to resent the attention. In the fall of 1933, Helen Worden happened on the farm while researching her travelogue *Round Manhattan's Rim*. Intrigued by the pumpkins, squash, and tomatoes piled high on the Benedettos' farm stand, Worden stepped over some bean sprouts and accosted a man with a hoe (probably Vincenzo) with questions about the place. The man shook his head and went into the house, whereupon, Worden wrote, Mary emerged yelling, "No stories, no stories! Every time the papers say this only farm in New York, man raises rent."

But gawkers kept showing up. They couldn't get over the novelty of it: A farm! On Broadway! "[Almost] every other week," the *Times* reported in 1935, "Signor di Benedetto awakes to find a junked auto toppled into his parsnips from the grassy banks of Broadway."

Vincenzo's ice routes melted with the advent of home refrigeration. By 1940, Patsy was operating a stationery store a few blocks from the farm with help from Vito, who manned the counter; Carlo was making deliveries for an embroidery company; and Vincenzo and Mary had sublet part of their farm to a used-car lot and converted another section into a parking lot, leaving only one-third of the block for farming. Vincenzo was listed on the 1940 Federal Census not as a farmer but as the parking lot's "watchman" and Mary as the "assistant watchman." That year the farm sold only about $50 worth of produce.

Vincenzo Benedetto died in 1943 at fifty-eight. The farm was sold about 1954, and by the following year an immense New York Telephone Company facility had been built on the site. That building is still there today, repurposed as an office complex that includes a branch of Manhattan Mini Storage, Hostos Community College, Everyday Christian Church, a law office, a violin maker's workshop, and a French grocery store that charges $6.90 for a jar of rhubarb jam.

JOSEPHINE LEFT HOME when she was still a teenager, and in looking back on her childhood wasn't nostalgic for the old family farm. "It was just someplace to live; let's put it that way," she said. Her upbringing in the midst of the Depression may have been hard, but Josephine could roam among rows of fruit trees and corn, smell the earth, and see expanses of sky, all of which made her childhood much closer to the experiences of New York children in the eighteenth and nineteenth centuries, when land was still measured in acres, than to that of twentieth- and twenty-first-century children confined within the strict boundaries of apartments and city blocks.

"You had freedom," Josephine remembered. "You didn't have to listen to your neighbors."

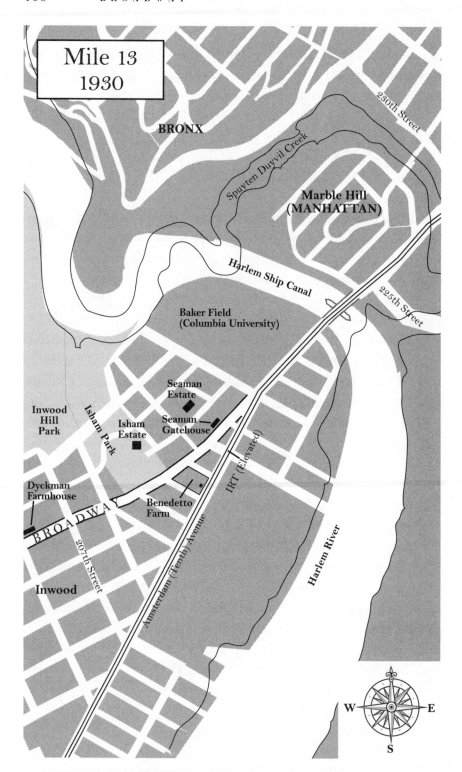

Mile 13
1930

BRONX

Spuyten Duyvil Creek

230th Street

Marble Hill
(MANHATTAN)

Harlem Ship Canal

225th Street

Baker Field
(Columbia University)

Seaman
Estate

Isham Park

Isham
Estate

Seaman
Gatehouse

Inwood
Hill
Park

IRT (Elevated)

Dyckman
Farmhouse

BROADWAY

Benedetto
Farm

207th Street

Amsterdam (Tenth) Avenue

Inwood

Harlem River

W   E

S

CHAPTER 49

INDIAN TRAIL

———

BROADWAY IS AN OLD INDIAN TRAIL—EVERYONE KNOWS that. Or is it? Martha Lamb didn't mention it in her three-volume *History of the City of New York: Its Origin, Rise, and Progress,* published in 1877, nor did Stephen Jenkins in his dense Broadway history *The Greatest Street in the World,* from 1911. (For her part, Lamb didn't think Manhattan's Lenape Indians were worth studying anyway: "It was not an interesting people whom the Dutch found in possession of Manhattan Island," she wrote. "They have ever been surrounded with darkness and dullness, and we can promise very little entertainment while we call them before us.")

The notion that Broadway began as a Lenape path picked up steam in 1922, when Reginald Pelham Bolton, an English-born engineer and self-trained archeologist, published *Indian Paths in the Great Metropolis,* which described Manhattan's Lenape traveling over an extensive network of roads beaten into the earth by, as he put it, "the patient art of the wild men." Bolton, father of Broadway playwright Guy Bolton (*Anything Goes, Lady Be Good, Girl Crazy*) lived for many years on 158th Street, where neighbors affectionately referred to him as the "No. 1 citizen of Washington Heights."

Much of Bolton's research was centered on the environs of Washington Heights and Inwood, where the relative lack of development made archeological digs possible. As a longtime member of the New-York Historical Society's "Field Exploration Committee," Bolton and colleague William L. Calver tramped around upper Manhattan in bowler hats and coats and ties, carrying picks and shovels and rescuing artifacts from construction sites. In Inwood they discovered not only Revolutionary War encampments strewn with bullets and buttons, but also Lenape gravesites, trash piles, and oyster "middens" (heaps of discarded shells).

Bolton reasoned that the Lenape must have had a system of pathways to get from place to place. He connected known sites of Lenape inhabitation with red lines and before long had uncovered, or rather designed, an entire network of Lenape roads crisscrossing Manhattan. *Indian Paths in the Great Metropolis* is almost pure conjecture—"probably" appears in the text thirty-three times, along with phrases such as "we can suppose" and "we can imagine"—but upon its publication was hailed as the definitive word on the subject. And it included the revelation that Broadway might have begun as what Bolton called the "ancient trail of the Red Men of Manhattan, known as the Weck-quaes-geek Path."

THE WICKQUASGECKS (or Weckquaskeeks or Weckquaesgweks—there isn't a definitive spelling) were a tribe of Lenape Indians that lived in present-day Westchester County. Bolton's "Weck-quaes-geek Path" appears to have been derived from a single reference in Dutch explorer David Pietersz De Vries's *Short Historical and Journal Notes of several Voyages Made in the Four Parts of the World, Namely, Europe, Africa, Asia, and America*, an account of his expeditions from 1632 to 1644. Originally published in 1655, it was translated by Henry C. Murphy and reprinted in New York in 1853 under the title *Voyages from Holland to America, A.D. 1632–1644.*

De Vries wrote that in 1642 a "harmless" Dutch wheelwright, Claes Cornelissen Swits, was transacting a business deal with a Wickquasgeck Indian when the Indian killed him with an axe, apparently in retaliation for the murder of the Indian's uncle by a Dutch settler some years before. (Swits's murder was one of the inciting incidents that led to Kieft's War, a bloodbath instigated by New Amsterdam's director-general Willem Kieft against the local Lenape.)

According to Murphy's 1853 translation, De Vries described Swits's murder as taking place in his house near "Densel-bay," apparently a misspelling of "Deutal," Old Dutch for a curved, scimitar-like blade that described the shape of a cove along the East River between present-day 46th and 47th streets. (Deutal Bay was corrupted into the English "Turtle Bay" and is still the name of a neighborhood there today, although the bay itself was filled in and forgotten in the early nineteenth century.) Swits's house, De Vries wrote, was "on the road, over which the Indians from Wickquasgeck passed daily."

In 1909, J. Franklin Jameson inserted De Vries's account into his massive *Narratives of New Netherland,* but in his version Swits's house was "on the Wickquasgeck road over which the Indians passed daily."

There is a critical difference between Jameson's version of that sentence and Murphy's translation of De Vries, who hadn't named the road in question nor described it as an Indian trail: In Murphy's translation De Vries simply called it a "road" that "Indians from Wickquasgeck," meaning Indians from Westchester, used on a daily basis—it could have been any road, including one built by the Dutch. In Jameson's version the road became the "Wickquasgeck road," implying a particular *kind* of road—an Indian path.

Other historians took up the cause, and soon the "Wickquasgeck road" seemed as real and well traveled as Broadway itself.

In 1928, the sixth and final volume of architect and historian Isaac Newton Phelps Stokes's masterful *The Iconography of Manhattan Island* went to press. A thick, heavy set of books—the term "doorstopper" is not adequate here—brimming with maps and reproductions of rare prints and documents, it offers a meticulous day-by-day chronology of life in the city, and an expansive bibliography. The *Iconography* remains without question the most ambitious and complete history of the city ever produced. It also furthered the connection between Broadway and the "Wickquasgeck road."

The *Iconography*'s sixth volume included a series of foldout maps depicting, in full-color overlays, the boundaries of Manhattan's original farms and land grants, accompanied by text chronicling how the land had been measured, partitioned, and conveyed from one generation to the next. Jennie F. Macarthy of Hackensack, New Jersey, who for forty years had worked as a researcher at the Title Guarantee & Trust Company and was an expert at deciphering city records, was the author of that section, and her work was, at least for those obsessed with the arcane trajectories of real-estate titles as they passed from generation to generation, riveting.

Since lower Broadway and the upland colonial highways it eventually absorbed—the Bloomingdale Road and parts of the Kingsbridge Road—often functioned as property lines in Manhattan's early settlement, Macarthy, in addressing its supposed origin, described in detail the supposed path of the "Wickquasgeck road."

"There is hardly a doubt," she wrote, but that Cryn Fredericksz, the Dutch West India Company's surveyor, had found an existing "Indian road" at the southern tip of the island and incorporated it into his plan for New Amsterdam. Macarthy figured that the road ran along the present-day line of Broadway from the Battery to City Hall Park, then branched off at Chatham Street (Park Row) to the Bowery and followed what was later called the Eastern, or Boston, Post Road to Harlem. From there, she guessed the path followed the Kingsbridge Road across the middle of the island and wound its way up to Spuyten Duyvil Creek.

Macarthy's version of the Wickquasgeck road only took into account Broadway's southern- and northernmost sections. What of its middle miles, the section from present-day 23rd to 147th streets that followed the path of the old Bloomingdale Road? Both Macarthy and Bolton believed that it, too, had begun as an Indian trail.

The Bloomingdale Road was one of several highways in Manhattan opened by "An Act for the Laying out Regulateing [sic] Clearing and preserving Publick Comon [sic] highways thro'out this Colony," passed on June 19, 1703, by the provincial legislature of the New York colony. The act appointed three commissioners, William Anderson, Clement Elsworth, and Pieter Oblinus, to complete a survey and report, which they turned in four years later, on June 16, 1707. Their report didn't mention any Indian trails but did include an enticing ambiguity in its description of the Bloomingdale Road's route: "From

the House at the End of New York lane [the Bowery], there is . . .
to lye a Road turning to the left hand the Course being Northerly
and so by Great Kills [a salt marsh along the Hudson River between
present-day 40th and 45th streets] & forward as the said Road now
lyes unto Theunis Edis's & Capt. D' Key's thro the said Edis's land."

"As the said Road now lyes" implies that sections of the Bloomingdale Road were already there in 1707, but it's unclear whether the
commissioners were referring to parts of the road that had been
built since their survey began in 1703, or whether they meant older
sections. Did Anderson, Elsworth, and Oblinus cut an entirely new
road up the West Side, or did they reuse an existing highway? And
if they did, was that highway so old that it had been there before the
Dutch arrived? At that point, the research trail goes cold.

And what of the Kingsbridge Road? It, too, as Bolton and Macarthy suggested, could have been an Indian path well before it was first
surveyed in 1707. Of all the various roads that were cobbled together
into modern Broadway, the Kingsbridge Road, straddling as it does the
narrow neck of upper Manhattan, seems most likely, for purely topographical reasons, to have once been a Lenape trail. The island gets
so skinny there, where else would the Lenape have walked but along
a path that must have at least occasionally coincided with the Kingsbridge Road? But there's no evidence that it *was* an Indian road, either,
other than its proximity to the Lenape habitation sites that Bolton
uncovered. As with every road, time brings incremental changes in
width, length, and direction, and the route of the Kingsbridge Road
changed dramatically around the time of the American Revolution,
when a leisurely loop that had brought the road from the middle of the
island to the edge of the Harlem River was closed in favor of a more
direct straight path to the King's Bridge over Spuyten Duyvil Creek.

SINCE BROADWAY'S HISTORY has been one of constant, tumultuous
change, it's reassuring to consider that America's most famous street
might lead not just uptown and downtown but also back in time.
Wouldn't it be nice, wouldn't it blunt the knife edge of unrelenting
progress a bit, if it turned out that not every ancient landmark had

been erased in the making of New York? What if an Indian highway was still there, right under the sidewalk? And what if not just any street had been an Indian trail, but *Broadway?*

"The white men did not remove it, but built upon it, so that today if the modern pavements were removed remains of the original path could still be found," the *New York Times* stated emphatically in 1922, soon after Bolton's *Indian Paths* was published. "Broadway an Indian Trail. Present Famous 'Bright Light' Pathway Used as Artery of Trade by the Aborigines," the *Pioneer Express* of Pembina, North Dakota, declared that same year, as what had been a local theory gradually became a national fact. It wasn't so much that an Indian trail had become Broadway but that Broadway had become an Indian trail.

CHAPTER 50

WHERE DOES THIS ROAD END?

———

L ET'S SAY YOU'RE A WICKQUASGECK INDIAN WITH AN URGENT need to leave Manhattan at the end of a long, hard day and get back home to Westchester. You'd find yourself at the edge of a stream where the waters of Spuyten Duyvil Creek—the name is Dutch for "Spitting Devil," which accurately described the creek's tumultuous currents—and the Harlem River joined at the northern tip of Manhattan. With no bridge across the creek, the Wickquasgecks were forced to wait for low tide and then wade across at a point called, of all things, the "wading place."

In 1693, Frederick Philipse built the first version of King's Bridge across the stream, connecting Manhattan to Westchester by way of the Kingsbridge Road. The bridge was rebuilt in 1713 a bit to the west of the original, destroyed several times during the Revolution, and again rebuilt after the war. Well into the nineteenth century the community that grew up around the bridge maintained a rustic quality—at least at first glance.

"The inhabitants near this bridge appear to be unsophisticated and primitive in their ways, but they are only superficially so," journalist Charles Dawson Shanly reported in the *Atlantic Monthly* in 1868. "They dredge their own oysters, which lends an air of self-support and independence to the place; but then they charge New

York prices for them, which shows that with them rural simplicity is but skin-deep."

The only craft that could navigate the shallow waters of the Spuyten Duyvil were canoes and skiffs, and for decades various plans had been put forth to replace the creek with a canal capable of admitting larger ships. The Erie Canal's opening in 1825 had inspired formation of the Harlem Canal Company, but that venture failed after only a few excavations had been made. But the idea of a canal across Manhattan wouldn't die: The year before the Erie Canal opened, Governor DeWitt Clinton had predicted that New York City would become the "granary of the world," and by the 1870s the city was exporting well over 100 million bushels of flour, corn, and other grains every year. Much of that grain was exported to Great Britain, which in the 1870s bought between 60 million and 70 million bushels of corn annually from the United States. A canal across upper Manhattan would expedite the exportation of grain and other products by creating a direct link from the Hudson River to Long Island Sound.

In 1875, the New York legislature turned the canal project over to the federal government, and in 1878, Congress authorized the first appropriations. But lawsuits brought by landowners, and the slow drip of congressional funding, delayed the project. The first scoopfuls of mud weren't dredged until 1888.

When work began, it was fully expected that the United States Ship Canal, or the Harlem River Ship Canal as everyone called it, would transform upper Manhattan into the center of shipping for the entire eastern seaboard, causing the commercial center of the city to shift to the north and transforming 125th Street into the most important thoroughfare in the city, the "Broadway of Harlem."

The project had three components: Removing rocks at the mouth of the Harlem River where it joined the East River; widening and dredging the Harlem River itself; and cutting a channel through Manhattan's neck. The cut was, by far, the most difficult proposition.

The first option was to go through Sherman's Creek and Dyckman Street straight across to the Hudson; the second to go through Sherman's Creek but bend north along the base of Inwood Hill to Spuyten Duyvil Creek; the third to dredge and widen the existing horseshoe curve of the Harlem River and Spuyten Duyvil Creek; and the fourth, the route engineers ultimately picked, to cut straight across Manhattan's neck for three-quarters of a mile, bypassing the S-curve of the Spuyten Duyvil and severing Marble Hill, a knoll at the tip of the island long known for its marble quarries, from the rest of the island.

The carving of the channel proceeded in two parts: One team of laborers, many of them Italian immigrants, made a cut from the Harlem River west to Broadway while a second team cut from Broadway to Spuyten Duyvil Creek. By 1890, passengers on New York Central trains traveling along the east side of the Harlem River were treated to a sight the *New York Sun* likened to the cellar of a titan's palace, a huge chasm of "astonishing breadth and depth" that had completely severed Manhattan's tip. Broadway was temporarily propped up on the wedge of rock that remained between the two excavations and was ultimately carried over the canal on an elegant new steel bridge.

When the canal finally opened, on June 17, 1895, city, state, and federal officials marked the occasion with a reenactment of the ecstatic "Wedding of the Waters" festivities that had inaugurated the Erie Canal seventy years earlier. A marine parade of steamers, yachts, tugs, rowboats, and the warship *Cincinnati* proceeded up the Hudson to Inwood, where they lined up in the river and then passed slowly and cautiously down the canal, sailing under bridges crowded with spectators. The flotilla emerged into the East River and Long Island Sound, whereupon Mayor William L. Strong, on the deck of the steamship *Elaine,* handed a ceremonial keg of Lake Erie water to one Grace McVeigh (someone's daughter; described in the *Evening World* as "pretty"), who poured it overboard amid much hoopla, just as officials had done in 1825. The pageant concluded with a banquet, speeches, and, later that evening, fireworks.

But the canal wasn't finished. It was estimated that two more years were needed to dredge the Harlem River to the proper depth. By 1903, the canal, its funding withheld, had filled with silt and even the captains of the smallest craft avoided it. Eventually the canal was satisfactorily dredged and, in 1938, straightened on the Spuyten

The opening ceremonies for the Harlem River Ship Canal,
June 17, 1895. The canal snipped off the end of Manhattan
and sutured it to the Bronx.

Duyvil side to allow for more direct passage to the Hudson. Hunts
Point, Port Morris, and Mott Haven, districts of the Bronx that lay
along the edge of the canal, did develop, as predicted, into centers of
manufacturing and shipping. But the commercial center of the city
never gravitated north to Harlem; the big stores, banks, and offices
remained far to the south on lower Broadway and Wall Street, and in
Midtown, where Penn Station and Grand Central Station disgorged
a constant stream of worker bees every minute of every day.

MARBLE HILL, CUT OFF from Manhattan by the canal, became an
island and, its quarries played out, slipped ever deeper into obscurity.
In 1914, the remaining section of Spuyten Duyvil Creek that wound
around the north edge of Marble Hill was filled in, so that it became,
geographically, part of the Bronx. But Marble Hill was still politically part of Manhattan, and residents kept rejecting referendums
to join the Bronx. When Bronx borough president James J. Lyons

defiantly planted the Bronx flag in Marble Hill in 1939, residents booed him.

Today, Marble Hill remains an insular community of winding streets and neat houses where residents tend to give visitors the once-over as they walk by. At the north end of the neighborhood, at the corner of Broadway and 228th Street, is No. 5249 Broadway, a C-Town supermarket and Broadway's northernmost building in Manhattan. It is the unremarkable flipside to No. 1 Broadway, the Washington Building that Cyrus W. Field built in 1882 in place of the old Archibald Kennedy mansion, where George Washington had reconnoitered with his generals in 1776. Poet Carl Sandburg once wrote that Broadway ends in the sea, but that's only true if you are heading south; if you go north, Broadway ends in a checkout line.

BUT BROADWAY DOESN'T really end there: It continues through the neighborhoods of Kingsbridge and Fieldston in the Bronx, where it forms the long western edge of the vast Van Cortlandt Park. Then, leaving New York City behind, it winds north through Yonkers, Hastings-on-Hudson, Dobbs Ferry, Sleepy Hollow, Ossining, Crotonville, Peekskill, Cold Spring, and Beacon. A ribbon of highway bounded by woods and open fields and suburbs, the upstate version of Broadway bears no resemblance to the Great White Way. North of Manhattan it follows the path of the eighteenth-century Albany Post Road—here and there, ancient mile markers still poke out from the side of the road—which in turn follows the even older Farmers' Turnpike. But it keeps digressing: Between Crotonville and Peekskill, it widens and is called the Croton Expressway, a smooth but lifeless artery that promises nothing more than a way to get quickly from one point to another. Maps may say that it's Broadway, but it's not: Broadway was never just a thoroughfare; it has always been, first and foremost, a place.

Broadway ends in Albany but continues, as Route 9, to the Canadian border. It is a perfectly fine road but hardly the confounding, multilayered, vexing, exhilarating, always-changing Broadway that is the centerline and lifeblood of Manhattan.

"Broadway," Walt Whitman once wrote, "will never fail in riches, arts, men, women, histories, stately shows, morals, warnings, wrecks, triumphs—the profoundest indices of mortality and immortality." That's fine for Whitman, but Stephen Jenkins, writing in 1911, was more to the point: He thought that Broadway was the place where New Yorkers felt most at home.

ACKNOWLEDGMENTS

I MUST FIRST AND FOREMOST THANK JOHN GLUSMAN, W. W. Norton's vice president and editor in chief, for editing this book with unerring insight and extreme patience. I must also thank John's assistant Lydia Brents, who patiently answered my thousands of questions. Thank you also to Norton's former president and current chairman Drake McFeely, former publisher Jeannie Luciano, sales director Steven Pace, director of publicity Louise Brockett, production manager Anna Oler, project editor Don Rifkin, copy editor Fred Wiemer, and Lydia's predecessors Alexa Pugh and Jonathan Baker.

Thank you to my friend Constance Rosenblum for reading and editing the book proposal and early drafts and offering nonstop encouragement. Thanks also to Andrew Dolkart, Robert Marx, Annie Polland, Barnet Schecter, and Carol Willis for reading the manuscript, in whole or in part, and offering insights and suggestions.

The Internet is truly a treasure trove of research material these days, and this book never would have been started, much less completed, without around-the-clock access to *Chronicling America*, the historical newspaper database at the Library of Congress, the New York Public Library Digital Collections, the Internet Archive, and other online sources. But I really prefer printed books, maps, prints, and documents, and so it was a pleasure to frequent New York's many remarkable libraries and archives, where I was assisted by some amazing people: Hector Rivera at the Manhattan Borough President's Map Room let me handle the original Randel Farm Maps; Thomas Lannan at the New York Public Library Manuscripts and Archives Division was enthusiastic and extremely helpful in granting access to manuscript diaries and surveying records; Thomas Lisanti, manager of the New York Public Library Permissions and Reproduction Services, and Eric Shows, manager of the New York Public Library Digitization Services, answered countless questions about the library's digital collections; Tammy Kiter, Joseph Ditta, and Joseph Festa at the New-York Historical Society's Patricia D. Klingenstein Library cheerfully helped me with manuscript diaries and city directories; and Assistant Commissioner of Records Kenneth Cobb, Municipal Archives director Sylvia Kollar, and researcher Barbara Hibbert at the New York City Department of Records helped me make sense of real-estate assessments and other inscrutable documents.

And then there are New York's wonderful bookstores, and I visited them often: Broadway doesn't have nearly as many bookstores as it once did, but, thank God, it does have the Strand and Book Culture. Thank you to Peter Miller at Freebird Books in Brooklyn, and a special thank you to Laura Ten Eyck and Richard Rosenblatt at Argosy Bookstore, prints department, where I whiled away many blissful afternoons rifling through stacks of *Harper's Weekly* and *Gleason's Pictorial Drawing-Room Companion*. And with considerable pangs I must also thank Christien Shangraw, Glenn Tranter, and the entire staff of my home-away-from-home, Brooklyn's late and deeply lamented BookCourt.

Teresa Fox of FoxPrint Design drew and redrew the book's maps, a process that continued for five years—mostly because I kept changing my mind. Thank you also to Katherine Slingluff for shooting me (the author photo, I mean).

I had barely begun this project when Pete Hogden of Grace Church took me on a memorable tour up into the rafters of James Renwick Jr.'s masterpiece at Broadway and 10th Street, a vertical jaunt that allowed me to see Renwick's genius up close. More recently Mary Miss has inspired me to look at Broadway from an entirely different angle through her ongoing project *Broadway: 1000 Steps*. Bernie Gelb of Ansonia Realty let me tag along while he inspected vacant apartments in the wondrous Ansonia. Don Rice and Naiomy Rodriguez at the Dyckman Farmhouse Museum Alliance answered my questions and gave me homemade cider.

Thank you to Walter L. Arnstein, Barbara Samuelson, Mary Sansone, and Gene Yellin for sharing their memories of Broadway with me, and to the incomparable Jeff Kisseloff, author of *You Must Remember This* (in my opinion the greatest book ever written about New York City), for graciously allowing me to quote from the original recordings of the oral histories he collected on cassette tapes in the 1980s and donated to the New York Public Library. Thanks also to Whitey Flynn at the Trinity Church Archives.

Partial funding for illustrations and permissions came from grants from the PSC-CUNY Research Foundation and from the Bernard and Anne Spitzer Endowment at the City College of New York School of Architecture, where I must also thank Jacob Alspector, George Ranalli, Julio Salcedo, Gordon Gebert, Peter Gisolfi, Alan Feigenberg, Michael Sorkin, Marta Gutman, Michael Miller, Camille Hall, and Erica Wszolek. Special thanks to Judy Connorton, Nilda Sanchez, and Taida Sainvil at the City College Architecture Library; Mayra Mahmood, who helped me dissect city directories and retrieved documents from the New York Public Library and the Municipal Archives; and all my astonishing students from my "Cities" and "Broadway" design studios.

I never would have embarked on, much less completed, this project without the guidance of my extraordinary agent Howard Morhaim, who not only saw me safely through the treacherous shoals of the proposal phase to the safety of Norton's harbor but also read draft after draft of the manuscript and offered insightful comments every step of the way. I lift a cup of decaf in your honor, Howard.

Thank you also to Camilla Crowe White, Tess Tomlinson, Lindsey Weaving, Nathan Sherwood, Beth Kolacki, Janice Campbell, Jacki Fischer, and Susan Goldstein.

And here's to my indefatigable family, Leigh, Ben, and Pete, who never complained when I went off to walk up Broadway one more time.

NOTES

"A SORT OF GEOGRAPHICAL VIVISECTION"

xiii **"The best way of finding out the inside of an orange"**: William Henry Rideing, "Life on Broadway," *Harper's New Monthly Magazine* LVI, no. 331 (December 1877), 229.

PREFACE

xv **a "mighty ever-flowing land-river"**: Jerome Loving, "'Broadway, the Magnificent!': A Newly Discovered Whitman Essay," *Walt Whitman Quarterly Review* 12 (Spring 1995), 210.
xv **Broadway as "a kind of animated mirror"**: Valerian Gribayedoff, "The 'Flaneur' on Broadway," *Illustrated American* XX, 352 (November 7, 1896), 619.
xvi **"Broadway's a great street when you're going up"**: Sidney Skolsky, *Times Square Tintypes*. New York: Ives Washburn, 1930, viii. Skolsky attributed the quote to McGuire, but it may be apocryphal.

CHAPTER 1. SOARING THINGS

3 **"Every window" . . . "appeared to be a paper mill"**: "The Sights and Sightseers," *New York Times*, October 29, 1886, 2.
4 **15,000 people marched in the parade**: "The Croton Jubilee," *New York Tribune*, October 15, 1842, 1.
4 **the tail end of the procession was still visible:** John Aspinwall Hadden diary, New York Public Library, Division of Manuscripts and Archives, 110.
4 **Field said he was overwhelmed:** "The Atlantic Telegraph Celebration. Procession, Festivities, Speeches, & c. A General Jubilee," *New York Evening Post*, September 2, 1858, 1.
4 **He was hailed as "Cyrus the Great":** Samuel Carter, *Cyrus Field: Man of Two Worlds*. New York: G. P. Putnam's Sons, 1968, 164.
5 **Laura Keene's Theatre:** Thomas Allston Brown, *A History of the New York Stage from the First Performance in 1732 to 1901*. Three volumes. New York: Dodd, Mead & Co., 1902, II, 132.

5 **Archbishop John J. Hughes buried:** Carter, *Cyrus Field*, 166.

5 **The "Atlantic Telegraph Polka":** Ibid., 169.

5 **a banquet in Field's honor:** Isabella Field Judson, *Cyrus W. Field: His Life and Work, 1819–1892*. New York: Harper Brothers, 1896, 117–120.

6 **"A carnivalesque appearance":** "The Cable Carnival," *New York Herald*, September 2, 1858, 1.

7 **Einstein insisted:** "Zionists Greet Einstein, Here for Palestine," *New York Tribune*, April 3, 1921, 1, 3. It is unclear whether ticker tape was involved in Einstein's parade.

7 **"New York has been kind":** "'Don't Worry,' Dr. Einstein Advises Public," *New York Tribune*, April 4, 1921, 9.

7 **the *Times* blamed "imps of office boys":** "The Sights and Sightseers," 2.

8 **acquired the decaying Washington Hotel:** "A Historical Building Sold. The Oldest Building in the City to Be Destroyed—Some Points in its History," *New York Tribune*, August 30, 1881, 8.

9 **a crank "with no moral sense":** "The Railroad Situation," *Real Estate Record & Builders' Guide* XXIX, 722 (January 14, 1882), 26.

9 **Field invited six architects:** "Mr. Field's New Building. Plans for the Offices to be Erected on Battery-place," *New York Times*, November 17, 1881, 8.

10 **"If I had the time":** "Seen and Heard on a Saturday Walk," *New York Tribune*, January 31, 1887, 5;

10 **machinations of Gould and Sage:** Carter, *Cyrus Field*, 342–343.

10 **"Leaning over the ship's rail":** Paul Bourget, *Outre-Mer: American Impressions*. London: T. Fisher Unwin, 1895, 17.

10 **He called the Equitable a "gigantic palace":** Ibid., 28.

11 **"At what time of day do they die here?":** Ibid., 26–27.

11 **"Sky-Scrapers":** I. N. Phelps Stokes, *The Iconography of Manhattan Island, 1498 to 1909*. Six volumes. New York: Robert H. Dodd, 1915–1928. Reprinted, New York: Arno Press, 1967, III, 967.

11 **"must be every inch a proud and soaring thing":** Louis H. Sullivan, "The Tall Office Building Artistically Considered," *Lippincott's Magazine* 57 (March 1896), 403–409.

CHAPTER 2. MUD AND FIRE

16 **"unconstitutional and oppressive":** *New York Post-Boy*, November 7, 1765. Quoted in I. N. Phelps Stokes, *The Iconography of Manhattan Island, 1498 to 1909*. Six volumes. New York: Robert H. Dodd, 1915–1928. Reprinted, New York: Arno Press, 1967, IV, 753.

16 **A "moveable Gallows" was erected:** Ibid.

17 **"The whole Multitude then returned to the Fort":** Ibid.

17 **"many Insults to the Effigy":** Ibid.

17 **"[It] soon kindled to a great Flame":** Ibid.

17 **he asked Captain Kennedy to move the paper:** Ibid., 754. Later, on December 24, 1765, a mob did threaten Kennedy's house but was "suppressed by the mayor." Quoted in ibid., 759.

18   **William Smith's house at No. 5 Broadway:** Barnet Schecter, *The Battle for New York: The City at the Heart of the American Revolution.* New York: Walker & Co., 2002, 21.

18   **captured and confined in Morristown:** Stokes, *The Iconography of Manhattan Island,* V, 1001.

18   **Washington stayed at first:** Thomas Jones, *History of New York During the Revolutionary War.* New York: New-York Historical Society, 1879, I, 85.

18   **"With a fair wind and rapid tide":** Henry Knox to William Knox, July 11, 1776, in Francis S. Drake, *Life and Correspondence of Henry Knox, Major-General in the American Revolutionary Army.* Boston: Samuel G. Drake, 1873, 28.

18   **"The city in an uproar":** Ibid.

20   **"I have nothing in particular to communicate":** George Washington to John Hancock, September 22, 1776, in *The Papers of George Washington, Revolutionary War Series, VI, 13 August 1776–20 October 1776,* Philander D. Chase and Frank E. Grizzard Jr., editors. Charlottesville: University Press of Virginia, 1994, 369–370.

21   **"as at noon day":** Joseph Henry, *The Campaign Against Quebec: Being an Accurate and Interesting Account of the Hardships and Sufferings of That Band of Heroes Who Traversed the Wilderness, by the Route of the Kennebec, and Chaudière River, to Quebec, in the Year 1775.* Watertown, N.Y.: Knowlton & Rice, 1844, 200–202.

21   **"If we could have divested ourselves":** Henry was among many eyewitnesses who saw several fires break out simultaneously, which some took as proof that Washington's agents had intentionally tried to burn the town to make things harder for the British. It is more likely that wind carried embers onto buildings far ahead of the flames, making it appear as if many fires were started at the same time. Henry, *The Campaign Against Quebec,* 200–202.

21   **In all, some 493 houses were destroyed:** D. T. Valentine, *Manual of the Corporation of the City of New-York.* New York: Edmund Jones & Co., 1866, 767. Since Trinity Church's losses were so staggering, many clergy and parishioners assumed the fire had been a plot aimed at the Church of England.

22   **"some good honest fellow":** George Washington to Lund Washington, October 6, 1776, in *The Papers of George Washington, Revolutionary War Series, VI, 13 August 1776–20 October 1776,* 493–495.

22   **"Had I been left to the dictates":** Ibid.

22   **moved into townhouses on broadway:** David C. Franks, *The New-York Directory.* New York, 1786 and 1787 editions; Robert Hodge, Thomas Allen, Samuel Campbell, *The New-York Directory and Register.* New York, 1789 and 1790 editions.

22   **the Alexander Macomb mansion:** In 1821 the Macomb mansion was converted into a hotel called Bunker's Mansion House.

23   **"All persons having demands":** *Gazette of the United-States,* September 1, 1790, 3. In 1789, Washington was listed in Hodge's *New-York Directory* as residing at 3 Cherry Street.

23   **"most convenient and agreeable part of the city":** William Winterbotham, *An Historical, Geographical, Commercial, and Philosophical View of the American United States, and of the European Settlements in America and the West-Indies.* London: J. Ridgway, H. D. Symonds, and D. Holt, 1795, II, 315.

23   **John Jacob Astor, then amassing:** *Longworth's American Almanac, New-York Register, and City Directory.* New York: Thomas Longworth. (Editions for 1798, 1803, 1813, 1826–1827, 1839.)

24   **In 1797, New York surpassed Philadelphia:** Robert Greenhalgh Albion, *The Rise of New York Port, 1815–1860.* New York and London: Charles Scribner's Sons, 1939, 8.

24   **Dead cats:** *Boston Gazette*, August 18, 1803. Quoted in Stokes, *The Iconography of Manhattan Island, 1498 to 1909*, V, 1412.

24   **"bottomless pit of finance":** *New York Gazette & General Advertiser*, November 4, 1805. Quoted in Stokes, *The Iconography of Manhattan Island*, V, 1439.

CHAPTER 3. PROMENADE

26   **"as much crowded as the Bond-street in London":** John Lambert, *Travels Through Canada and the United States of North America, in the Years 1806, 1807 & 1808.* London: Baldwin, Cradock & Joy, 1816, II, 58–59.

26   **"[Dressed] in their best":** John J. Sturtevant memoir, Manuscripts and Archives Division, New York Public Library, Astor, Lenox, and Tilden Foundations, 51.

27   **"Yes, everyone walked in those days":** John Flavel Mines, *A Tour Around New York and My Summer Acre: Being the Recreations of Mr. Felix Oldboy.* New York: Harper & Brothers, 1893, 56.

27   **"We walked everywhere, and saw everything":** George Kirwan Carr diary, Manuscripts and Archives Division, New York Public Library, Astor, Lenox, and Tilden Foundations, 74–75.

27   **Broadway "might be taken for a French street":** Frances Trollope, *Domestic Manners of the Americans.* Second edition. London: Whittaker, Treacher & Co., 1832, II, 211.

27   **"Broadway became a desert":** McDonald Clarke, *Afara: or, The Belles of Broadway.* New York: s.n., 1829, 23.

28   **Shillings were valued differently:** Hopper Striker Mott, *The New York of Yesterday.* New York and London: G. P. Putnam's Sons, 1908, 193.

29   **"On one occasion we met in Broadway a young negress":** Trollope, *Domestic Manners of the Americans*, II, 211. Slavery was outlawed in New York in 1827, and the sense of newfound freedom among the city's black community was perhaps reflected in Frances Trollope's observations of blacks promenading on Broadway two years later.

29   **accused Zion's congregation of rude manners and insobriety:** Untitled letter, *New York Evening Post*, October 25, 1825, 2.

29   **"If a white person were to walk arm in arm":** Isaac Candler, *A Summary View of America: Comprising a Description of the Face of the Country, and of Several of the Principal Cities; and Remarks on the Social, Moral, and Political Character of the People: Being the Result of Observations and Enquiries During a Journey in the United States.* London: T. Cadell, 1824, 280–281.

30   **"Heaven save the ladies, how they dress!":** Charles Dickens, *American Notes for General Circulation.* Paris: Baudry's European Library, 1842, 100.

30 **New York City's population:** John Disturnell, *A Gazetteer of the State of New-York*. Albany: J. Disturnell, 1842, 281.

30 **"Twice a week they come":** Untitled, *New York Aurora*, February 2, 1842, 2.

31 **"There, amid the splendour of Broadway":** Lydia Maria Child, *Letters from New-York*. New York and Boston: Charles S. Francis & Co., 1843, 1.

31 **"It's a pity we've no street but Broadway":** New-York Historical Society. BV Strong, George Templeton—MS 2472. Journal entry, October 11, 1840, I, 413.

31 **Dickens went for a tour of the city:** Dickens, *American Notes for General Circulation*, 106.

31 **"These are the city scavengers, these pigs":** Ibid., 107. Pigs remained a fixture on New York streets, including on Broadway, into the Civil War era, and laws prohibiting their roaming remained on the books until 1897.

32 **"Then the water leaped joyfully":** Lydia Maria Child, *Letters from New York. Second Series*. New York and Boston: C. S. Francis & Co., 1845, 80. Those who could afford to pay a fee—anywhere from $10 to $40 a year ($285 to $1,142 in today's dollars), depending on the kind of dwelling—had Croton water piped directly into their homes. Builders were kept busy adding bathrooms to houses, and daily showers became the latest fad. Everyone else had to make do with public hydrants.

CHAPTER 4. FIRE AND PROGRESS

36 **his death in 1875:** Strong's brief but gracious obituary in the *New York Tribune* commended him for his work as treasurer of the United States Sanitary Commission during the Civil War, but noted that Strong "was not the author of any extensive literary work." "Obituary. George Templeton Strong," *New York Tribune*, July 22, 1875, 5. His journal, which is now in the collection of the New-York Historical Society, wasn't discovered until the 1930s.

36 **"like an earthquake":** New-York Historical Society. BV Strong, George Templeton—MS 2472. Journal entry, July 19, 1845, II, 137.

37 **"[The] roof moved":** Augustine E. Costello, *Our Firemen: A History of the New York Fire Departments*. New York: Augustine E. Costello, 1887, 238.

37 **Somehow Hart survived:** "The Great Fire—Full Particulars of the Buildings Burnt—Names of the Sufferers—Probable Loss of Stores and Merchandize from Five to Seven Millions of Dollars—Over Three Hundred Buildings—Several Lives Lost," *New York Tribune*, July 21, 1845, 2.

37 **the fire leapt across Broadway:** New-York Historical Society. BV Strong, George Templeton—MS 2472. Journal entry, July 19, 1845, II, 137.

37 **"Drays, carts and wheelbarrows, hastily loaded":** "The Great Fire—Full Particulars of the Buildings Burnt," 2.

38 **"not even the daring firemen could venture":** Ibid.

38 **The volunteers of Engine Company No. 8:** John Doggett Jr., *The Great Metropolis: or, Guide to New-York for 1846*. New York: H. Ludwig, 60.

38 **"a chaos of ruin and smoke":** New-York Historical Society. BV Strong, George Templeton—MS 2472. Journal entry, July 19, 1845, II, 137.

38 **a prairie fire:** *New York Evening Post*, July 23, 1845. Quoted in I. N. Phelps

Stokes, *The Iconography of Manhattan Island, 1498 to 1909.* New York: Robert H. Dodd, 1915–1928. Reprinted, New York: Arno Press, 1967, V, 1792.

38 **The fire displaced at least 400 residents:** John Doggett Jr., *Supplement to Doggett's New-York City Directory.* New York: John Doggett Jr., viii.

38 **"Bank notes of the denomination":** Doggett, *The Great Metropolis,* 60; and *Supplement to Doggett's New-York City Directory,* 2.

38 **"[Our] bountiful supply of Croton Water":** "The Great Fire of Saturday," *New York Tribune,* July 21, 1845, 2.

39 **"Throw down our merchants ever so flat":** *The Diary of Philip Hone, 1828–1851,* Bayard Tuckerman, editor. New York: Dodd, Mead & Co., 1889, II, 261.

39 **the city wouldn't be "crushed":** "The Great Fire of Saturday," 2.

39 **an "abundance of capital":** *New York Evening Post,* July 23, 1845. Quoted in Stokes, *The Iconography of Manhattan Island,* V, 1792.

40 **"cunningly carved":** New-York Historical Society. BV Strong, George Templeton—MS 2472. Journal entry, May 15, 1844, II, 78.

41 **"It rivals the accurate taste of the best works":** Arthur D Gilman, "American Architecture," *North American Review,* LVIII (1844), 465. Quoted in William H. Pierson Jr., *American Buildings and Their Architects, Volume 2: Technology and the Picturesque: The Corporate and the Early Gothic Styles.* New York and London: Oxford University Press, 1978, 162.

42 **Strong couldn't find a seat:** New-York Historical Society. BV Strong, George Templeton—MS 2472. Journal entry, May 21, 1846, II, 181.

42 **worth a reported $800,000:** Moses Yale Beach, *The Wealth and Biography of the Wealthy Citizens of the City of New York.* New York: New York Sun, 1846, 26.

42 **dry goods amounted to about one-third of American imports:** Robert Greenhalgh Albion, *The Rise of New York Port, 1815–1860.* New York and London: Charles Scribner's Sons, 1939, 58–59.

43 **Philip Hone scoffed at the extravagance:** *The Diary of Philip Hone, 1828–1851,* Bayard Tuckerman, editor, II, 284.

43 **"notoriously fatal to the female nerve":** Henry James, *A Small Boy and Others.* New York: Charles Scribner's Sons, 1913, 66.

CHAPTER 5. BARNUM

44 **"Broadway was the feature and the artery":** Henry James, *A Small Boy and Others.* New York: Charles Scribner's Sons, 1913, 64.

44 **"dusty halls of humbug":** Ibid., 155–156.

44 **"Electric Fluid":** "The DEAD restored to apparent animation!!" Advertisement, *New York Evening Post,* March 31, 1807, 2.

45 **"some of the finest views in the City":** Edwin Williams, editor, *New York as It Is, In 1834; and Citizens' Advertising Directory.* New York: J. Disturnell, 1834, 187–188.

45 **To attract business:** Advertisements, *New York Evening Post,* July 20, 1833, 3; *New York Tribune,* May 5, 1841, 3; and Williams, *New York As It Is, in 1834; and Citizens' Advertising Directory,* 187–188.

45 **a top hat made of felted rabbit fur:** The Barnum Museum in Bridgeport, Connecticut, has in its collection Barnum's hat, made in Hartford ca. 1830.

46 **the $1,000 he had paid:** Phineas Taylor Barnum, *The Autobiography of P. T.*

Barnum, Clerk, Merchant, Editor, and Showman; with His Rules for Business and Making a Fortune. Second edition. London: Ward & Lock, 1855, 56.

47 **A typical afternoon in Barnum's "lecture hall":** Advertisement, *New York Tribune*, June 22, 1842, 3.

47 **"The public appeared to be satisfied":** Barnum, *The Autobiography of P. T. Barnum*, 91. The "Feejee Mermaid" was displayed not at the American Museum but at the Concert Hall, later known as the Minerva Rooms, just up the block at 404 Broadway.

48 **The screams of panicked animals:** "Great Conflagration. Barnum's Museum in Ashes," *New York Tribune*, July 14, 1865, 1; "Disastrous Conflagration. Destruction of Barnum's Museum," *New York Sun*, July 14, 1865, 1, 4.

49 **a "graceful sinking motion":** "Disastrous Conflagration. Destruction of Barnum's Museum," 4.

49 **"Don't fret a bit over the Museum":** Ibid.

50 *Harper's Weekly* **called him "Phoenix T. Barnum":** Quoted in advertisement, *New York Sun*, March 21, 1873, 4. In 1871, Barnum had organized "P. T. Barnum's Great Travelling Museum, Menagerie and World's Fair," which featured wild animals, circus acrobats, snake charmers, musical and mechanical automatons, and various "Freaks of Nature." Barnum attractions included "Wild Fiji Cannibals," "Admiral Dot," advertised as four times smaller than Tom Thumb, a bearded child, and a woman with no arms. He called it the "Greatest Show on Earth." In 1875, Barnum opened the "Roman Hippodrome" on the site of the old New York & Harlem Railroad terminal (the future site of the first Madison Square Garden) at the corner of Fourth (Park) Avenue and 26th Street, opposite the northeast corner of Madison Square. Advertisement, *Wheeling (West Virginia) Daily Intelligencer*, June 1, 1872, 2.

CHAPTER 6. TRAFFIC

51 **One drawing in *Harper's Weekly* in 1860:** "View of Broadway, Opposite Fulton Street, New York," *Harper's Weekly*, IV, 164 (February 18, 1860), 104–105.

51 **Traveling on Broadway:** Isabella Lucy Bird, *The Englishwoman in America.* London: John Murray, 1856, 337.

51 **Walt Whitman loved the "tramp of the horses":** Jerome Loving, "'Broadway, the Magnificent!': A Newly Discovered Whitman Essay," *Walt Whitman Quarterly Review* 12 (Spring 1995), 209–216.

54 **Broadway's colorful omnibus drivers:** Walt Whitman, *Specimen Days & Collect.* Philadelphia: Rees Welsh & Co., 1882, 18–19.

54 **"It is true here and there a church":** "How to Relieve Broadway," *Harper's Weekly* I, 51 (December 19, 1857), 808–809.

54 **"Scarcely a day passes":** "City Items: Reckless Driving," *New York Tribune*, October 22, 1859, 10.

54 **and crowds began gathering:** Fairfax Downey, "Traffic Regulation from Then Until Now," *New York Tribune*, Part V (Magazine Section), January 15, 1922, 3.

54 **"laughed at and condemned":** "Traffic at a Dead-Lock," *New York Tribune*, December 24, 1867, 5.

54 **The men of the Broadway Squad:** "Sergt. John P. Day, Police Hero for 25

Years, Retires To-Night," *New York Evening World*, June 15, 1922, 9; "The City," *New York Tribune*, June 1, 1869, 8.

55 **"They are generally handsome":** "Broadway During a Thaw," *Harper's Weekly* XVI, 793 (March 9, 1872), 189.

55 **"Traffic had to be physically enforced":** Downey, "Traffic Regulation from Then Until Now," 3.

55 **"Tall and handsome fellow":** "The Broadway Policeman" (poem), *Harper's Weekly* III, 139 (August 27, 1859), 554.

57 **"This din, this driving, this omnibus thunder":** "Anti-Broadway Railroad Meeting," *New York Times*, September 8, 1852, 4.

57 **Beach ran the pneumatic car:** Advertisement, *New York Tribune*, May 12, 1870, 7.

58 **workers digging the tunnel:** Robert Daley, "Alfred Ely Beach and his Wonderful Pneumatic Underground Railway," *American Heritage* XII, 4 (June 1961), 54–89.

CHAPTER 7. ACROSS THE MEADOWS

63 **it was called "Hell's Hundred Acres":** Fire Commissioner Edward F. Cavanagh coined the nickname following a major fire on November 18, 1960, in the old Lord & Taylor's store at Broadway and Grand Street. Ralph Katz, "Violations Found Before Loft Fire," *New York Times*, November 22, 1960, 37.

64 **Broadway's Stone Bridge became a familiar landmark:** Thomas A. Janvier, "Lispenard's Meadows," *Harper's New Monthly Magazine* LXXXVII, 521 (October 1893), 746–754.

64 **"You must not cross the bridge":** John J. Sturtevant memoir, Manuscripts and Archives Division, New York Public Library, Astor, Lenox, and Tilden Foundations, 55a.

65 **the Common Council spent $13,000:** *Minutes of the Common Council of the City of New York, 1784–1831.* City of New York, 1917, III, 280, 525.

65 **a "very offensive and irregular mound":** John Randel Jr., "City of New York, north of Canal street, in 1808 to 1821," in D. T. Valentine, *Manual of the Corporation of the City of New York.* New York: Edmund Jones & Co., 1864, 849.

66 **In 1809, Broadway was paved:** *SoHo-Cast Iron Historic District Designation Report*, New York City Landmarks Preservation Commission, 1973, 5.

66 **By 1812 there were still only forty:** New York City Municipal Archives, *Assessed Valuation of Real Estate*, 6th Ward, 1808–1827, Microfilm Roll 27; 8th Ward, 1808–1822, Microfilm Roll 38.

66 **Blackwell & McFarlan's Union Air Furnace:** *New York Journal*, August 20, 1767. Mentioned in I. N. Phelps Stokes, *The Iconography of Manhattan Island, 1498 to 1909.* New York: Robert H. Dodd, 1915–1928. Reprinted, New York: Arno Press, 1967, V, 777; and Thomas Longworth, *Longworth's American Almanac, New-York Register, and City Directory.* New York: Thomas Longworth, 1826.

66 **a coterie of prosperous downtown merchants:** Residents in 1812 included prominent merchants Benjamin Hyde, George Fairclough, Benjamin Sands, Edward Kirby, David and Andrew Ogden, Peter Hatterick, Peter Talman, and Martin Hoffman. New York City Municipal Archives, *Assessed Valuation of Real Estate*, 8th Ward, 1808–1822, Microfilm Roll 38.

66 **the "healthy part of Broadway":** Advertisement, *New York Evening Post*, June 25, 1823, 1.

67 **lots on Broadway in 1812:** At first, it wasn't Astor but Abijah Hammond, obscure today but in his day well known in New York, who acquired much of the land along Broadway's second mile and on adjacent streets. In 1812, Hammond owned the entire block on the west side of Broadway between Grand and Broome streets, plus 38 additional lots on Mercer Street, 41 on Greene Street, and 49 on Wooster Street. Like Astor, Hammond wasn't in any hurry to develop his land, and in 1812 there wasn't a single building on any of Hammond's 142 lots on or near Broadway's second mile. Over the next five years the value of vacant lots on Broadway between Canal and Houston streets grew exponentially, and Hammond's Broadway lots, worth a total of $8,400 in 1812, were worth $20,000 only two years later. (By 1817 Hammond had sold all but four of his Broadway lots.) New York City Municipal Archives, *Assessed Valuation of Real Estate*, 6th Ward, 1808–1827, Microfilm Roll 27; 8th Ward, 1808–1822, Microfilm Roll 38.

67 **by 1822 there were twice as many houses:** New York City Municipal Archives, *Assessed Valuation of Real Estate*, 6th Ward, 1808–1827, Microfilm Roll 27; 8th Ward, 1808–1822, Microfilm Roll 38.

67 **By 1825 the 8th Ward:** "Census Memorandum," *New York Evening Post*, October 25, 1825, 2. The population of the 8th Ward grew from 13,766 in 1820 to 24,285 in 1825, but the growth would have been even more dramatic had the 8th Ward not lost much of its territory to the newly created 10th Ward. As the city developed, new wards were created by subdividing old ones. Within a generation most of the houses built in the 1820s building boom along Broadway's second mile were torn down to make way for stores, warehouses, and office buildings. Only one of them remains today: 423 Broadway, built by shipmaster Benjamin Lord on the west side of the street between Canal and Howard streets in 1822.

CHAPTER 8. "A GLANCE AT NEW YORK"

69 **"I ain't a goin' to run":** Thomas Allston Brown, *A History of the New York Stage from the First Performance in 1732 to 1901*. New York: Dodd, Mead & Co., I, 284. The published version of *A Glance at New York* printed Chanfrau's pronouncement as "I've made up my mind not to run wid der machine any more." Benjamin A. Baker, *A Glance at New York: A Local Drama, in Two Acts*. New York and London: Samuel French & Son, 1890, 9.

69 **popular actor Frank Chanfrau:** Chanfrau was supposedly the son of a Bowery grocer, and therefore a favorite of newsboys and Bowery toughs. Whether Chanfrau was actually a product of the Bowery is debatable: A "Raymond Chanfraud, grocer," was listed in *Longworth's Directory* at various Bowery addresses between 1822 and 1833, and he certainly could have been Chanfrau's father. No one with that surname appeared in directories between 1834 and 1838. "Raymond Chanfraud, clerk," is listed at various addresses on the Lower East Side beginning in 1839. Beginning in 1844, the spelling of his name as listed changes from "Chanfraud" to "Chanfrau." Other people named "Chanfrau" began appearing in city directories around that time, including Henry, Peter, Jane, and Joseph Chanfrau.

The actor Frank Chanfrau doesn't appear in directories until 1849, when he is listed as a boarder at the New England House hotel.

69   **"Fellow citizens":** Baker, *A Glance at New York*, 17.

70   **"I declare," she exclaims:** Ibid., 7.

70   **Chanfrau supposedly based the Mose character:** Humphreys was listed in *Longworth's Directory* as a dresser of morocco leather, which was used in book-binding, from 1824 to 1838–39, and, beginning in 1839, as a printer. From 1824 to 1828–29 he lived on William Street, from 1829 to 1830 on Grand Street, and on Mulberry Street after that.

72   **William Makepeace Thackeray:** Frank Kernan, *Reminiscences of the Old Fire Laddies and Volunteer Fire Departments of New York and Brooklyn: Together with a Complete History of the Paid Departments of Both Cities.* New York: M. Crane, 1885, 63.

72   **"How comes it I find you":** Baker, *A Glance at New York*, 10.

72   **"The fire-boys may be a little rough":** Ibid., 20.

73   **Tattersall's famous horse market:** Tattersall's, 442–448 Broadway, occupied the old Broadway (West's) Circus building next door to Mitchell's. It was demolished in the fall of 1850 to make way for stores and, in the rear, the City Assembly Rooms, designed by John M. Trimble. "The Metropolis. . . No. V. Architectural Improvements," *New York Tribune*, October 5, 1850, 1–2.

73   **"Mr. Mitchell has, with great tact":** *A Picture of New-York in 1846: With a Short Account of Places in Its Vicinity; Designed as a Guide to Citizens and Strangers.* New York: Roman & Ellis, 1846, 66.

74   **an influx of "market boys":** Stephen C. Massett, *Drifting About; or, What Jeems Pipes of Pipesville Saw-and-Did.* New York: Carleton, 1863, 50–52.

74   **"Boys, if you misbehave":** Brown, *A History of the New York Stage*, I, 271.

74   **Massett, who was known professionally:** Massett, *Drifting About*, 49.

74   **a calf's head, "white as milk":** Ibid., 53; "Olympic Wit," *Illinois Free Trader and LaSalle County Commercial Advertiser*, June 30, 1843, 4.

74   **In 1855 there were still twelve theaters:** In 1859, Wood's Marble Hall, at Broadway and Prince Street, was turned into the Merchants and Manufacturers' Bank, and the Broadway Theatre was torn down and replaced by a store, even though it was only twelve years old. Panorama Hall, the Apollo Rooms, and Wallack's Theatre suffered similar fates. Brougham's Lyceum, 485 Broadway, was demolished in 1869 to make way for a dry goods store.

74   **Just before Christmas in 1854:** "Terrible Conflagration," *New York Tribune*, December 21, 1854, 5.

CHAPTER 9. MILLIONAIRES AND MURDERERS

75   **The interior furnishings:** "Metropolitan Hotel," *New York Times*, March 4, 1852, 2; "Mirrors Extraordinary," *New York Tribune*, January 20, 1852, 5.

75   **Dances called "hops":** Untitled, *New York Times*, October 7, 1852, 1.

76   **"the largest and most elegant hotel":** "The New-York State Agricultural Society Fair," *New York Tribune*, September 26, 1854, 3.

76   **Visitors entered from Broadway:** Isabella Lucy Bird, *The Englishwoman in America.* London: John Murray, 1856, 341–342.

76 **Off to the side was a "gentlemen's drawing-room"**: "The St. Nicholas Hotel," *New York Times*, January 7, 1953, 6.

76 **$50 a night**: "The Bridal Chamber," *Spirit of the Times* (Ironton, Ohio), February 8, 1853, 3.

77 **"Who could think of sitting down to a dinner"**: Thomas Butler Gunn, *The Physiology of the New York Boarding-Houses*. New York: Mason Brothers, 99.

77 **"The man who sits beside you at dinner"**: Ibid., 98.

78 **that guidebooks were published**: *Directory to the Seraglios in New York, Philadelphia, Boston and All the Principal Cities in the Union. Edited and Compiled by a Free Loveyer.* New York: s.n., 1859.

78 **"The practice of carrying concealed arms"**: Bird, *The Englishwoman in America*, 339.

78 **Graham drew a concealed sword**: "Manslaughter at the St. Nicholas Hotel," *New York Tribune*, August 3, 1854, 7.

79 **"You need not be at all afraid to go there"**: "The New-York State Agricultural Society Fair," 3.

79 **Thomas R. White of Augusta**: "The Stabbing Case at the St. Nicholas Hotel—Postponement of Examination," *New York Times*, July 5, 1854, 8.

79 **Captain J. J. Wright attempted to strike Robert S. Dean**: "The Affray at the St. Nicholas Hotel," *New York Times*, September 18, 1855, 4.

79 **"beat his face"**: "A Brutal Outrage in Broadway," *New York Times*, October 23, 1851, 1.

79 **a Whig Party operative**: "The Whig General Committee, the Whig Party, and the U.S. Senator," *New York Tribune*, February 13, 1851, 4; "Political Notices," *New York Tribune*, October 29, 1851, 8. The Broadway House stood on the site of Abraham Davis's earlier tavern.

80 **Poole ran his own barroom**: "Death of Bill Poole," *New York Tribune*, March 9, 1855, 7.

81 **Stanwix Hall specialized in terrapin soup**: "Board and Rooms," advertisement, *New York Tribune*, March 8, 1855, 2.

82 **John Lyng's barroom**: "The Murder of Wm. Poole. Coroner's Inquest. The Funeral on Sunday," *New York Tribune*, March 12, 1855, 6. Lyng's "public house" was reportedly at 39 Canal Street. City directories of the time list a "John R. Lyng, carpenter," at 49 Canal Street, three doors west of Broadway.

82 **shot him on the heart**: "The Murder of Wm. Poole. Coroner's Inquest. The Funeral on Sunday," 6.

82 **"I die a true American"**: "Funeral of the Late William Poole," *New York Tribune*, March 12, 1855, 6.

84 **"It is generally conceded"**: Ibid.

84 **"We are so young a People"**: New-York Historical Society. BV Strong, George Templeton—MS 2472. Journal entry, November 8, 1854, III, 68.

CHAPTER 10. "BROADWAY IS NEVER FINISHED"

85 **"in the hands of contractors"**: "City Improvements. Migration of the Mercantile Community," *New York Tribune*, June 9, 1860, 5.

86 **544 buildings in Manhattan**: Daniel D. Badger, *Illustrations of Iron Architec-*

ture, Made by the Architectural Iron Works of the City of New York. New York: Baker & Godwin, 1865, 25–33.

87 **the E. V. Haughwout & Company store:** In 1941, Robert Moses designated Broome Street as the conduit for the proposed Lower Manhattan Expressway, an elevated highway designed to connect the Williamsburg Bridge and the Holland Tunnel across Manhattan, bisecting Broadway's second mile. The project called for the demolition of hundreds of buildings along Broome Street, including the old Haughwout's store. In 1965, the city's new Landmarks Preservation Commission included Haughwout's as one of the first eight buildings designated as historic landmarks, which meant the building was protected from demolition and the expressway would have to be rerouted. The expressway project was finally canceled once and for all in 1971.

88 **a Henry Frederick Metzler sculpture of Atlas:** The Atlas Clock followed Tiffany's with each subsequent uptown move. Today it is part of the façade of Tiffany's famous store at 727 Fifth Avenue.

88 **Lord & Taylor spent $180,000:** "City Improvements. Migration of the Mercantile Community," 5.

89 **the "latest Paris novelties":** Advertisement, *New York Tribune*, March 14, 1860, 1.

89 **a typical dress of the era:** "Begin Centennial of Lord & Taylor," *New York Times*, February 2, 1926, 10.

89 **"suitable for promenade":** Advertisement, *New York Tribune*, December 30, 1861, 1.

89 **"Will Broadway ever be finished?":** "The Metropolis . . . No. V. Architectural Improvements," *New York Tribune*, October 5, 1850, 1–2.

89 **"Broadway is always being built":** Henri Junius Browne, *The Great Metropolis: A Mirror of New York.* Hartford: American Publishing Co., 1869, 339.

CHAPTER 11. THE BEND

94 **perhaps New York's most powerful merchant:** Ron Chernow, *Alexander Hamilton.* New York: Penguin, 2004, 32.

94 **Watts brushed them aside:** *Minutes of the Common Council of the City of New York, 1784–1831,* III, 338–339.

95 **in 1804 proposed that Broadway should bend:** Ibid., 585.

96 **a group of landowners headed by Henry Spingler:** Ibid., 549.

96 **The following August:** *Minutes of the Common Council of the City of New York, 1784–1831.* New York: City of New York, 1917, IV, 70–71, 139.

96 **"Mr. Dunham still occupies his house":** Ibid., 465.

96 **the immediate removal of Dunham's house:** Ibid.

97 **Hunn visited her house:** Ibid., 620.

97 **New York City had never seen as prosperous a year:** Robert Greenhalgh Albion, *The Rise of New York Port, 1815–1860.* New York and London: Charles Scribner's Sons, 1939, 8.

97 **Hunn recommended pushing ahead:** *Minutes of the Common Council of the City of New York, 1784–1831,* IV, 687–688.

98 **they recommended extending Broadway:** Ibid., 694.

98 **Spingler claimed that he had "misconceived" the terms:** Ibid., 692.

98   **Fish, Slidell, and Kip confessed:** *Minutes of the Common Council of the City of New York, 1784–1831,* V, 16.

98   **the Common Council ordered Dunham:** Ibid., 29–30.

98   **Then Spingler and six of his neighbors:** "Reasons of several land holders in Broad Way against the payment of the Sums assessed upon them for Opening the Same, Submitted to the Honorable the Mayor & Corporation of the City & County of New York," New York City Municipal Archives, *New York City Common Council Papers (1670–1831),* 1807, "Street Commissioner: Accounts-Assessments," Box 31, Folder 858, Microfilm Roll 31.

98   **Henry Brevoort:** The Brevoort family tree comes from *The Story of the Brevoort Family: From Farm to Savings Bank.* Brooklyn: Brevoort Savings Bank, 1964.

99   **only 11 acres remained:** Jennie F. Macarthy, "Original Grants, and Farms," in I. N. Phelps Stokes, *The Iconography of Manhattan Island, 1498 to 1909.* New York: Robert H. Dodd, 1915–1928. Reprinted, New York: Arno Press, 1967, VI, 80–81.

99   **"of large size":** Robert Manning, *Book of Fruits: Being a Descriptive Catalogue of the Most Valuable Varieties of the Pear, Apple, Peach, Plum & Cherry, for New-England Culture.* Salem: Ives & Jewett, 1838, 102. There is also a mention of Brevoort's plums in U. P. Hedrick, *The Plums of New York.* Albany: J. B. Lyon Company, 1911, 408.

99   **"[The Brevoort Purple Washington] is a handsome and most productive plum":** Andrew Jackson Downing, *The Fruits and Fruit Trees of America; or, the Culture, Propagation, and Management, in the Garden and Orchard, of Fruit Trees Generally; with Descriptions of All the Finest Varieties of Fruit, Native and Foreign, Cultivated in This Country.* London: Wiley & Putnam, 1845, 290.

99   **"One of the richest":** Ibid., 472.

99   **having served three consecutive terms:** D. T. Valentine, *Manual of the Corporation of the City of New-York.* New York: Edmund Jones & Co., 1847, 165; *Minutes of the Common Council of the City of New York 1784–1831,* III, 151. Brevoort's name was among those of the Common Council carved into the cornerstone of City Hall when construction began in 1803.

100   **Brevoort was named one of twenty-seven inspectors:** *Minutes of the Common Council of the City of New York, 1784–1831.* New York: City of New York, 1917, IV, 289.

100   **"A merry old Dutchman was Uncle Brevoort":** Gideon J. Tucker, "The Old Brevoort Farm," *Legends of the Netherlands to Which Are Added Some Legends of Manhattan Island.* New York: Concord Cooperative Printing Co., 1892, 171–176.

101   **selling four of the lots to John Jacob Astor:** *Memoranda as to the Will of Henry Brevoort,* undated, Box A0240, Folder 2, Brevoort Family Papers (1760–1879), Brooklyn Historical Society.

101   **gave his father's prized long gun to Irving:** George S. Hellman, editor, *Letters of Henry Brevoort to Washington Irving.* New York: G. P. Putnam's Sons, 1915, II, 114.

102   **calculating how much the Brevoort farm was worth:** *The Diary of Philip Hone, 1828–1851,* Bayard Tuckerman, editor. New York: Dodd, Mead & Co., 1889, II, 85.

102   **encouraged his children to sell:** "Last Will & Testament of Henry Brevoort," 1836, Box A0240, Folder 2, Brevoort Family Papers (1760–1879), Brooklyn Historical Society.

CHAPTER 12. GRACE

103 **selling the old church for $65,000:** *The Diary of Philip Hone, 1828–1851,*
Bayard Tuckerman, editor. New York: Dodd, Mead & Co., 1889, II, 252.

103 **while paying only $35,000:** George S. Hellman, editor, *Letters of Henry
Brevoort to Washington Irving Together With Other Unpublished Brevoort Papers.*
New York: G. P. Putnam's Sons, 1916, II, 170.

103 **Renwick Jr. hadn't yet opened a proper architecture office:** Throughout the
1840s, Renwick was listed in *Doggett's Directory* as working out of his father's
office on the campus of Columbia College. By 1854 he was working at 21 Fifth
Avenue, his parents' house on the old Brevoort property. In 1857 he opened an
office at 88 Wall Street. Dennis Steadman Francis, *Architects in Practice: New
York City, 1840–1900.* Committee for the Preservation of Architectural Records,
American Institute of Architects, 1979.

103 **a "monstrosity":** New-York Historical Society. BV Strong, George Templeton—
MS 2472. Journal entry, July 19, 1843, II, 15.

104 **"Have you seen the magnificent** *kaleidoscope":* "City Items," *New York Tribune,* January 30, 1846, 2.

104 **"[We] were not prepared to find [Renwick] capable":** Ibid.

105 **Grace suffered from an "unhappy straining":** New-York Historical Society.
BV Strong, George Templeton—MS 2472. Journal entry, August 1, 1845, II, 139.

105 **tormenting Strong with pontifications:** New-York Historical Society. BV
Strong, George Templeton—MS 2472. Journal entry, April 16, 1847, II, 218.

105 **"That most windy of all the bags":** Ibid.

105 **Mrs. Jervis's Cold Candy:** "More—More—More!—Proof of the good effects
of Mrs. Jervis's Cold Candy," advertisement, *New York Tribune,* December 24,
1846, 2.

105 **"This is to be the fashionable church":** *The Diary of Philip Hone, 1828–1851,*
Bayard Tuckerman, editor, II, 269.

106 **"The bidding was quite lively and spirited":** "City Items," *New York Tribune,*
January 29, 1846, 2.

106 **she was twice ejected:** "Consecration of Grace Church," *New York Evening
Post,* March 9, 1846, 2.

106 **"The effect of the light":** "City Items," *New York Tribune,* March 9, 1846, 2.

107 **"This grace our Churches want":** Margaret Fuller, "Consecration of Grace
Church," *New York Tribune,* March 11, 1846, 1; Fuller's contributions weren't
signed, but have been attributed and collected in Judith Mattson Bean and Joel
Myerson, *Margaret Fuller, Critic: Writings from the New-York Tribune, 1844–1846.*
New York: Columbia University Press, 2000, 372–373. In 1856, Grace built a
"free" chapel (meaning that pews weren't sold) on 14th Street, and began to
reach out to the city's poor residents.

CHAPTER 13. UNION

109 **Randel remembered that the name came about:** John Randel Jr., "City of
New York, north of Canal street, in 1808 to 1821," in D. T. Valentine, *Manual of the
Corporation of the City of New-York.* New York: Edmund Jones & Co., 1864, 850.

109 **When landowners around the Forks discovered:** In late April of 1811, Ephraim Jennings, who held twenty-one-year leases on two lots situated between Broadway and the Bowery, within the theoretical boundaries of Union Place, sent a memorial to the Common Council. Jennings was typical of the many tenants who had recently entered into long-term leases and spent money on their improvement, only to find that the Commissioners' Plan was about to negate everything. Jennings suggested two equally difficult propositions: that the city either immediately take the land and pay him for the improvements he had already made there, or let him stay for the full term of the lease. In response, the Council formed a committee to consider "measures respecting Union Place." *Minutes of the Common Council of the City of New York, 1784–1831*, New York: City of New York, 1917, VI, 567.

109 **an "Act making certain Alterations in the Map":** Henry E. Davies, *A Compilation of the Laws of the State of New York, Relating Particularly to the City of New York*. New York: City of New York, 1855, 582. The legislature decided that Union Place should "cease to be or be deemed to be a public square or place."

109 **"It is worthy of remark":** *Documents of the Board of Assistants*. New York: City of New York, 1837, I, 154.

111 **Union Place was only:** Ibid.

111 **a neat Greek Revival house at 24 Union Place:** The houses that Ruggles built along Union Square weren't much bigger than the supposedly outmoded residences flanking Washington Square and St. John's Park. They were a bit taller but weren't, in general, wider or longer, and most of them maintained the 25-foot width that had become ubiquitous for New York row houses.

112 **Peter Goelet's house wasn't demolished until 1896:** I. N. Phelps Stokes, *The Iconography of Manhattan Island, 1498 to 1909*. New York: Robert H. Dodd, 1915–1928. Six volumes. Reprinted, New York: Arno Press, 1967, V, 2023.

112 **"This is now the *fashionable quarter*":** James Disturnell, *A Gazetteer of the State of New York*. Albany: J. Durnell, 1842, 271.

112 **"That's the way to live in New York":** Henry James, *Washington Square*. New York: Harper & Brothers, 1881, 36–37.

113 **"I bought an extra and cross'd to the Metropolitan hotel":** Walt Whitman, *Specimen Days & Collect*. Philadelphia: Rees Welsh & Co., 1882, 21.

113 **a recruiting office opened at 613 Broadway:** This was the same office that a mob later burned during the 1863 Draft Riots.

113 **an American flag to be hoisted:** "Public Sentiment in the City," *New York Tribune*, April 20, 1861, 5; New-York Historical Society. BV Strong, George Templeton–MS 2472. Journal entry, April 19, 1861, III, 377–378.

113 **Spier & Co., 187 Broadway:** Advertisement, *New York Tribune*, April 23, 1861, 1.

113 **"A beautiful bonnet made by Miss A. M. Stuart":** "Public Sentiment in the City," 5.

113 **"At the command *forward*":** Egbert L. Viele, *Hand-Book for Active Service; Containing Practical Instructions in Campaign Duties*. New York: D. Van Nostrand, 1861, 24; Advertisement, *New York Tribune*, April 23, 1861, 1.

114 **hawked portraits of Anderson:** Advertisements, *New York Tribune*, April 20, 1861, 1.

114 **Music publishers rushed out:** Ibid.

114 **"a heaving multitude"**: "Departure of the Seventh Regiment. Splendid Ovation," *New York Tribune*, April 20, 1861, 5, 8. The storied 7th Regiment was the same unit that had opened fire on civilians during the Astor Place Riot of 1849.

114 **"The scene that burst upon the view"**: "Departure of the Sixth Regiment," *New York Herald*, April 22, 1861, 1.

115 **Semmons & Company:** Advertisement, *New York Tribune*, April 20, 1861, 1.

115 **guaranteed regiments "an enormous supply"**: Advertisement, *New York Tribune*, April 23, 1861, 1.

115 **Devlin, Hudson & Company offered "military clothing"**: Advertisement, *New York Tribune*, April 23, 1861, 1; Devlin, Hudson & Co. became Devlin & Co. later that year. Their two stores were at 253, 259, and 260 Broadway, corner of Warren Street, and 459-461 Broadway, corner of Grand Street.

116 **"southerners sighing for their sunny homes"**: Isabella Lucy Bird, *The Englishwoman in America*. London: John Murray, 1856, 342.

116 **B. F. Palmer & Company, manufacturer:** Palmer promised that prosthetics would be "provided for mutilated soldiers *of very limited means*, at prime cost, and in *extreme cases at less than cost.*" *Trow's Directory*, 1863, 965. By 1864 the company was offering "the 'Best' Patent Limbs to Soldiers—Free!" Advertisement, *New York Tribune*, November 29, 1864, 5.

117 **"stained with fire"**: "The Great Meeting This Afternoon," *New York Tribune*, April 20, 1861, 4.

117 **"our grieved brethren of the slave states"**: "Message of Mayor Wood," *New York Sun*, January 8, 1861, 1.

117 **Spontaneous, unscheduled speakers:** "Close of the Meeting," *New York Tribune*, April 22, 1861, 6.

117 **The *Sun* noted:** Untitled (first news column), *New York Sun*, April 23, 1861, 1.

117 **The blocks surrounding the formerly tranquil square:** Professions compiled from Lawrence G. Goulding, *Goulding's Business Directory of New York, Brooklyn, Newark, Paterson, Jersey City, and Hoboken*. New York: Lawrence G. Goulding, 1875.

119 **Hats were thrown in the air and pistols fired:** "Our Greatest Fourth," *New York Sun*, July 4, 1876, 1; "The City in Gala Dress," *New York Tribune*, July 4, 1876, 1; "One Hundred Years," *New York Herald*, July 4, 1876, 2.

119 **"There were men, women, and children"**: "Our Greatest Fourth," 1.

119 **Ruggles still lived in his original row house:** *Trow's New York City Directory*, 1872.

119 **"Oh! checkered train of years, farewell"**: "Dawn of a New Century," *New York Tribune*, July 5, 1876, 1.

CHAPTER 14. THE RIALTO

120 **The Academy of Music:** Thomas Allston Brown, *A History of the New York Stage from the First Performance in 1732 to 1901*. New York: Dodd, Mead & Co., 1902, II, 24–113.

121 **"unsurpassed riders, gymnasts, posture masters, & c."**: Ibid., 353–355.

121 **"Why not at once set about dyking the sidewalks"**: "The Canalization of Broadway," *New York Times*, February 25, 1860, 4. The *Times* noted another

advantage to the plan: "Then, too, when people got themselves murdered in the street, as they will insist upon doing, it would be so simple to drop them into the water, there to drift out of sight and remembrance."

122 **"Hello, Granville":** "The Rialto, Old and New," *New York Sun*, September 8, 1895, 14.

122 **He was born in New York around 1837:** "Antoni Paster," barber, 147 Fulton St., was listed in *Longworth's Directory* in 1827; Antonio Pastor, haircutter, 165 Greenwich Street, was listed in 1839. See also Brown, *A History of the New York Stage*, II, 170–172.

122 **As an eight-year-old:** "Tony Pastor Dead," *New York Tribune*, August 27, 1908, 7.

122 **"family theater":** Advertisement, *New York Tribune*, October 29, 1875, 9.

122 **Pastor had a way with a song:** "Invented the Name of Lillian Russell," *New York Tribune*, August 30, 1908, 53.

123 **"[When] the weather's fine":** Ibid.

123 **the popular liniment St. Jacob's Oil:** Advertisement, *New York Sun*, December 3, 1881, 4.

123 **in 1881, Pastor was mobbed:** "Very Bad for Mr. Conkling," *New York Sun*, May 31, 1881, 1.

123 **the Tony Pastors unwisely challenged the Mutuals:** "The Ball and Bat. How the Mutuals Waxed the Tony Pastors," *New York Sun*, May 17, 1871, 1.

124 **160 actors:** Advertisement, *New York Tribune*, October 29, 1875, 9.

125 **Huber's Museum on 14th Street:** Advertisements, *New York Evening World*, July 11, 1893, 5; *New York Evening World*, October 13, 1890, 3.

125 **James Meade's Midget Hall:** Brown, *A History of the New York Stage*, II, 593, 595.

CHAPTER 15. INCENDIARY SPEECH

126 **Ruggles once described Union Square:** *Address by the Hon. Samuel B. Ruggles, at Union Square, on the Opening of the Metropolitan Fair, April 8th, 1864.* New York: C. A. Alvord, 1864, 11.

127 **Goldman waved a red flag:** "Anarchists Spoil the Meeting. Wrangling Mars the Labor Demonstration in Union Square," *New York Tribune*, May 3, 1892, 1; Emma Goldman, *Living My Life.* New York: Alfred A. Knopf, 1931. Reprinted, New York: Dover Publications, 1970, I, 79–80.

127 **Her theatrical performance:** "Anarchists in Hiding," *New York Tribune*, July 25, 1892, 1.

127 **4,000 unemployed:** "Emma at the Bar," *New York Evening World*, October 4, 1893, 1.

127 **remarks of an "incendiary character":** "Emma Goldman on Trial," *New York Sun*, October 5, 1893, 7.

127 **"She is small":** "Emma at the Bar," 1.

128 **"distinctly pudgy":** "Emma Goldman on Trial," 7.

128 **a "dangerous woman":** "Emma Goldman's Sentence," *New York Sun*, October 17, 1893, 5.

128 **Selig Silverstein attempted to throw:** "Bomb Kills One; Police Escape," *New York Times*, March 29, 1908, 1.

129 **"I want to say it's about time the working class":** *Mother Earth* IX, 5 (July 1914), 145–146.

129 **Edelsohn, wearing a black dress and red stockings:** "1,000 Men Hold Reds in Order at Funeral for Bomb Victims," *New York Sun*, July 12, 1914, 6.

129 **"[I] am for violence":** *Mother Earth* IX, 5 (July 1914), 153–154.

129 **"[While] we are approaching the Social Revolution":** Ibid., 140. The *Sun*, no friend to the anarchists, printed Berkman's line as the more inflammatory "We are on the verge of social revolution. We are not quite ready yet, but when the time comes we will not stop short of bloodshed to gain our ends." "1,000 Men Hold Reds in Order at Funeral for Bomb Victims," 6.

130 **"That was pretty hot stuff":** "1,000 Men Hold Reds in Order at Funeral for Bomb Victims," 6.

130 **"[The police] were always there":** Mary Sansone, personal interview, Brooklyn, August 19, 2015. Crisalli joined the IWW soon after immigrating from Italy to New York in 1911, the same year as the horrific Triangle Shirtwaist Company fire, which killed 146 mostly female garment workers in Greenwich Village. He organized sweatshops and often led striking workers to Union Square to picket.

130 **"The place was mobbed":** Ibid.

130 **"The police were bastards":** Ibid.

130 **35,000 protestors assembled in Union Square:** "Police Pummel Reds in Second Invasion of City Hall Park," *New York Times*, March 2, 1930, 1.

131 **"I saw no reason for perpetuating":** "Leaders of Red Riot Held Without Bail. Fight for Release," *New York Times*, March 8, 1930, 2.

131 **"From all parts of the scene":** "Reds Battle Police in Union Square; Scores Injured, Leaders Are Seized. Two Dead, Many Hurt in Clashes Abroad," *New York Times*, March 7, 1930, 2.

131 **The police moved in:** "Police Battle Reds in Union Square Riot," *New York Times*, August 2, 1930, 1, 4.

132 **One typical May Day:** "May Day Balloons Disperse 'Brotherhood Seeds' Here," *New York Times*, May 2, 1958, 3.

133 **"a graveyard of memories":** "Labor Day Puts Little Fervor into Thin Crowds at Union Sq.," *New York Times*, September 6, 1960, 30.

133 **Black Lives Matter:** Emily Ngo, "Hundreds of Black Lives Matter Protestors March to Union Square," *Newsday*, July 10, 2016.

CHAPTER 16. LADIES' MILE

137 **"We are all satisfied":** "The Art of Shopping," *Emporia News* (Emporia, Kansas), December 28, 1861, 1.

137 **Broadway's "silks and velvets":** Moses King, *King's Handbook of New York City*. Second edition. Boston: Moses King, 1893, 843.

137 **past "pictures, jewelry, silks":** Jerome Loving, "'Broadway, the Magnificent!': A Newly Discovered Whitman Essay," *Walt Whitman Quarterly Review* 12 (Spring 1995), 211.

138 **a "woman out of the house":** William Henry Rideing, "Life on Broadway," *Harper's New Monthly Magazine* LVI, 331 (December 1877), 235.

138 **"A woman who gets adrift on Broadway"**: (Mrs.) George Washington Wylles, "The Theory of Shopping," *Bolivar Bulletin* (Bolivar, Tennessee), May 11, 1867, 1. Reprinted from the *American Phrenological Journal*.

138 **"On they go, on they go"**: "Broadway," *Harper's Weekly* II, 79 (July 3, 1858), 428.

138 **But there were rules**: George Ellington, *The Women of New York; or, The Under-World of the Great City*. New York: New York Book Co., 1869, 36.

139 **S. M. Peyser's dry goods**: S. M. Peyser was located at 487 Broadway, southwest corner of Broome Street. In 1858, Peyser placed a notice in the *Tribune* that tried to clarify rumors he had sold his business. It was his brother, Frederick M. Peyser, an importer who had operated a wholesale store farther south at the corner of Broadway and Franklin Street (363 Broadway), who had gone out of business that spring. "I am now the only Peyser doing business on Broadway," S. M. Peyser stated. Advertisement, *New York Tribune*, October 5, 1858, 1. Both brothers are listed in Rode's *Directory for 1854–55*.

139 **"Believe me, young ladies"**: "Broadway," *Harper's Weekly* I, 35 (August 29, 1857), 545–546.

139 **one young woman who walked down Broadway**: Ibid.

139 **the "vicissitudes of trade"**: Undated clipping, Thomas Hunt & Co. ledger. Manuscripts and Archives Division, New York Public Library, Astor, Lenox, and Tilden Foundations.

139 **Broadway's shopping district was defined**: Fourteen blocks is about six blocks less than a mile, but descriptions of Ladies' Mile often extended past Madison Square, or included the long block along 23rd Street leading to the stores on Sixth Avenue. It might also have been interpreted as a half a mile up one side of Broadway and a half a mile down the other.

140 **"a white house in the skies"**: "A New Mercantile Palace. Opening of Arnold and Constable's New Store," *New York Tribune*, March 29, 1869, 5.

142 **"The commerce of the world is here embodied"**: Ellington, *The Women of New York*, 40.

142 **"The clerk from behind his moustaches"**: Ibid., 344.

142 **"If you need exercise"**: Wylles, "The Theory of Shopping," 1.

CHAPTER 17. THE "MERRY CHAIR WAR"

144 **In 1794 the land was appropriated by the city**: *Minutes of the Common Council of the City of New York, 1784–1831*, New York: City of New York, 1917, II, 92.

145 **The park appeared in its present rectangular form**: See foldout map in John Disturnell, *A Guide to the City of New York, Containing an Alphabetical List of Streets, & c.* New York: J. Disturnell, 1837.

145 **singing to them from sheet music**: Elizabeth Story Palmer, *My Memories of Old New York*. New York: Edwin S. Gorham, 1923, 3.

145 **Madison Square Presbyterian Church**: The church was a Gothic Revival gem designed by Richard M. Upjohn, son of the renowned Trinity Church architect. Built in 1854, it was torn down in 1909.

145 **a layer of "cold chocolate sauce"**: Edith Wharton, *The Age of Innocence*. New York and Los Angeles: Windsor Editions by arrangement with D. Appleton & Co., 1920, 69.

145 **"without great churches or palaces"**: Edith Wharton, *A Backward Glance.* New York and London: D. Appleton-Century Co., 1934, 54.

146 **"This is the most interesting spot in the city"**: Richard Harding Davis, "Broadway," *Scribner's Magazine* IX, 5 (May 1891), 596.

146 **chained himself to a streetcar**: "Man Pulls Broadway Car," *New York Tribune,* April 27, 1903, 4.

147 **"up and down, up and down"**: Stephen Crane, "In the Broadway Cars," *New York Sun,* July 26, 1896, 3.

147 **Conductors careered around the southwest corner**: Fairfax Downey, "Traffic Regulation from Then Until Now," *New York Tribune,* Part V (Magazine Section), January 15, 1922, 3; "Cable Car Passengers Hurt," *New York Sun,* July 16, 1896, 9; "Thrown Off at Dead Man's Curve," *New York Sun,* September 12, 1896, 1.

147 **"the most charming of the smaller parks"**: Moses King, *King's Handbook of New York City.* Boston: Moses King, 1893, 218.

147 **the "people's roof-garden"**: Davis, "Broadway," 602.

148 **"[Only] on the rarest of occasions"**: "Pay Chairs and Hygiene," *New York Sun,* July 14, 1901, 6.

148 **"a port of missing men"**: Theodore Dreiser, *The Color of a Great City.* New York: Boni & Liveright, 1923, 217.

148 **Thousands slept**: "Sleeping on the Beach," *New York Tribune,* June 30, 1901, 1.

148 **spraying water on each horse**: "Humane Son of a Prizefighter. 'Charlie' Pool Relieves the Sufferings of Horses as They Pass in the Street," *New York Tribune,* July 4, 1901, 3.

149 **calling the whole affair an "outrage"**: "Didn't Pay for Park Seat," *New York Tribune,* July 2, 1901, 5.

149 **"When the policeman told me to sit on the bench"**: Ibid.

149 **the city's parks were free and "for the people"**: "The Parks Are Free," *New York Tribune,* July 3, 1901, 6.

149 **"The citizens of this community own the parks"**: "Murphy Hits Chair Privilege," *New York Sun,* July 4, 1901, 7.

149 **a "thin, nervous, wiry little man"**: "Pay Seats in City Parks Wanted Only by Clausen," *New York Evening World,* June 26, 1901, 5.

150 **"I believe a certain class of people"**: "Spate Muses and Loses," *New York Tribune,* July 10, 1901, 1.

150 **The Fourth of July dawned warm**: "A Cool Wind Fans City," *New York Tribune,* July 5, 1901, 1.

150 **a crowd of 300 to 400**: "Green Chairs Cause Row," *New York Sun,* July 7, 1901, 7.

150 **Six or seven men from the crowd**: "Spate Man Mobbed in Madison Square," *New York Evening World,* July 6, 1901, 2.

150 **"Save me! They're going to lynch me!"**: "Tries to Lynch Spate Man," *New York Tribune,* July 7, 1901, 1.

150 **children heckled Spate's hapless attendants**: "Merry Park Seat War," *New York Sun,* July 8, 1901, 3.

151 **insults "favoring the immediate extinction of aristocrats"**: Ibid.

151 **"Spate! Spate! Clausen and Spate!"**: "Spate Chairs Cause Riot," *New York*

Tribune, July 9, 1901, 7; "All Day Park Chair Scrap," *New York Sun*, July 9, 1901, 3.

151 **a violent game of beanbags:** "End of Pay Park Chairs," *New York Sun*, July 10, 1901, 1.

151 **"Smash it! Break it up!":** Ibid.

151 **Some drivers even reversed direction:** "Spate's 5-Cent Chairs Cause a Riot. Mob Jeers Police in Madison Square," *New York Evening World*, July 9, 1901, 2.

CHAPTER 18. THE FREAK BUILDING

153 **the last section of Broadway's cable traction system:** Between 1898 and 1901 the cable traction system was replaced with electricity on the Broadway, Columbus, and Lexington Avenue lines of the Metropolitan Street Railway Co. The last cable was removed on May 25, 1901. *Street Railway Journal* XVI, 830; XVII, 681. Quoted in I. N. Phelps Stokes, *The Iconography of Manhattan Island, 1498 to 1909*, New York: Robert H. Dodd, 1915–1928. Six volumes. Reprinted, New York: Arno Press, 1967, V, 2043.

154 **"At the present rate of improvement":** "Adopt Proskey's Plan," *New York Tribune*, May 18, 1901, 16.

154 **He gave tours of his shambles of a home:** Untitled, *New York Tribune*, May 22, 1901, 6.

154 **"Only five flights more":** "Proskey's 'Comforts,'" *New York Tribune*, May 21, 1901, 4.

154 **a federal court ruling forced him to surrender his keys:** "Col. Proskey Gets Out," *New York Tribune*, June 6, 1901, 14; "Another Effort to Oust Proskey," *New York Tribune*, May 30, 1901, 4. The following year Proskey married, claiming he was tired of hotel rooms and the bachelor life. "Evicted, He Is Driven to Wed," *New York Evening World*, March 16, 1903, 3.

155 **the "Freak Building":** "Thugs Hold Up Flatiron Man," *New York Evening World*, April 20, 1903, 3; "Gale Strews Harbor with Shipwrecks," *New York Evening World*, September 16, 1903, 1.

156 **compared the project to the Tower of Babel:** Charles F. McKim to Daniel H. Burnham, April 30, 1902. Quoted in Charles Moore, *Daniel H. Burnham, Architect, Planner of Cities*. Boston and New York: Houghton Mifflin Co., 1921, I, 180–181.

157 **"It appeared to be moving toward me":** Quoted in Dorothy Norman, *Alfred Stieglitz, An American Seer*. New York: Random House, 1973, 45.

157 **"As one looks through the bars of the cage":** Montgomery Schuyler, "Architectural Appreciations—No. II," *Architectural Record* XII, 5 (October 1902), 535.

157 **"[It] is a great pity":** Ibid.

158 **Chief Joseph:** "Chief Joseph's Adventures in New York," *New York Sun*, October 4, 1903, 7.

158 **stacks of newspapers flying everywhere:** "Hurricane Corner," *Leslie's Weekly* XCVI, 2477 (February 26, 1903), cover illustration.

158 **the "Home of the Winds":** "Blaze at the Big Flatiron," *New York Evening World*, April 10, 1903, 2.

158 **"Winds not only blow"**: "'Rubbering' at Flatiron Legal," *New York Evening World*, February 9, 1903, 1, 12.

159 **the "Flatiron Girl"**: "The 'Flatiron' Girl in a Snowstorm," *New York Evening World*, February 18, 1903, 13.

159 **and began making arrests**: "City in a Wet Gale. Pranks Played by the Wind at Flatiron Storm Centre," *New York Tribune*, April 15, 1903, 3.

160 **"Now, two minutes is a reasonable time"**: "'Rubbering' at Flatiron Legal," 1, 12.

160 **The *Evening World* interpreted Mayo's decision**: Ibid.

160 **"Women's skirts flapped over their heads"**: Bruce St. John, editor, *John Sloan's New York Scene*. New York: Harper & Row, 1965, 123. Sloan's studio was at 165 West 23rd Street, at Seventh Avenue. The diary he kept from 1906 to 1913 remains one of the most vivid descriptions of everyday life in New York in the years leading up to World War I.

CHAPTER 19. THE "LIGHT CURE"

161 **"About 10 o'clock are now to be seen the Pleiades"**: Richard Albert Edward Brooks, editor, *The Diary of Michael Floy Jr. of Bowery Village, 1833–1837*. New Haven: Yale University Press, 1941, 263.

162 **During an especially impressive shower**: "City Items," *New York Tribune*, August 16, 1855, 7. "[The meteors] have been noticed and spoken of by the most casual observers—those whose eyes apparently, as well as thoughts, are so generally directed earthward that they seem to be unmindful in their evening walks that there is a celestial panorama right over their heads and presented every evening with no charge for witnessing it."

162 **"Bat, bat! Come under my hat!"**: John J. Sturtevant memoir, Manuscripts and Archives Division, New York Public Library, Astor, Lenox, and Tilden Foundations, 57.

162 **in the "Darke time of ye Moon"**: *Minutes of the Common Council of the City of New York, 1675-1776*. New York: Dodd, Mead & Company, 1905, II, 21.

162 **Broadway was lighted above Canal Street**: *New York Daily Advertiser*, April 14, 1800. Quoted in I. N. Phelps Stokes, *The Iconography of Manhattan Island, 1498 to 1909*. New York: Robert H. Dodd, 1915–1928. Six volumes. Reprinted, New York: Arno Press, 1967, V, 1376.

162 **4,519 of the city's 11,239 streetlights**: "Mayor's Message," *New York Tribune*, May 9, 1849, 4.

163 **"When all the rest of the city is asleep"**: William Henry Rideing, *Harper's New Monthly Magazine* LVI, 331 (December 1877), 229.

163 **In Wabash, Indiana, Brush mounted**: "Light from the Wires," *New York Sun*, September 29, 1880, 3; "Report of the Tifflin City Council Investigating Committee," *Salt Lake Daily Herald*, September 17, 1880, 3.

164 **"While Edison has been busy"**: Untitled, *New York Sun*, October 1, 1880, 2.

164 **Brush built a power station**: "New Lights in Broadway," *New York Times*, December 20, 1880, 1; "Under the Electric Arc. The First Trial of the New Lights in New York Streets," *New York Sun*, December 21, 1880, 3. The *Times* reported that the steam engine was 100 horsepower, the *Sun* that it was 125.

164 **traveling to Menlo Park:** "The Electric Light. Tests in This City and at Menlo Park," *New York Tribune*, December 21, 1880, 1.

164 **A. A. Hayes Jr. gave the signal:** "Under the Electric Arc," *New York Sun*, December 21, 1880, 3.

165 **"white, steady glare":** "Lights for a Great City. Brush's System in Successful Use Last Night," *New York Times*, December 21, 1880, 2.

165 **Startled pedestrians:** "Lights for a Great City," 2. The *Sun*, meanwhile, reported very different reactions to the Brush experiment: "There was no excitement in crowded Broadway as the lights blazed up the line, for nobody could take in the entire view at one time." "Under the Electric Arc," 3.

165 **"The great white outlines of the marble stores":** "Lights for a Great City," 2.

165 **the old gaslights suddenly seemed "sickly yellow":** "Under the Electric Arc," 3.

165 **From their office windows:** "Lights for a Great City," 2.

165 **the Brush Company was awarded a city contract:** "City and Suburban News," *New York Times*, May 14, 1881, 8.

165 **Brush mounted lights on 150-foot-tall towers:** "Electric Lights in the Parks," *New York Tribune*, July 1, 1881, 8.

165 **an unearthly green tint:** Richard Harding Davis, "Broadway," *Scribner's Magazine*, IX, 5 (May 1891), 602.

165 **An 1882 illustration:** Charles Graham, illustrator, "The Electric Light in Madison Square, New York," *Harper's Weekly* XXVI, 1308 (January 14, 1882), 25.

167 **"infested by drowsy tramps":** "Home News. New-York City," *New York Tribune*, December 27, 1880, 8.

167 **"I've come from a rump precinct":** "Lively Record of the Tenderloin, Which Wants a New Station House," *New York Sun*, December 4, 1904, Second Section, 2.

168 **In 1881, property owners:** "A Neighborhood Full of Thieves," *New York Tribune*, July 1, 1881, 8.

168 **"where the gay Bohemians dwell":** Bob Cole and Billy Johnson, "The Czar of the Tenderloin." New York: George L. Spaulding, 1897. Music Division, New York Public Library.

168 **In 1899 two black men:** "White Men Mob Negroes," *New York Times*, October 22, 1899, 9.

168 **"the forbidden ground of Broadway":** Davis, "Broadway," 596.

169 **"There are some who will tell you":** Ibid., 598.

169 **"traversing the avenues":** Charles H. Parkhurst, *Our Fight with Tammany*. New York: Charles Scribner's Sons, 1895, 55.

169 **50 percent of prisoners held:** "Lively Record of the Tenderloin, Which Wants a New Station House," 2.

169 **The victim was businessman James B. Craft:** "Murderer Beheads Slain Man," *New York Evening World*, September 27, 1902, 1; "Head Hacked Off in a Dive," *New York Sun*, September 28, 1902, 1; "Butchered in a Low Resort," *New York Tribune*, September 28, 1902, 1.

170 **turned into a one-act play:** "Vaudeville in Yiddish. The Empire Garden Murder Played in a One-Act Sketch," *New York Sun*, November 24, 1902, 7. *The Empire Garden Tragedy* opened at the new Oriental Music Hall, 624 Grand Street, on November 22, 1902.

170 **Tobin was convicted:** "Death Sentence for Beheader," *New York Evening World*, December 22, 1902, 12; "Death for Tobin, Craft's Murderer," *New York Tribune*, December 23, 1902, 6.

170 **"One of the most troublesome":** William McAdoo, *Guarding a Great City.* New York and London: Harper & Brothers, 1906, 93.

170 **"All of these mixed-race places":** Ibid., 95.

170 **"You can't have too much light on crime":** "White Lights Vs. Red," *New York Evening World*, September 2, 1904, 12.

172 **"The Tenderloin isn't what it used to be":** "Lost Lights of the Tenderloin," *New York Evening World*, April 28, 1903, 13.

172 **"The midnight throng on Broadway":** "New York That Never Sleeps," *New York Times*, Magazine Section, January 8, 1905, 2.

172 **New Tenderloins took root:** McAdoo, *Guarding a Great City*, 91.

CHAPTER 20. GREAT WHITE WAY

175 **What was so great:** The most direct influence on Broadway's famous nickname may have been *The Great White Way*, a 1901 adventure novel by Albert Bigelow Paine that is long forgotten but was heavily advertised and extensively reviewed at the time of its publication. The story is set not on Broadway, although Broadway is mentioned here and there, but in Antarctica, which a group of explorers from New York reach after much difficulty. Surely Paine's use of the title *Great White Way* as a description not of Broadway but of Antarctica means that Broadway wasn't yet known, or at least wasn't widely known, as the "Great White Way." Four years later the nickname was still obscure enough that the *New York Times* put it in quotes: "[It] is at night, at the dinner hour, that Broadway—or the 'Great White Way,' as it is frequently called—assumes its distinctive character." "New York That Never Sleeps," *New York Times*, Magazine Section, January 8, 1905, 2.

176 **George M. Cohan wrote plays at a borrowed desk:** Ward Morehouse, *George M. Cohan, Prince of the American Theater.* Philadelphia and New York: J. B. Lippincott Co., 1943, 59.

177 **Edison mounted light bulbs on the heads:** "Sixty Thousand in Line. The Grandest Parade Ever Seen in New-York," *New York Tribune*, November 1, 1884, 1.

179 **Theodore Dreiser noticed Corbin's sign:** Theodore Dreiser, *The Color of a Great City.* New York: Boni & Liveright, 1923, 121.

180 **"[Electric signs] have become so numerous:** "Ugly Electric Signs Mar Fifth Avenue," *New York Times*, July 8, 1910, 6.

180 **It was so extraordinary:** David E. Nye, *Electrifying America: Social Meanings of a New Technology.* Cambridge and London: MIT Press, 1990, 52.

181 **"This is the best day":** "Epworth Leaguers Dine. Bishop Quayle Says New York Looks Good to Him," *New York Tribune*, November 12, 1910, 7.

181 **"[Let us] get together":** "A 'Great White Way' Would Be Our Biggest Advertisement," *Richmond Daily Register* (Richmond, Kentucky), September 29, 1919, 2.

181 **One real-estate company in tiny Newberry:** Advertisement, Southeastern Realty Co., *Herald and News* (Newberry, South Carolina), February 10, 1920, 5.

181 **"At the touch of a button":** "Texas Street—El Paso's Main Thoroughfare," *El Paso Herald,* Texas Street and White Way Business Section, October 2, 1920, 8B.

181 **"For many years Omaha has waged a war":** "Signs That Dispel Darkness and Command Attention in Omaha," *Omaha Daily Bee Home Magazine,* September 17, 1911, 2–3.

182 **"Less than a year ago Columbia":** "Viewpoints," *University Missourian* (Columbia, Missouri), October 10, 1913, 2.

CHAPTER 21. EDEN

183 **It passed through various estates:** H. Croswell Tuttle, *Abstracts of Farm Titles in the City of New York, Between 39th and 73rd Streets, West of the Common Lands, Excepting the Glass House Farm.* New York: Spectator Co., 1881, 115–125.

184 **In 1803, Wortman lost the farm:** Ibid., 365. In the 1830s Astor expanded his holdings in the area when he foreclosed on the former John Cosine farm just to the north, which ran from Broadway west to the Hudson River between 54th and 55th streets, for $59,740.

184 **relinquishing for $4,346 a substantial swath:** Ibid., 125.

184 **the Estate was worth $20 million:** Burton J. Hendrick, "The Astor Fortune," *McClure's Magazine* XXIV, 6 (April 1905), 573.

185 **the Estate was divided:** Ibid.

187 **"You wouldn't have to work, would you?":** Advertisement, *Real Estate Record & Builder's Guide* 109, 23 (June 10, 1922), 714.

187 **invented a bicycle brake and an engine that burned peat:** John D. Gates, *The Astor Family.* New York: Doubleday & Co., 1981, 179.

188 **Jack's vision of New York in 2000:** John Jacob Astor, *A Journey in Other Worlds: A Romance of the Future.* New York: D. Appleton & Co., 1894, 43.

188 **"twentieth-century stage-coaching":** Ibid., 69.

188 **and Jack correctly predicted that a municipal subway system:** Ibid., 52–79.

188 **Overnight, real-estate prices in the vicinity of Broadway:** I. N. Phelps Stokes, *The Iconography of Manhattan Island, 1498 to 1909.* Six volumes. New York: Robert H. Dodd, 1915–1928. Reprinted, New York: Arno Press, 1967, III, 819.

189 **office boy for the *Knoxville Chronicle*:** "Adolph S. Ochs," *New York Times,* April 9, 1935, 20.

189 **circulation jumped from 22,000 to 100,000:** Ibid., 21.

191 **The station's most arresting feature:** "Big Sign in Times Station," *New York Times,* October 28, 1904, 5.

191 **"The new name proposed is awkward":** "Don't," *New York Tribune,* March 26, 1904, 8.

192 **"Why should not each of our other daily papers":** "Object to Times Square. Protest of the American Scenic and Historic Preservation Society," *New York Tribune,* June 19, 1904, 2.

192 **"it makes one dizzy to look":** "William Waldorf Astor, Englishman, Who Is on a Trip Here to View His New York Fortune," *New York Evening World,* September 9, 1903, 3.

192 **The *Washington Times* suggested he wear:** "Points in Paragraphs," *Washington Times,* September 10, 1904, 4.

192 **Willie's Hotel had cost:** "A $9,000,000 Hotel," *Barre Daily Times* (Barre, Vermont), September 10, 1904, 3.

193 **"From there I could see the city as it slept":** "Prince Louis Sees Big Financiers," *New York Evening World*, November 13, 1905, 2.

CHAPTER 22. TIMES SQUARES TYPES

195 **a "parade ground with elastic boundaries":** "The Rialto, Old and New," *New York Sun*, September 8, 1895, 14.

195 **The building was far from finished:** "Amusements. Opening of the New Casino," *New York Sun*, October 22, 1882, 5.

196 **"promenade, sup, sip wine, flirt":** "A Series of Surprises. Novel Features of the Casino—A Double Theatre, Double Stage, and Two-Tier Summer Garden," *New York Tribune*, June 19, 1883, 2.

196 **an "operatic war":** "The Italian Opera Season. Successful Opening Last Night. Both Temples of Music Well Patronized," *New York Tribune*, October 23, 1883, 5.

196 **leased, for $1,200 per season:** "Opening of the Italian Opera Season," *New York Tribune*, October 21, 1883, 9.

196 **"Palace on Broadway":** "Crowding to Both Operas," *New York Sun*, October 23, 1883, 1.

196 **"Where to go is this year":** "Opening of the Italian Opera Season," 9.

196 **The Met's opening-night throng:** "Crowding to Both Operas," 1; "The Italian Opera Season. Successful Opening Last Night. Both Temples of Music Well Patronized," 5.

197 **"Diamonds glittered in all directions":** "The Italian Opera Season. Successful Opening Last Night. Both Temples of Music Well Patronized," 5.

197 **crowd's aggregate wealth at $450 million:** "Opening of the Italian Opera Season," 9.

197 **Caroline Astor outdid them:** Ibid.; "Crowding to Both Operas," 1.

198 **"Is New-York to become 'the city of theatres'?":** "Theatrical Incidents and News Notes," *New York Tribune*, April 26, 1903, p. 9.

198 **"Dishonest Abe":** Allen Churchill, *The Great White Way*. New York: E. P. Dutton & Co., 1962, 166.

198 **he once chastised George M. Cohan:** Ward Morehouse, *George M. Cohan, Prince of the American Theater*. Philadelphia and New York: J. B. Lippincott Co., 1943, 74.

198 **Hammerstein leased the Theatre Republic to David Belasco:** William Winter, *The Life of David Belasco*. New York: Moffat, Yard & Co., 1918, II, 179.

199 **"[Erlanger] told me":** Ibid., 22.

199 **"impalliable trash":** Ibid., 339.

199 **Belasco was born:** "The Most Picturesque Career of David Belasco," *New York Times Magazine*, September 29, 1907, 7.

200 **At the groundbreaking ceremony:** Winter, *The Life of David Belasco*, II, 235–236.

201 **The studio was stuffed:** David Belasco, *The Theatre Through Its Stage Door*. New York and London: Harper & Brothers, 1919, 10 (facing); Winter, *The Life*

of David Belasco, II, 241–243; *The Collection of the Late David Belasco.* New York: American Art Association, Anderson Galleries, 1931.

201 **The hammer fell for an entire week:** *The Collection of the Late David Belasco*, i.

203 **they seemed "kaleidoscopic":** "The New Plays. 'Governor's Son' Made Over for Roof Garden Use," *New York Evening World*, June 5, 1906, 8.

203 **"Speed! Speed!":** George M. Cohan, *Twenty Years on Broadway and the Years It Took to Get There.* New York: Harper & Brothers, 1925, 185.

204 **By 1905, "Give My Regards to Broadway":** "The Hit of the Season," *Daily Telegram* (Clarksburg, West Virginia), April 14, 1906, 5.

204 **Songs about Broadway:** Advertisement, *New York Evening World*, November 16, 1905, 11.

204 **"What is Broadway?":** John McCabe, *George M. Cohan: The Man Who Owned Broadway.* New York: Doubleday & Co., 1973, 120–121.

206 **"I guess Broadway, for me, was everything":** Ibid., 121.

CHAPTER 23. BROADWAY GHOSTS

207 **"Do you like music?":** Advertisement, *Los Angeles Herald*, April 2, 1906, 8.

208 **"I am a girl eighteen years old":** David Belasco, *The Theatre Through Its Stage Door.* New York and London: Harper & Brothers, 1919, 2.

208 **"Success," Belasco wrote :** Ibid., 10.

208 **called Broadway the "Street of Broken Hearts":** *Daily Telegram* (Clarksburg, West Virginia), August 8, 1915, 26.

209 **"I do not ask whether they are married":** "Stranger in New York?—Feel Safe with Alice, the Girl Escort," *Day Book* (Chicago), November 21, 1916, 14.

209 **"The lure of New York beckons":** "Grace Le Gendre Says New York Women Are Hitting Up the Booze," *Day Book* (Chicago), December 5, 1913, 29.

209 **The story ran in newspapers all over:** "Winter Garden Chorus Girl and Escort Killed When Autos Crash. Two Owners of Cars Held," *New York Sun*, September 15, 1915, 16; "Broadway's Old Story Retold in Girl's Death," *Washington Times*, September 15, 1915, 7; "Story of Ida Brown Typical of Numerous 'Careers' on Stage," *Daily Capital Journal* (Salem, Oregon), September 15, 1915, 1; "Broadway Lights Are Not for Her," *Grand Forks Daily Herald* (Grand Forks, North Dakota), September 16, 1915, 2; "Dares City's Clamor, Goes Home in Coffin," *Barre Daily Times* (Barre, Vermont), September 16, 1915, 3.

210 **Broadway the "port of missing maidens":** "New York Sees Fight to Vanquish the System That Gobbles Girls," *Day Book* (Chicago), February 28, 1917, 14-15.

210 **"The glamour of the Gay White Way":** "Gay Old Broadway Is No More! Joy Palaces Go to the Side Streets," *Day Book* (Chicago), October 19, 1916, 14.

211 **who was later gunned down:** "Larry Fay Is Slain in His Night Club. Doorman Is Hunted," *New York Times*, January 2, 1933, 1.

212 **three drunken women singing "Bye Bye Blackbird":** Stephen Graham, *New York Nights.* New York: George H. Doran Co., 1927, 92.

213 **Guinan . . . lived with a parrot:** Sidney Skolsky, *Times Square Tintypes.* New York: Ives Washburn, 1930, 25–27.

CHAPTER 24. THE BOULEVARD

218 **a "road or public drive":** *Documents of the Assembly of the State of New York*, IX, 148. Albany: Weed, Parson & Co., 1880, 998–1003.

218 **"I found today that 'labor was rest,'":** Richard Albert Edward Brooks, editor, *The Diary of Michael Floy Jr. of Bowery Village 1833–1837*. New Haven: Yale University Press, 1941, 74.

219 **gave it "peculiar value":** Andrew H. Green, *Communication to the Commissioners of the Central Park, Relative to the Improvement of the Sixth and Seventh Avenues, from the Central Park to the Harlem River; the Laying Out of the Island Above 155th Street; the Drive from 59th St. to 155th St., and Other Subjects*. New York: Wm. C. Bryant & Co., 1866, 59.

220 **became Sherman Square:** Sherman Square was named in 1891, after the death of William Tecumseh Sherman, who lived nearby at 75 West 71st Street; Lincoln Square was named in 1906.

220 **"The law of the street is motion, not rest":** Andrew H. Green, *Communication to the Commissioners of the Central Park*, 63.

220 **"The boulevards and new avenues [of Paris]":** "Improvement of Cities," *New York Sun*, May 21, 1867, 2.

222 **thirteen lodges in New York City with some 1,300 members:** "A Riot Impending. The Orangemen's Twelfth of July Parade," *New York Tribune*, July 10, 1871, 1.

222 **the Orangemen . . . broke into the anti-Catholic anthem:** "A Riot Impending. The Orangemen's Twelfth of July Parade," 1. The song "Croppies Lie Down" dated to the Irish Rebellion of 1798. The Orange Order had assisted the British Army in suppressing the uprising; "Croppies" referred to Catholics who had cut their hair short during the rebellion. The song characterized Irish Catholics as murderous cowards, and Catholics, naturally, considered the song highly offensive.

223 **"[I] have heard only one sentiment":** New-York Historical Society. BV Strong, George Templeton—MS 2472. Journal entry, July 13, 1871, IV, 323.

CHAPTER 25. "DOWN THERE"

224 **saw goats:** Charles Dawson Shanly, "Along the Hudson River at New York," *Atlantic Monthly* XXII, 129 (July 1868), 3.

224 **"with unerring accuracy":** Jacob A. Riis, *The Battle with the Slum*. New York: Macmillan Co., 1902, 111.

224 **Newspapers called the neighborhood the "declivity":** "The Naughty Negroes of San Juan Hill," *New York Sun*, August 6, 1905, 19.

225 **Another riot erupted:** "Negroes Again Rioting," *New York Tribune*, July 18, 1905, 1.

226 **"If the police will only differentiate":** "Preacher on the Riots," *New York Tribune*, July 24, 1905, 12.

226 **the "lawless colored element":** "Handy to Riot District," *New York Tribune*, July 25, 1905, 8.

226 **"They are without exception the worst lot":** "The Naughty Negroes of San Juan Hill," 19.

CHAPTER 26. CHICKENS ON THE ROOF

229 **electricity "free at all hours":** *The World's Loose Leaf Album of New York Apartment Houses.* New York: New York World, 1910, 48.

229 **"black as slate in the fog":** Saul Bellow, *Seize the Day.* New York: Penguin, 1965, 3.

230 **a menu of littleneck clams:** Ansonia lunch menu, Rare Book Division, the Buttolph Collection of Menus, New York Public Library Digital Collections, 1907.

230 **There was a barbershop:** "Big Private Telephone Exchange," *New York Times,* February 11, 1902, 13.

230 **the "Most Superbly Equipped House":** Postcard, 1909, Art and Picture Collection, New York Public Library.

231 **Babe Ruth:** "Ruth Develops New Talent. Learns to Play Saxophone," *New York Times,* December 23, 1927, 24.

231 **as little as $900 per year:** Advertisements, *New York Tribune,* September 8, 1907, 11; August 23, 1908, 13.

232 **Stokes family:** William Earle Dodge Stokes was the son of James Boulter Stokes; his brother was merchant and philanthropist Anson Phelps Stokes, and his nephew was architect Isaac Newton Phelps Stokes, author of *The Iconography of Manhattan Island.*

232 **dumped the Ansonia's waste:** "Stokes's Ash Heap Stirs His Neighbors," *New York Times,* April 5, 1908, 8.

232 **"the diseased offscouring":** W. E. D. Stokes, *The Right to Be Well Born.* New York: C. J. O'Brien, 1917, 57.

232 **"Our pure healthy New England blood":** Ibid., 48.

232 **In 1903, Stokes was hospitalized:** "Lawyer Fixed Up Alibi," *New York Tribune,* October 18, 1903, 2.

233 **Robert Reinhart, whose family:** "The Ansonia Remembered," *New York Times,* Real Estate Section, November 7, 1971, 1.

233 **Gene Yellin, who grew up:** Gene Yellin, personal interview, New York, January 27, 2016.

233 **The building was still full:** The Ansonia was rescued from certain demolition in 1971, when tenants petitioned the city's Landmarks Preservation Commission for protection as a city landmark. Today the Ansonia has been largely restored to its original condition and converted to condominiums.

CHAPTER 27. HARSENVILLE

234 **94 prime acres of Dyckman's land:** H. Croswell Tuttle, *Abstracts of Farm Titles in the City of New York, Between 39th and 73rd Streets, West of the Common Lands, Excepting the Glass House Farm.* New York: Spectator Co., 1881, 547.

235 **Pew-holders in the church:** Hopper Striker Mott, *The New York of Yesterday.* New York and London: G. P. Putnam's Sons, 1908, 178, 184–186.

235 **sang hymns to a tuning fork:** Ibid., 163.

235 **"walk and conversation":** Ibid., 169.

236 **"Mme. d'Auliffe" surrounded herself:** Ibid., 87–89.

236 **"Auliffe" was actually a mispronunciation:** Margaret A. Oppenheimer, *The Remarkable Rise of Eliza Jumel.* Chicago: Chicago Review Press, 2016, 48.

237 **kicked out of an inn in Virginia:** Samuel Griswold Goodrich, *Life of Louis-Philippe, Late King of the French.* Boston: J. B. Hall, 1848, 21.

CHAPTER 28. THE RAVEN OF SPECULATION

241 **docked at Pier 2:** Steamboat schedule, *A Picture of New-York in 1846, with a Short Account of Places in Its Vicinity; Designed as a Guide to Citizens and Strangers.* New York: Roman & Ellis, 1846, 94.

241 **Poe wrote to Muddy the next morning:** Edgar Allan Poe to Maria Clemm, April 7, 1844. Quoted in *The Letters of Edgar Allan Poe*, John Ward Ostrom, editor. New York: Gordian Press, 1966, I, 251–252.

242 **James Gordon Bennett dismissed Poe's hoax:** "Beach's Last Hoax," *New York Herald*, April 15, 1844, 2.

242 **Beach printed a retraction:** "Balloon," *New York Sun*, April 15, 1844. Quoted in Dwight Thomas and David K. Jackson, *The Poe Log: A Documentary Life of Edgar Allan Poe, 1809–1849*. Boston: G. K. Hall & Co., 1987, 460.

242 **"There is nothing put forth":** Quoted in Jacob E. Spannuth and Thomas Ollive Mabbott, editors, *Doings of Gotham by Edgar Allan Poe*. Pottsville, Pa.: Jacob E. Spannuth, 1929, 31.

242 **he was feeling ill and depressed:** Edgar Allan Poe to Nathaniel Parker Willis, May 21, 1844. Quoted in Thomas and Jackson, *The Poe Log*, 462.

242 **the future 84th Street:** The Brennan house was located approximately at present-day 206 W. 84th Street.

243 **Poe's room had a fireplace:** Theodore F. Wolfe, "Poe's Life at the Brennan House," *New York Times Saturday Review of Books*, January 4, 1908, 10.

243 **"I have been roaming far and wide":** Quoted in Spannuth and Mabbott, *Doings of Gotham by Edgar Allan Poe*, 25.

243 **"The perfumery department is especially rare":** Ibid., 48.

243 **Poe stopped in a tobacco store:** Thomas and Jackson, *The Poe Log*, 472.

243 **the incessant "din of the vehicles":** Quoted in Spannuth and Mabbott, *Doings of Gotham by Edgar Allan Poe*, 61.

243 **"I have . . . rambled and dreamed":** Edgar Allan Poe to James Russell Lowell, July 2, 1844. Quoted in Ostrom, *The Letters of Edgar Allan Poe*, I, 256.

244 **Poe had withdrawn so thoroughly:** Edgar Allan Poe to Frederick W. Thomas, September 8, 1844. Quoted in Ostrom, *The Letters of Edgar Allan Poe*, I, 262.

244 **Stationed at a desk in the corner:** Nathaniel Parker Willis, *Home Journal*, October 30, 1858; cited in Thomas and Jackson, *The Poe Log*, 473.

244 **To travel the six miles:** As an alternative, Poe could have stayed on the Bloomingdale stage to Tryon's Row near City Hall Park, then walked a few blocks south to his office. See omnibus and stage routes in *A Picture of New-York in 1846*, 95–96.

244 **on January 29 published a new poem:** "The Raven," *New York Tribune*, February 4, 1845, 4.

245 **the *Journal* moved to new offices:** John Doggett Jr., *Doggett's New York City Directory*, 1845–46, 429; advertisement, *New York Tribune*, May 2, 1845, 3.

245 **"perhaps a little jaded":** Walt Whitman, *Specimen Days & Collect*. Philadelphia: Rees Welsh & Co., 1882, 29.

246 **"disposed of his interest":** "City Items," *New York Tribune*, January 1, 1846, 2.

246 **found him in a tavern in Baltimore:** Thomas and Jackson, *The Poe Log*, 844.

246 **Mary Brennan was listed:** *Trow's New York City Directory*, 1879.

246 **By the mid-1880s the Brennan farm:** *Robinson's Atlas of the City of New York*. New York: E. Robinson, 1885, Sheet 24, New York Public Library Map Collection.

246 **Hemstreet took the mantel home:** William Hemstreet, "'Raven' Mantel Is in Brooklyn," *New York Times Saturday Review of Books*, December 21, 1907, 843.

246 **donated it to Columbia University:** "Columbia Receives the Poe Mantel," *New York Times*, January 5, 1908, 8; "After a Part in Poe's 'Raven,' the Dust of Obscurity," *New York Times*, August 11, 2012, A16.

246 **dotted with elm, locust, buttonwood:** John Flavel Mines, *A Tour Around New York and My Summer Acre: Being the Recreations of Mr. Felix Oldboy*. New York: Harper & Brothers, 1893, 227.

247 **the decrepit Apthorp mansion as "debased":** Charles Dawson Shanly, "Along the Hudson River at New York," *Atlantic Monthly* XXII, 129 (July 1868), 2.

247 **"threatened on all sides":** Mines, *A Tour Around New York and My Summer Acre*, 227–229.

247 **"[The] air was thick with the shadows":** Ibid.

248 **"In some thirty years every noble cliff":** Quoted in Spannuth and Mabbott, *Doings of Gotham by Edgar Allan Poe*, 26.

248 **"Going! Going! Gone!":** Mines, *A Tour Around New York and My Summer Acre*, 225.

CHAPTER 29. BOOMTOWN

251 **compared the district to London:** Egbert L. Viele, *The West End Plateau of the City of New York*. New York: Johnson & Platt, 1879, 17.

251 **"in wretched condition":** "West Side Property Holders," *New York Times*, July 12, 1885, 12.

251 **"desultory and scattered":** "The Wonderful West Side," *New York Sun*, March 23, 1889, 5.

251 **mail was still carried by a lone rider:** "The Big West Side of Town," *New York Sun*, March 31, 1889, 6.

251 **the only commuter disembarking at 93th Street:** Ibid.

251 **from 9 million to 46 million:** Samuel Carter, *Cyrus Field: Man of Two Worlds*. New York: G. P. Putnam's Sons, 1968, 339.

252 **the Mutual Life Insurance Company:** "The Wonderful West Side," 5.

252 **"They were mistaken":** "The Big West Side of Town," 6.

252 **In 1889 a vacant lot on the Boulevard:** Ibid.

252 **only 27 percent of the lots:** George W. Bromley and Walter S. Bromley, *Atlas of the City of New York*. Philadelphia: G. W. Bromley & Co., 1891, sheets 23, 25, 26, 36, 37, 38.

252 **"The demand is constantly for more":** "The Wonderful West Side," 5.

253 **"Boulevard" sounded too foreign:** "No More 'Boulevard,'" *New York Tribune*, February 16, 1899, 8.

253 **"Hundreds of men, red-shirted and grimy":** "No Longer Lies Dormant. Boulevard Vitalized by Better Buildings and Transit," *New York Tribune*, May 16, 1899, 3.

254 **"They are making an underground trolley":** Horatio Sweetser to Theodore Sweetser, May 28, 1899. Manuscript letter. Courtesy of Richard and Kathleen Hage.

254 **Broadway had no transit at all:** "Delay That Is Ruinous," *New York Tribune*, November 12, 1899, 2.

255 **"ATTENTION, BARGAIN HUNTERS":** Advertisement, *New York Tribune*, November 14, 1899, 10.

255 **In 1899 a small lot:** "No Longer Lies Dormant. Boulevard Vitalized by Better Buildings and Transit," 3.

255 **so vast in scope, the *Tribune* marveled:** "New-York the Empire City," *New York Tribune*, December 31, 1902, Part II, 8.

256 **"as if they had been doing it all their lives":** "Our Subway Open, 150,000 Try It," *New York Times*, October 28, 1904, 1.

256 **one station every six blocks:** The 91st Street station was considered too close to the 86th and 96th street stations and was abandoned in 1959.

257 **Apartments often came equipped:** "The West Side's Newest Apartment Buildings," *New York Tribune*, Sunday Real Estate Section, September 3, 1899, 6.

257 **rents in Broadway's new apartment houses:** Ibid.; advertisement, *New York Tribune*, Sunday Real Estate Section, October 22, 1899, 9.

257 **"elegant" suites of six to ten rooms:** "The Wonderful West Side," 5.

258 **"magnificent human hives":** "Millions Invested in Homes," *New York Tribune*, December 31, 1902, Real Estate Section, 9.

258 **189 vacant lots:** George W. Bromley and Walter S. Bromley, *Atlas of the City of New York*. Philadelphia: G. W. Bromley & Co., 1898 (corrections up to 1902), 1911, 1920–1922.

CHAPTER 30. HOMETOWN

260 **"the large and opulent class":** Egbert L. Viele, *The West End Plateau of the City of New York*. New York: Johnson & Platt, 1879, 15. In 1879 many of the wealthiest Jewish Grand Dukes still lived on the East Side well below Lenox Hill: Adolph Lewisohn and David, Henry, James, and Jesse Seligman all lived between East 46th and 55th streets. The northward migration to Lenox Hill began in earnest in the 1880s, when Meyer Lehman moved to East 62nd Street and Jacob H. Schiff built a large mansion at Fifth Avenue and East 74th Street. *Trow's New York City Directory*, 1882.

260 **the "great west side plateau":** Viele, *The West End Plateau of the City of New York*, 16.

260 **the "Jewish Fifth Avenue":** Stephen Birmingham, *"Our Crowd": The Great Jewish Families of New York*. New York: Harper & Row, 1967. Reprinted 1996, Syracuse University Press, 258–259.

260   **400,000 people:** "Big Wave of Jews Coming," *New York Tribune*, December 17, 1905, Part V, 1.

260   **"There is room for all of them":** Ibid.

260   **By then 750,000 residents:** Ibid.

261   **"The reason the Jews ran out of Harlem":** Jeff Kisseloff oral history interviews. Manuscripts and Archives Division, New York Public Library, Astor, Lenox, and Tilden Foundations.

261   **"[We] were upwardly mobile":** Ibid.

262   **By 1930, an estimated one-third of the West Side's population:** Federation of Jewish Philanthropies, Demographic Study Committee, *The Estimated Jewish Population of the New York Area, 1900–1975.* New York, 1959, 26; Welfare Council of New York City, Research Bureau, *Population in Health Areas, New York City, 1930*, Health Districts 27–35, Manhattan. Quoted in Selma Cantor Berrol, "The Making of a Neighborhood: The Jewish West Side," New York Neighborhood Studies, Working Paper No. 4. New York: Division of Urban Planning, Graduate School of Architecture and Planning, Columbia University, ca. 1982, 1.

262   **epicenter at Broadway and 86th Street:** Aaron M. Frankel, "From the American Scene: Back to Eighty-Six Street," *Commentary* II, 2 (August 1, 1946).

262   **"[My father] was too lenient":** Jeff Kisseloff oral history interviews. Manuscripts and Archives Division, New York Public Library, Astor, Lenox, and Tilden Foundations.

262   **"We were always, constantly, considering survival":** Ibid.

262   **the West Side's population increased:** Russell Porter, "Our Changing City: Along Manhattan's West Side," *New York Times*, July 4, 1955, 13.

262   **over 100,000 Puerto Ricans:** Ibid.

262   **"To the Irish, the Italians were guineas":** Jeff Kisseloff oral history interviews. Manuscripts and Archives Division, New York Public Library, Astor, Lenox, and Tilden Foundations.

263   **The Alamac was the quintessential:** Barbara Samuelson, personal interview, New York, April 25, 2016.

265   **"Mainly the West Side then was small shops":** Ibid.

265   **Zabar's grocery, which Louis Zabar:** Christopher Gray, "Zabar's, Broadway between 80th and 81st Street; As Its Horizons Widened, It Never Left Home," *New York Times*, November 10, 2002, www.nytimes.com.

265   **Aaron Chinitz, a Jewish immigrant:** "Aaron Chinitz, Founder and President of Two Restaurants Here, Is Dead," *New York Times*, April 6, 1945, 15.

265   **They featured almost identical menus:** C & L Restaurant and Tip Toe Inn menus. Rare Book Division, Buttolph Collection of Menus, New York Public Library Digital Collections, 1954–1955.

265   **well over a million were consumed:** "Bagel Famine Threatens in City; Labor Dispute Puts Hole in Supply," *New York Times*, December 17, 1951, 1.

265   **where locals stuffed themselves with chopped herring:** Steinberg's Dairy menu. Rare Book Division, Buttolph Collection of Menus, New York Public Library Digital Collections, 1941.

265   **Walter Matthau used to get a rise:** Joann Stang, "How They Survive," *New York Times*, July 25, 1965, Section 2, 1.

266 **Hidden beneath the new sign:** www.ephemeralnewyork.wordpress.com. Accessed September 28, 2016.

270 **fragments of the Bloomingdale Road:** A nondescript alley on 97th Street, just behind the Powellton apartment house on Broadway, is actually a fragment of the road; another small fragment exists out of view behind the Barnard Court apartment building at the corner of Claremont Avenue and 116th Street. And farther to the north, two fragments of the road survive as Old Broadway and Hamilton Place.

270 **Harlem Heights or Vandewater Heights:** Andrew S. Dolkart, *Morningside Heights: A History of Its Architecture & Development*. New York: Columbia University Press, 1998, 4.

271 **Eddy recommended that New York Hospital:** James Hardie, *The Description of the City of New-York, Containing Its Population, Institutions, Commerce, Manufactures, Public Buildings* . . . New York: Samuel Marks, 1827, 259–261. New York Hospital opened in 1791 and was demolished in 1869.

271 **to "relieve the melancholy mind":** *A Picture of New-York in 1846; with a Short Account of Places in Its Vicinity; Designed as a Guide to Citizens and Strangers*. New York: Roman & Ellis, 1846, 43.

271 **an act prohibiting 115th through 120th streets:** "Refusing to Close a Street," *New York Times*, June 27, 1884, 8.

271 **the asylum followed the Retreat model:** Hardie, *The Description of the City of New-York*, 262.

272 **Philip Hone was an asylum trustee:** *The Diary of Philip Hone, 1828–1851*, Bayard Tuckerman, editor. New York: Dodd, Mead & Co., 1889, I, ix, 9.

272 **Of the 4,182 patients:** J. H. French, *Historical and Statistical Gazetteer of New York State*. Syracuse: R. Pearsall Smith, 1860, 432.

272 **"At Bloomingdale":** Margaret Fuller, "Our City Charities. Visit to Bellevue Alms House, to the Farm School, the Asylum for the Insane, and Penitentiary on Blackwell's Island," *New York Tribune*, March 19, 1845, 1. Quoted in Judith Mattson Bean and Joel Myerson, *Margaret Fuller, Critic: Writings from the New-York Tribune, 1844–1846*. New York: Columbia University Press, 2000, 101.

273 **Olmstead predicted, land values in the area would skyrocket:** "West Side Property Holders," *New York Times*, July 12, 1885, 12.

273 **In 1879, Olmstead suggested:** "A Site for the World's Fair," *New York Times*, October 2, 1879, 8.

273 **Olmstead argued that since the asylum charged:** "Refusing to Close a Street," 8.

273 **Olmstead and Bixby demanded:** "Insane Asylum Methods," *New York Times*, March 25, 1888, 11.

273 **Olmstead and Bixby brought to the stand:** "Bloomingdale Taxes. The Senate Committee Investigating the Institution's Standing," *New York Times*, March 11, 1888, 16.

273 **"The Bloomingdale Lunatic Asylum has damned":** "Insane Asylum Methods," 11.

273 **John Brewer, who owned lots:** Ibid.

273 **"People won't live in the neighborhood of a madhouse":** Ibid.

274 **Agent William Cruikshank testified:** "Bloomingdale's Claims. Defending Itself Before the Senate Committee," *New York Times*, April 1, 1888, 14.

274 **"Do you ever go up there?":** Ibid.

274 **On May 3 the senate committee:** "The Bloomingdale Asylum. A Report Adverse to Cutting Streets Through Its Grounds," *New York Times*, May 4, 1888, 1.

274 **the result of a mysterious "tacit agreement":** "To Go to White Plains. Bloomingdale Insane Asylum to Be Moved," *New York Times*, May 19, 1888, 5.

274 **"The lunatics in the asylum":** "The Big West Side of Town," *New York Sun*, March 31, 1889, 6.

274 **With the asylum out of the way:** "West Side Property Holders," 12.

CHAPTER 32. ACROPOLIS

276 **King's College was chartered in 1754:** Brander Matthews, *A History of Columbia University, 1754–1904.* New York: Columbia University Press, 1904, 18.

276 **"with the utmost Decency and Propriety":** *New-York Gazette*, August 30, 1756. Quoted in Matthews, *A History of Columbia University, 1754–1904*, 20–21.

276 **"Husbandry, Commerce, and Government":** Matthews, *A History of Columbia University*, 444.

276 **The college's "Laws and Orders":** "Laws and Orders of the College of New York." Quoted in Matthews, *A History of Columbia University*, Appendix B, 446–447.

277 **Low transformed Columbia into a modern university:** Andrew S. Dolkart, *Morningside Heights: A History of Its Architecture & Development.* New York: Columbia University Press, 1998, 109.

277 **he engineered Columbia's purchase, for $2 million:** Ibid., 109.

277 **The asylum's main building:** One building from the asylum still exists: Macy Villa, which serves as Columbia's Buel Hall.

278 **drawing equally well with either hand:** "Charles Follen McKim," *Bulletin of the Metropolitan Museum of Art* IV (October 1, 1909), 173; Henry Bacon, "Charles Follen McKim: A Character Sketch," *The Brickbuilder* XIX, 2 (February, 1910), 38–39.

279 **"Roman weight":** Royal Cortissoz, "Some Critical Reflections on the Architectural Genius of Charles F. McKim," *The Brickbuilder* XIX, 2 (February 1910), 33.

280 **Seth Low had been:** Dolkart, *Morningside Heights*, 109.

280 **Columbia hired McKim:** Ibid., 125.

280 **McKim's plan for Columbia:** Originally the campus was bounded on the south by 116th Street, which opened from Tenth Avenue to the Boulevard in 1889 and closed to traffic in 1953. Today it is the main east-to-west axis of the campus and is known as "College Walk."

281 **Low Library had room for 600,000 volumes:** Dolkart, *Morningside Heights*, 151.

282 **"enveloping serious ideas in garments"**: Cortissoz, "Some Critical Reflections on the Architectural Genius of Charles F. McKim," 32.

282 **Low had been calling it "Morningside Heights"**: Dolkart, *Morningside Heights*, 5.

284 **the "temples of the white man"**: "Ground Has at Last Been Broken for the Stately New Buildings of the College of the City of New York, Which Will Crown St. Nicholas Terrace," *New York Tribune Illustrated Supplement*, March 8, 1903, 8, 9.

CHAPTER 33. GOD'S SKYSCRAPERS

285 **"Morningside Heights has entered a new era"**: "New York's Acropolis Grows in Glory," *New York Times Magazine*, March 7, 1926, 5, 23.

286 **Columbia remained a male bastion:** In 1886, Columbia initiated the Collegiate Course for Women, which resulted in a certificate, not a degree. That program ended with the founding of Barnard College in 1889. From there, women were gradually admitted to Columbia's professional schools and allowed to take some undergraduate courses but weren't fully admitted until 1983.

286 **In 1890 there had been only four:** *Bromley's Atlas*, Lionel Pincus and Princess Firyal Map Division, New York Public Library, 1891, Sheet 38.

287 **In 1841, Philip Hone called:** *The Diary of Philip Hone, 1828–1851*, Bayard Tuckerman, editor, II, 97.

287 **Five Points orphans and newsboys:** Advertisement, *New York Evening Express*, December 22, 1855, 4.

287 **"I saw the great audience with dismay"**: Edward Waldo Emerson and Waldo Emerson Forbes, *The Journals of Ralph Waldo Emerson.* Boston and New York: Houghton Mifflin Co., 1912, VIII, 448–449.

287 **Demonstrations of mesmerism:** In January of 1844, Lydia Maria Child went to the Tabernacle to listen to an introductory lecture on "Phreno-Mnemotechny," which promised to strengthen the memory in ten hour-long lessons. Child, *Letters from New York. Second Series.* New York and Boston: C. S. Francis & Co., 1845, 57.

287 **Rynders broke down in tears:** Untitled, *New York Tribune*, April 13, 1857, 4.

287 **"The church may be dead"**: "Where Are the Great Preachers? Does New York Know Her Own Pulpits?" *New York Tribune*, May 12, 1919, 13.

288 **"We should use in church buildings"**: "Proposed Skyscraper Cathedral of Church Meets Opposition," *South Bend News-Times*, January 15, 1922, 14.

288 **plans for a skyscraper church on Broadway:** "Reisner to Tell of Temple Plans," *New York Times*, September 13, 1925, 6E.

288 **little evidence of Christianity in New York's skyline**: "Links Lawlessness to Lack of Religion: Dr. Reisner Declares Conditions Better in Europe Than Here Because of Training of Youth," *New York Times*, December 10, 1928, 30.

289 **Oscar Konkle broke ground:** "Tallest Building in World Is Begun," *New York Times*, January 19, 1926, 15.

289 **Blasting began at the corner:** "Blast for Skyscraper," *New York Times*, February 26, 1926, 23; "Tallest Building in World Is Begun," 15.

290 **Ten percent of the building's earnings:** "65-Story Hotel Here to Be Part Church," *New York Times*, September 1, 1925, 1.

290 **were crushed to death:** "Huge Rock Kills 5 In Pit on Broadway," *New York Times*, March 31, 1926, 8.

290 **administered last rites:** Ibid.

CHAPTER 34. "HONEST TO GOODNESS SLUM LAND"

295 **On October 28:** Mardges Bacon, *Le Corbusier in America: Travels in the Land of the Timid.* Cambridge, Mass., and London: MIT Press, 2001, 67. Le Corbusier lectured at Columbia on October 28 and November 19.

295 **Empire State Building "too small":** H. I. Brock, "Le Corbusier Scans Gotham's Towers," *New York Times Magazine*, November 3, 1935, 10.

295 **Returning to Columbia on November 19:** Bacon, *Le Corbusier in America*, 93.

295 **"swift and nervous":** Talbot Faulkner Hamlin, *Columbia University Quarterly* 28 (March 1936), 68–69. Quoted in Bacon, *Le Corbusier in America*, 93. Le Corbusier's sketches from the Columbia lectures are in the collection of Columbia's Avery Library. Some of them are reproduced in Bacon, plates 2, 5, 6, 8.

296 **Students were warned away from the park:** "Woman Slain in Park," *New York Times*, July 16, 1935, 11.

296 **"Columbia has lost conviction":** Lewis Mumford (uncredited), "Bricks of the City," in *New York Panorama*. New York: Random House, 1938, 222.

296 **Morningside Heights had devolved:** Wayne Phillips, "Slums Engulfing Columbia Section," *New York Times*, June 9, 1958, 25.

296 **"obsolete design":** Elizabeth R. Hepner, *Morningside-Manhattanville Rebuilds . . .* New York: Morningside Heights, Inc., 1955, 2.

297 **"nothing short of substantial rebuilding":** Ibid.

297 **Moses informed Rockefeller:** Ibid.

297 **The valley is a geological fault line:** Eric K. Washington, "St. Mary's Protestant Episcopal Church (Manhattanville), Parish House, and Sunday School," Designation Report, New York City Landmarks Preservation Commission, May 19, 1998, 2.

298 **Irish and German immigrants:** Ibid.

298 **the neighborhood's black population had doubled:** Howard Brown Woolston, *A Study of the Population of Manhattanville.* New York: Columbia University Press, 1909, 89.

298 **"no exceptional incidence of [over]crowding":** Hepner, *Morningside-Manhattanville Rebuilds . . .* , 8.

299 **"hysterical":** Bert Horwitz, "Building Plans Objected to by Housing Group," *Columbia Daily Spectator*, December 3, 1951, 1–2.

299 **"[The] aim of the redevelopment":** Ibid.

300 **on November 12 the city announced plans:** "Morningside Groups Clarify Issues," *Columbia Daily Spectator*, December 14, 1951, 3.

300 **for the "upset price" of $1,302,046:** Hepner, *Morningside-Manhattanville Rebuilds . . .* , 23.

300 **A mass exodus:** Ibid., 24.

300 **"After one or two futile attempts":** Ibid., 24.

302 **"The people on the hill":** Gertrude Samuels, "Rebirth of a Community," *New York Times Magazine*, July 4, 1955, 26.

CHAPTER 35. MURDERVILLE

303 **Seventy-five percent of the site's buildings:** Ira Henry Freeman, "Morning-side Site Is Set for Co-Op," *New York Times*, September 16, 1955, 25.

305 **Jane Jacobs . . . called"buoyancy":** Jane Jacobs, *The Death and Life of Great American Cities*. New York: Vintage Books, 1961, 146.

306 **our "complicated and ornery society":** Ibid., 4, 9.

306 **One-third of them came:** Charles Grutzner, "City's 'Acropolis' Combating Slums," *New York Times*, May 21, 1957, 37, 40.

306 **Seventy-five percent of Morningside Gardens':** Charles Grutzner, "Moses Backs Sale of Slum Project," *New York Times*, June 21, 1957, 27.

306 **In 1982, twenty-five years:** Deirdre Carmody, "After 25 Years, Co-op Endures as Stable Sign," *New York Times*, October 16, 1982, www.nytimes.com.

306 **The Grant Houses opened:** Charles Grutzner, "5 Families Move to Grant Houses," *New York Times*, August 21, 1956, 31.

306 **the Housing Authority spelled out** HELLO: Charles Grutzner, "'Hello' to Gleam at Grant Houses," *New York Times*, August 20, 1956, 23.

307 **in September of 1962 battalions of tenants:** Peter Kihss, "Tenants Recruit Volunteer Guard," *New York Times*, September 11, 1962, 35.

307 **Anna Ayala:** "Girl, 12, Slain in Harlem Project as City Is Agreeing to Guard It," *New York Times*, September 13, 1962, 35.

307 **The Housing Authority's response:** Franklin Whitehouse, "200 Guards Hired for City Housing," *New York Times*, September 13, 1962, 35.

307 **"The tenants are afraid to leave their apartments":** Emanuel Perlmutter, "Vigil Is Begun in Harlem Project for More Police," *New York Times*, April 16, 1968, 37.

307 **In 1980 twenty women reported being raped:** "2 Indictments Allege Sex Assaults on 7," *New York Times*, May 2, 1980, 31; "Police Seek a Rapist," *New York Times*, April 21, 1980, 23; Glenn Fowler, "A Suspect in 4 Rapes at 2 Housing Projects in Harlem Is Arrested," *New York Times*, April 24, 1980, 37.

307 **In 1994 the decomposed bodies:** Seth Faison, "Woman and 3 Children Found Killed in Harlem," *New York Times*, May 2, 1994, 31.

307 **In 1997 a dispute between neighbors:** David Kocieniewski, "Tenant Is Held In Explosion at Apartment," *New York Times*, March 25, 1997, www.nytimes.com.

307 **eighteen-year-old Tayshana Murphy:** Dmitry Kiper and Joseph Goldstein, "Heralded Girls Basketball Star Is Shot to Death in Manhattan," *New York Times*, September 11, 2011, A21; Corey Kilgannon, "Housing Project Feud Cited in Killing of Basketball Star," *New York Times*, September 14, 2011, A25; Sarah Maslin Nir, "Two Arrested in the Killing of a Student," *New York Times*, September 21, 2011, A25.

CHAPTER 36. THE HOUSE ON THE HILL

314 **"little retreat":** Alexander Hamilton to Elizabeth Hamilton, June 8, 1800, in *The Papers of Alexander Hamilton*, Harold C. Syrett, editor. New York: Columbia University Press, 1976, XXIV, 587–588.

314 **Eliza and Hamilton were married:** Ron Chernow, *Alexander Hamilton*. New York: Penguin, 2004, 148.

316 **"You have forgot to send me the plans"**: Philip Schuyler to Alexander Hamilton, July 17, 1800, in *The Papers of Alexander Hamilton*, Harold C. Syrett, editor, XXV, 41–42.

317 **"Don't forget to visit the *Grange*"**: Alexander Hamilton to Elizabeth Hamilton, January 18, 1801, in *The Papers of Alexander Hamilton*, Harold C. Syrett, editor, XXV, 327–328.

318 **"You see, I do not forget the Grange"**: Ibid., 159–160.

318 **the house "rocked like a cradle"**: William Kent, *Memoirs and Letters of James Kent*. Boston: Little, Brown & Co., 1898, 143.

318 **"friendly and amiable"**: Ibid.

318 **Hamilton was $50,000 to $60,000 in debt**: Chernow, *Alexander Hamilton*, 724–725.

318 **"[Schuyler] knows well"**: "Alexander Hamilton's Explanation of His Financial Situation," in *The Papers of Alexander Hamilton*, Harold C. Syrett, editor, XXVI, 289.

319 **he was, like Hamilton, in debt**: Chernow, *Alexander Hamilton*, 724–725.

319 **"I pray God that something may remain"**: "Obsequies of Mrs. Hamilton," *New York Herald*, November 12, 1854, 12.

319 **worth about $25,000**: "Statement of My Property and Debts, July 1, 1804," in *The Papers of Alexander Hamilton*, Harold C. Syrett, editor, 1979, XXVI, 284.

319 **On April 8, 1805, it fetched $30,500**: *Mercantile Advertiser*, April 9, 1805. Quoted in I. N. Phelps Stokes, *The Iconography of Manhattan Island, 1498 to 1909*. Six volumes. New York: Robert H. Dodd, 1915–1928. Reprinted, New York: Arno Press, 1967, V, 1434.

319 **Pendleton, Fish, Church bought it back**: Chernow, *Alexander Hamilton*, 724–725.

319 **Gouverneur Morris solicited subscriptions**: Ibid., 725.

319 **Congress passed "An Act"**: "Alexander Hamilton's Explanation of His Financial Situation," in *The Papers of Alexander Hamilton*, Harold C. Syrett, editor, XXVI, n288.

319 **Eliza wore widow's black the rest of her life**: "Obsequies of Mrs. Hamilton," 12.

319 **she never mingled in Washington's fashionable circles**: Ibid.

319 **credited Eliza with teaching him**: "In Memory of Hamilton," *New York Tribune*, July 13, 1904, 1.

319 **rented out as pasture for horses**: Advertisement, *New York Herald*, August 9, 1868, 1.

319 **In 1887, De Forest subdivided**: "The Great Auction Sale of the Magnificent Hamilton Grange Property," advertisement, *New York Evening World*, October 17, 1887, 4.

319 **De Forest declared he was unhappy**: "Small Demand for Hamilton Grange Lots," *New York Sun*, October 26, 1887, 2.

320 **De Forest went bankrupt**: "W. H. De Forest Fails," *New York Sun*, January 10, 1888, 1.

320 **In the 1880s it was painted**: "Where a Statesman Died," *New York Evening World*, November 28, 1887, 3.

320 **The original carriage drive**: "Alexander Hamilton's Old Home," *New York Evening World*, November 7, 1887, 4.

320 **The back corner of the house intruded**: Ibid.

320 **Isaac H. Tuthill, St. Luke's pastor**: "And Old St. Luke's Must Go," *New York Evening World*, January 3, 1889, 2.

321 **when three generations of Hamilton's descendants**: "In Memory of Hamilton," *New York Tribune*, July 13, 1904, 1.

321 **The last trunk was cut down**: Stokes, *The Iconography of Manhattan Island*, V, 2072.

321 **That same year the American Scenic and Historic Preservation Society**: Clarence Dean, "City Hopes to Put Hamilton Grange Back in the Sun," *New York Times*, March 4, 1955, 25.

322 **the Grange might be moved to Riverside Drive**: "Substitute Urged for Claremont Inn," *New York Times*, May 16, 1950, 33.

322 **a plan in 1955 to move the Grange**: Dean, "City Hopes to Put Hamilton Grange Back in the Sun," 25.

322 **During thunderstorms**: Eric Sloane and Edward Anthony, *Mr. Daniels and the Grange*. New York: Funk & Wagnalls, 1968, 16.

322 **"The Grange is a sad house"**: Ibid.

323 **the Wolfe movers used hydraulic jacks**: www.wolfehousebuildingmovers.com. Accessed June 2, 2016.

323 **the 298-ton Grange**: David W. Dunlap, "Witnessing a House, and History, on the Move," *New York Times*, June 8, 2008, A38.

323 **chains were wrapped around it**: www.wolfehousebuildingmovers.com. Accessed June 2, 2016.

323 **calculated the Grange's speed at .04 miles an hour**: Dunlap, "Witnessing a House, and History, on the Move," A38.

324 **"may be regarded as fluid"**: "Spires on Morningside," *New York Times*, February 13, 1926, 12.

324 **There were 682 visitors**: "Summary of Visitor Use by Month and Year (1979—Last Calendar Year)," Park Reports, National Park Service Visitor Use Statistics, http://irma.nps.gov. Accessed November 2, 2016.

CHAPTER 37. NECROPOLIS

326 **commonplace deaths**: "Weekly Report of Deaths," *New York Herald*, 1830s–1860s.

326 **the churchyard was already "crowded with the dead"**: John Lambert, *Travels Through Canada and the United States of North America, in the Years 1806, 1807 & 1808*. London: Baldwin, Cradock & Joy, 1816, II, 88.

326 **"One would think there was a scarcity of land"**: Ibid.

327 **killed over 4,000**: J. H. French, *Historical and Statistical Gazetteer of New York State*. Syracuse: R. Pearsall Smith, 1860, 428.

327 **the city's Board of Health recommended**: Edward Miller, *Report on the Malignant Disease, Which Prevailed in the City of New-York in the Autumn of 1805*. New York: s.n., 1806, 35.

327 **held thousands of corpses**: Records indicate 11,864 burials in the churchyard, but this doesn't take into account missing records before 1777 and between 1783 and 1800. Whitey Flynn, Trinity Church Archives, email message to author, July 13, 2017.

328 **"A more desirable excursion for schools"**: Advertisement, *New York Herald*, August 27, 1845, 3.

330 **"How humbling to one with a heart and a soul"**: John Augustus Shea, "The Ocean," in *Famous Fugitive Poems*, Rossiter Johnson, editor. New York: Henry Holt & Co., 1909, 307.

CHAPTER 38. MINNIE'S LAND

332 **"pour[ing] forth his melody"**: Excerpt from Audubon's *Ornithological Biography*. Quoted in Rufus W. Griswold, *The Prose Writers of America*. Philadelphia: Porter & Coates, 1870, 193–194.

332 **"I am part Frenchman, part American"**: Untitled, *New York Herald*, July 7, 1837, 2.

333 **Audubon had some difficulty in securing subscribers**: Richard Rhodes, *John James Audubon: The Making of an American*. New York: Alfred A. Knopf, 2004, 273.

333 **"His bird pictures reflect his own temperament"**: John Burroughs, *John James Audubon*. Boston: Small, Maynard & Co., 1902, 125.

334 **the "most splendid book ever published"**: *The Diary of Philip Hone, 1828–1851*, Bayard Tuckerman, editor. New York: Dodd, Mead & Co., 1889, I, 73.

334 **"an interesting man"**: Ibid. Audubon visited Hone on March 30 or 31, 1833.

334 **"Audubon, the great naturalist"**: Untitled, *New York Herald*, July 7, 1837, 2.

334 **Bennett ran into Audubon on a steamship**: "Sailing of the Packet Ship England," *New York Herald*, July 19, 1837, 2.

334 **volunteer firemen presented a copy to Jenny Lind**: Augustine E. Costello, *Our Firemen: A History of the New York Fire Departments*. New York: Augustine E. Costello, 1887, 181.

334 **the edition earned $36,000**: Rhodes, *John James Audubon*, 430.

335 **Samuel F. B. Morse visited**: George Bird Grinnell, *Audubon Park: The History of the Site of the Hispanic Society of America and Neighboring Institutions*. New York: Hispanic Society of America, 1927, 14.

336 **a "secluded house . . . unpretending in its architecture"**: Parke Godwin, "Audubon," in *Homes of American Authors*. New York: G. P. Putnam & Co., 1853, 4.

336 **Shown into a ground-floor studio**: Ibid., 5.

336 **"How kind it is [of you] to come see me"**: Ibid., 6.

336 **then returned to Minnie's Land full of energy**: Rhodes, *John James Audubon*, 429–430.

336 **"all in ruins"**: John Bachman to Maria Martin, May 11, 1848. Quoted in Rhodes, *John James Audubon*, 433.

337 **To make ends meet**: George Bird Grinnell, "Recollections of Audubon Park," *The Auk*, 37 (July 1920), 372–373.

337 **Audubon Park grew into a small community**: Grinnell, "Recollections of Audubon Park," 372; Grinnell, *Audubon Park*, 17.

337 **"If you have nothing to do"**: Grinnell, "Recollections of Audubon Park," 379.

337 **Grinnell remembered sylvan days of fishing**: Ibid., 376.

337 **"worn and shabby"**: Ibid., 374.

337   **Eventually fences went up:** Grinnell, *Audubon Park*, 18.

338   **Their father's house was offered for rent:** Advertisement, *New York Herald*, May 2, 1861, 11.

338   **Lucy, always in financial straits:** Rhodes, *John James Audubon*, 436–438.

338   **By 1909, Grinnell's father:** Grinnell, *Audubon Park*, 21.

338   **Audubon's house survived:** It was roughly at the position of present-day 765 Riverside Drive.

338   **"If there is such a thing as communication":** "More Buried Treasure in a Noted Basement," *New York Tribune*, March 11, 1917, 5.

CHAPTER 39. THE HEIGHTS

344   **"All the redoubts and forts":** John Randel Jr., "City of New York, North of Canal Street, in 1808 to 1821," in D. T. Valentine, *Manual of the Corporation of the City of New-York*. New York: Edmund Jones & Co., 1864, 855.

344   **though "hardly visible":** Wilson Cary Smith, "The Roger Morris House," *Magazine of American History* VI (1881), 103.

344   **They thought it "improbable":** Gouverneur Morris, Simeon DeWitt, and John Rutherfurd, "Remarks of the Commissioners for Laying Out Streets and Roads in the City of New York, Under the Act of April 3, 1807." Quoted in I. N. Phelps Stokes, *The Iconography of Manhattan Island, 1498 to 1909*. Six volumes. New York: Robert H. Dodd, 1915–1928. Reprinted, New York: Arno Press, 1967, I, 472–473.

344   **"impracticable . . . ruinous to land owners":** Statute 1860, Ch. 201, *Documents of the Assembly of the State of New York* IX, 148, 994.

345   **They envisioned "Fort Washington Park":** "The Commissioners of Washington Heights," *New York Herald*, July 26, 1860, 5.

345   **"We trust that the Commissioners":** "Grand Suburban Park at Washington Heights," *New York Herald*, August 27, 1860, 4.

345   **"[Some] two thousand blocks were provided":** Frederick Law Olmsted and J. James Croes, "Preliminary Report of the Landscape Architect and the Civil and Topographical Engineer, upon the Laying Out of the Twenty-third and Twenty-fourth Wards," 1876. Quoted in Albert Fein, editor, *Landscape into Cityscape: Frederick Law Olmsted's Plans for a Greater New York City*. Ithaca: Cornell University Press, 1967, 352.

345   **"rich and cultivated":** Frederick Law Olmsted to Henry H. Elliott, August 27, 1860, in *Frederick Law Olmsted: Writings on Landscape, Culture, and Society*, Charles E. Beveridge, editor. New York: Library of America, 2015, 141, 144.

346   **Washington Heights would be overrun:** Ibid., 137, 139.

346   **"Our right unquestionably is to control matters":** Calvert Vaux to Frederick Law Olmsted, May 12, 1865, Frederick Law Olmsted Papers, Library of Congress, Reel 32. Quoted in Melvin Kalfus, *Frederick Law Olmsted: The Passion of a Public Artist*. New York: New York University Press, 1990, n391.

346   **In 1866 they proposed a new boulevard:** Calvert Vaux and Frederick Law Olmsted, "Preliminary Report to the Commissioners for Laying Out a Park in Brooklyn, New York: Being a Consideration of Circumstances of Site and

Other Conditions Affecting the Design of Public Pleasure Grounds," 1866. Quoted in Albert Fein, editor, *Landscape into Cityscape: Frederick Law Olmsted's Plans for a Greater New York City*, 126–127.

347 **"This is the most picturesque route":** Charles Dawson Shanly, "Along the Hudson River at New York," *Atlantic Monthly* XXII (July 1868) 129, 1.

CHAPTER 40. HILLTOPPERS

351 **"enough diamonds in the shirt fronts":** "New Team Wins First Game—Beat Washington 6 to 2," *New York Tribune*, May 1, 1903, 5.

351 **The Americans went on to win 6 to 2:** Ibid.

351 **It was the golden era of great baseball nicknames:** www.baseball-reference .com. Accessed July 26, 2016.

352 **"If the new baseball team is to have a name":** "Name for the American New Yorks," *New York Sun*, May 7, 1903, 8.

352 **attendance was well over 20,000:** "Yankees Start Well; Beat Boston in Twelfth," *New York Tribune*, April 15, 1906, 8.

CHAPTER 41. THE FOURTH REICH

354 **Malcolm X was assassinated:** In the early 1990s, half of the Audubon was demolished and the surviving half repurposed as a biomedical research facility. The front façade is intact.

354 **"Ruination," he cried:** Charles Darnton, "Popular Priced Theatres Unite Families by Keeping Men Out of Saloons, Says Fox," *New York Evening World*, November 12, 1912, 5.

355 **a "long, unending monotone":** Rian James, *All About New York: An Intimate Guide*, 1931. Quoted in David W. Dunlap, *On Broadway: A Journey Uptown over Time*. New York: Rizzoli, 1990, 293–296.

355 **locals were calling the neighborhood *das vierte Reich*:** "School Plan Used to Decrease Bias," *New York Times*, September 16, 1945, 42.

355 **"Byzantine-Romanesque-Indo-Hindu":** Dunlap, *On Broadway*, 306.

355 **"Negro-white antagonism [is] sharp":** "School Plan Used to Decrease Bias," 42.

355 **took fifth-graders and members of the PTA:** Ibid.

356 **"I was walking along Dyckman [Street]":** Jeff Kisseloff, *You Must Remember This: An Oral History of Manhattan from the 1890s to World War II*. Baltimore and London: Johns Hopkins University Press, 1999, 243–244.

356 **"[The automat] was really a blessing":** Jeff Kisseloff oral history interviews. Manuscripts and Archives Division, New York Public Library, Astor, Lenox, and Tilden Foundations.

356 **"We had a marvelous view":** Ibid.

356 **By 1940 . . . his income had risen:** 1940 United States Federal Census, National Archives and Records Administration. New York, New York: Enumeration District 31-2030, p. 63A, www.1940census.archives.gov.

357 **"This is the way people used to do it":** Jeff Kisseloff oral history interviews.

CHAPTER 42. THE BRIDGE

360 **"The scheme of building on the North [Hudson] River":** *American Citizen,*
January 27, 1808. Quoted in I. N. Phelps Stokes, *The Iconography of Manhattan Island, 1498 to 1909.* Six volumes. New York: Robert H. Dodd, 1915–1928. Reprinted, New York: Arno Press, 1967, V, 1485–1486.

360 **Lindenthal and Rea continued to advocate:** "Samuel Rea, Retiring at Age 70, Foresees a New Rail Era," *New York Times,* September 20, 1925, Section 9, 1, 14.

360 **Real-estate agents accosted passersby:** Advertisement, *New York Tribune,* March 19, 1910, 10.

361 **"the dream of every New York motorist":** "The Dream of Every New York Motorist," *New York Tribune,* August 14, 1921, Section 7, 1.

362 **Secretary of War James William Good:** "Bars Hudson Span as Planned Too Low," *New York Times,* May 30, 1929, 1, 12.

362 **four immense cables, each 36 inches:** Frank W. Skinner, "George Washington Bridge a Feat of Man's Ingenuity," *New York Times,* October 18, 1931, Section 20, 6. John A. Roebling & Sons, the world's oldest manufacturer of steel wire, fabricated the cables; the company's founder, John A. Roebling, had, of course, designed the Brooklyn Bridge.

363 **Letters flooded into the Authority's offices:** "Washington Leads as Name for Bridge," *New York Times,* February 12, 1931, 14; "Would Name New Span Verrazano Bridge," *New York Times,* February 9, 1931, 39.

364 **The bridge was dedicated:** "Two Governors Open Great Hudson Bridge as Throngs Look On," *New York Times,* October 25, 1931, 1, 30.

364 **two Bronx kids:** "Two Schoolboys on Skates First to Cross the New Bridge," *New York Times,* October 25, 1931, 30.

364 **the George Washington was always his favorite:** Michael Aaron Rockland, *The George Washington Bridge: Poetry in Steel.* New Brunswick, N.J., and London: Rivergate Books, 2008, 52.

364 **"It is blessed":** Le Corbusier, *When the Cathedrals Were White.* New York: Reynal & Hitchcock, 1947, 75.

CHAPTER 43. THE CUT

365 **In 1925, Port Authority chairman Julian A. Gregory:** "Take Fight to Estimate Board: Washington Heights Taxpayers Prepare a Petition Against the Fort Lee Span," *New York Times,* March 30, 1925, 3.

365 **Two churches with large:** Chelsea Methodist, led by the celebrity pastor Christian F. Reisner, moved south to the still-incomplete Broadway Temple on Broadway between 173rd and 174th streets.

365 **The work displaced 3,000 people:** "Apartment Houses Must Go for Hudson Bridge Approach," *New York Times,* October 27, 1929, Real Estate Section, 1.

366 **"the free flow of traffic":** Robert Moses, "Highways for a Better New York," *New York Times Magazine,* November 11, 1945, 10.

366 **the project involved demolition:** Joseph C. Ingraham, "New Bridge Links Planned Uptown," *New York Times,* February 18, 1957, 1.

366 **tenants from Washington Heights:** Paul Crowell, "Engineers Favor Bridge-Link Plan," *New York Times*, May 16, 1957, 33.

367 **"The rest is battling obstructionists":** Robert Moses, "Highways for a Better New York," 10.

367 **people he called "eagle[s] with vision":** Robert Moses, "It's Going to Be Quite a Town," *New York Times Magazine*, February 16, 1947, 7.

367 **Ammann, eighty-three:** Joseph C. Ingraham, "Lower Deck of George Washington Bridge Is Opened," *New York Times*, August 30, 1962, 1, 59.

CHAPTER 44. MR. BILLINGS

374 **"Mr. Billings's connection with the turf":** "Chatter of the Clubs," *New York Times Magazine*, September 27, 1903, 7.

375 **He and wife Blanche:** "Natives of New York Still Own Upper Fifth Avenue," *New York Times Magazine*, May 26, 1907, 5.

375 **Billings hired Boston architect Guy Lowell:** "Real Estate," *New York Tribune*, December 19, 1901, 6.

375 **Billings moved in his prized trotters:** "Gossip of the Trotters," *New York Tribune*, August 21, 1901, 8.

375 **In the spring of 1903:** "Lowell Mills Closed; 17,000 Persons Idle," *New York Times*, March 29, 1903, 1; "Strikers Close Restaurants," "Eighteen Arrested for Strike Violence," "J. P. Morgan Is Bullish," *New York Times*, March 31, 1903, 1; "Six Killed in a Furnace," *New York Times*, April 1, 1903, 1; "Minimum Wage Law Void," *New York Times*, April 2, 1903, 1.

376 **But when details of the festivities:** "Guests to Ride Wooden Horses," *New York Evening World*, March 28, 1903, 3; "Abandons Hobby Horse Dinner," *New York Tribune*, March 29, 1903, 5.

376 **Billings substituted real horses:** "Luncheon in a Stable," *New York Times*, March 30, 1903, 14.

376 **The horses ate too:** Ibid.

376 **Peoples Gas was trading at over $100 a share:** Stock tables, *New York Times*, April 4, 1903, 13.

377 **destroyed a well-preserved section of the fort:** "Want Customs Records Kept," *New York Tribune*, October 29, 1902, 5. In 1909, Billings paid to have a bronze plaque honoring Margaret Corbin installed at the site of the fort. It is still there in what is today Fort Tryon Park.

377 **Built of brick:** Barr Ferree, *Fort Tryon Hall*. New York: C. K. G. Billings, 1911.

378 **Lou Dillon, the first horse:** "Lou Dillon Sold for $12,500," *New York Tribune*, May 13, 1903, 5.

378 **the servants (generally English, Scottish):** 1910 United States Federal Census; New York, New York; Ward 12, Enumeration District 0675, pp. 4A and 4B, www.ancestry.com.

CHAPTER 45. MR. MOLENAOR

380 **between $300 million and $500 million:** "'Squatter' Claims $300,000,000 Realty," *New York Times*, May 13, 1913, 1.

380   **The shack had low ceilings:** Eleanor Booth Simmons, "The Last Days of Squatter Sovereignty," *New York Herald*, Section 8 (*Books and Magazine*), December 3, 1922, 16–17, 37.

380   **"I expect to stay here quite some time":** "'Squatter' Claims $300,000,000 Realty," 1.

380   **"You are hereby notified":** "A Claim for Millions," *New York Sun*, February 1, 1878, 3.

381   **A Catholic priest:** Ibid.

381   **"I was not long in getting that notice off my building":** "Lively Times at Kingsbridge," *New York Sun*, February 6, 1878, 1.

381   **"The Molenaors are poor":** "A Claim for Millions," 3.

381   **"an army of lawyers":** "'Squatter' Claims $300,000,000 Realty," 1.

381   **then went to Flagstaff, Arizona:** 1900 United States Federal Census; Flagstaff, Coconino, Arizona Territory; Enumeration District 0014, p. 5B, www .ancestry.com.

382   **he had lived in Manhattan, on Bleecker:** "Wants $300,000,000 Worth of Harlem," *New York Sun*, March 16, 1913, Section 7, 7.

382   **During the Civil War:** 1900 United States Federal Census; Flagstaff, Coconino, Arizona Territory; Enumeration District 0014, p. 5B, www.ancestry.com.

382   **In 1872, Molenaor's brother Andrew visited him:** "Wants $300,000,000 Worth of Harlem," 7.

382   **opened a jewelry business on Fulton Street:** "Martin M. Molenaor" was listed in an 1882 directory as a jeweler at 1053 Fulton Street in Brooklyn. George T. Lain, *The Brooklyn Directory for the Year Ending May, 1882.* New York: George T. Lain, 1882, 772.

382   **"good horse and chaise":** "Wants $300,000,000 Worth of Harlem," 7.

382   **invested heavily in the Harlem Canal Company:** Ibid.

382   **His land had been put up as security:** Henry Edward Smith, "Story of a Forty-Year Fight for $300,000,000," *Pittsburg Press, Sunday Press Illustrated Magazine*, August 19, 1917, 1.

382   **listed as "None":** 1850 United States Federal Census; New York, New York; Ward 17, p. 115A, www.ancestry.com.

382   **He died in 1858:** "Died," *New York Times*, February 3, 1858, 5.

382   **"To my eldest son":** "Wants $300,000,000 Worth of Harlem," 7.

383   **"[The defendants], as I understand it, do not contest":** William V. R. Erving, reporter, *The Miscellaneous Reports: Cases Decided in the Courts of Record of the State of New York.* Albany: J. B. Lyons Co., XCVIII (1917), 697.

384   **"To this extraordinary construction":** Ibid.

384   **"He sits at evening in the door of his cabin":** Smith, "Story of a Forty-Year Fight for $300,000,000," 1.

384   **Norton began excavating anyway:** "Heir to Millions Soon to Lose Hut," *New York Herald*, April 25, 1921, 20; "Waiting in Shack for Tunnel to Evict Them," *New York Herald*, April 26, 1921, 4.

385   **"Undermine our home, will you?":** Simmons, "The Last Days of Squatter Sovereignty," 37.

385   **But the stress of being threatened:** Ibid.

385   **"All that . . . is mine":** Ibid.

CHAPTER 46. MR. BARNARD

386   **In 1926 the château burned down:** "Billings Mansion Destroyed by Fire; Loss Near $1,000,000," *New York Times*, March 7, 1926, 1, 20.

386   **Landscape painter Eric Sloane:** Eric Sloane and Edward Anthony, *Mr. Daniels and the Grange*. New York: Funk & Wagnalls, 1968, 6–7.

387   **"human dynamo":** "George Grey Barnard," *New York Times*, April 26, 1938, 20.

387   **compared him favorably to Michelangelo:** "Barnard, Sculptor, Is Dead Here at 74," *New York Times*, April 25, 1938, 1, 3.

387   **"I was getting $2,000 a week":** "What Is Happening in the World of Art," *New York Sun*, December 6, 1914, 4.

387   **cabled Barnard to "come home":** Ibid.

387   **Joseph Miller Huston, and four others:** "Huston Goes to Prison," *New York Times*, May 24, 1911, 1.

388   **He began by bicycling around the French countryside:** "What Is Happening in the World of Art," 4.

388   **"I went into every cellar":** Ibid.

388   **"stealing the soul of France":** "Barnard, Sculptor, Is Dead Here at 74," 3.

388   **But others praised Barnard:** J. L. Schrader, "George Grey Barnard: The Cloisters and the Abbaye," *Metropolitan Museum of Art Bulletin* XXXVII, 1 (Summer 1979), 43.

388   **He called the museum the Cloisters:** Advertisement, *New York Sun*, December 14, 1914, 16.

388   **an "intellectual Coney Island":** Schrader, "George Grey Barnard: The Cloisters and the Abbaye," 45.

389   **Barnard put the Cloisters up for sale:** Ibid., 36.

389   **greeted guests in a velvet jacket and bow tie:** Ibid., 42.

390   **closed on February 9, 1936:** Ibid., 47.

390   **Among those paying tribute was Mathilda Burling:** "Artists Present at Barnard Rites," *New York Times*, April 28, 1938, 23.

390   **well over 4,000 had filed through:** "4,473 Visit the Cloisters," *New York Times*, May 15, 1938, 4.

CHAPTER 47. LIFE AND DEATH IN INWOOD

395   **One tenant's rent consisted only of one hen:** "Old Dyckman Farm Becomes City's Newest Recreation Ground," *New York Sun*, October 10, 1915, Section 7, 5.

396   **wait for his regular "Tubby Hookers":** Eleanor Booth Simmons, "Where Cobwebs Thrive on Manhattan Isle," *New York Tribune*, November 6, 1921, Magazine Section, 5, 7.

396   **McCreery didn't take the train to work:** Ibid.

396   **"Among the rocks and forest trees":** T. Addison Richards, "New York Circumnavigated," *Harper's New Monthly Magazine* XXIII, 134 (July 1861), 178.

397   **"utterly without salt and savor":** "What's in a Name?" *New York Tribune*, August 22, 1867, 4.

397 **continued to announce "Tubby Hook!":** Ibid.

397 **By 1867 the Hudson River Railroad:** "Local Intelligence. Suburban Homes: How to Reach them by Rail and Steamboat—Number of Trains and Commutation Rates of Fare—The Pleasant Villages of Manhattan, Long Island and New-Jersey—A Helping Word to Home Seekers," *New York Times*, March 11, 1867, 2.

397 **"Inwood seems, by its beautiful situation":** "The West Side," *New York Tribune*, May 22, 1868, 2.

397 **there were still virtually no buildings of any kind:** *Robinson's Atlas of the City of New York.* New York: E. Robinson, 1885, sheet 32, Lionel Pincus and Princess Firyal Map Division, New York Public Library, New York Public Library Digital Collections.

397 **"unchanged by the march of improvement":** Wilson Cary Smith, "The Roger Morris House," *Magazine of American History* VI (1881), 102.

398 **"The teachers had no business":** "Put in the Marsh to Die," *New York Sun*, June 15, 1887, 1.

399 **The mutilated body of a pregnant Italian woman:** "Hairs Clutched in Hand of Girl Brutally Slain. New Clue in the Mystery," *New York Evening World*, August 11, 1913, 1–2.

399 **For years the Joseph Keppler house stood vacant:** Simmons, "Where Cobwebs Thrive on Manhattan Isle," 5, 7.

399 **"quaint houses with cupolas and pillars":** Ibid.

399 **"And what do ye be after?":** Helen Worden, *Round Manhattan's Rim*. Indianapolis: Bobbs-Merrill Co., 1934, 169.

399 **Dwyer let Worden inside the old mansion:** Ibid., 171–172.

CHAPTER 48. THE LAST FARM

401 **filled with family mementos:** Bashford Dean and Alexander McMillan Welch, *The Dyckman House: Park and Museum, New York City, 1783–1916*. New York: Gilliss Press, 1916, 40.

401 **hung with antiquated implements:** Ibid., 36.

401 **The first Dyckman in the New World:** "Old Dyckman Farm Becomes City's Newest Recreation Ground," *New York Sun*, October 10, 1915, Section 7, 5; Dean and Welch, *The Dyckman House*, 22.

402 **By the 1860s the "Dyckman Tract" had grown:** Dean and Welch, *The Dyckman House*, 21.

403 **probably the largest land sale in Manhattan's history:** "Auction Bids the Beginning of Broadway Values," *New York Sun*, December 1, 1912, 25; advertisement, *New York Tribune*, May 31, 1871, 7.

403 **Hugh and Mary Drennan, who had arrived:** 1880 United States Federal Census; New York, New York; Enumeration District 535, p. 451D, www.ancestry.com.

403 **the Drennans' second-oldest daughter:** "Postmaster in 1880 Dies," *New York Times*, March 3, 1951, 13. In 1900, Mary and Elizabeth Drennan were listed in *Trow's Directory* as living on Broadway near 210th Street.

403 **"with an unkempt yard and slovenly surroundings":** Sarah Comstock, "Old Homesteads in Upper New York," *New York Times*, July 9, 1916, Section 2, 8.

404 **"There is, perhaps, not a city in the world":** Dean and Welch, *The Dyckman House*, 7.

404 **"You will probably come upon it with a start":** Comstock, "Old Homesteads in Upper New York," 8.

405 **$30 a month:** 1930 United States Federal Census; New York, New York; Enumeration District 31-1164, p. 16A, www.ancestry.com.

405 **The farm had good soil:** Jeff Kisseloff oral history interviews, Manuscripts and Archives Division, New York Public Library, Astor, Lenox, and Tilden Foundations.

405 **1930 had been an especially hard year:** "Farm," *Time* XVI, 11 (September 15, 1930), 70.

406 **300 of them in just two apartment buildings:** 5000 Broadway had 187 residents in 1930; 5008 Broadway had 114. 1930 United States Federal Census; New York, New York; Enumeration District 31-1164, pp. 8B-11A, www.ancestry.com.

406 **"No stories, no stories!":** Helen Worden, *Round Manhattan's Rim*. Indianapolis: Bobbs-Merrill Co., 1934, 166. Mary Benedetto's fears of Fellman raising the rent were well founded: A photograph of the farm taken in 1933 shows large billboards positioned at the street corners, advertising the entire block for sale or lease. The Benedettos' grasp on their farm was, it seems, always tenuous.

407 **"[Almost] every other week:** "City Is 'Going Rural' Fast, Census Shows; Leads the State in Rate of Farm Increase," *New York Times*, May 21, 1935, 21.

407 **Patsy was operating a stationery store:** 1940 United States Federal Census, National Archives and Records Administration; New York, New York; Enumeration District 31-1974, p. 4A, https://1940census.archives.gov.

407 **Vincenzo was listed:** Ibid.

407 **about $50 worth of produce:** "Farm Here Fades; Census Job Gone," *New York Times*, April 3, 1940, 4.

407 **Vincenzo Benedetto died in 1943:** "Vincenzo Benedetto," obituary, *New York Times*, August 1, 1943, 38.

407 **"It was just someplace to live":** Jeff Kisseloff oral history interviews, Manuscripts and Archives Division, New York Public Library, Astor, Lenox, and Tilden Foundations.

407 **"You had freedom":** Ibid.

CHAPTER 49. INDIAN TRAIL

409 **"It was not an interesting people":** Martha Lamb and Burton Harrison, *History of the City of New York: Its Origin, Rise, and Progress*. New York: A. S. Barnes & Co., 1896, I, 36.

409 **"the patient art of the wild men":** Reginald Pelham Bolton, *Indian Paths in the Great Metropolis*. New York: Museum of the American Indian, Heye Foundation, 1922, 16.

409 **the "No. 1 citizen of Washington Heights":** "Reginald Bolton, Engineer, Author," *New York Times*, February 19, 1942, 19.

410 **"ancient trail of the Red Men of Manhattan":** Reginald Pelham Bolton, *The Path of Progress*. New York: Central Savings Bank, 1928, 7.

410 **a "harmless" Dutch wheelwright:** David Pietersz de Vries, *Voyages from Hol-*

land to America, A.D. 1632–1644, translated from the Dutch by Henry C. Murphy. New York: s. n., 1853, 149–150. De Vries gave the victim's name as Claes Rademaker (Dutch for "Wheelmaker").

411 **"on the road, over which the Indians"**: Ibid.

411 **"on the Wickquasgeck road"**: J. Franklin Jameson, editor, *Narratives of New Netherland, 1609–1664*. New York: Charles Scribner's Sons, 1909, 213.

412 **Jennie F. Macarthy:** "Affidavit of Jennie F. Macarthy," January 7, 1931. *Robert Read et al v. the Rector, Church Wardens and Vestrymen of Trinity Church in the City of New York and John Doe and Richard Doe*. Supreme Court of the State of New York, Appellate Division, First Department, County Clerk's File No. 1046, 1931, 12–15.

412 **"There is hardly a doubt"**: Jennie F. Macarthy, "Original Grants, Farms: Introduction," in I. N. Phelps Stokes, *The Iconography of Manhattan Island, 1498 to 1909*. Six volumes. New York: Robert H. Dodd, 1915–1928. Reprinted, New York: Arno Press, 1967, VI, 67-b.

412 **Macarthy figured that the road:** The Post Road, which began in 1669 as the "Road to Harlem," branched away from the Bowery at present-day 23rd Street and ran up the east side of the island past Turtle Bay on its way to the village of Harlem. The Post Road was superseded by the 1811 Commissioners' Plan and closed in stages between 1839 and 1852.

412 **The Bloomingdale Road was one of several highways**: *Colonial Laws, New York*, I, 532. Quoted in Stokes, *The Iconography of Manhattan Island*, IV, 445.

412 **"From the House at the End of New York lane"**: "Minutes of the General Sessions of the Peace," manuscript, 129–130. Quoted in Stokes, *The Iconography of Manhattan Island*, IV, 458; and in D. T. Valentine, *Manual of the Corporation of the City of New-York*. New York: Edmund Jones & Co., 1862, 518.

414 **"The white men did not remove it"**: "Prehistoric Broadway," *New York Times*, September 10, 1922, Section 6, 8.

414 **"Broadway an Indian Trail"**: "Broadway an Indian Trail: Present Famous 'Bright Light' Pathway Used as Artery of Trade by the Aborigines," *Pioneer Express* (Pembina, North Dakota), December, 29, 1922, 7.

CHAPTER 50. WHERE DOES THIS ROAD END?

415 **"The inhabitants near this bridge"**: Charles Dawson Shanly, "Along the Hudson River at New York," *Atlantic Monthly* XXII, 129 (July 1868), 1.

416 **"granary of the world"**: "Address of the Committee to Mr. Clinton and his Answer," in David Hosack, *Memoir of De Witt Clinton*. New York: J. Seymour, 1829, 478.

416 **well over 100 million bushels:** "Harlem Ship Canal," *New York Herald*, May 6, 1878, 4.

416 **A canal across upper Manhattan:** Ibid.

416 **the "Broadway of Harlem"**: "Work on the Harlem Canal," *New York Tribune*, January 10, 1888, 1; "Harlem Canal Opened," *New York Evening World*, June 17, 1895, 1.

417 **a huge chasm of "astonishing breadth and depth"**: "Harlem Ship Canal," 20.

417 **handed a ceremonial keg:** "Harlem Canal Opened," 1.

417 **It was estimated that two more years:** Ibid.

417 **By 1903, the canal:** "The Harlem Ship Canal Has Become a Jest Among Pilots Because of Neglect—Government Urged to Complete the Partly Constructed Waterway," *New York Tribune, Illustrated Supplement*, May 31, 1903, 8.

419 **a C-Town supermarket:** Since the line dividing Manhattan from the Bronx is midway between 228th and 230th streets, the northernmost building on Broadway in Manhattan is actually the southernmost building of the Marble Hill Houses, a public housing project. But since it's set back from the street, perhaps it's not technically "on" Broadway anyway.

420 **"Broadway," Walt Whitman wrote:** Jerome Loving, "'Broadway, the Magnificent!': A Newly Discovered Whitman Essay." *Walt Whitman Quarterly Review* 12 (Spring 1995), 215.

420 **where New Yorkers felt most at home:** Stephen Jenkins, *The Greatest Street in the World: The Story of Broadway, Old and New, from the Bowling Green to Albany.* New York and London: G. P. Putnam's Sons, 1911, vi.

BIBLIOGRAPHY

BOOKS

Albion, Robert Greenhalgh. *The Rise of New York Port, 1815–1860*. New York and London: Charles Scribner's Sons, 1939.

Astor, John Jacob. *A Journey in Other Worlds: A Romance of the Future*. New York: D. Appleton & Co., 1894.

Bacon, Mardges. *Le Corbusier in America: Travels in the Land of the Timid*. Cambridge: MIT Press, 2001.

Badger, Daniel D. *Illustrations of Iron Architecture, Made by the Architectural Iron Works of the City of New York*. New York: Baker & Godwin, 1865.

Barnum, Phineas Taylor. *The Autobiography of P. T. Barnum, Clerk, Merchant, Editor, and Showman; with His Rules for Business and Making a Fortune*. London: Ward & Lock, 1855. Second Edition.

Barnum, Phineas Taylor. *The Life of P. T. Barnum, Written by Himself*. London: Sampson Low, Son & Co., 1855.

Beach, Moses Yale. *The Wealth and Biography of the Wealthy Citizens of the City of New York*. New York: New York Sun, 1846.

Bean, Judith Mattson, and Joel Myerson, editors. *Margaret Fuller, Critic: Writings from the New-York Tribune, 1844–1846*. New York: Columbia University Press, 2000.

Belasco, David. *The Theatre Through Its Stage Door*. New York and London: Harper & Brothers, 1919.

Bellow, Saul. *Seize the Day*. New York: Penguin, 1965.

Beveridge, Charles E., editor. *Frederick Law Olmsted: Writings on Landscape, Culture, and Society*. New York: Library of America, 2015.

Bird, Isabella Lucy. *The Englishwoman in America*. London: John Murray, 1856.

Birmingham, Stephen. *"Our Crowd": The Great Jewish Families of New York*. Syracuse: Syracuse University Press, 1967.

Bolton, Reginald Pelham. *Indian Paths in the Great Metropolis*. New York: Museum of the American Indian, Heye Foundation, 1922.

Bourget, Paul. *Outre-Mer: American Impressions*. London: T. Fisher Unwin, 1895.

Brooks, Richard Albert Edward, editor. *The Diary of Michael Floy Jr. of Bowery Village, 1833–1837*. New Haven: Yale University Press, 1941.

Brown, Thomas Allston. *History of the American Stage.* New York: Dick & Fitzgerald, 1870.

Brown, Thomas Allston. *A History of the New York Stage from the First Performance in 1732 to 1901.* Three volumes. New York: Dodd, Mead & Co., 1902.

Browne, Henri Junius. *The Great Metropolis: A Mirror of New York.* Hartford: American Publishing Co., 1869.

Burroughs, John. *John James Audubon.* Boston: Small, Maynard & Co., 1902.

Candler, Isaac. *A Summary View of America: Comprising a Description of the Face of the Country, and of Several of the Principal Cities; and Remarks on the Social, Moral, and Political Character of the People: Being the Result of Observations and Enquiries During a Journey in the United States.* London: T. Cadell, 1824.

Carman, Harry James. *The Street Surface Railway Franchises of New York City.* New York: s. n., 1919.

Carter, Samuel. *Cyrus Field: Man of Two Worlds.* New York: G. P. Putnam's Sons, 1968.

Censer, Jane Turner, editor. *The Papers of Frederick Law Olmsted. Volume IV, Defending the Union: The Civil War and the U.S. Sanitary Commission, 1861–1863.* Baltimore and London: Johns Hopkins University Press, 1986.

Chambers, Whittaker. *Witness.* Washington, D.C.: Regnery Publishing, 1980.

Chase, Philander D., and Frank E. Grizzard Jr., editors. *The Papers of George Washington, Revolutionary War Series, VI, 13 August 1776–20 October 1776.* Charlottesville: University Press of Virginia, 1994.

Chernow, Ron. *Alexander Hamilton.* New York: Penguin, 2004.

Child, Lydia Maria. *Letters from New-York.* New York: Charles S. Francis & Co.; Boston: James Munroe & Co., 1843.

Child, Lydia Maria. *Letters from New York. Second Series.* New York and Boston: Charles S. Francis & Co., 1845.

Churchill, Allen. *The Great White Way.* New York: E. P. Dutton & Co., 1962.

Cohan, George M. *Twenty Years on Broadway and the Years It Took to Get There.* New York: Harper & Brothers, 1925.

Costello, Augustine E. *Our Firemen. A History of the New York Fire Departments.* New York: Augustine E. Costello, 1887.

Crowe, Eyre. *With Thackeray in America.* New York: Charles Scribner's Sons, 1893.

De Vries, David Pietersz. *Voyages from Holland to America, A.D. 1632–1644.* Translated from the Dutch by Henry C. Murphy. New York: s. n., 1853.

Dickens, Charles. *American Notes for General Circulation.* Paris: Baudry's European Library, 1842.

Dolkart, Andrew S. *Morningside Heights: A History of Its Architecture and Development.* New York: Columbia University Press, 1998.

Downing, Andrew Jackson. *The Fruits and Fruit Trees of America: Or, the Culture, Propagation, and Management, in the Garden and Orchard, of Fruit Trees Generally; with Descriptions of All the Finest Varieties of Fruit, Native and Foreign, Cultivated in This Country.* London: Wiley and Putnam, 1845.

Drake, Francis S. *Life and Correspondence of Henry Knox, Major-General in the American Revolutionary Army.* Boston: Samuel G. Drake, 1873.

Dreiser, Theodore. *The Color of a Great City.* New York: Boni & Liveright, 1923.

Dunlap, David W. *On Broadway: A Journey Uptown over Time.* New York: Rizzoli, 1990.

Ellington, George. *The Women of New York; or, The Under-World of the Great City.* New York: The New York Book Co., 1869.

Emerson, Edward Waldo, and Waldo Emerson Forbes. *The Journals of Ralph Waldo Emerson.* Volume VIII. Boston and New York: Houghton Mifflin Co., 1912.

Fein, Albert, editor. *Landscape into Cityscape: Frederick Law Olmsted's Plans for a Greater New York City.* Ithaca: Cornell University Press, 1967.

Finch, John. *Travels in the United States of America and Canada.* London: Longman, Bees, Orme, Brown, Green & Longman, 1833.

Gates, John D. *The Astor Family,* New York: Doubleday & Co., 1981.

Godwin, Parke. *Homes of American Authors.* New York: G. P. Putnam & Co., 1853.

Goldman, Emma. *Living My Life.* Two volumes. New York: Alfred A. Knopf, 1931. Reprinted, New York: Dover Publications, 1970.

Goodrich, Samuel Griswold. *Life of Louis-Philippe, Late King of the French.* Boston: J. B. Hall, 1848.

Graham, Stephen. *New York Nights.* New York: George H. Doran Co., 1927.

Green, Asa. *A glance at New York: Embracing the City Government, Theatres, Hotels, Churches, Mobs, Monopolies, Learned Professions, Newspapers, Rogues, Dandies, Fires and Firemen, Water and Other Liquids, & c. & c.* New York: A. Greene, 1837.

Grinnell, George Bird. *Audubon Park: The History of the Site of the Hispanic Society of America and Neighboring Institutions.* New York: Hispanic Society of America, 1927.

Griswold, Rufus W. *The Prose Writers of America.* Philadelphia: Porter & Coates, 1870.

Gunn, Thomas Butler. *The Physiology of New York Boarding-Houses.* New York: Mason Brothers, 1857.

Hardie, James. *A Census of the New Buildings Erected in the City, in the Year 1824.* New York: S. Marks, 1825.

Hardie, James. *The Description of the City of New-York, Containing Its Population, Institutions, Commerce, Manufactures, Public Buildings . . .* New York: Samuel Marks, 1827.

Hedrick, U. P. *The Plums of New York.* Albany: J. B. Lyon Co., 1911.

Hellman, George S., editor. *Letters of Henry Brevoort to Washington Irving.* Two volumes. New York: G. P. Putnam's Sons, 1916.

Hellman, George S., editor. *The Letters of Washington Irving to Henry Brevoort.* Two volumes. New York: G. P. Putnam's Sons, 1915.

Henry, Joseph. *The Campaign Against Quebec: Being an Accurate and Interesting Account of the Hardships and Sufferings of That Band of Heroes Who Traversed the Wilderness, by the Route of the Kennebec, and Chaudière River, to Quebec, in the Year 1775.* Watertown, N.Y.: Knowlton & Rice, 1844.

Hobbs, William Herbert. *The Configuration of the Rock Floor of Greater New York*, U.S. Geological Survey. Washington, D.C.: Government Printing Office, 1905.

Holmes, Isaac. *An Account of the United States of America, Derived from Actual Observation, During a Residence of Four Years in That Republic.* London: Caxton Press, 1823.

Hosack, David. *Memoir of De Witt Clinton.* New York: J. Seymour, 1829.

Jacobs, Jane. *The Death and Life of Great American Cities.* New York: Vintage Books, 1961.

James, Henry. *A Small Boy and Others.* New York: Charles Scribner's Sons, 1913.

James, Henry. *Washington Square.* New York: Harper & Brothers, 1881.

Jameson, J. Franklin, editor. *Narratives of New Netherland, 1609–1664.* New York: Charles Scribner's Sons, 1909.

Jenkins, Stephen. *The Greatest Street in the World: The Story of Broadway, Old and New, from the Bowling Green to Albany*. New York and London: G. P. Putnam's Sons, 1911.

Jones, Thomas. *History of New York During the Revolutionary War*. New York: New-York Historical Society, 1879.

Judson, Isabella Field. *Cyrus W. Field: His Life and Work, 1819–1892*. New York: Harper & Brothers, 1896.

Kalfus, Melvin. *Frederick Law Olmsted: The Passion of a Public Artist*. New York: New York University Press, 1990.

Kent, William. *Memoirs and Letters of James Kent*. Boston: Little, Brown & Company, 1898.

Kernan, Frank. *Reminiscences of the Old Fire Laddies and Volunteer Fire Departments of New York and Brooklyn: Together with a Complete History of the Paid Departments of Both Cities*. New York: M. Crane, 1885.

Kisseloff, Jeff. *You Must Remember This: An Oral History of Manhattan from the 1890s to World War II*. Baltimore and London: Johns Hopkins University Press, 1999.

Lamb, Martha, and Burton Harrison. *History of the City of New York: Its Origin, Rise, and Progress*. Three volumes. New York: A. S. Barnes & Co., 1896.

Lambert, John. *Travels Through Canada and the United States of North America, in the Years 1806, 1807 & 1808*. Two volumes. London: Baldwin, Cradock & Joy, 1816.

Landau, Sarah Bradford, and Carol W. Condit. *Rise of the New York Skyscraper, 1865–1913*. New Haven and London: Yale University Press, 1996.

Le Corbusier. *When the Cathedrals Were White*. New York: Reynal & Hitchcock, 1947.

Manning, Robert. *Book of Fruits: Being a Descriptive Catalogue of the Most Valuable Varieties of the Pear, Apple, Peach, Plum & Cherry, for New-England Culture*. Salem, Mass.: Ives & Jewett, 1838.

Massett, Stephen C. *Drifting About, or What Jeems Pipes of Pipesville Saw-and-Did*. New York: Carleton, 1863.

Matthews, Brander. *A History of Columbia University, 1754–1904*. New York: Columbia University Press, 1904.

McAdoo, William. *Guarding a Great City*. New York and London: Harper & Brothers, 1906.

McCabe, John. *George M. Cohan: The Man Who Owned Broadway*. New York: Doubleday & Co., 1973.

Mesick, Jane Louise. *The English Traveller in America, 1785–1835*. New York: Columbia University Press, 1922.

Mines, John Flavel. *A Tour Around New York and My Summer Acre: Being the Recreations of Mr. Felix Oldboy*. New York: Harper & Brothers, 1893.

Moore, Charles. *Daniel H. Burnham, Architect, Planner of Cities*. Two volumes. Boston and New York: Houghton Mifflin Co., 1921.

Morehouse, Ward. *George M. Cohan, Prince of the American Theater*. Philadelphia and New York: J. B. Lippincott Co., 1943.

Mott, Hopper Striker. *The New York of Yesterday*. New York and London: G. P. Putnam's Sons, 1908.

Nevins, Allan, editor. *The Diary of Philip Hone, 1828–1851*. New York: Dodd, Mead & Co., 1936.

Nye, David E. *Electrifying America: Social Meanings of a New Technology*. Cambridge and London: MIT Press, 1990.

Oppenheimer, Margaret A. *The Remarkable Rise of Eliza Jumel.* Chicago: Chicago Review Press, 2016.

Ostrom, John Ward, editor. *The Letters of Edgar Allan Poe.* Two volumes. New York: Gordian Press, 1966.

Palmer, Elizabeth Story. *My Memories of Old New York.* New York: Edwin S. Gorham, 1923.

Parkhurst, Charles H. *Our Fight with Tammany.* New York: Charles Scribner's Sons, 1895.

Pierson, William H., Jr. *American Buildings and Their Architects. Volume 2, Technology and the Picturesque: The Corporate and the Early Gothic Styles.* New York and London: Oxford University Press, 1978.

Rhodes, Richard. *John James Audubon: The Making of An American.* New York: Alfred A. Knopf, 2004.

Riis, Jacob A., *The Battle with the Slum.* New York: Macmillan Co., 1902.

Rockland, Michael Aaron. *The George Washington Bridge: Poetry in Steel.* New Brunswick, N.J., and London: Rivergate Books, 2008.

Salwen, Peter. *Upper West Side Story.* New York: Abbeville Press, 1989.

Schecter, Barnet. *The Battle for New York: The City at the Heart of the American Revolution.* New York: Walker & Co., 2002.

Skolsky, Sidney. *Times Square Tintypes.* New York: Ives Washburn, 1930.

Sloane, Eric, and Edward Anthony. *Mr. Daniels and the Grange.* New York: Funk & Wagnalls, 1968.

Spannuth, Jacob E., and Thomas Ollive Mabbott, editors. *Doings of Gotham by Edgar Allan Poe.* Pottsville, Pa.: Jacob E. Spannuth, 1929.

St. John, Bruce, editor. *John Sloan's New York Scene.* New York: Harper & Row, 1965.

Stokes, I. N. Phelps. *The Iconography of Manhattan Island, 1498 to 1909.* New York: Robert H. Dodd, 1915–1928. Six volumes. Reprinted, New York: Arno Press, 1967.

Stokes, W. E. D. *The Right to Be Well Born: or, Horse Breeding in Its Relation to Eugenics.* New York: C. J. O'Brien, 1917.

Syrett, Harold C., editor. *The Papers of Alexander Hamilton.* Twenty-seven volumes. New York: Columbia University Press, 1955–1987.

Thomas, Dwight, and David K. Jackson. *The Poe Log: A Documentary Life of Edgar Allan Poe, 1809–1849.* Boston: G. K. Hall & Co., 1987.

Trollope, Frances. *Domestic Manners of the Americans.* Two volumes. Second edition. London: Whittaker, Treacher & Co., 1832.

Tucker, Gideon J. *Legends of the Netherlands to Which Are Added Some Legends of Manhattan Island.* New York: Concord Cooperative Printing Co., 1892.

Tuckerman, Bayard, editor. *The Diary of Philip Hone, 1828–1851.* Two volumes. New York: Dodd, Mead & Co., 1889.

Tuttle, H. Croswell. *Abstracts of Farm Titles in the City of New York, Between 39th and 73rd Streets, West of the Common Lands, Excepting the Glass House Farm.* New York: Spectator Co., 1881.

Van Hoogstraten, Nicholas. *Lost Broadway Theatres.* Revised edition. New York: Princeton Architectural Press, 1997.

Viele, Egbert L. *Hand-Book for Active Service, Containing Practical Instructions in Campaign Duties.* New York: D. Van Nostrand, 1861.

Ward, Susan Hayes. *The History of the Broadway Tabernacle Church from Its Organi-

zation in 1840 to the Close of 1900, Including Factors Influencing Its Formation. New York: Trow Print, 1901.

Wharton, Edith. *The Age of Innocence.* New York and Los Angeles: Windsor Editions by arrangement with D. Appleton & Co., 1920.

Wharton, Edith. *A Backward Glance.* New York and London: D. Appleton-Century Company, 1934.

Whitman, Walt. *Specimen Days & Collect.* Philadelphia: Rees Welsh & Co., 1882.

Winter, William. *The Life of David Belasco.* Two volumes. New York: Moffat, Yard & Co., 1918.

Winterbotham, William. *An Historical, Geographical, Commercial, and Philosophical View of the American United States, and of the European Settlements in America and the West-Indies.* Four volumes. London: J. Ridgway, H. D. Symonds & D. Holt, 1795.

Woolston, Howard Brown. *A Study of the Population of Manhattanville.* New York: Columbia University Press, 1909.

Worden, Helen. *Round Manhattan's Rim.* Indianapolis: Bobbs-Merrill Co., 1934.

MANUSCRIPTS AND SPECIAL COLLECTIONS

Brooklyn Historical Society:
  Brevoort Family Papers (1760–1879)
New York City Municipal Archives:
  Assessed Valuation of Real Estate
  New York City Common Council Papers (1670–1831)
New-York Historical Society:
  George Templeton Strong diary, 1835–1875. Four volumes.
New York Public Library, Manuscripts and Archives Division, Astor, Lenox, and Tilden Foundations:
  Jeff Kisseloff oral history interviews
  George Kirwan Carr diary
  John Aspinwall Hadden diary
  John J. Sturtevant memoir

JOURNALS, MAGAZINES, AND NEWSPAPERS

Architectural Record
Atlantic Monthly
The Auk
Ballou's Pictorial Drawing-Room Companion
Barre Daily Times (Barre, Vermont)
Bolivar Bulletin (Bolivar, Tennessee)
The Brickbuilder
Bulletin of the Metropolitan Museum of Art
Columbia Daily Spectator
Columbia University Quarterly
Daily Capital Journal (Salem, Oregon)
Daily Telegram (Clarksburg, West Virginia)

Day Book (Chicago)
El Paso Herald (El Paso, Texas)
Emporia News (Emporia, Kansas)
Frank Leslie's Popular Monthly
Gazette of the United-States
Gleason's Pictorial Drawing-Room Companion
Grand Forks Daily Herald (Grand Forks, South Dakota)
Harper's Weekly
Harper's New Monthly Magazine
Herald and News (Newberry, South Carolina)
Illinois Free Trader and LaSalle County Commercial Advertiser (LaSalle County, Illinois)
Illustrated American
Illustrated News
Lippincott's Magazine
Los Angeles Herald
Magazine of American History
McClure's Magazine
Mother Earth
New York Aurora
New York Evening Express
New York Evening Mirror
New York Evening Post
New York Evening World
New York Herald
New York Journal
New York Mirror
New York Municipal Gazette
New York Sun
New York Times
New York Tribune
North American Review
Omaha Daily Bee (Omaha, Nebraska)
Phrenological Journal & Life Illustrated
Pioneer Express (Pembina, North Dakota)
Real Estate Record & Builder's Guide
Richmond Daily Register (Richmond, Kentucky)
Salt Lake Daily Herald (Salt Lake City, Utah)
Scribner's Magazine
South Bend News-Times (South Bend, Indiana)
University Missourian (Columbia, Missouri)
Washington Times
Wheeling Daily Intelligencer (Wheeling, West Virginia)

DIRECTORIES

Biographical Directory of the State of New York. New York: Biographical Directory Co., 1900.

Boyd, William Henry. *Boyd's Pictorial Directory of Broadway: In Which Will Be Found an Alphabetical, a Business, and a Numerical or Street Directory, Giving the Names of the Occupants of Every Building on Broadway.* New York: W. H. Boyd, 1859.

Doggett, John, Jr. *Doggett's Double Directory.* New York: John Doggett Jr., 1851.

Doggett, John, Jr. *Doggett's New-York City Directory.* New York: John Doggett Jr. (Editions for 1842, 1845, 1845–1846, 1846–1847, 1847–1848, 1848–1849.)

Duncan, William. *The New-York Directory and Register for the Year 1791.* New York: T. and J. Swords, 1791.

Elliot, William. *Elliot's Improved New-York City Double Directory.* New York: William Elliot, 1812.

Francis, Dennis Steadman. *Architects in Practice: New York City 1840–1900.* Committee for the Preservation of Architectural Records, American Institute of Architects, 1979.

Franks, David C. *The New-York Directory for 1786.* New York: Shepard Kollock, 1786. Reprinted, New York: John Doggett Jr., 1851.

Franks, David C. *The New-York Directory.* New York, 1787.

Goulding, Lawrence G. *Goulding's Business Directory of New York, Brooklyn, Newark, Paterson, Jersey City, and Hoboken.* New York: Lawrence G. Goulding, 1875.

Hodge, Robert, Thomas Allen, and Samuel Campbell. *The New-York Directory and Register for the Year 1789.* New York: Hodge, Allen & Campbell, 1789.

Lain, George T. *The Brooklyn Directory for the Year Ending May, 1882.* New York: George T. Lain, 1882.

Longworth, Thomas. *Longworth's American Almanac, New-York Register, and City Directory.* New York: Thomas Longworth. (Editions for 1798, 1803, 1813, 1826–1827, 1839.)

Mercein, William A. *Mercein's City Directory, New-York Register, and Almanac.* New York: William A. Mercein, 1820.

Phillips' Business Directory of New York City. New York: W. Phillips & Co., 1883.

Prall, John P. *The New-York Mercantile Register, for 1848–49, Containing the Cards of the Principal Business Establishments.* New York: John P. Prall, 1848.

Rode, Charles R. *The New-York City Directory for 1854–1855.* New York: Charles R. Rode, 1854.

The Trow (Formerly Wilson's) Copartnership and Corporation Directory of the Boroughs of Manhattan and the Bronx, City of New York. Volume XLVIII. New York: Trow Directory, Printing & Bookbinding Co., 1900.

Wilson, H., *Trow's New York City Directory for the Year Ending May 1, 1857.* New York: John Trow, 1856.

GUIDEBOOKS, GAZETTEERS, AND MANUALS

Beldon, E. Porter. *New-York: Past, Present, and Future, Comprising a History of the City of New-York, a Description of its Present Condition, and an Estimate of Its Future Increase.* New York: G. P. Putnam, 1849.

Disturnell, John. *A Gazetteer of the State of New-York.* Albany: J. Disturnell, 1842.

Disturnell, John. *A Guide to the City of New York, Containing an Alphabetical List of Streets, & c.* New York: J. Disturnell, 1837.

Doggett, John, Jr. *The Great Metropolis: or, Guide to New-York for 1846.* New York: H. Ludwig, 1846.

French, J. H. *Historical and Statistical Gazetteer of New York State.* Syracuse: R. Pearsall Smith, 1860.

King, Moses. *King's Handbook of New York City.* Second edition. Boston: Moses King, 1893.

Mitchill, Samuel L. *The Picture of New-York: or, The Traveller's Guide Through the Commercial Metropolis of the United States.* New York: I. Riley & Co., 1807.

New York Panorama. New York: Random House, 1938.

A Picture of New-York in 1846; with a Short Account of Places in Its Vicinity; Designed as a Guide to Citizens and Strangers. New York: Roman & Ellis, 1846.

Sights and Wonders in New York: Including a Description of the Mysteries, Miracles, Marvels, Phenomena, Curiosities, and Nondescripts, Contained in That Great Congress of Wonders, Barnum's Museum . . . New York: J. S. Redfield, 1849.

Spafford, Horatio Gates. *A Gazetteer of the State of New-York.* Albany: H. C. Southwick, 1813.

Valentine, D. T. *Manual of the Corporation of the City of New-York.* New York: Edmund Jones & Co., 1841–1866.

Williams, Edwin, editor. *New York As It Is, in 1834; and Citizens' Advertising Directory.* New York: J. Disturnell, 1834.

The World's Loose Leaf Album of New York Apartment Houses. New York: New York World, 1910.

ARTICLES

Berrol, Selma Cantor. "The Making of a Neighborhood: The Jewish West Side." New York Neighborhood Studies, Working Paper no. 4. New York: Division of Urban Planning, Graduate School of Architecture and Planning, Columbia University, ca. 1982.

Daley, Robert. "Alfred Ely Beach and his Wonderful Pneumatic Underground Railway," *American Heritage,* XII (June 1961), 4.

Frankel, Aaron M. "From the American Scene: Back to Eighty-Six Street," *Commentary,* II, 2 (August 1, 1946).

Loving, Jerome. "'Broadway, the Magnificent!': A Newly Discovered Whitman Essay." *Walt Whitman Quarterly Review,* 12 (Spring 1995).

Schrader, J. L. "George Grey Barnard: The Cloisters and the Abbaye," *Metropolitan Museum of Art Bulletin,* XXXVII, 1 (Summer 1979).

Zabar, Lori. "The Influence of W. E. D. Stokes's Real Estate Career on West Side Development," M.S. thesis, Columbia University, 1977.

BOOKLETS AND PAMPHLETS

Baker, Benjamin A. "A Glance at New York: A Local Drama, in Two Acts." New York and London: Samuel French & Son, 1890.

Bolton, Reginald Pelham. *The Path of Progress.* New York: Central Savings Bank, 1928.

Clarke, McDonald. *Afara: or, The Belles of Broadway.* New York: s.n., 1829.

The Collection of the Late David Belasco. New York: American Art Association, Anderson Galleries, 1931.

Daly, Peter F. *Present Value of Real Estate in New York City (By Wards), Compared with That of 1842.* New York: Peter F. Daly, 1884.

Dean, Bashford, and Alexander McMillan Welch. *The Dyckman House: Park and Museum, New York City, 1783–1916.* New York: Gilliss Press, 1916.

Directory to the Seraglios in New York, Philadelphia, Boston, and All the Principal Cities in the Union. Edited and Compiled by a Free Loveyer. New York: s.n., 1859.

Ferree, Barr. *Fort Tryon Hall.* New York: C. K. G. Billings, 1911.

Hepner, Elizabeth R. *Morningside-Manhattanville Rebuilds . . .* New York: Morningside Heights, Inc., 1955.

Ruggles, Samuel B. *Address by the Hon. Samuel B. Ruggles, at Union Square, on the Opening of the Metropolitan Fair, April 8th, 1864.* New York: C. A. Alvord, 1864.

The Story of the Brevoort Family: From Farm to Savings Bank. Brooklyn: Brevoort Savings Bank, 1964.

Viele, Egbert L. *The West End Plateau of the City of New York.* New York: Johnson & Platt, 1879.

REPORTS AND RECORDS

1915 New York State Census. www.ancestry.com.

1850 United States Federal Census. www.ancestry.com.

1880 United States Federal Census. www.ancestry.com.

1910 United States Federal Census. www.ancestry.com.

1930 United States Federal Census. www.ancestry.com.

1940 United States Federal Census. National Archives and Records Administration. www.1940census.archives.gov.

Davies, Henry E. *A Compilation of the Laws of the State of New York, Relating Particularly to the City of New York.* New York: City of New York, 1855.

Documents of the Board of Assistants. Volume I. New York: City of New York, 1837.

Erving, William V. R., reporter, *The Miscellaneous Reports: Cases Decided in the Courts of Record of the State of New York.* Volume XCVIII. Albany: J. B. Lyons Company, 1917.

Green, Andrew H. *Communication to the Commissioners of the Central Park, Relative to the Improvement of the Sixth and Seventh Avenues, from the Central Park to the Harlem River; the Laying Out of the Island Above 155th Street; the Drive from 59th St. to 155th St., and Other Subjects.* New York: Wm. C. Bryant & Co., 1866.

Green, Andrew H. *Eleventh Annual Report of the Board of Commissioners of the Central Park, for the Year Ending December 31, 1867.* New York: William Cullen Bryant, 1868.

Minutes of the Common Council of the City of New York, 1675–1776. Eight volumes. New York: Dodd, Mead & Company, 1905.

Peterson, A. Everett, editor. *Minutes of the Common Council of the City of New York, 1784–1831.* Nineteen volumes. New York: City of New York, 1917.

Proceedings of the Boards of Aldermen and Assistant Aldermen, and Approved by the Mayor, Volume I. New York: City of New York, 1835.

SoHo–Cast Iron Historic District Designation Report. New York: New York City Landmarks Preservation Commission, 1973.

Washington, Eric K. "St. Mary's Protestant Episcopal Church (Manhattanville), Parish House, and Sunday School," *Designation Report.* New York: New York City Landmarks Preservation Commission, May 19, 1998.

ILLUSTRATION CREDITS

INDEX